SPLITTING
THE
DIFFERENCE

Jordan Lectures in Comparative Religion, 1996–97

School of Oriental and African Studies
University of London

SPLITTING

THE

DIFFERENCE

Gender and Myth in
Ancient Greece and India

Wendy Doniger

The University of Chicago Press

Chicago and London

Wendy Doniger is Mircea Eliade Professor of the History of Religions in the Divinity School and a professor in the Department of South Asian Languages and Civilizations at the University of Chicago. She is the author of several books, including *Women, Androgynes, and Other Mythical Beasts* (1980) and *Other Peoples' Myths: The Cave of Echoes* (1988). She is also the editor of *Mythologies,* an English-language edition of Yves Bonnefoy's *Dictionnaire des Mythologies.*

The University of Chicago Press, Chicago 60637
The University of Chicago Press, Ltd., London
© 1999 by The University of Chicago
All rights reserved. Published 1999
08 07 06 05 04 03 02 01 00 99   1 2 3 4 5
ISBN: 0-226-15640-0 (cloth)
ISBN: 0-226-15641-9 (paper)

Library of Congress Cataloging-in-Publication Data

Doniger, Wendy.
    Splitting the difference : gender and myth in ancient Greece
and India / Wendy Doniger.
        p.   cm.—(Jordan lectures in comparative religion)
    Includes bibliographical references and index.
    ISBN 0-226-15640-0 (alk. paper)
    ISBN 0-226-15641-9 (pbk. : alk. paper)
    1. Sex—Mythology—Comparative studies.   2. Mythology,
Greek.   3. Mythology, Hindu.   I. Title.   II. Series.
BL325.S42 D65   1999
291.1'78343—dc21   98-47996
                                                                   CIP

♾ The paper used in this publication meets the minimum requirements of the American National Standard for Information Sciences—Permanence of Paper for Printed Library Materials, ANSI Z39.48-1992.

for Annie Dillard

CONTENTS

ACKNOWLEDGMENTS

The central text in this book is what I have come to recognize as my own personal Sanskrit *bija mantra* ("seed text"): the story of Saranyu. My constant if not eternal return to this story is a demonstration of the fact, which I have argued elsewhere,[1] that storytellers tend to go back to the same story for different meanings, drawing again and again from the same well. For the tale of Saranyu seems to keep getting into what I write, just as King Charles's head kept getting into the memoirs of Mr. Dick in Dickens's *David Copperfield*. I touched upon it in *Siva: The Erotic Ascetic* (1973) and *The Origins of Evil in Hindu Mythology* (1976), translated it in *Hindu Myths* (1975), analyzed it in *Women, Androgynes, and Other Mythical Beasts* (1980) and in *Dreams, Illusion, and Other Realities* (1984)—always, as here, using different variants and devising different interpretations. The story of Saranyu always makes me say, when I hear it, "That's the story of my life."[2] Yet it still accuses me of not even beginning to plumb its depth.

Over the course of this long obsession, I used earlier and, I hope, now unrecognizable versions of pieces of this book as lectures and articles, and I am grateful to the people and journals that published them for permission to reprint the following fragments. Parts of "Interlude: Saranyu" (chapter 1) appeared as "Sexual Doubles and Sexual Masquerades: The Structure of Sexual Symbols," Arizona State University Lecture in Religion, April 1986; "Sexual Doubles and Sexual Masquerades: The Structure of Sex Symbols," *Annual of Psychoanalysis* 17 (1989): 263–80; "Sexual Masquerades in Hindu Myths: Aspects of the Transmission of Knowledge in Ancient India," in *The Transmission of Knowledge in South Asia*, edited by Nigel Crook (Delhi: Oxford University Press, 1996), 28–48; and "Saranyu/Samjna: The Sun and the Shadow," in *Devi: Goddesses of India*, edited by John Stratton Hawley and Donna Wulff (Berkeley and Los Angeles: University of California Press, 1996), 154–72, copyright © 1996 The

Regents of the University of California. Parts of the conclusion to chapter 4, "Put a Bag over Her Head," appeared in " 'Put a Bag over Her Head': Beheading Mythological Women," in *Off with Her Head! The Female Head in Myth, Religion, and Culture*, edited by Howard Eilberg-Schwartz and Wendy Doniger (Berkeley and Los Angeles: University of California Press, 1995), 14–31, copyright © 1995 The Regents of the University of California. Parts of "Sita" and "Helen" (chapter 1) and "Indra as Gautama with Ahalya" and "Zeus as Amphitryon with Alcmena" (chapter 2) appeared in "Sita and Helen, Ahalya and Alcmena: A Comparative Study," in *History of Religions* 37:1 (August 1997), 21–49. Parts of "Damayanti's Dilemma" and "The Sign of the Bed" (chapter 3) were used in "The Homecomings of Odysseus and Nala," in *Literary Imagination, Ancient and Modern: Essays in Honor of David Grene*, edited by Todd Breyfogle (Chicago: University of Chicago Press, in press). Parts of "The Mortal Foot" (chapter 3) appeared as "The Immortal Foot: The 1997 Ingersoll Lecture," *Harvard Divinity Bulletin* 27 (1998): 16–21. Parts of chapter 6, "Bisexual Transformations," appeared in "Transsexual Masquerades in Ancient India: The Myth of Ila," in *India and Beyond: Aspects of Literature, Meaning, Ritual and Thought*, edited by Dick van der Meij (Amsterdam: International Institute for Asian Studies, 1997), 128–47.

I am indebted to the participants in the fine seminars that followed each of the Jordan lectures in London during the week of October 28–November 1, 1996—particularly to Richard Gombrich, Sasha Piatigorsky, Julia Leslie, Dominik Wujastik, Simon Weightman, Aidan Southall, and Marina Warner for their insights. And I owe a great deal to the suggestions of two readers of this book, Ann Grodzins Gold and Gregory Nagy, and to my editor, Alan Thomas, for his invariably sound and tactful advice. I also want to thank the participants in the seminar on "Transformations of the Self," sponsored by the Einstein Forum, on the Sea of Galilee in April 1998 (particularly David Shulman, Galit Hasan-Rokem, Wei-yi Li, Janet Gyatso, Guy Stroumsa, Charles Malamoud, Sara Sviri, and Moshe Idel), and of the seminar on "The Sexual Divide: Human and Divine," at Mishkenot Sha'ananim in Jerusalem, also in April 1998 (particularly Maurice Olender, Lydia Flem, Allan Grapard, and Tikva Frymer-Kensky, and, again, Galit Hasan-Rokem and Moshe Idel), where I presented parts of chapter 6. And again I must thank Katherine Ulrich for her inspired sleuthing in the stacks and for making the index.

I owe so much to Kirin Narayan, first for a generous and sensitive reading of this text, and then for supplying the perfect image for its cover: a print of a poster of Randhal-ma (Saranyu), the caste goddess of the Gujjar Sutars of Kutch (Kirin's father's caste), who trace their descent from Vishvakarma (Tvashtri), Randhal-ma's father. The poster was found in the puja-cupboard of Kirin's grandmother, Kamalabai Ramji, in 1997, and probably dates from around 1970. Randhal-ma, who is invited to all caste ritual events, is usually represented by two coconuts with faces; this two-dimensional, semipermanent representation is rare.

Finally, I am grateful to Nasser Elian for guiding me through an epiphanic voyage in Jordan, sometimes on camelback, while I was finishing these (appropriately Jordan) lectures. It seems doubly auspicious to have finished this book about doubles on the simultaneous eve of Passover and Easter, April 1998 at Petra, Jordan, and Jerusalem, Israel.

Zwei Seelen wohnen, ach! in meiner Brust.

Goethe, *Faust* (1112)

Comparing Texts
Comparing People

Hindu and Greek mythologies teem with gendered narratives of doubling and bifurcation, stories that people (mostly but certainly not only men) have told about other people (mostly but certainly not only women) who have been split in half in various ways: split into an original and a double or a male and a female (in tales of androgyny and/or bisexuality), or severed head from body (or mind from body, soul from body, or left from right), or seduced by gods who appear as the doubles of mortals. These stories address questions that concern many different cultures, including our own: What is the connection between rape and the fantasy of the double? Why do the women depicted in myths fool men more than men fool women? How can you tell a human from a god? Why prefer a human lover or spouse to a god? What is the mythological source of the expression, "Put a bag over her head"?

The part of my title that might, with some indulgence, be called post-colonic *(Gender and Myth in Ancient Greece and India)* sets out an agenda that is double in several respects: I intend to discuss the duality, the *two*-ness, of *two* genders (male and female) of *two* bodies of creatures (mortal and immortal) in *two* bodies of mythology (from ancient India[1] and Greece). I will trace each set of texts from the earliest textual period (the Vedas in India, Homer in Greece) roughly to the present, in contemporary India and Europe, touching down in passing in Victorian England (where the cultures of India and Greece interacted vividly with England at the hub of the empire) and sometimes invoking in the conclusions stories from other cultures as well, including "double features" from the Hammer Studio variants of *Jekyll and Hyde* to John Woo's *Face/Off.*

The six chapters will consider six related plots, some about split women, others about women forced to tell the difference between split men. Chapter 1 is about the shadow Sita and the phantom Helen, and about their relationship to the Vedic myth of Saranyu and her Shadow. Chapter 2 compares the Hindu Ahalya (seduced by the god Indra in the form of her husband Gautama) with the Greek Alcmena (seduced by Zeus in the form of her husband Amphitryon). Chapter 3 begins with the dilemma of the Hindu princess Damayanti, like that of Ahalya, in telling her husband Nala from a god, and then her dilemma, like that of the Greek noblewoman Penelope, in trying to recognize her much-changed husband after a long absence. The fourth and fifth chapters are about transposed heads, of women—the Hindu Mariatale (split in two and given the head of an Outcaste woman) and the Greek twin monsters Scylla and Charybdis, together with their Victorian descendant, Lucy Westenra—; and of men—the Hindu tale of the men with the transposed heads. Chapter 5 is also about the Greek Narcissus and his Victorian descendants, Dr. Jekyll and Dorian Gray. Chapter 6 is about transsexual transformations of males and females, human and divine: the Hindu Ila and Amba, Vishnu/Mohini and Shiva, and the Greek Teiresias. The six chapters deal with six kinds of splitting and doubling of men and women: one woman splits into two; one male doubles another; one man appears in two forms; one woman is cut in half horizontally; then one man is cut in half first horizontally, then vertically, then androgynously; and then men and women double themselves bisexually.

The pre-colonic part of the title, *Splitting the Difference,* suggests another set of double agendas. This is a book about what postmodern scholars call *fragmentation,* a problem that (premodern) myths tackle in ways that are often surprisingly supportive of many postmodern approaches.[2] It is fragmented on the double levels of form and content: in form, the multiple facets of the myth present a fragmented view, patriarchal and antipatriarchal, tragic and comic, that gives the postmodern lie to the Enlightenment search for one truth. And in content, the fragmentation focuses on sexuality, for reasons eloquently expressed by Maurice Olender: "Sexuality, for mortals as well as gods, is a matter of cutting and splitting, falling apart and meeting up again. It is a matter of division and recomposition allowing both distance and closeness, absence and presence, death and birth. . . . Sexuality is double and divided."[3]

Splitting may be a transitive verbal noun ("causing someone else to split") or intransitive ("splitting oneself"). (The intransitive meaning also carries over into a slang sense of *splitting*—walking out on one's spouse and/or family—that is also highly relevant to this corpus of myths.) Both

men and women intransitively split themselves in two—sometimes willingly to get what they want, sometimes against their will to avoid what
they do not want—, but they also transitively split other people in two,
often for these very same reasons. Yet another bifurcation appears when
we note that within the stories, women as subjects may split themselves in
order to avoid men, while outside the story, on the level of the text,
women as objects are split by (usually male) authors in their imaginations.
That is, within the stories, men often force women to split in half, while
outside the texts, men split women in half by composing texts that depict
them as intrinsically split from the start. For instance, in Bram Stoker's
Dracula, Lucy Westenra, who is both villain and victim of the piece, splits
herself in two in order to have it both ways—prim in the light, lascivious
in the dark—but she is also an imaginary male construction of a polarized
woman. Male authors imagine that women by their very nature have
placed them upon the horns of a dilemma—often the horns of cuckolding—, but it is the men who have made the horns, and the dilemma, in
these texts.

The And splitting splits into two significantly different forms: sloughing
and dividing. Chapters 1 through 3 are about splitting in the sense of
sloughing, inside from outside, real from unreal; 4 and 5 are about splitting as dividing, horizontally, head from body, soul or mind from body;
and chapter 6 is about splitting vertically (left from right) or sexually
(male from female). In each category, myths about men (sloughing in
chapters 2 and 3, dividing in chapter 5, and doubling in chapter 6) are
contrasted with myths about women (sloughing in chapter 1, dividing in
chapter 4, and doubling in chapter 6).

The "differences" in the title are also various: within the texts we may
note differences between the parts of a man or a woman and between men
and women, mortals and immortals; outside the texts we may note differences between individual authors within a culture and between the two
cultures of Hinduism and Greece. The contributions of individual authors
emerge particularly vividly from the contrast between different tellings of
the same story to enrich the total picture produced by its combined cross-
cultural spread. Other differences may be explained in terms of the influence of very different cultural factors: Greek history made the stories take
one form, Indian history another, not only in plot but in emotional tone
and literary style. These differences, however, become apparent only as
they emerge from a framework of resemblances between tales told in India

and Greece—and beyond them, in other cultures as well. The similarity must be established before we can go on to the difference; we must acknowledge that there is something to compare before we can compare it.[4] This methodological concern is mirrored within the texts by the problems faced by the characters in the myths: how two halves of a single man or woman or two different men or women both are and are not the same.

I will argue here not for universal but cross-cultural comparisons, stressing factors that two cultures, ancient Greek and Hindu, have in common. The resemblances occur on two levels and can be explained by two very different sorts of theories, requiring a kind of split-level methodology. Certain features shared by the two sets of stories—such as the recurrence of equine twins in the mythologies of Saranyu, Sita, and Helen—are shared cultural assumptions that result from historical connections between Greece and India. But the fact that an ancient Japanese source, the *Kojiki*, tells a story that incorporates a stunning number of the elements of the tale of Saranyu should make us hesitate before limiting even those aspects of this story to the confines of India and Greece, or even to the Indo-European world (about which more below).

On the other hand, other shared features—such as the theme of the beheaded woman or the wounded foot, or the assumption that women are dangerous and dichotomous—are the result of more widely shared human bonds and assumptions that transcend these cultural barriers. I am arguing first that ancient Greeks and Indians are cousins and then that all women are sisters. Moreover, in my conclusion I argue that if we compare images of women in different cultures, their cultural differences (as cousins) are outweighed by their gendered resemblances (as sisters), thus privileging sisters over cousins.

The cousins argument, the argument for historical connections, can itself be split into two parts, emphasizing either common origin or later historical contacts.[5] The historical correspondences between the Greek and Indian stories were explained by Georges Dumézil and Emil Benveniste in terms of an original proto-Indo-European source from which both Greece and India derived their languages and certain basic cultural paradigms.[6] Nowadays, however, we are more inclined to speak of analogues, influences, and borrowings than of sources and diffusions. For these correspondences can also be explained in terms of later historical contacts between Greece and India that took place during the centuries after the period in which the relationship between the Indo-European cultures may have operated to produce the original shared cultural artifacts. Sailors, Buddhist proselytizers, armies, merchants, and many others left various sorts of evidence: the writings of Megasthenes, records of Alexander the Great, archaeology, epigraphy, coins, loan words, etc. Constant miscellaneous interchange between two neighboring cultures is always possible and is necesssary to explain the more specific correspondences. Moreover, many contemporary scholars, even while acknowledging that India and Greece are historically connected, jettison the Dumézilian emphasis on shared language in favor of a shared geography that made possible historical connections with the ancient Mediterranean world (Jews and Egyptians) and beyond.

Acknowledging historical contact does not commit us to the sorts of simple, one-way arguments that some scholars have made: the Greeks—or, for that matter, the Vedic Indians—as source, everyone else as recipient. On the contrary, I want to argue that *all* cultures—or, at the very least, all of the ones that concern us here—are recipients. Sheldon Pollock has made this point eloquently:

> No form of literary culture is "indigenous." "Indigenous" is always the conceptual consequence—in the end, a dangerous consequence—of a deficiency of historicization. Indigenism inhibits us from seeing that all literary cultures participate in what turn out to be networks, ultimately globalized networks, of borrowing, appropriating, reacting, imitating, emulating, rivaling, defeating, albeit, by way of corollary, that literary traditions often construct themselves by sublating this history and affirming, stubbornly, a specious autochthony. From this processual perspective, "culture" or "civilization" (as in "Indian Civilization 101") becomes nothing but an arbitrary moment—a still frame in a film—illegitimately generalized; each of these moments is in fact only an instance of exchange, a point of trans-shipment, a site for reprocessing cultural goods that are always-already other.[7]

It is not necessary either, on the one hand, to explain the resemblances between the cultures I am comparing by historical diffusion or linguistic links, or, on the other hand, to rule out the possibility that some of the shared details of the stories in question may have been introduced or at least reinforced by contacts between Greeks and Indians.

I have argued elsewhere that myths derive a great deal of their power and endurance from their ability to express a deeply troubling paradox that everyone in the community shares and no one can solve.[8] Telling a myth, even to just one other person, gives a kind of comfort: we are all in this together; it's not just me, not just my problem. But here, as ever, we must ask who "we" are. The siblings argument (without the gendered bias implicit in "sisters") in comparative studies stresses the ways in which "we" are all humans; the cousins argument, whether it is expressed, explicitly or implicitly, by the texts themselves or is imposed upon them by European scholars, may construct "us" in ways that emphasize political units: "we" may be we Indo-Europeans (a.k.a. Aryans), Greeks and Indians, together against the world (the Dumézilian stance), or simply "we" Greeks against you Indians.

Why select the mythologies of India and Greece to compare at all, let alone the intracultural variants, if the ultimate goal is a broader cross-cultural comparison? Because, even though texts from Greece and India share a large percentage of related cultural constraints (beginning with language), they still manage to deviate dramatically. And we need to understand history in order to explain those deviations; cousins are not twins; even sisters are not twins. But, on the other hand and at the other end of the spectrum, it is also interesting to note how much the Greek and Hindu stories have in common with traditions with which they share relatively little else, such as our own or that of Victorian England or even Japan. The differences between them are balanced by other sorts of human perceptions that transcend the barriers not only between Greece and India but between their shared historical ground and that of other cultures that do not have such close historical connections. I made the methodological case for siblings in my last book, *The Implied Spider*, and will apply it in my forthcoming book, *The Bedtrick* (which began life as the other half of the present volume: appropriately, they split into twin projects—a book-trick?). I will not, therefore, argue it explicitly here; but it is implicit in the cross-cultural analyses that go beyond the Greek and Hindu texts in the main body of each chapter and in the more general morphological conclusions.

When we consider not the more specific details (the connection between the words *ashva* in Sanskrit, *equus* in Latin, *hippos* in Greek) but the broader patterns (the connection between the false Sita and the false Helen) it would be as useful for my ultimate purpose—the broader cross-cultural case for sisterhood—to argue that the shared stories came from an older shared period, or were even independently conceived in reaction to the same patterns of gender and sexuality, as to argue that they are to be explained by later historical contacts. Indeed, both historical diffusion and independent origination depend in the end upon a shared human predilection for some sorts of stories over others, and the two processes must therefore ultimately be explained in the same way.

My most basic purpose is therefore to show the astonishing volume and power of stories that depict men and women as dichotomized in violent and highly gendered ways. My argument is that myth responds to the complexities of the human condition by splitting its characters into two unequal halves, and that these sloughed and cloven selves animate myriad permutations of character and plot, centering on two primal topics: sex and death. Myths, being themselves transformations (of other myths, variants), are particularly well equipped to express transformations (of people, metamorphoses). Over and above this general concern, however, I intend to make *two* more particular points about the stories from India and from Greece: first, what they have in common, and second, how they differ. The stories, like the men and women that they bring to life for us, are both cousins and sisters.

O N E

The Shadow Sita and the Phantom Helen

~~✤~~

Once upon a time, a great king (named Rama, or Menelaus) fought a great battle to retrieve his abducted wife (named Sita, or Helen) from the rival who had carried her off (the demon Ravana, or prince Paris). This might stand as the bare-bones, Cliff's Notes version of either the ancient Hindu epic, the Sanskrit *Ramayana* attributed to Valmiki, or the ancient Greek epic, the *Iliad* of Homer. The early tellings agree in a number of significant details: Rama, like Menelaus, expresses doubts about the woman he has retrieved, regarding her as compromised—in reality or reputation—by her long sojourn with another man. Menelaus, like Rama, says that he fought not to bring his woman back, but merely to punish the man who had carried her off—to defend his own honor, not hers. Rama tells Sita that he went to war against Ravana, "not for your sake, but to protect my own reputation and expunge the scandal against my own family, not out of any attachment to you but for my own fame."[1] Menelaus, in a later text, says much the same, and adds that people are wrong to think that he fought for Helen.[2] Menelaus wants to kill Helen, and Rama subjects Sita to a potentially fatal trial by fire.

More impressive correspondences arise in the course of the revisions of the stories. Subsequent retellings in both traditions sidestepped the question of the defilement of the returned queen by maintaining that the real queen had never been carried off at all: an identical double had been abducted, while the real queen remained safely in hiding. Thus both Sita and Helen became the subjects of a series of texts which denied the presence of the woman at the scene of the crime. How could the same story, the story of the shadow double, have been constructed and applied to the hated adulteress of ancient Greece and the revered chaste wife of ancient India? Let us consider them one by one, and then together.

SITA

The *Ramayana* is a much retold story,[3] of which I will cite just a few variants. The earliest recorded version, in the Sanskrit text of Valmiki (c. 200 B.C.E.–200 C.E.), establishes this basic plot:

> Sita, the wife of Prince Rama, had been born from a furrow of the earth. The demon king Ravana stole Sita from Rama and kept her captive on the island of Lanka for many years. When Rama finally killed Ravana and brought Sita back home with him, he said he feared that his people worried that her reputation, if not her chastity, had been sullied by her long sojourn in the house of another man. Rama forced Sita to undergo an ordeal by fire: she swore that she had always been faithful to Rama, called on the fire to protect her, and entered the blazing flame; but the god of Fire placed her in Rama's lap, assuring him that Sita had always been pure in thought as well as deed. Rama reinstated her, but when he doubted her again she disappeared forever back into the earth.[4]

Another episode in Valmiki's *Ramayana* (the latest part, probably a section of afterthoughts) tells us why Ravana did not rape Sita when he had her in his power:

RAVANA RAPES RAMBHA[5]

> One day, when Ravana was full of passion, he saw the celestial courtesan Rambha and went mad with lust for her. She reminded him that she was his daughter-in-law, more precisely the wife of Nalakubara, the son of his brother Vaishravana. But Ravana replied, "You say you are my daughter-in-law. For those who have but one husband, this argument is valid, but in their world, the gods have established a law said to be eternal, that celestial courtesans have no appointed consorts, nor are the gods monogamous." Then he raped her. When he released her she ran home, trembling with fear, and told her husband, who said, "Since he raped you brutally, despite your lack of desire for him, he will never be able to approach another young woman unless she shares his desire. If, carried away by lust, he does violence to any woman who does not desire him, his head will split into seven pieces." When Ravana learned of the curse his hair stood on end and he ceased to indulge in uniting himself with those who had no desire for him. And the chaste married women whom he had raped rejoiced when they heard this curse.[6]

And that's why Ravana never raped Sita.

Rambha, a celestial courtesan *(apsaras),* is passive and helpless in this episode. Accused by her seducer of promiscuity, though not toward him, she is raped and cannot avenge herself, and her husband is the one who makes the curse. Ravana here invokes the double standard not of men and women but of immortals and mortals; as the appropriately mythological Latin saying goes, "What is permitted to Zeus is not permitted to a bull" (Quod licet Jovi non licet bovi).

The same pattern prevails when Ravana rapes another celestial courtesan, Punjikasthali, as he tells a friend:

> Ravana said, "This is a secret about me, something that happened to me a long time ago. One day I saw Punjikasthali gliding through the sky going to the house of the Grandfather [the Creator, Brahma]. I stripped her and raped her by force. When she got to the home of the Self-Created [Brahma] he knew what had happened, and in a fury he said to me, 'From today, if you force any other woman, then your head will split into a hundred pieces.' It is in fear of that curse that I do not force Sita to my bed."[7]

Now the rape is more brutal, preceded by no attempt to persuade; and now it is not merely the husband but the Creator himself who curses Ravana. In accordance with the Creator's greater power, the head is to be shattered into not merely seven but a hundred pieces.

Elsewhere in the *Ramayana*, Ravana gets a more specific curse for lusting not for a courtesan but for a good woman named Vedavati; when she resists him he warns her that she will soon lose her youth, but she insists that she wants to marry Vishnu; infuriated, Ravana seizes her by the hair, which she cuts off with her hand that has become a sword; she throws herself into the fire and promises to be reborn for his destruction—and she is reborn as Sita.[8] This passage sexualizes Sita by giving her a sexual past (as a woman whom Ravana attempted to rape) and then limits that sexuality by attributing to the woman the very power that Sita herself has: the power of her chastity. In contrast with the helpless courtesan in the earlier variant, this woman is empowered by her goodness, which both protects her from being raped and gives her the ability to make the curse herself; indeed, she has no husband to do it for her. Where Sita, like Damayanti,* can swear only by her fidelity to her husband, Vedavati has a chastity that the text regards as a kind of marital fidelity *in potens*: she is faithful to the man she intends to marry, Vishnu. (Here and throughout, I will use an asterisk to indicate a topic discussed elsewhere in the book and noted in the index.) Vedavati therefore has not only the power of a chaste woman but the power of the text, the power of the author's knowledge that she must not be touched. The courtesans and the good women thus face the same problem (male sexual violence) but have very different options in dealing with it. This raises a question that we would do well to bear in mind throughout this inquiry: Who is the agent? Does the woman split or double herself of her own will or does someone else force her to do it?

In another passage, Ravana conflates all three rapes when he says, "Vedavati cursed me when I raped her before; she has been reborn as Sita; and what Uma, Rambha, and Punjikasthali predicted . . . has now come to pass."[9] In this passage, Ravana says he actually raped *(dharshita)* Vedavati, but no details are given. A Freudian would have said that Ravana's inability to rape Sita is overdetermined.[10] Now Rambha and Punjikasthali are given the agency to pronounce a prediction, if not a curse. Presumably, all the courtesans take satisfaction in the curse, just like the chaste married women who "rejoiced when they heard this curse." Vedavati too curses Ravana in this text but does nothing more dramatic; she has therefore lost, where the courtesans gained, power; they have all drawn closer together in a paradigm that erases the contrast between the virtuous woman and the whore.

A later Sanskrit Puranic text, composed between 750 and 1500 C.E., attributes even greater power to Vedavati:

SITA'S FORMER LIFE

A beautiful maiden named Vedavati was granted her wish that she would marry Vishnu in her next life. She went into the mountains to meditate but Ravana came to her, grabbed her with his hand, and attempted to rape her. She, being a good woman, paralyzed him with her angry gaze; he became impotent in his hands and feet and unable to say anything. Then, by the power of her yoga, she died and was reborn as Sita.[11]

Here, as in the *Ramayana*, Vedavati protects herself and is reborn as Sita; though she does not curse Ravana, she uses her gaze to silence his voice— a powerful reversal of the general pattern in other myths of rape and seduction, such as the tale of Ahalya,* in which the woman is the victim of the male gaze, and is silenced. It seems that some of these objects of Ravana's lust protect themselves while others fail to do this but make a curse that will later protect Sita in the same situation.

But already in the Valmiki text there is evidence that Sita is sexually vulnerable. Before Ravana comes to abduct her, successfully masquerading as a human ascetic, he sends the demon Marica to her in the form of a golden deer, an illusion created by the demons precisely in order to lure Rama away so that Ravana can capture Sita. Sita is fooled and insists that Rama go after the deer; she is also fooled when the demon mimics Rama's voice calling for help, and she insists that Rama's brother Lakshmana go to him, ignoring Lakshmana's wise warning that it is probably just a demonic imitation. Indeed, she adds insult to injury by implying that Lakshmana desires her and therefore wishes for Rama's death.[12] A Tibetan text of uncertain provenance states that when Sita sent Lakshmana after Rama she not only accused him of having designs on her but added a curse: "Perhaps the younger brother thinks in his mind that, when the elder brother is dead, he will live together with me. If I do not want it, then, let whoever will touch me be burned."[13] And it was this curse, uttered by Sita herself, that protected her, not against the innocent Lakshmana, but against Ravana, who when he arrived "knew that, if he touched the queen, he would be burned." Sita herself here assumes one aspect of the roles played by Rambha and Vedavati in the Sanskrit texts—she curses her potential rapist even before he exists, just as Vedavati swears by her still nonexistent husband.

The fifteenth-century *Adhyatma-ramayana* found it necessary to exculpate Sita not only from being present in Ravana's home but from the weakness of asking Rama to capture the golden deer for her. This illusory deer, however, may have inspired the *Adhyatma-ramayana* to create the illusory Sita who now desires the deer:

THE ILLUSORY DEER OF THE ILLUSORY SITA

Rama, knowing what Ravana intended to do, told Sita, "Ravana will come to you disguised as an ascetic; put a shadow *[chaya]* of yourself outside the hut, and go inside the hut yourself. Live inside fire, invisible, for a year; when I have killed Ravana, come back to me as you were before." Sita obeyed; she placed an illusory Sita *(mayasita)* outside and entered the fire. This illusory Sita saw the illusory deer and urged Rama to capture it for her.[14]

Rama then pretends to grieve for Sita, pretends to fight to get her back, and lies to his brother Lakshmana, who genuinely grieves for Sita. Sita herself is never subjected to an ordeal at all: after Ravana has been killed and the false Sita brought back and accused, the illusory Sita enters the fire and vanishes forever, while the real Sita emerges and remains with Rama.[15] But Rama seems to forget what he has done; he orders the illusory Sita into the fire as if she were real. Probably in order to maintain the power of the narrative, the author has Rama seem to forget about the shadow at crucial moments; only when the gods come and remind him of his divinity (as they do in the Valmiki text) does Fire (incarnate as the god Agni) return Sita to Rama, remarking, "You made this illusory Sita in order to destroy Ravana. Now he is dead, and that Sita has disappeared."[16] Thus Rama both has and does not have the agency in this text: he creates the shadow but suffers as if he had been helpless to protect his wife. And where Sita's desire for the deer in the Valmiki text proves that she can't recognize a substitute deer, in this text she gets a substitute who can't recognize the substitute deer.

Other texts—the *Mahabharata, Harivamsha, Vishnu Purana,* and several other Puranas—omit the ordeal of Sita,[17] but Tulsi Das's fifteenth-century Hindi version, the *Holy Lake of the Acts of Rama (Ramacaritamanasa),* retains the motif and expands upon it:

SITA'S ORDEAL

[Rama said to Sita,] "Listen, beloved wife, beautiful, faithful, and amiable; I am about to act an alluring human part; let fire then be your dwelling place until I have completed the extirpation of the demons." No sooner had Rama finished speaking than she impressed the image of the Lord's feet on her heart and entered into the fire, leaving her image there, of exactly the same appearance and the same amiable and modest disposition. Not even Laksman knew the secret of what the Lord had done. [Ravana stole Sita, Rama brought her back, and a great celebration took place]. The real Sita had earlier been lodged in the fire, and now the Blessed Lord who witnesses the secrets of all hearts sought to bring her back to light. For this reason the All-merciful addressed some reproachful words [i.e., he commanded Sita to undergo the fire ordeal], on hearing which the female demons all began to grieve. . . . Sita rejoiced at heart to see the fiercely blazing flames, and felt no fear. "If in thought and word and deed," she said, "I have never set my heart on anyone other than Raghubira [Rama], may this Fire, who knows the thoughts of all, become as cooling as sandal-paste" . . . Both her shadow-form as well as the stigma of public shame were consumed in the blazing fire; but no one understood the secret of the Lord's doings. Even the gods, adepts, and sages stood gazing in the heavens. Then Fire assumed a bodily form and, taking by the hand the real Shri

[Sita], famed alike in the Vedas and the world, escorted her and committed
her to Rama.[18]

This episode simultaneously justifies Rama's "reproachful words" in sub-
jecting Sita to the ordeal (by pointing out that he knew it wasn't the real
Sita all along, and that the flames were cool) and quells the uneasiness that
the reader (or hearer) may well share with Rama at the thought of Sita living in Ravana's house for so long (the "public shame" that is burnt up in
the fire). Tulsi argues that Rama never intended or needed to test Sita
(since he knew she wasn't in Ravana's house at all) but had the shadow
Sita enter the fire merely in order to bring the real Sita back from the fire,
to make her visible again.[19] The shadow Sita protects the real Sita from the
trauma of life with Ravana as well as with Rama. It is Rama, not Sita, who
has the idea, and the power, to create Sita's double.

But in borrowing this motif from the *Adhyatma-ramayana*, Tulsi also
seems to have borrowed that text's tendency to forget (or to depict Rama
as forgetting) that the real Sita has been replaced; Rama appears genuinely
to grieve for Sita. Tulsi's double lacks reality, or, to put it differently, the
real Sita never loses her reality. As Frank Whaling points out, "Sita is very
much a woman of flesh and blood in her interviews with Ravana . . . Tulsi
seems to have forgotten the shadow Sita as soon as he has introduced
her."[20]

The double is, however, real enough to be the object of sympathy; like
Rama and Sita, she suffers. She is "a counterfeit or surrogate Sita, condemned to undergo the trials of Lanka—including the painful immersion
in fire at the end of the *Ramayana* war—without ever winning the reward
of suffering, in the form of union with Rama."[21] Thus the double created
in order to spare the original from suffering becomes a new original who
suffers even more than the first original, because she cannot have what
that original was saved *for*. (An illuminating contrast is provided by mainstream Christianity, which rejected the legend that it was Simon of Cyrene
who bore the cross on his shoulder and the crown of thorns upon his
head, while Christ, totally insensitive to the suffering of poor Simon crucified in his place, watched him from heaven and laughed at the fools who
thought that he was the one on the cross.[22] The fact that docetism, along
with other Gnostic beliefs about surrogates for God, was condemned as a
heresy indicates a major difference between Christian and Greek or Hindu
attitudes to divine doubles.)

But Hinduism did express, from time to time, compassion for the sexual double who suffers in place of the original. The idea of the subjectivity of the surrogate is developed in the Puranic text in which the shadow Sita goes on to have a life of her own as a woman notorious for her sexuality:

THE FUTURE LIFE OF THE SHADOW SITA

One day when Sita and Rama were in the forest, the god of Fire came to Rama, took the true Sita, constructed an illusory shadow Sita, with qualities, form, and limbs equal to hers, and gave her to Rama. He told Rama not to divulge the secret to anyone; even Rama's brother Lakshmana did not know. Eventually, Rama subjected Sita to the ordeal of fire and Fire restored the real Sita to Rama.

But then the shadow Sita asked Rama and Fire, "What shall I do?" Fire told her to go to the Pushkara shrine, and there she generated inner heat and was reborn as Draupadi. In the Golden Age she is called Vedavati; in the Second Age, she is [the shadow] Sita. And in the Third Age, the shadow is Draupadi. This shadow, who was in the prime of her youth, was so nervous and excited with lust when she asked Shiva for a husband that she repeated her request five times. And so she obtained five husbands, the five Pandavas.[23]

Here it is Fire rather than Rama who constructs the double; Rama has lost some of his agency. And it is Fire who gives the shadow Sita a sexual future; for when she has saved the original Sita from contact with Ravana, she goes on to have a sex life of her own: she is reborn as Draupadi, heroine of the other epic, the *Mahabharata,* and of many contemporary cults—a woman with five husbands, unheard of in polygynous, but never polyandrous, Hinduism. Significantly, too, Draupadi, like the shadow Sita in some variants, is born of a fire;[24] indeed, it may have been this episode in her history that attracted Draupadi from her own epic into Sita's story in the other epic, as if Hamlet somehow popped up as a character in *King Lear.* In the past, Sita herself (as Vedavati) was the victim of a promiscuous man (Ravana), and in the future her shadow (as Draupadi) will be accused of promiscuity. In the present, Vedavati becomes the shadow who undergoes Sita's ordeal not only with Ravana but with Rama.

A contemporary Tamil text attempts not only to save Sita (by using the surrogate) but to reward the double with a sexually satisfying future incarnation that is not, however, promiscuous:

THE MARRIAGE OF SITA'S DOUBLE

Once Ravana had behaved in an unseemly manner toward a virtuous woman named Vedavati. She became angry and cursed him saying, "I will destroy your entire clan," and then she sought refuge with Lord Agni [Fire]. Lord Agni consoled her and offered her protection. [When Ravana came to abduct Sita], Lord Agni transformed Vedavati, who was in his care, into the likeness of Sita and carried away the real Sita, leaving Vedavati in her place. After Lord Rama had defeated Ravana and recovered Sita he was unable to bear the rumors of scandal, and so he commanded Sita, who in reality was Vedavati, to undergo trial by fire. Vedavati entered the fire as Lord Rama ordered, and at that moment Lord Agni appeared with Vedavati and the real Sita, who had been living under his protection. When he saw two identical Sitas, Lord Rama was astonished. The real Sita said, "My Lord, this woman's name is Vedavati. . . . She went with Ravana in my place and suffered unbearable hardships in Lanka. You must marry this woman who suffered so much in the Ashoka grove [of Ravana's palace] on our behalf." Rama answered, "O queen, you are undoubtedly aware that I have vowed that in my present incarnation as Rama I will have just one wife. But during the Kali Yuga I will assume the form of Venkateshwara. At that time this Vedavati will be born as Padmavati, and I will marry her."[25]

Again Fire rather than Rama is the agent, but this time Rama is so far from masterminding the double that he does not even understand what has happened at all. Unlike the Sanskrit texts we have just seen, this text has Rama confront the two doubles together. And this Sita does not merely use the surrogate to protect herself, but protects the surrogate, assuming that the surrogate's sensibilities are like her own and that she too has rights. Generously she suggests that Rama marry them both. Rama prefers, however, to postpone this marriage to yet another incarnation in the future. Vedavati is then reborn not as Draupadi but as Padmavati, an important deity worshipped in Tirupati; thus the double takes on a persona and a rebirth, a life of her own in South India, where some sources say that the god Vishnu set her free after he married her; she roams the world as an autonomized fragment of his divinity.[26] One can imagine these texts continuing to proliferate in an infinite regress caused by the suspension of the original assumption that the double is not real, does not count, has no feelings: once that assumption is gone, each double can create a double just as the original did.

Tulsi also relates another episode in which Sita is impersonated, this time by Sati, the wife of the god Shiva:

THE SHADOW SATI

[Sati, traveling with Shiva, met Rama when he was searching for Sita after Ravana had taken away the shadow Sita.] A great doubt arose in her mind. . . . "Can he wander in search of his wife like an ignorant man, he who is a repository of knowledge?" . . . Though [Sati] did not open her lips, yet Shiva, who knows the secrets of all hearts, came to know everything. . . . [He said,] "If you have a grave doubt in your mind, why not go and put the matter to the test?" . . . After many an anxious thought Sati assumed the form of Sita and moved ahead on the same road by which the king of men (Rama) was coming. . . . All-perceiving and acquainted with the secrets of all hearts, the Lord of gods, Rama, took no time in detecting Sati's disguise.

[Sati returned and lied to Shiva, pretending that Rama had mistaken her for Sita; but Shiva knew the truth.] "Sati took Sita's form," Shiva thought in deep despondency; "if now I treat Sati as my wife, the faith I follow will be all lost, and I shall be committing a sin. Sati is too pure to be abandoned; yet it were great sin to show my love. . . . I will not touch Sati in the body she now wears." . . . Sati guessed that the omniscient Shiva knew all she had done. "I have deceived [Shiva]," she thought, "stupid and senseless woman that I am. . . ." In her infatuation, she did not listen to Shiva's advice and was beguiled into assuming the form of Sita. [Shiva] deserted her because she had offended him by taking the form of Sita.[27]

Sati's question is wiser than she knows, since she is apparently unaware of the shadow Sita: she merely asks, Why should Rama be grieving for Sita?, where we might ask, Why should Rama be grieving for Sita, *when he knows it is not the real Sita?* But she chooses to test him by an impersonation the purpose of which is unclear: Is she trying to prove that Rama could not tell the difference between a real woman and an illusion (which would imply that she *did* know about the shadow Sita)? Or just that he is not in fact omniscient? In any case, the trick backfires; she does not fool Rama, but as a result of her action, which invites the intimacy of another man even though it is not consummated, Shiva treats her precisely as Rama treated Sita in the parallel situation: he rejects her. Or, to put it differently, Shiva can no longer treat Sati as his wife because she has taken the form of another man's wife. Sati, like Draupadi, may have been attracted to the tale of Sita by the shared theme of fire, even more closely shared by Sati than by Draupadi: in a famous myth, Sati willingly enters a fire for the sake of her husband, committing suicide in this way to be reborn in the next life as Parvati, Shiva's wife.[28] A later Sanskrit text spares

Sati this trauma by lending her Sita's trick of using a surrogate when she enters the fire: when Sati was about to commit suicide, she created a shadow who entered the fire and died, while the real Sati was reborn as Parvati.[29] Tulsi's Sati, however, does not create a shadow but becomes a shadow herself; like Valmiki's Sita, she must enter the fire before she can return to her husband.

Another Tamil text gives Parvati a shadow of her own:

THE SHADOW PARVATI

Ravana asked Shiva to give Parvati to him, and Shiva was forced to grant this wish to this powerful devotee. But as Ravana was carrying Parvati south to Lanka, Vishnu took the form of a sage and said to Ravana, "Shiva gave you Illusion *(maya)* and told you she was his wife." Ravana believed him and went off to a river to meditate in order to get the "real" Parvati, leaving the "false" one behind in the sage's care. As soon as Ravana was gone, Vishnu raced away with Parvati, bringing her to Shiva.

When Ravana returned to the grove, to find the sage and the goddess missing, he followed the footprints but could not find Parvati, for she was with Shiva, who had rendered her invisible to Ravana by a wall of sacred ash. Shiva then appeared and gave Ravana a woman that he called Illusory Power (*mayashakti* [Shakti being another name of the wife of Shiva]). Ravana, believing that he now had the real Shakti, Shiva's wife, put Illusion in his chariot and went to Lanka. On the way, he saw the sage again, and the sage said, "All this was illusion. Now you have received a real boon of a beautiful woman, there is no doubt of that." Ravana was content and went to Lanka with Illusion.[30]

Ravana, the master of illusion, is hoist by his own petard. He abducts Parvati instead of Sita, and he does not even manage to get the real Parvati. This text removes Sita very far indeed from the touch of Ravana: she is not even in the story at all.

And it went on. A different sort of shadow Sita was constructed for the opposite purpose, not to protect the real Sita from sexual contact but to allow the false Sita to achieve sexual contact with Rama. This shadow is conjured up by the demoness Shurpanakha, who, in the Valmiki text, attempts to seduce Rama in her own ugly form and is repulsed by Lakshmana, who cuts off her nose.[31] In Kamban's Tamil version of the *Ramayana,* composed in the twelfth century C.E., Shurpanakha impersonates Sita for Rama, who, as in Tulsi, sees through the trick:

THE DEMONIC SHADOW SITA FAILS

The demoness Shurpanakha, the sister of Ravana, well aware of her ugliness, fell in love with Rama, who rejected her and instructed his brother to mutilate her by cutting off her nose, ears, and breasts. She then transformed herself into the image of the divine form of Sita. When the real Sita appeared, Shurpanakha told Rama that the other woman [the real Sita] was a deceitful, man-eating demoness who was skilled in the arts of illusion and had adopted a false form. Rama knew who was who but continued to tease Shurpanakha. When Sita ran to Rama and embraced him, Rama rejected Shurpanakha.[32]

The poet makes explicit the demoness's motive; she reasons, "He will never look at me while she who has no equal is near him. / Best for me to run there fast, take her and hide her away somewhere quickly / and then I will assume that form that he loves and I will live with him."[33] But she does not in fact hide Sita away; the two Sitas, the original and the double, stand there side by side.

A fourteenth-century Nepalese dramatization of this episode turns it entirely on its head: this time Rama is completely fooled by the apparition and has to resort to tests of her identity. Here is a summary of the first act:

THE DEMONIC SHADOW SITA SUCCEEDS

Now Shurpanakha comes looking for Rama. Shurpanakha admires the big arms of Rama and wants to embrace him, but seeing Sita she gets angry and waits for an opportunity to embrace Rama. Sita wakes up and suddenly embraces Rama. She has seen a bad dream: a fearful ogress [rakshasi] came to eat her up. Rama tells her that she need not be frightened when both he and Lakshmana are there; she should take a bath in the Godavari and thus remove the bad effect of the dream. Sita asks Lakshmana to show her the path and they both leave. Sita gets into the river and Lakshmana goes to collect fruits and roots. Now Shurpanakha approaches Rama in the guise of Sita. Rama too is getting impatient without Sita. Seeing Shurpanakha in Sita's guise Rama takes her to be the real Sita and thinks that Sita has come back after the bath. Shurpanakha embraces Rama and asks him to kiss her. Rama is a little perplexed at the behavior of Sita and says, "It is not proper for people like us to engage in sexual [gramya, literally "village, vulgar, or sexual"] activity in the day; let us wait for the night." Now the real Sita enters. Shurpanakha asks Rama to protect her, saying that Sita is an ogress in her [Sita's] form; Shurpanakha embraces Rama.

Rama, believing that the real Sita is the ogress, attempts to kill her. Sita shouts for Lakshmana to help her. Lakshmana arrives, but, though he cannot decide which is the real Sita, he stops Rama from killing the presumed ogress. Then Lakshmana gets an idea: whichever of the two Sitas brings a *parijata* flower from Indra's heaven is the real one. The real Sita, who does not know where she can get this flower, faints, while the other Sita goes and brings the flower. But since Lakshmana knows that only an ogress could get the flower so easily, he recognizes the ogress, catches her by the hair, and wants to kill her. Rama tells him to punish her without killing her, and Lakshmana cuts off her nose. She resumes her fierce form and curses them, while Rama consoles the real Sita.[34]

Rama here behaves not only unlike a god but even unlike a man: the words in which he meditates on his suspicions of his wife reflect, and may well have been borrowed from, the strikingly similar words in which a woman, Ahalya,* meditates on her suspicions of the man posing as her husband Gautama ("We should not make love in the daytime"). Not only that: where Ahalya used that logic to figure out that her bed partner was *not* her true spouse, Rama draws precisely the wrong conclusion and goes on with the lovemaking.

The logic of the test that Lakshmana finally sets[35] is taken from another Hindu tradition, the tales of Mariatai Raman,* in which the impostor betrays himself by succeeding in the test of supernatural powers. Though Rama is, as in Valmiki's text, the one who condemns Shurpanakha to mutilation rather than death, Lakshmana here prevents Rama from committing an even more terrible crime, against Sita herself, and the superiority of Lakshmana's discernment over Rama's in this text is one of several strong hints that Rama here is very definitely not God. His failure to recognize his own wife, even after embracing the impostor, is a far cry from his omniscience in Tulsi's text.

Kamban's Tamil text also constructs an even more elaborate shadow Sita, this time in the mind of the demon Ravana himself. Here is R. K. Narayan's retelling of this incident:

THE DEMON'S SHADOW SITA AND RAMA

In that utter darkness Ravana suffered hallucinations of Sita's figure approaching and receding, and addressed it endearingly. . . . Still doubting his own vision, he ordered, "Fetch my sister at once. . . . I see this woman before me. Is this the one you meant?" [Shurpanakha] looked hard and said, "Oh, no. The person who stands before us is not a woman at all. It's

Rama, that—that man. I don't see Sita here. You are only imagining. . . ."
"If it's mere imagination on my part, how is it you see Rama here?" [Shur-
panakha] merely said, "Ever since the day he did this damage to me, I find
it impossible to forget him," trying not to be too explicit about her feelings
for Rama, equivocating her meaning.[36]

This text presents us with a remarkable reification of fantasy: Ravana and
his sister carry on a long argument about a figment of Ravana's imagination that both of them can see—or, more precisely, that they see simultaneously as a figment of his imagination and hers.

Shurpanakha goes on to explain what has happened to Ravana: "As
your consciousness, obsessed, fixes on nothing else, / and your great desire, spreading wide, burns within you, / everywhere that your eyes turn,
they light on her, / and she appears for you! Look! This is an old story."[37]
The translator suggests that the reference to the "old story" means that
"since everyone knows that Ravana has a weakness for beautiful women, it
is natural that he should mistakenly see Sita everywhere." Or does everyone do it, not just Ravana? Or is the idea of multiple Sitas itself the "old
story"?

A different sort of permutation occurs in a Malay version of the *Ramayana* in which the demon tries to abduct both Rama's wife and his
mother:

THE SHADOW OF RAMA'S MOTHER

Mandudari was the wife of Dasarata, and the mother of Rama and Lak-
samana. The giant Rawana came to ask Dasarata for her. From the secre-
tion from her skin, Mandudari made a frog that transformed itself into a
beautiful woman in her likeness. The double, called Mandudaki, was given
to Rawana. Dasarata, however, managed to sleep with Mandudaki first; she
later gave birth to a daughter, Sita dewi. Rawana tried to kill her, exposed
her in a chest on a river, but she was saved, raised by an ascetic, and married Rama; she and Rama were transformed into monkeys and gave birth
to Hanuman. Rawana then abducted Sita, but Rama retrieved her with the
help of Hanuman.[38]

Ravana first tries to abduct Rama's mother and is fooled by her double, as
he is fooled in other texts when he tries to get Rama's wife, Sita. But since
Rama's father has already begotten Sita upon the double, Sita is Rama's
half sister and wife and Ravana's stepdaughter (and, if he had his way,
wife). In this text, the double, far from protecting Sita, both leaves her fully

exposed (since she has no double of her own) and doubles Ravana's sin in stealing Sita: she is not merely the wife of another man (who happens to be her half brother) but Ravana's own stepdaughter.

In the Tibetan text cited above, Sita is not Ravana's stepdaughter but his daughter, whom he throws into a river; a farmer finds her in the watery channel of a furrow and adopts her, giving her the name of Rolrnedma, "Found in a Furrow." But this time a quite unmagical double actually precipitates Sita's ordeal at Rama's hands instead of protecting her from it. After Sita's return from Lanka, Rama (here called Ramana) begins to suspect her chastity when he hears a husband quarreling with his promiscuous wife, who defends herself by saying that other women are like that too, citing the case of Sita and concluding, "Do you know the nature of all women?":

> King Ramana heard this and thought in his mind: "Alas, it is true that my wife has slept with the demon." He was full of doubt and dejected. He thought: "In connection with her saying: 'Do you know the nature of women?,' it is likely to be different from that of men. I must examine the wife of [that husband]." [He slept with her.] He asked her: "Fair one, you said the nature of women is not like that of men. How is it?"[39]

She replied that while women do sleep with men other than their husbands, they fear "shame," and thus, though they "obtain the object of [their] desire even with a stranger," they do so in a solitary place. Men, in contrast, "though feeling blame, do not feel ashamed."[40] The distinction that anthropologists once made between "shame" and "guilt" cultures is here made between women and men, together with a cunning if twisted logic for the double standard, the gender asymmetry that haunts these myths. There are no magical doubles in this down-to-earth telling, just an anonymous woman who can double for Sita because all women are alike. But women are different from men; they act the same, but their minds are different, and because, unlike men, they know infidelity is wrong, it *is* wrong—for *them*. Ramana is convinced by his own infidelity (with the promiscuous wife) that Sita has been unfaithful (with the demon), and so he banishes her.

Why did the authors of these later texts feel that they had to give the real Sita a double—indeed, more and more doubles? Perhaps in response to the shift in the nature of Rama. In Valmiki's *Ramayana,* Rama is by very definition an incarnate god, but he keeps forgetting that he is god, flickering in and out of an ambiguous divinity. Readers and hearers were bothered for a long time by his shabby treatment of Sita, but only when he came to be the object of widespread worship, an unambiguous, full-fledged man/god/king, did the tellers of his story feel that they could no longer portray the hollowness implicit in his mistrust of his wife's honesty and/or chastity.

Attitudes to women changed too, and the growing Hindu obsession with the chastity of women reached a particularly fanatical climax after the Turkic invasions, the time in which the Hindi and Tamil texts were composed. As Sheldon Pollock remarks of this process, "Ravana is not only 'other' in his reckless polygyny—'others' always threaten to steal 'our' women—but is presented without question as a tyrant, perhaps even as a kind of 'Oriental despot' constructed by a preform of Orientalism."[41] The need to protect Sita's chastity from demons (read: Hindu women's chastity from Muslims) was answered by the appropriation of the motif of the surrogate, which had long been available in the literature, as we shall see.

In Valmiki's text Sita has some agency—she leaves Rama, in the end—and Rama himself admits (when he claims that he knew all along that she was chaste, and made her enter the fire only to prove it to everyone else), "Ravana could not even think of raping Sita, for she was protected by her own energy." Yet that very verb, meaning "to rape, assault, or violate," is used when Ravana grabs Sita by the hair.[42] This Sita seems to lack Vedavati's power to paralyze Ravana with her glance. Why? The Valmiki text does not raise this question, let alone answer it, but we might speculate that Vedavati's (or Rambha's) earlier curse on Ravana both made it unnecessary for Sita to defend herself and rendered her powerless to prevent Ravana from violating her in the mildest sense of the word. We might go one step further and suggest that it was precisely in order to sidestep this issue—to make it possible for Ravana to carry off Sita so that Rama could get her back—that later texts invented the shadow Sita, who had the form of the real Sita but not her chaste power.

On the other hand, another Hindu tradition assumes that good women can*not* be doubled. This tradition glosses a Vedic text that tells us that the Pleiades, the wives of the Seven Sages (Ursa Major), were kept from intercourse with their husbands because the Seven Sages rise in the North and the Pleiades in the East, and Agni (the god of fire) mated with them.[43] The *Mahabharata* (the other great Sanskrit epic, composed between about 400 B.C.E. and 400 C.E.) gives this story a new twist:

FIRE, THE WIFE OF FIRE,
AND THE WIVES OF THE SEVEN SAGES

Agni fell in love with the wives of the Seven Sages, but since he knew that they were not in love with him he went away to the forest. Svaha fell in love with him and was looking for a weak spot; when she found out that he was in love with the sages' wives she decided to take their forms and to seduce him; then both of them would obtain their desires. Assuming the form of each of the wives in turn, she made love with Agni, but she could not take the form of Arundhati because of Arundhati's great fidelity. And because Svaha worried that anyone who saw her in her transformation would falsely accuse the sages' wives of adultery, she took the form of a bird to leave the forest each time, carrying in her hand the seed of Fire, which eventually became the god Skanda. Nevertheless, even when they learned the truth, the Seven Sages abandoned their wives—all but Arundhati; Skanda made them into the Pleiades. Then Agni married Svaha.[44]

Agni, who was the agent of Sita's doubling, does not himself produce or become a double of the husband in this situation, as other gods in his position might do (such as Indra, to seduce Ahalya*); Agni honors the wishes of the women, a rare consideration, and then becomes the victim of the serial doublings of Svaha (whose name represents the oblation of butter offered into the sacrificial fire). Equally considerate is Svaha's concern for the reputation of the women she imitates, who are usually falsely accused in variants of this myth; indeed, despite her efforts they are still dishonored and given, at the end, the boon (or punishment?) of becoming stars. The implication is that since Arundhati's chastity prevented Svaha from imitating her for unchaste purposes, the chastity of the other women must have been somehow flawed. This implication does not, apparently, apply to Sita in the post-Valmiki *Ramayana* tradition; the authors of the stories about Shurpanakha as Sita, or indeed of the shadow Sita, were apparently unaware of the Arundhati syndrome or chose to ignore it—or silently allowed it to cast doubt on the purity of Sita.

Agni plays a more active role in a later retelling of this myth that omits Svaha almost entirely:

FIRE AND THE WIVES OF THE SEVEN SAGES

Agni wanted to seduce the sages' wives, but since they were protected by a curse, he made images of them and, unable to control his mounting desire, shed his seed in a golden pot; but he could not make the form of Arundhati because of her fidelity to her husband. Assuming the form of a bird,

he carried the pot to a mountaintop, where it became the god Skanda. It
was because Agni did not enjoy making love to Svaha that he made the imitation Pleiades and seduced other women.[45]

Agni is apparently married to Svaha before this story begins, but he explicitly rejects her, nor is she able to reach him this time through a series of
doubles. Yet she is implicitly present through the assumed paradigm of
sacrificial symbolism:[46] Agni places his semen in the golden pot, just as
the sacrificer places the melted butter (Svaha) in the sacrificial fire (and as
Rama uses a golden* image of Sita in his fire sacrifices). A curse keeps
Agni from taking the women (like the curse that accounts for Ravana's re-
straint toward Sita), so that he himself must produce the doubles; he even
becomes a bird, like Svaha. But instead of taking the forms of their husbands (which would be the logical parallel to what Svaha did in the earlier
text) he makes images of *them,* just as Svaha had done, and apparently
makes love to the images, the consoling replicas. The story of Agni and the
(presumably golden) images of the sages' wives is an instance of the theme
of the artistic image* that, like the shadow, stands in for the unattainable
or lost beloved.

The pattern of Agni's seduction of the sages' wives was revived centuries later in a popular corpus of myths in which the wives of the
cowherds leave the beds of their husbands to join the god Krishna, who
produces two sets of doubles in order to accommodate them. Krishna is
heir to much of the mythology of Indra and Agni, but there is an important difference between them: whereas Indra and Agni, who are great gods
in the *Rig Veda,* c. 1000 B.C.E., were worshipped only in high-caste Vedic
sacrifices by the time of the story of Ahalya and the tales of the sages'
wives, c. 200 B.C.E., Krishna was regarded as God with a capital *G* and worshipped by people at all levels of society at the time of the myths of his
adultery. This means that we will have to look for different sorts of meanings in the Krishna myths, as well as some of the same meanings as those
of the Indra and Agni myths. Krishna (himself the son of doubled parents)[47] produces doubles that really *are* Krishna, for he divides himself
into as many parts as there are women; each woman gets the real thing,
not a fake replica. But Krishna also provides, conveniently, doubles of
them to stay at home in bed with their husbands while they cavort with
him, and the implication is that the husbands do not get the real thing,
that they are fooled.

The locus classicus for this event is the *Bhagavata Purana,* composed in about the tenth century C.E.: "The cowherd men did not become jealous of Krishna, for they were deluded by his magic power of illusion *[yoga-maya]* and each one thought that his own wife was lying beside him."[48] A later commentator argued that Krishna's illusory power *[yoga-maya],* here incarnate as a goddess, "in order to protect Krsna's eternal wives from the sexual approaches of others, created duplicate forms of them which their so-called husbands saw by their sides."[49] In the *Bhagavata Purana,* this duplication is said to have taken place on the night of the erotic dance, but this commentator says that it extended, retroactively, as it were, to the entire period of the married life of the cowherd women.

The commentator even cites the story of the double created to protect Sita when Ravana abducted her, and adds, "As the same rule is seen to take effect for any devoted wife in similar circumstances by the power of her devotion to her husband, then why would Maya, who serves the husband of the *gopis,* not especially protect them in the way that Rama's fire protected Sita?"[50] But there is a double danger here, both that Krishna might pollute the honor of other men by sharing their wives and that his contact with other mens' wives might pollute him. This may have troubled the mind of another commentator who goes even farther: "The *gopis* are the wives of these cowherds only in the sense that the latter claim possession of them, but that is all. In fact, they rarely even see one another."[51] Still later, and still more fastidious, commentaries, in an attempt to distance the god even more from any possible implication of adultery, reversed the situation described in the *Bhagavata Purana* and argued that the real women remained at home with their husbands, while Krishna made love to the doubles.[52] Thus, where Western tales of adultery have a mere eternal triangle, the Hindu myth gives us an eternal mandala.

The storyteller Urmilaji, in present-day Kangra, explained Krishna's multiplicity to Kirin Narayan this way:

WHY KRISHNA HAS SO MANY WIVES

Krishna was always falling in love with women. Before he was born as Krishna, he had taken birth as Ramchandra [Rama]. At the gathering of princes when Sita chose her groom, it was Ramchandra whom she got. All her girlfriends were absolutely incredulous. "Where did you get this groom from? Look at him! He's incomparable. . . ." So Ramchandra gave them a boon. He said, "In my next life, I'll marry you all."

> Radha is one of them, and there are many others that he married
> too . . . , it's said.[53]

Krishna, who reciprocates the women's desire, multiplies himself in order
to give copies to the losers. Thus the contrast between the chastity of
Rama and Sita, on the one hand, and the promiscuity of Krishna and the
cowherd women, on the other, is resolved by reincarnation: the paradigmatic chaste husband doubles himself, as it were, in the paradigmatic
adulterous god. In this scenario, Sita, though paradigmatically chaste, is
not so chaste as either to prevent or not to need the creation of a double to
protect her chastity.

The impulse to create an illusory Sita may stem from a desire either to
affirm the reality of the original Sita or to reject her reality. If an illusory
Sita substitutes for a Sita who is originally illusory herself, the Sita who is
captured is a double illusion, *maya* squared—or, if two negatives cancel
one another out, a reality. Whaling states the first case, arguing for the reality of Sita in the *Ramayana*:

> If the phenomenal Sita were mere illusion, there would be no point in an il-
> lusory Sita entering the fire so that another illusory Sita could do duty for
> her in the tense parts of the story. It is because the phenomenal Sita is real
> at the phenomenal level that her real form must be protected. Although at
> the highest level Rama and Sita are not humans, at the phenomenal level
> they are [and] the real Sita has to be protected within the fire while the illu-
> sory Sita goes to Lanka. The illusory Sita of Lanka is the guarantee of the
> real Sita of the whole story. The *Adhyatma* "improves" the original story in
> order to safeguard the moral character of the principals.[54]

There were ways of protecting Sita by devising other stratagems, without
creating a magical double, as both Kamban's Tamil *Ramayana* and the Tibetan *Ramayana* demonstrate.[55] But the double Sita was the preferred device because of its deep resonance with other aspects of the *Ramayana*.

There are illusory Sitas, shadow Sitas, even in Valmiki's Sanskrit text.
Ravana's son Indrajit produces a false image of Sita and kills it, fooling
Hanuman and, through Hanuman's report, Rama;[56] Indrajit cuts the illusory Sita in half diagonally, from one shoulder to the other hip—"along
the path of the sacred thread," the poet tells us, with a vivid image of simultaneously horizontal and vertical splitting. A very different sort of
double appears at the end of the *Ramayana,* after Sita's final disappear-
ance: "Rama never sought another consort, but in every sacrifice a golden

image of Sita took the place of the wife."[57] In Bhavabhuti's retelling, in a chapter actually entitled "Shadow" *[Chaya]*, Sita learns of this golden image and, touched, comes into Rama's presence, invisible; he feels her touch but cannot see her, a vivid and moving reversal of all the other doubles, which are visible but not truly palpable.[58]

The agency of the women, and the men, shifts in the course of history. In the Valmiki text, Vedavati is able both to protect herself from rape and to curse Ravana, and Sita herself takes the initiative in leaving Rama and plunging into the earth; but this final act of rebellion on her part is generally omitted from later tellings, in which she becomes more and more subservient to Rama. Unlike Vedavati, and like the courtesan Rambha, Sita after Valmiki is protected by a series of doubles created by males, first by Rama and then—in one Puranic text when he too loses his agency—by Fire incarnate. (The Nepalese text, in which Rama is certainly neither omniscient nor omnipotent, depicts him as the helpless victim of the ogress's illusory Sita.) But once Rama has become fully divine in Tulsi's text and the *Adhyatma-ramayana*, he takes over and commands Fire to produce the false Sita.

The complex doublings of Sita grow in part out of the doctrine of illusion that is woven throughout all *Ramayanas*.[59] But they are also inspired by a deep ambiguity in the attitude to Sita's sexuality. On the one hand, she is the epitome of female chastity. On the other hand, the demoness Shurpanakha is able to double for Sita, David Shulman suggests, because both of them are highly sexual women[60]—a quality that, as I have suggested, may also explain why Ravana is able to carry her off in the first place. Indeed, as the *Ramayana* came to play a major role in political rhetoric in later Indian history, Sita began to look too good to be true—or too good to be good. Thus, according to one reinterpretation by a South Indian author, keen to mock North Indian piety: "Sita . . . is Ravana's paramour who did not resist but 'clung like a vine' when she was abducted."[61] Whether Sita resisted or clung became, like many other points in this epic, a matter for bitter, even violent dispute, as it was in the reception of the texts about the seduction of Ahalya and Alcmena.*

HELEN

A close narrative parallel to the shadow Sita is provided by the story of Helen of Troy and her phantom double (called an *eidolon* in Greek, a ghost or shadow or image—and, eventually, an idol, whence our own term).[62] The plot is basically the same: a phantom surrogate is found for the abducted heroine; the king must retrieve his abducted wife and kill her abductor. But there is an essential difference between the two stories: where Sita was innocent of the sexual betrayal of which she is accused, Helen is guilty: Homer tells us, in both the *Iliad* and the *Odyssey* (composed in the ninth or eighth century B.C.E.), that Helen fell for the Trojan Paris and ran off with him, leaving her Greek husband, King Menelaus, in Sparta and thereby triggering the Trojan War, ostensibly fought to bring her back to Greece.

Homer says nothing of another Helen taking her place in Troy, but his Helen is duplicitous in the basic sexual sense of the word: she has two men, her husband and her lover. Indeed, already in Homer she has two lovers; when Paris dies, she replaces him with his brother Deiphobus.[63] (As Froma Zeitlin nicely sums it up, "Helen, it seems, can never be single—at least, for long.")[64] In later Greek mythology, Helen continues to seduce or be seduced by new lovers: besides Paris and Deiphobus, there are Theseus, Enarsophoros the son of Hippokoon, Idas and Lynkeus, Korythos, and Achilles.[65] Helen also has two fathers—Zeus and Tyndareus—, and two mothers—Leda and Nemesis. Roberto Calasso says that "doubleness is the distinguishing mark of her entire tradition" and that "Helen was a phantom before she was a woman."[66] Moreover, Helen is both doubling and doubled, both mimicked and mimicking.

Homer certainly seems to assume that the real Helen went to Troy with Paris, leaving Menelaus with no wife at all. Aeschylus, however, in the *Agamemnon* (458 B.C.E.), speaks of Menelaus as having a kind of shadow Helen while the real Helen was, presumably, in Troy (as she is in Homer's telling):

THE PHANTOM HELEN IN SPARTA

Through yearning for the one gone over the sea,
a ghost *[phasma]* will seem to rule the house . . .
Fancies haunt him in dreams persuasively;
theirs is a grace without substance.
Unsubstantial it is, when one sees,
and dreaming reaches to the touch,
and the vision *[opsis]* is gone,
quickly slipping through his hands,
as it follows the winged paths of sleep.[67]

Other Greeks, from Homer on, assumed that Menelaus was left with no wife at all when Paris took her away. But where was she?

Herodotus (also in the fifth century B.C.E.) maintained that the real Helen was not in Troy:

HELEN NOT OF TROY

[Helen had run off with Paris, but a storm had cast them ashore in Egypt; she was kept there, protected by Proteus, while Paris returned home empty-handed. The Greeks laid siege.] But when they captured the walls—there was no Helen! . . . Menelaus came to Egypt and sailed up to Memphis, told the truth of what had happened, and received great hospitality and took back Helen, quite unhurt. . . . If Helen had been in Ilium, she would have been given back to the Greeks, whether Alexander wanted it so or not.[68]

Herodotus, who accuses Homer of knowingly suppressing the story of Helen's absence from Troy, says nothing about a false Helen; the whole point of his story is that there was *no* Helen in Troy, not even a phantom, that the entire Trojan War was fought for a woman who did not even appear to be there. Nor does Herodotus save the real Helen from being seduced by Paris; Proteus takes Helen only after the lovers have presumably consummated their adultery on the way to Egypt (though Herodotus remarks, ambiguously, that Helen was brought back from Egypt "unhurt," more literally, "without having experienced anything bad *[apathea kakon]*").[69] Elsewhere, Herodotus says that the Persians said that Helen (like other abducted women) *willingly* ran off with Paris: "Clearly, the women would not have been carried off had they no mind to be."[70] Herodotus certainly would not have called it a rape, or even, perhaps, a seduction, by Paris; Helen was, as men say, asking for it.

Hesiod too seems to have gotten Helen as far as Egypt with Paris.[71] The phantom Helen, who absolves the real Helen of adultery, is first mentioned in a palinode by Stesichorus, known to us primarily from its citations by Plato, in the fourth century B.C.E., in two separate dialogues:

THE PHANTOM OF HELEN AT TROY

When he was struck blind for accusing Helen, Stesichorus, unlike Homer, recognized the cause, for he was well educated, and immediately he composed his Palinode: "The story *[logos]* is not true. You did not board the well-benched ships. You did not reach the towers of Troy."[72] . . . Stesichorus says the phantom of Helen was fought for at Troy through ignorance of the truth.[73]

These two pieces, patched together, tell a story that agrees with Herodotus in asserting that Helen was absent from Troy. But where Herodotus got Helen as far as Egypt with Paris, Stesichorus does not tell us where she was but states that she had a phantom stand-in at Troy. Pausanias, in the second century C.E., does not explicitly mention the phantom Helen in his account: Helen announced to Stesichorus that he had lost his eyes because he had infuriated her; and so Stesichorus recanted.[74] Pausanias says that Homer too was struck blind,[75] as other Greek traditions maintain.[76] If Stesichorus was believed to have been blinded for accusing Helen, Homer's blindness too may have been attributed to his statement that the real Helen went to Troy—particularly if (as Herodotus argued) Homer knew that she didn't and nevertheless said that she did.

Stesichorus' tale of the phantom Helen implies that Paris was fooled, while Menelaus never had to be fooled, since he never had the double. (Paris, who bedded the false Helen, failed that test as he had failed another famous test, when he was asked to distinguish between not the identities but the qualities of three goddesses: Aphrodite, Athena, and Hera—a failure that led directly to the debacle with Helen.) Greek honor is saved. But is the problem really solved? Norman Austin thinks not: "The Palinode's project, to remove the dishonor from the traditional story by ascribing all Helen's ambiguity to her simulacrum, far from resolving Helen's ambivalences, had the unwitting effect of making Helen into a ghost of her own ghost, the negative of a negative. . . . The only reason for this Helen's being was to be not-Helen of Troy."[77] Helen is the negative of a negative, as Sita was the illusion of an illusion; that is, Helen becomes able to impersonate herself.[78] The big question then is, "Was Helen ever in another man's bed who was not her husband? Sparta, Egypt, Troy—who cared about the place? The question was not *where* but *whether*."[79]

The Phantom Helen in Sparta and at Troy

In Euripides' *The Trojan Women* (415 B.C.E.), Helen has no double; Menelaus says he went to Troy not to get Helen but to kill Paris, and he plans to bring Helen back to Sparta to kill her; Helen herself, as in Homer, blames Aphrodite for her seduction by Paris, and now she also claims that Deiphobus took her by force, though Hecuba mocks these defenses and Menelaus is unmoved. But Euripides tells the story quite differently just a few years later, in *Helen* (412 B.C.E.), a play that reconciles the assertions of Herodotus (that Helen was not at Troy, but in Egypt) and Stesichorus (that Helen herself was not at Troy, but her phantom *eidolon* was), by adding an essential strategic detail: the phantom replaced

Helen in Sparta and was taken to Troy, so that the real Helen not only never reached Egypt with Paris, as Herodotus had said she did, but never even slept with Paris: she was magically transported directly from Sparta to Egypt.

The Helen of *Helen* is no longer the willing adulteress, as she was in Homer and Herodotus (and *The Trojan Women*); she was carried off against her will, it is implied (though never actually stated), and the phantom was created to save her from an alliance she did not want. Helen herself claims at the start of the play:

> Hera gave Paris not me, but a breathing image *[eidolon]* made in likeness to me, made out of air, and he thinks he has me, but has a useless seeming. Hermes caught me up in folds of air, veiled by cloud, and set me down in the halls of Proteus . . . and I will still make my home in Sparta with my husband, and he will know I never went to Troy, never spread a bed for any man.

Menelaus had captured the phantom Helen at Troy and kept her in a cave for seven years (never noticing the difference); then he came to Egypt and met the real Helen. At that moment, the gods dissolved the phantom back into mist, and Helen announced that the "evil thing" that had been sent to Troy in her place, the piece of cloud, had now been returned to the ether.[80] Later, Helen—the real Helen—is sexually harassed by Theoklymenos, the son of the very man—Proteus—assigned to guard her chastity; she resists him, without the help of a double.

Here, first Paris and then Menelaus gets the double, while the real Helen dreams on in Egypt. Menelaus says that he seized Helen from Troy and hid the woman" in "the depths of a cave,"[81] a phrase reminiscent simultaneously of the oversexed women who lurk in hollow caves throughout the *Odyssey* (Calypso* and Scylla*)[82] and of the shadow images in Plato's caves.* But Helen tells Menelaus that Hera made her image out of air so that Paris would not have her, and that he, Menelaus, had had in the cave "a figment of the gods. . . . a changeling,"[83] a creature that functions, in Austin's words, "as a most subtle deus ex machina, floating in and out of the play to resolve the complications."[84] This is rather hard on poor Menelaus, as Austin complains:

> At the risk of being thought ungracious, we might question the motives for such bed making, which leaves Menelaus with a cloud for his bedmate in order to punish Paris. . . . He may have mistakenly fought at Troy for a

phantom—the woman-as-name—since he did not see her but only as-sumed she was in Troy. But to ask him to believe that for the past seven years he has enjoyed not Helen's body but her name is to impose on him an ontology too steep for his comprehension.[85]

Indeed, Menelaus is understandably confused. He "recognizes that he has been sleeping with but a name, compounded of conceits and lies," and he admits that he was "tricked by the gods" when he held in his arms "a miserable piece of cloud."[86] In this episode, as in Aeschylus's *Agamemnon*, Menelaus is fooled by the phantom. When he sees Helen he says things like "I never saw a more resembling form" and "I see you as most like Helen, my lady." But when she remarks on his astonishing resemblance to Menelaus, and welcomes him back, "after such a long time, to the arms of your wife," Menelaus shies away and tells her to take her hands off him. He insists that he has only one wife, "the one hidden in the cave," though he admits that Helen's body is very much like that woman's (which is not surprising, since Helen has apparently not aged a day since she left Sparta).[87] Menelaus is finally convinced only when one of the doubles vanishes back into the ether from which it came (apparently he assumes that the Helen frail enough to vanish was the false one): a messenger comes and says that his "wife" just now vanished from the secret cave, declaring that she was nothing but a phantom, an empty *eidolon,* and saying, "You thought Paris had Helen, but he never did. The daughter of Tyndareus did nothing, though evil things are said of her." Only then does Menelaus say, "The stories *[logoi]* told by this woman fit, and are true"—which is, together with Helen's insistence that "I never went to the land of Troy,"[88] an almost verbatim repetition of Stesichorus's recantation: "The story *[logos]* is not true. You did not go to Troy."

In Euripides' *Helen,* as in all Greek tragedies, the parts of women were played by men. In Aristophanes' *Thesmophoriazousae,* composed shortly after *Helen* (c. 411 B.C.E.), the men play the women's parts in the play within the play, and the playwright Euripides appears as a character in the play:

Helen in Drag

Euripides persuaded his brother-in-law Mnesilochos to dress in women's clothes in order to spy on the women who were plotting against him; but when Mnesilochos was discovered he offered to play Helen in Euripides' play, while Euripides himself played Menelaus. The two spoke a number of lines from Euripides' play but were interrupted by comic remarks from other characters who refused to accept the stage convention that the actors were people other than their real identities. Mnesilochos was seized by women who discovered his true sex, but Euripides rescued him by promising never again to revile women in his plays.[89]

Where, in Euripides' *Helen,* the joke was that that there were two Helens with one name, here the joke lies in the flat-footed refusal to let one actor play two parts with two names (his real-life identity and the character in the play). As Zeitlin puts it:

> The *eidolon* of Helen is neither visible nor even mentioned in the parody. Nevertheless, as the personification of illusion itself, the phantom figure hovers over the entire scene. . . . In satirizing Euripides' theatrical innovations in the *Helen* and in presenting a parody with metatheatrical dimensions, Aristophanes reaffirms, as it were, through the tradition that goes back to Stesichorus, the perennial utility of Helen as the figure upon whom can be focused the poetic problem of imitation itself.[90]

The ultimate reduction to the absurd is a Helen impersonated not by a perfect image of the perfect woman but by the hilariously imperfect image of a drag queen. Wavering between tragedy and comedy, Euripides' play may have opened the door to satires on Helen, supplying the comic inspiration not only for Aristophanes but for Plautus,[91] perhaps for his telling of the story of Alcmena and the double Amphitryons.

The problems left unresolved in Euripides' story of Helen were finally resolved in *Die ägyptische Helena* ("The Egyptian Helen," or "Helen in Egypt"), an opera composed by Richard Strauss in 1926, with a libretto by Hugo von Hofmannsthal. It begins, like Euripides, with Menelaus sailing back from Troy with Helen—but this time, as in Homer, he has the real Helen; there *is* no phantom Helen. Menelaus has not forgiven Helen for her adultery (indeed, now he accuses her of having slept with Paris's brothers, after the death of Paris), nor has he slept with her during the voyage back from Troy. When he approaches her, she thinks he wants to make love to her at last, but soon she realizes that he intends to kill her (as in Euripides' *Trojan Women*). In order to save her, an Egyptian nymph named Aithra ("Air," the very word that Euripides uses for the substance with which Hera made the phantom Helen)[92] wrecks their ship and brings them to shore in Egypt, where she further distracts Menelaus by conjuring up not only a phantom Helen but a phantom Paris, both of whom Menelaus attacks and believes that he kills. Then the nymph tells what Hofmannsthal, in a commentarial essay,[93] calls "a fairy tale" *(Märchen):*

HELEN IN EGYPT

Aithra tells Menelaus that the moment that Paris made a play for Helen, while Menelaus was out hunting, the gods replaced her with an image made of air, an airy ghost that looked just like her, an image with which they fool mortal men. It was this that flirted with Priam's sons, so that for ten years Menelaus, together with all the Greeks, was the victim of a phantom. Meanwhile, the gods guarded the real Helen in Egypt, in the city of Aithra's father, so that she did not age but slept through the whole decade, dreaming that she was in his arms. And it was this ghost, Aithra insists, that Menelaus had dragged out of the city and carried over the sea.

In fact, the real Helen has aged, but Aithra gives her a drug of forgetfulness that which makes her forget her guilt and, therefore, makes her look young and innocent: "As you feel, so will you be," says Aithra, and Helen glances in a mirror and says she looks as she did on her wedding night. Under the influence of the same drug of forgetfulness (which Aithra advises Helen to keep, as she might need to give it to him—or to herself—from time to time, "so that the evil will remain forgotten, buried"), Menelaus comes to believe that he now has, for the first time in ten years, the real Helen. Helen lays her head on Menelaus's shoulder with maidenly innocence, he embraces her, and the curtain falls.

But then comes the second act. Menelaus awakens and becomes, as usual, confused; now, on the morning after, he believes that the woman with whom he spent that night was the phantom, a mirror image or temptress made of air. Perversely, he fears that he has betrayed the real Helen (whom he thinks he has killed) by sleeping with the phantom on the night just passed. Part of his argument is precisely that the woman in his arms looks too young, that she resembles an eternally young goddess; she looks too good, with a face "too untouched by life," while the real Helen would have aged. Suspicious now, he muses that "[a] man who goes hunting and returns home to his wife cannot know if he will find her the same woman."

Helen is now jealous of the Helen that Menelaus thinks he has killed, the adulterous Helen ("He spurns me! He loves the other one!"). Apparently Menelaus not only prefers the Helen who went to Troy, the adulterous ghost, but even feels guilty that he didn't notice the difference; and he is ashamed that he went to Troy to get the ghost—leaving the real Helen in Egypt. But when Helen complains to Aithra, "He thought I was a stranger, a woman that you had brought him for the night; he thought he had betrayed Helen with me, Helen whom he had killed," Aithra simply remarks, "Lucky you" [Du Selige]. Helen, however, rejects this "empty joy" and resolves to win her husband back by administering an antidote to the amnesiac drug, a drug of remembering that is another shadow double: Aithra has warned Helen that the two vials of drugs look so alike that one might mistake one for the other. Helen must persuade Menelaus that she is the real Helen, who really deceived him with Paris. And so, once she has disenchanted him they return to Sparta to rule as king and queen.[94]

Thus Hofmannsthal reduces the long tradition of the phantom Helen to a campfire ghost story, a lie told to Menelaus to keep him from killing the real, never-doubled, Helen. The fairy tale is precisely the story that Euripides tells in *Helen;* apparently Aithra (or Hofmannsthal) has read Greek tragedies. Poor Menelaus is being asked to believe that, although he hasn't been sleeping with Helen for ten years, she's been sleeping with him (in her dreams), not with Paris. The fact that Helen is, as usual, unflawed, unaged, here becomes a problem, not a solution; it makes Menelaus worry not only that she is not human, but that she is not *his* human. The drug he drinks, inspired by the amnesiac drug that Homer's Helen says she brought back from Egypt,[95] is compounded by the effects of the drug that Helen drinks: hers works by projection,* so that someone else (Menelaus) will see the illusion that she is young. Like Dorian Gray,* she stays young because she forgets her guilt. And although the antidote makes him believe just what he believed at the start of the play—that Helen, the real Helen, his Helen, committed adultery—, the experience of killing one phantom (or, perhaps, the experience of sleeping with what he took to be another) somehow makes him forgive her for everything.

Helen of Clay

One late variant of the story tells us that when Paris and Helen arrived in Egypt, and Proteus took her away from Paris, out of compassion Proteus gave the frustrated Paris an image *(eidolon)* of Helen "painted on a tablet so that gazing at it, he would be consoled of his love."[96] Austin refers to this as "an art object to pacify a lover's unfulfilled libido,"[97] and Zeitlin comments: "In this romanticized and indeed partially inverted reading, the phantom has turned into a portrait; the insubstantial double is now a permanent sign of presence, always available to the lover's desiring embrace."[98]

Plato used Helen as an example in his arguments about the ability of art to capture unreal images—the context in which he quotes Stesichorus.

He mocks what he calls *skiagraphia,* "painting with shadow," which he equates both with the visual and intellectual illusions of *hoi polloi* and with the illusory form of Helen of Troy:

> And are not their pleasures inevitably commingled with pains, phantoms of true pleasure, illusions of painting with shadows, so colored by contrary juxtaposition as to . . . beget mad loves of themselves in senseless souls, and to be fought for, as Stesichorus says the phantom of Helen was fought for at Troy, through ignorance of the truth?[99]

Helen herself is a work of art, hence a fake; her phantom double is a fake of a fake, twice removed from reality; and this is what Plato likens to both shadow painting (the illusory cave shadows of Platonic reality)[100] and the false pleasures of the people. This aesthetic line of thought reached its apogee in the seventeenth century, when Giovanni Pietro Bellori argued that since the real Helen, like all natural products, must have been flawed, "therefore the Trojan War in reality must have been fought over a statue of a woman."[101] But it is precisely as a symbol of unflawed beauty that Helen (or perhaps the statue of Helen, the phantom of the phantom Helen) became the touchstone against which all other women were measured. In Jean Giraudoux's telling of the tale of Amphitryon, Alcmena says to Leda, the mother of Helen: "One only has to see you to realize that you're not so much a woman, you're one of those living statues whose marble progeny will one day grace all the beautiful corners of the world." Leda, like Helen, is proleptic: she is the form of future copies of herself.

The goddess Hera is the one who commissions the phantom Helen (sometimes with the help of Hermes), according to most versions of the story; an exception is Apollodorus, writing in the first century C.E., who replaces Hera with Zeus: "Some people say that Hermes, in obedience to the command of Zeus, stole Helen and brought her to Egypt and gave her to Proteus to guard, while Alexander took a phantom Helen made of clouds and brought her to Troy."[102] The idea of the surrogate statue made by Zeus was also turned around and applied not to Helen but to Hera herself. According to Pindar, writing at the beginning of the fifth century B.C.E., Ixion was fooled by an image of Hera that Zeus made out of clouds, out of air, just like the phantom Helen:

Hera of Air

In his delirious heart [Ixion] loved Hera, dedicated to the high couch of Zeus. . . . in the great secret chambers of Zeus he strove to ravish the

> Queen. . . . It was a cloud *[nephela]* he lay with, and he in his delusion was
> given the false loveliness. A phantom *[eidos]* went in the guise of that high-
> est daughter of Uranian Kronos; a deceit visited upon him by the hands of
> Zeus, a fair evil thing.[103]

Zeus then crucified Ixion upon a wheel, but the cloud Hera gave birth to
Kentauros, who coupled with mares to create a breed that resembled their
parents *[omoioi tokeusi]*, the mother (the mare) below, the father ("man-
like") above—centaurs. The ambivalence of the centaur answers to the
ambivalence of the mare goddess (Saranyu, Demeter*) who creates an
equine double in a vain attempt to resist a rape.

 Apollodorus tells the story of Ixion a bit differently:

> Ixion fell in love with Hera and tried to rape her, and when Hera told him,
> Zeus, wishing to know if the matter was in fact like that, made a cloud that
> looked like Hera and laid it beside Ixion; and when Ixion boasted that he
> had made love with Hera, Zeus tied him to a wheel on which he is whirled
> by winds through the air. And the cloud, impregnated by Ixion's seed, gave
> birth to Kentauros.[104]

This time, apparently, Zeus does not believe Hera's story of the attempted
rape, and has to stage an episode of entrapment in order to verify her account. Endymion, too, attempted to rape Hera but was thwarted by "an *eidolon* of a cloud" in her form.[105] Similarly, Demeter's rape by Iasion was
later retold in such a way that Iasion got only a phantom—an *agalma* or
phasma—, and was struck by lightning to boot.[106]

 One double was created not to keep Hera from being taken away by
someone else but to get her back, when Zeus and Hera had one of their
usual marital squabbles and Hera went off in a huff:

HERA OF WOOD

> Zeus was advised to pretend to marry someone else. The other woman was
> a block of oak carved in the shape of a girl and draped in veils like a bride.
> They called her Daedala. When the celebrations had begun, Hera came
> down from Cithaeron in anger and jealousy and ran to confront Zeus. But
> when the image was revealed, she laughed and led the bride forward her-
> self.[107]

Hera discovers not her rival but her double, and laughs; her narcissism has
defused her jealousy. The double is a *xoanon*, which Calasso describes as
"one of those endless blocks of wood kept in temples all over Greece. . . .

They called her Daedala, which is as much as to say Artifact, because she was the first creature who embodied art in herself."[108]

The story of the thefts and abductions of Helen may also have inspired (or have been inspired by) the closely related tradition of the thefts and abductions of the statue of Athena known as the Palladion (or Palladium), which Zeus or Athena gave to Troy, and Odysseus and Diomedes stole from Troy.[109] Euripides fancies that the Trojans referred to the Trojan horse as a sacred wooden image—*hieron xoanon*—and wanted to carry it to Athena; thus the wooden idol that was stolen *into* Troy paved the way for the idols of Athena stolen *from* Troy. And in one telling, Odysseus argues that he is just taking it *back* from Troy, since Paris had already stolen it[110] (as he had of course stolen Helen) from Greece. According to some of these tellings, multiple images were made to "baffle a would-be thief and require his ability to discriminate between the counterfeit and the real"; Helen herself was sometimes identified with the Palladion or depicted holding it, and there is a "tradition that Paris stole the Palladion from Argos along with Helen, thereby redoubling his theft of a female figure."[111] Calasso points out the confusion that this tradition inspired:

> When the Achaeans began their siege of Troy, the Trojans immediately decided to make an identical copy of the Palladium. Thus, if the Greeks managed to steal it, Troy would not fall. Odysseus and Diomedes did break into Athena's temple and ran off with the Palladium. But, as with every audacious exploit, there are a host of different versions. Was it the real Palladium? Or did they steal two, one real and one false? Or were there, as some suggested, any number of Palladiums, the real one being the smallest? Or were the two Palladiums the two heroes stole both false, the only real one being the one Cassandra clutched in her hand the night Troy was sacked . . . ?[112]

Calasso goes on to relate the goddess's reaction to this duplication, the doubling of the phantom Palladium in a number of Palladia: "The double takes its revenge by reproducing itself as an image, first in the one true Palladium, . . . but likewise in the endless other Palladiums to be found all over the world, all false."[113] Like Sita and Helen, the statue, once doubled, could proliferate endlessly.

Helen in Europe

Euripides' Helen is called a copy *(mimema)* or a sculpted image *(agalma)* or a "cloud image" *(nepheles agalma).* Euripides' Helen says, "I wish that like an image *(agalma)* I had been erased and remade without this beauty."[114] Euripides distinguishes between Helen's presence and Helen's name; Helen worries that even if she were to return to Sparta with Menelaus, everyone would take her for the false Helen, the Helen of her name. Yet, "Though she has now been revised out of the story, she must still pay for the transgressions of her *eidolon*, while being innocent of all actions imputed to it. She might as well have been the phantom Helen if she was to be blamed for its misbehavior."[115] And indeed, the subsequent history of the theme has proved Helen's doubts well founded. As Calasso remarks, "When people speak of Helen, we can never know whether they are referring to her body or her phantom copy."[116]

For centuries, European literature alluded to Helen as a kind of double, an artistic ideal of beauty against which an individual human woman could be measured. Shakespeare evokes this trope: "The lover . . . Sees Helen's beauty in a brow of Egypt."[117] "Egypt" here means primarily "dark" in contrast with "fair," but it may also carry overtones of that other Helen, the illusory Helen who was kept in Egypt, the false woman for whom the lover mistakes his real (but false in the sense of adulterous) love. In Goethe's *Faust*, Helen becomes a metaphor for erotic projection, like the projection of forgetfulness that Hofmannsthal's Helen casts upon Menelaus; Faust sees her as a reflection in a magic mirror that dissolves into a mist when he attempts to draw her, like the Helen made of air; and when Mephistopheles gives Faust the transformative drug he remarks that Faust will soon be seeing Helens everywhere. Helen says, "As an idol I joined myself to him as an idol. It was a dream, so the very words themselves said. Now I vanish from here and become an idol to myself."[118]

Shakespeare gave the name of Helena to the sexual trickster in *All's Well That Ends Well*, a woman who calls herself "the shadow of a wife"; he calls our attention to Helena's Greek associations with a specific reference to the "fair face" that caused the sack of Troy, a reference surely reinforced in his *Troilus and Cressida* by the sensual and heartless figure of Helen of Troy, who "hath launched above a thousand ships."[119] The figure of a thousand, in Christopher Marlowe's *Dr. Faustus*, signals Helen's multiplicity, her power not merely to double but to multiply destruction, even into the thousands: "Was this the face that launch'd a thousand ships / And burnt the topless towers of Ilium?"[120] This famous line inspired my late colleague, Arthur Adkins, to joke that the most precise measure in Greek philology is the milli-helen, the quantity of energy it takes to launch one ship.[121] The cliché tells us that once you start numbering women,[122] you lose the sense of individualism and are dealing with ideal types, stereotypes, as is appropriate for the woman who came to symbolize ideal beauty and treachery, the essence of the misogynist view of women.

In John Erskine's *The Private Life of Helen of Troy,* however, Helen rightly, if literal-mindedly, points out that it was Menelaus, not she, who launched the ships—neither a normal nor a sensible reaction to a simple case of adultery. She also argues explicitly against the Herodotean version, which placed her in Egypt without a double: "Now, if I allowed you to believe that shabby story about Egypt, I should be shirking the blame for all the wretchedness at Troy. I was there, and I was the cause of it all; to deny it would be to deny myself—to exist in falsehood." (But she also mocks Menelaus for being, together with his brother, "the poorest sailors I ever met. Menelaos steered right into Egypt, trying to get home to Sparta.") Instead, she argues that not she but Paris was illusory, that love itself, though never a mistake, is always an illusion; and so, after running off with Paris she discovered, "It wasn't the real Paris."[123] In James Branch Cabell's mythological novel, *Jurgen: A Comedy of Justice,* three men see Helen of Troy, and each thinks that she is the exact image of his first, lost love (though the three women do not resemble one another at all). One of the men explains this: "For the woman whom when we were young we loved in vain is the one woman that we can never see quite clearly, whatever happens. So we might easily, I suppose, confuse her with some other woman."[124] By this argument, women look alike not only if they are too low (in the dark all cats are gray)[125] but if they are too high. Helen's double (and the miniature city in Virgil's *Aeneid,* built to resemble Troy) may also have inspired William Butler Yeats to double the city that she destroyed; his poem about Maude Gonne, "No Second Troy," ends: "Was there another Troy for her to burn?"

The theme of the phantom Helen is brilliantly developed in Iris Murdoch's novel about illusory love, *The Sea, The Sea,* in which a man named Charles finds his childhood sweetheart, Hartley, after many years and believes that they should be together once again. The self-deluding nature of this love is presented in several stages, culminating in the story of the false Helen, told to Charles by his brother James:

> The heroes at Troy fought for a phantom Helen, according to Stesichorus.
> Vain wars for phantom goods. . . . As we know ourselves we are fake objects,

fakes, bundles of illusions. . . . Some kinds of fruitless preoccupation with the past can create simulacra, and they can exercise power, like those heroes at Troy fighting for a phantom Helen. . . . [Hartley] is real, as human creatures are, but what reality she has is elsewhere. She does not coincide with your dream figure. [And finally, when he has lost Hartley, Charles himself comes to understand the meaning of Helen:] When did I begin to relax my hold upon Hartley, or rather upon her image, her double, the Hartley of the mind? . . . What has become of that light now? It has gone and was at best a flickering flame seen in a marsh, and my great "illumination" a kind of nonsense. She is gone, she is nothing, for me she no longer exists, and after all I fought for a phantom Helen.[126]

Like Menelaus, and Rama, and so many others.

Thus Helen becomes another sort of double, an evil succubus, the phantom of all losses, the phantom of beauty and perfection, a pain like the pain that amputees feel in a phantom limb. When, in a 1995 film, Dr. Jekyll finally produces a female Hyde,* her name is, of course, Helen. And when the protagonist in the film *The Truth about Cats and Dogs* (1996) tries to explain why she sent her more beautiful friend in her place to meet a man who had fallen in love with her voice on the radio but had never seen her, she insists that she must go on with the masquerade, since beauty is what matters to men; and her concluding argument is simply: "The truth is—Helen of Troy." The illusory beautiful woman (Helen, the double) is the true image of the idealized self, the voice. But if Helen is "the truth," the truth (about sex) is a lie. Writing in 1998 about the sexual harassment suit brought against President Clinton involving Paula Jones and Monica Lewinsky, Jeffrey Toobin casually remarked, "As is demonstrated by the history of scandal from Helen of Troy to Monica of Beverly Hills, sex has a way of befogging the higher intellectual faculties." And Edward Jay Epstein, writing in the *New Yorker,* suggested that the White House issue an "alien-abduction" or "Two Clinton" explanation of the affair: "It was a substituted Clinton clone, not our Commander-in-Chief, who was visited numerous times by Monica Lewinsky in the Oval Office. . . . In this happy rendering, all the humans are telling the truth."[127] Epstein was referring explicitly to alien body snatchers and implicitly to all those films about dead ringers that Bette Davis and Jeremy Irons specialized in; but he might just as well have been quoting Stesichorus and Plato.

Interlude: Saranyu and the Sun and the Shadow

The key to the relationship between Sita and Helen lies, I think, in two verses recorded in the *Rig Veda* some three thousand years ago, centuries before the recension of either the *Ramayana* or the *Iliad:*[128] the story of Saranyu, who left a shadow double in her place when she abandoned her husband, the Sun. Our earliest known record of the myth of Saranyu, in the *Rig Veda,* assumes rather than narrates the plot, which concerns the artisan of the gods (Tvashtri), his daughter (Saranyu), her husband the Sun (Vivasvant), and their equine twin sons (the Ashvins):

The Riddle of Saranyu

"Tvashtri is giving a wedding for his daughter": people come together at this news. The mother of twins, the wedded wife of the great Vivasvant, disappeared. They hid the immortal woman from mortals. Making a similar female, they gave her to Vivasvant. What she became bore the twin equine gods, the Ashvins, and then she abandoned the two sets of twins—Saranyu.[129]

The cryptic form of the text is explained by the likelihood that it is a riddle, a genre that recurs throughout the *Rig Veda.*[130] No explanation is given for the hiding away of Saranyu; instead, a series of hints is presented and at the end, her name—the answer to the riddle in so many folktales (such as Rumpelstiltskin or Lohengrin): "Who am I? What is my name?" But one thing is clear: Saranyu is explicitly an immortal and her husband a mortal (one of those from whom "they" hid her). The similar or resembling double is literally of-the-same-kind *(sa-varna),* of the same *varna*—sort, or type, or appearance, or color, or class, or, finally, "kind" in the sense of "kin" (as Hamlet puns about his wicked stepfather-uncle, "A little more than kin, and less than kind" [*Hamlet* 1.2]—a remark that applies well to the "similar" mother in later variants). The term may function here as a double entendre, implying that the double is in some ways like Saranyu and in others like Vivasvant (the Sun): like Saranyu in appearance, but like the Sun, and unlike Saranyu, in character or class or even mortality.

The mortal Sun is regarded as an inadequate husband for Saranyu in a later telling in the *Harivamsha* (the appendix to the great Sanskrit epic, the *Mahabharata*), composed a few centuries after the final recension of the *Mahabharata,* perhaps in 600 C.E.—a millennium and a half after the *Rig*

Veda. Here, Saranyu's name is been changed to *Samjna*,[131] which becomes the more usual form in all later texts; she is double even in her name. (*Samjna* is a hard word for English speakers to pronounce, but an acceptable approximation is "Sangya.") Now, too, her surrogate is no longer said to be of the same kind or class, but is rather her mirror reflection or shadow (*chaya,* related to the Greek *skia*)—a creature who is not exactly like her but is her opposite in terms either of left-right orientation (the reflection) or of color (the shadow):

SAMJNA AND HER SHADOW

The Sun married Samjna, the daughter of Tvashtri. She had beauty and youth and virtue, and she was not satisfied by the form of her husband. For Samjna was filled with her own bright ascetic heat, and the form of the Sun, burnt by his own fiery brilliance in all his limbs, was not very attractive; excessive, it constantly overheated the three worlds. The Sun produced a daughter and two sons: first came Manu the Son of Vivasvant, and then the twins Yama and Yamuna. When Samjna saw that the form of the Sun had a dark color, she was unable to bear it; transforming her own shadow into a similar, earthly female, a Samjna that was made of magic illusion, she said to her, "I am going to my father's house; you stay here in my house. Treat my three children well, and do not tell this to my husband." The similar female replied, "Even if I am dragged by the hair, even if I am cursed, I will never tell your husband. Go wherever you like, goddess."

Somewhat embarrassed, the wise woman went to her father's house. Her father, however, reviled her and kept telling her, "Go back to your husband," and so she hid her form by taking the form of a mare. Meanwhile the Sun, thinking, "This is Samjna," produced in the second Samjna a son who was his equal. And because the Sun thought, "This one looks like the Manu who was born before," the son's name was "Manu the Similar." The earthly shadow Samjna gave extra affection to her own child and did not behave in the same way to the older children. Manu put up with her but Yama could not. In his anger and childishness, and through the force of future destiny, Yama threatened the shadow Samjna with his foot. Then the similar mother, who was very unhappy, cursed him in anger: "Let that foot of yours fall off."

Terrified by the curse and agitated by the shadow Samjna's words, Yama reported this to his father. "Turn back the curse!" he said to his father; "a mother should behave with affection to all her children, but this one rejects us and is good to the younger one. I lifted my foot at her but I did not let it fall on her body. You should forgive what I did out of childishness or delusion." The Sun said, "You must have had very good cause indeed if anger possessed you who know dharma and speak the truth. But I can't make your mother's words fail to come true. Worms will take flesh [from your foot] and go to the surface of the earth. Thus your mother's words will come true, and you will be protected from the blow of the curse."

But then the Sun said to the similar Samjna, "Why do you show excessive affection [to one] among your children when they are all equal?" She avoided this question and said nothing to the Sun, but when he wanted to curse her to destroy her she told him everything, and he became angry and went to Tvashtri. Tvashtri mollified the Sun's anger and trimmed him on his lathe, removing his excessive fiery brilliance. Then the Sun was much better to look at.

He saw his wife the mare by concentrating his powers in yoga, for no creature could look at her because of her brilliance. Then he took the form of a horse and coupled with her by joining with her in her mouth, for she was struggling against mating with him in her fear that it might be another male. She vomited out that semen of the Sun from her nose, and two gods were born in her, the Ashvins, called the Nasatyas. Then the Sun showed her his handsome form, and when she saw her husband she was satisfied.[132]

The mortality and/or mutilation of the Sun is a pivotal point of this myth. The *Rig Veda* tells us that Aditi, the Sun's mother, bore eight sons: "With seven she went forth among the gods, but she threw Martanda, the sun, aside. . . . so that he would in turn beget offspring and then die."[133] (Indeed, the daily rising and setting of the sun was seen by many cultures as a continual process of death and rebirth; the sun dies every day.) Other Vedic texts, the Brahmanas, composed around 800 B.C.E., tell us that, even in the womb, the Sun was inadvertently mutilated and consciously rejected by his own mother, who miscarried him and pushed him away as an unshaped lump: "[The Sun] was an unshaped lump, as broad as it was high, the size of a man. His brothers, however, shaped him so that he was not lost; they cut the flesh away from him and threw it into a lump."[134]

It may have been on this occasion that, as the *Harivamsha* tells us, the Sun's father saved him: " 'Let him not be dead while he is still in the egg,' his father, Kasyapa, had said in love and ignorance, and so he became known as 'Dead-Egg' [or 'Dead-in-the-Egg,' Martanda]."[135] But Kasyapa's protest "in love and ignorance" is precisely what causes the Sun's mother to miscarry and thus inadvertently hurts him, according to a rather different version of the episode told in the *Markandeya Purana*, c. 700 C.E.:

> When Aditi was pregnant, she undertook several difficult vows, knowing that she was carrying a divine embryo. But her husband Kasyapa spoke to her with words that stumbled in anger, saying, "Why are you killing the egg in your womb with this constant fasting?" She said to him in anger, "Look at the egg in my womb. It hasn't been killed, but it will kill our enemies." And in fury at her husband's words she brought forth the embryo. But because Kasyapa had said that the egg was dead, the child was called "Dead Egg."[136]

These texts shift the blame for the Sun's deformity from his mother to his father; fathers, even well-meaning fathers, can also mutilate.

And so can fathers-in-law. The first attempt to shape the Sun appears to have been insufficient; only later does his father-in-law, the archetypal artisan and sculptor, succeed in transforming the Sun from raw brilliance that his wife cannot look at into an artistic form that she can bear. Some later versions say that Samjna rejected the Sun not because he was too hot, or too dark, or excessive in any way, but because he was too round—inhumanly perfect: "In the old days he did not take the form of a man when he made love to his wife *[bhajati]*,"[137] or, "Samjna saw that the form of the Sun was a ball *[golakaram]*."[138] The trimming here humanizes the abstract Sun. (The *Mahabharata* avoids this awkwardness on a similar occasion by stating that when the Sun raped Kunti, he took the trouble to split himself into two by his yoga, so that he came to Kunti presumably in the form of a man but still went on shining in the sky with his celestial body.)[139] Thus the Sun is rejected first by his mother and then by his wife; and each time, he is mutilated.

Inadvertently mutilated by his father and his father-in-law, the Sun saves his own son, Yama, from death, though not from mutilation. Yama is caught between his three parents: his mother abandons him, his stepmother curses him, and his father blesses him—with mortality. Yama is therefore liminal in the most basic way: immortal (he is one of the World-protectors, deities who guard the four directions, his being the inauspicious south), he brings death into the world and reigns over it. Yama becomes a mortal immortal: already in the Veda, he is the first mortal, the one who willingly chose death, the first king, the king and god of the dead.[140] And where Yama is mistreated by his stepmother (the Shadow),

Manu is abandoned by his true mother. Samjna and the Shadow are therefore the paradigmatic absent mother and cruel stepmother, who inflict
upon their children and stepchildren injuries that are both theologically
and psychologically significant.

Samjna in the *Harivamsha* is more beautiful than her husband, and
perhaps more powerful; but the nature of his power, and her reaction to it,
have now become ambiguous, as has the nature of the person whom the
Shadow resembles, Samjna or the Sun. Samjna in this text perceives herself
as literally of a different class *(varna)*, in the sense of mortal versus immortal, from that of both her husband and her double. Thus the *Harivamsha* refers to the Shadow as "earthly," belonging to the earth, in
contrast with the other mother, the heavenly mother. But over the centuries that passed between the *Rig Veda* and the *Harivamsha*, the word
varna had come primarily to denote "class" in a sociological rather than
purely morphological sense, reflecting the hardening of the lines separat-
ing the social classes (called *varna*s) and the increasingly overt class overtones of "color" (also designated by *varna*). This shift in the meaning of
varna may explain why the "similar" female *(sa-varna)* of the Veda becomes a "look-alike" *(sadrisha)* or a "shadow" *(chaya)* in later texts: the
ambiguity of *chaya*, as either bright reflection or dark shadow, linked the
class of the shadow goddess either with her brilliant prototype (as a bright
reflection) or with her dark-skinned husband (as a dark shadow).

Samjna in the *Harivamsha* is explicitly said to have her own brilliance;
when she is a mare, perhaps her true form, no creature can look at her (or,
in a significant alternate reading, rape her),[141] because of her brilliance,
and her husband can see her (or rape her) only by resorting to yoga. But
he has his brilliance too, though his apparently gives literally more heat
than light. The *Harivamsha* is a transitional text in this respect: Samjna
still has her Vedic power, but now it begins to be subordinated to her husband's power in some portions of the story. The word for the Sun's "brilliance" *(tejas)* is also a word for semen; Samjna in her anthropomorphic
form avoids the Sun's brilliance, while in her mare-form she tries (in vain)
to avoid the stallion's semen.[142] But as the myth develops through time,
the relative status, and hence the relative brilliance, of the god and the
goddess is inverted.[143] The *Markandeya Purana* does not mention
Samjna's brilliance but simply states that she left her husband because she
could hardly bear *his* brilliance (or semen: *tejas*) and that she also feared
his anger; when her father threw her out of his house she took the form of

a mare, "not wanting the Sun's heat and frightened of his brilliance/se-men."[144]

This reversal is no accident but part of a consistent pattern in which Hindu women and goddesses become increasingly subservient to their husbands. (Thus Sita sinks in power as Rama rises.) It continues through the medieval texts and pops up in the contemporary version that is, for many Hindu children today, their primary source of this and other Hindu myths: the Amar Chitra Katha comic book, closely modeled on the American Classic Comics. This telling of the tale of Sanjna (as it calls her) goes even farther in moving from female to male "brilliance." When Manu grew up, we are told, "Surya and Sanjna were proud of him." The proud father remarked, "He is brilliant!" to which his mother replied, "Like his father!"[145] Thus the Sanskrit pun on *tejas* as brilliance or semen is given a third twist, "brilliance" in the sense of intellectual power; and the cosmic question of resemblance is transferred from the second son, Manu the Similar, applied to the first, Manu the son of the Sun, and reduced to the cliché compliment/complement of resembling, look-alike fathers and sons: "Chip off the old block." The resemblance between mother and shadow is overshadowed by the resemblance between father and son.

Was Saranyu, in the *Rig Veda,* hidden to conceal her light, because she was too bright for her husband to look at? Was she the first too-bright woman in recorded history? We cannot know, but the (male) Indologist Maurice Bloomfield nervously remarked that Saranyu's immortal nature and equine character make her too hot even for the Sun to handle:

> The feeling that she is the victim of a *mésalliance* grows more and more. . . . Possibly the story aims to convey a more special form of Saranyu's dissatis-faction, which peeps out not only in her abandonment of her husband, but more clearly in her metamorphosis into a mare: Vivasvant in his human ca-pacity may have failed to satisfy the instincts of the goddess, which were probably laid out on too large a scale for his mortal capacities.[146]

Where some (women?) might see the disparity with Vivasvant in Saranyu's immortality, or in his inadequacy (or color), Bloomfield sees it in her insa-tiability.

This insatiability is the telltale characteristic of the mare in Hindu mythology,[147] and Samjna's horsiness is an essential clue to the nature of her flight from marriage and motherhood. The sexual freedom of the mare is actually said, in one manuscript of the *Harivamsha,* to be the reason for Samjna's choice of that particular form. This short passage, expanding upon the statement that "her father reviled her and kept telling her, 'Go back to your husband,' and so she hid her form by taking the form of a mare," describes Samjna's thoughts about the nature of human women's subordination to men:

> She became very worried, and thought, "Damn this behavior of women." She kept blaming herself and her own womanhood: "No one should remain a woman, ever; damn this life with no independence. In her childhood, youth, and old age, a female is in danger from her father, husband, and sons, respectively. It was stupid of me to abandon my husband's house; that was a mistake. Even though I have not been recognized, I have suffered now in my father's house, and there she is, the similar female, with all her desires fulfilled. I have lost my husband's house because of my naive stupidity, and it is no better here in my father's house."[148]

And with that, she decided to become a mare, perhaps because she shared the common Hindu belief that mares, unlike human women, are free, both to reject unwanted stallions and to indulge their unbridled sexuality.[149] This may have been what Samjna had in mind when she paraphrased, and perhaps mocked, the famous verse in *The Laws of Manu*: "In childhood a woman should be under her father's control, in youth under her husband's, and when her husband is dead, under her sons'. She should not have independence."[150] But Samjna speaks of danger rather than of control, and as for freedom, she is raped by the Sun stallion and brought home again, in vivid contrast to the *Rig Veda* verse that clearly implies that she abandons her husband and children forever. As a mare she may have agency and subjectivity and even the illusion of freedom for a while, but in the end she must submit to her husband's sexual demands, just like a human woman.

The *Harivamsha* passage just cited strikes a contemporary reader as a strange mix of a quasi-feminist perception of male persecution and a male chauvinist justification for that persecution, projected (by the author of the text) into the mind of the subject (the woman). A feminist might well read the myth of Samjna as a parable of male domination. Yet the Sun is surely a most pathetic victimizer, and the real brilliance and energy (perhaps even the real power) in most versions of the myth seem embodied (sometimes literally embodied) in the tricky females. If this myth is about victimization, then it is certainly equally, if not more, about subversion.

The subversion, however, is gradually eroded. At first, in the early period, Saranyu/Samjna actually gains agency: someone other than Saranyu herself (one of the gods, we assume) makes the similar female in the *Rig Veda* and hides Saranyu, but the grammarian Yaska, a few centuries later, tells us that Samjna herself, after giving birth to twins, produced the substitute, the similar female, who gave birth to Manu,[151] and it is Samjna herself who fashions all subsequent doubles. But though she gains agency, she loses power; the shift from female power to male power that begins in the *Harivamsha*, with Samjna's loss of "brilliance," continues through all subsequent texts. It appears in other, related myths, too; in a text composed about 900 B.C., right after the *Rig Veda*, a male god rather than a goddess creates by means of his own shadow: "He emitted these waters and looked and saw his own reflection *(chaya)* in them. And as he was looking at it, he emitted his semen in the waters."[152] Here the desired shadow is not his wife's, like the Shadow that the Sun unknowingly and passively receives, but his own reflection, which he knowingly and actively creates and impregnates.

A similar shift, specifically linked, as in the case of Samjna, to the issue of energy/semen, occurs in the mythology of the celestial courtesan and swan maiden Urvashi. In the *Rig Veda*, Urvashi leaves her mortal husband, Pururavas, complaining that he made love to her too often ("You pierced me with your rod three times a day, and filled me even when I had no desire. I did what you wanted") and concluding, "Once each day I swallowed a drop of butter, and even now I am sated with that."[153] So too, Samjna as the mare is filled when she has no desire and unwillingly swallows the Sun's seed. In a text composed some three centuries later, however, Urvashi *begs* Pururavas to make love to her just that often ("You must strike me with the bamboo reed three times a day"), though she has the forethought to add, "but never approach me when I have no desire."[154] Moreover, she stays with him, just as Samjna stays with the Sun in the later telling, though she threatens to leave him when he fails to keep his promise not to let her look upon *him* naked. Now, since this is an inversion of the usual, and more logical, pattern (as in the tale of Cupid and Psyche),[155] according to which the mortal must not look at the immortal, it may snag an inconsistency in an incomplete transitional stage of the myth: Urvashi is beginning to be treated, in this one detail, like a mortal woman married to an immortal man.

In the course of her long history in India, Saranyu not only loses her own intrinsic power (if not her agency) but accumulates more and more co-wives, who implicitly further limit both her individuality and her power. Some texts give the Sun *five* wives, two in addition to Samjna, the Shadow, and, presumably, the mare: Rajni and Prabha[156] or Dyaus.[157] Another text says that the Sun had two wives, both daughters of Tvashtri, named Samjna and Shadow (Chaya), and a third wife, named Mare (Vadava).[158] Thus Samjna and Shadow and Mare (not Samjna's shadow and a horse, but just a woman named Shadow and another named Mare) are three separate people; the Sun is happily polygynous, and no one has any problems at all. The same Euhemeristic tendency that makes the Shadow a woman rather than a shadow and the mare a woman named Mare also inspired the late text that makes Chaya simply Samjna's maid, whom Samjna sends to the Sun disguised in her (Samjna's) clothing[159]—like countless heroines in folklore throughout the world. This text also demonstrates another trend, bleeding the story of its tragedy as well as its theology.

A delightfully cheerful and down-to-earth interpretation of the myth is current in a caste that still worships Samjna, under the name of Randhal-ma; one woman in this caste remarked that Randhal-ma is doubled because, "When does a woman go do things alone? Two women like to go out and do things together. It is strange to think of Samjna and the Shadow as two girlfriends out shopping."[160] The comic book, too, makes the two women pals in the end: Sanjna says, "I shall never again wander away from home," and the Sun adds: "Chhaya [the Shadow] shall be forgiven and shall live with us." And then: "So Surya and Sanjna went back to his abode in the skies and lived there in happiness with Chhaya and the children." And all of the children, of both generations and both mothers, are depicted in a final happy family snapshot. This text has traveled a long way from the Sanskrit corpus in which the tragic story of Samjna and Manu attributes the origin of the human race, and death, to an abandoning mother.

Saranyu remains important in Hinduism because of her children: the child that she abandons is Yama, king of the dead, consigned to rule over Hell, and the child of the shadow double is Manu, the ancestor of the human race. "Manu" means "Man" and is later said to be connected with the verb *man*, "think," hence, "the wise one." Thus *manava* ("descended from Manu") becomes a common word for "human" (which, in terms of the lexical meaning of Manu as "wise," might also be the Sanskrit equivalent of *Homo sapiens*); he is the first sacrificer and father of many descendants, the ancestor of the human race,[161] the Hindu Adam. Manu is also connected with *manas*, "mind-and-heart," which, Gregory Nagy argues, is precisely the part of a human being that survives death, the part that is able to regenerate itself through progeny.[162] Since, as we have seen, the Sun is regarded as mortal in Hindu mythology, while Saranyu in the *Rig Veda* is expressly said to be immortal, this story raises the question of the generic differences between gods and humans, and the ways of telling them apart.* But that is not all that is at stake here.

Samjna functions as a trope for verbal deception, the deception of texts. The word *samjna* means "mutual understanding" or "consciousness," or, by extension, "sign" or "image" or "name," or, finally, "recognition." (It contains the verbal root *jna*, "to know," cognate with the Greek *gnosis*, English *know*, *ignore*, etc.) Samjna is the Signifier. Since the image or name is the double of the thing or person, Samjna is her own double from the start. And perhaps it is relevant to note here that "shadow" *(chaya)* is also used in much later Sanskrit tradition to refer to a commentary on a text.[163] Thus their names render both of the mothers of the human race unreal in one sense or another: one is "the Sign," the other "the Shadow." If Samjna is the text, the Shadow is the commentary; if Samjna is the dream, the Shadow is the secondary elaboration. Stella Kramrisch speaks of "idea and image. . . . the polarity of name and form, . . . great likeness and just the difference of non-identity" between Samjna and the Shadow. Between Samjna and her shadow, "there is a difference for which only the gods can account but which man endeavours to make up for."[164] Yet it should be recalled that names and images in Hinduism are regarded as in many ways isomorphic with reality or even able to create reality; this consideration gives greater meaning to the female who is "just" an image.[165]

Samjna may also be a riddle term for *sandhya*, the twilight; if Samjna is the dawn, the doppelgänger woman is the evening twilight, and the two twilights are the two wives of the Sun.[166] The parallels between Samjna and Sandhya are suggestive: each is a wife of the Sun and is incestuously connected with her father,[167] and each is a term of art designating an ambiguity: just as *samjna* means "sign" or "image," so *sandhya* becomes the term for the "twilight speech" of later Hindi and Urdu poetry, a speech marked by riddles, inversions, and paradoxes.

What sort of a mother is the double? Usually the double cleverly avoids calling herself a mother at all and merely claims, correctly, to be Yama's father's wife. But who, then, is Manu's mother? The various texts that tell this story disagree. The *Rig Veda* riddle verses do not mention Manu, but there is reason to suppose that Yama and Manu may have been twins in related texts that preceded the *Rig Veda*,[168] which might make Manu the other, unnamed twin born of Saranyu. At least one *Rig Veda* passage identifies Manu with a patronymic that makes him the son of Vivasvant, but other passages give him the name (a matronymic?) of Similar (*savarnya* and *savarni*),[169] implying that, already in the *Rig Veda*, there was a Manu who was himself similar to someone or was the son of someone similar.

This ambiguity is resolved when Yaska tells us that the similar female gave birth to Manu.[170] But the resolution does not last long; the *Harivamsha*, as we have seen, says that the first wife bore Manu (son of the Sun) and the twins, while the second wife, the double, bore another Manu, a double of Manu, called Manu the Similar, who will reign in the future. And since, according to many subsequent texts, this second Manu is our ancestor, the tradition implies that we are descended not only from a replicated mother, a mother who was nothing but a copy, a fake, but now from a replicated Manu as well. The epithet *Similar* is therefore a pun, indicating both a similar mother and a son "similar (to his brother)." In fact, the second Manu is not merely a double but a triple: he is similar to his replicated mother, his older brother (son of the true mother) and his (mortal, dark) father. The fact that it is Manu's father who gives him the epithet of *Similar* may indicate that he is somehow aware of the pun and of the substitution at which it hints, perhaps through a displaced awareness that the double he lives with is not his real wife, an unconscious realization expressed in a Freudian error that makes him name his son not, as he explicitly states, after the son's elder brother, but after his false mother.

The splitting of Manu into two Manus may represent an attempt to combine two creation stories, one about Yama and one about Manu, for each is regarded in some texts as the primeval human.[171] But this is just the beginning. Later texts tell us that there have been many Manus, beginning with Manu the son of Brahma the Self-Created, continuing, past other Manus, through Manu the son of Vivasvant and Manu the Similar, and on to many more.[172] And the many Manus are matched by a series of other children, as well. The Shadow bears Manu and, almost as an afterthought, the inauspicious planet Saturn;[173] then she gives birth to a daughter, Tapati ("the Heater"),[174] who plays a crucial role in the *Mahabharata* as the mother of Kuru, ancestor of the epic heroes;[175] and the Shadow has yet another child, named Vishti ("Drudgery, Slavery"),[176] a horrible creature who represents the slave labor inflicted upon sinners in Hell, where her half-brother Yama reigns.

Some texts, including the *Harivamsha,* make us the descendants of the first Manu, born of the real mother, Samjna herself, not the similar mother.[177] This may simply indicate that some authors could not bear to believe that we might be the children of a fake mother. But, then, why did such texts go to such trouble in constructing a false mother, if only to make her the parent of people who are quite peripheral to our interests (one son who is a planet, another who will reign in the future, as well as a series of problematic daughters)? No, the central metaphysical issue was pinpointed by Stella Kramrisch: "When Vivasvant knows Savarna, man is born with the imperfection and memory of his descent."[178]

That Saranyu and her double are regarded as the mothers of the two ancestors of the human race, Yama and Manu, the authors of death and of procreation, respectively, is even more significant a fact than might at first appear. For Saranyu marks the dividing line between abstract goddesses who have children and anthropomorphic goddesses who do not. Before her, Aditi and Tvashtri produce immortal children, as do Sky and Earth and a few other deities. After her, some goddesses give birth to divine children by themselves, through a kind of parthenogenesis,[179] but never anthropomorphically, and never through sexual union with a god. In fact, later texts tell stories to explain why all the goddesses are barren, sometimes as the result of a curse.[180] But this is an afterthought, a back-formation to explain what had already long been taken for granted, namely, that immortals do not have children simply because they are immortal; if you don't die, there is no need to reproduce yourself. Or, to put it the other way around, as the myth often does, if you have sex, you must have death. This explains why, although Hindu gods and goddesses often marry—the *hieros gamos* is after all a major mythological theme—, they do not usually procreate with their spouses. Instead, gods seduce mortal women, and celestial courtesans (*apsarases*), rather than goddesses, seduce mortal men.* The Saranyu myth marks the transition between these two patterns: mating with a liminal husband who is both a mortal and a god, she herself functions like the Vedic goddess Aditi and produces a god (Yama, king of the dead), while her double, functioning like one of the later celestial courtesans, produces his mortal brother (originally his mortal twin brother)—Manu, the founder of the human race.

Moreover, the story of Samjna and her shadow stands at the threshold of another tradition, the beginning of the incorporation of the worship of the Goddess into Sanskrit texts. The fact that the most ancient and best-known prayer to the Goddess in Sanskrit, the *Devimahatmya* of the *Markandeya Purana,* already knows a thousand of her names, most of which encapsulate either a myth or an attribute, suggests that she must already have been around for quite a while in the non-Sanskrit world before this hymn assembled the pieces of her traditions, just as the myth describes how the gods assembled the pieces of her powers (out of parts of the male gods). The very first verse of this Hymn to the Goddess Durga begins: "Savarni the son of Surya is called the eighth Manu, born through the power of the Great Illusion."[181] Since the *Markandeya Purana* tells the tale of Samjna not once but twice and regards her as the mother of the Manu who rules in our age, the whole *Devimahatmya* is, in a sense, a footnote to the story of the shadow Saranyu.

COMPARISON: SITA AND HELEN
The Afterimage of Epic Doubles in History

Whatever their origins, common or disparate, and however divergent their historical developments, both Hindu and Greek traditions resorted to the story of the surrogate double to generate a revisionist history of a rape or a seduction in the epic. Both traditions were able to recant, to change their stories just as Stesichorus and Euripides, as individuals, changed theirs, because, for very different reasons, the earliest texts of the epics (the *Ramayana* and the *Iliad* and *Odyssey*) were not dogmatically fixed. The Hindu text was regarded as part of *smriti,* human memory, and hence malleable (in contrast with *shruti,* divinely inspired texts such as the Vedas, of which not a syllable could be changed).[182] The Greek text was part of a tradition that was, from the start, of variable piety[183] (as Paul Veyne pointed out in his well-named study, *Did the Greeks Believe in Their Myths?*) and that inspired a kind of cultural reverence but no religious piety to sustain it in the modern European revisions; more important, Greek tradition from Plato on seriously challenged the Homeric version of Greek mythology. In both cultures, the myths moved through a number of different genres (from epic to Purana to devotional poetry to satire, in the Hindu tradition; from epic to drama to satire, in the Greek and European) in which changes were inevitable—in which they were, indeed, the whole point of the exercise.

Moreover, both epics provide examples of doubles of men who might have served as models for the postepic doubles of women. (Closer to our theme, however, there are also some exceptional doubles of women: Athena makes an *eidolon* of Penelope's sister and sends her to Penelope in a dream,[184] and there are other sorts of double Sitas.) We have noted the aural double of Rama's voice in the *Ramayana;* in Homer's *Iliad,* too, there are doubles—designed to save men, not women. Often a deity protects a hero by removing him from the battlefield and putting a double in his place; sometimes the deity himself (or, more often, herself) becomes the double, and sometimes a lesser mortal is substituted for a greater hero. Athena, for instance, takes the form of Deiphobus, Helen's second lover, in order to trick Hector, and Aphrodite creates an airy mist to hide Paris (!) from the enemy while she whisks the real man out of a tight fix (she does the same for Aeneas, and Apollo saves him with an *eidolon*).[185]

How did these overwhelmingly male paradigms then come to be transferred to women? In both traditions, subsequent texts generate doubles of the central woman, but the two traditions tell the same story about two diametrically opposed women. Was Freud right about the connection between the whore and the madonna? Valmiki's Sita is innocent of any lust, merely the victim of Ravana's lust; Helen is less seduced against than seducing (though even in Homer Aphrodite urges Helen to her sin, as Penelope recalls, a reading that makes Helen not a victimizer but a victim). Sita never does sleep with Ravana in any of the South Asian texts that we have considered (or in fact, in any ancient South Asian text that I know); Helen certainly does sleep with Paris in Homer, if not in all later Greek texts. Valmiki's Sita proves her chastity and in some texts vanishes forever, leaving Rama miserable (and, one hopes, very sorry that he behaved so badly); Homer's Helen acknowledges her promiscuity and lives again with Menelaus; we meet them in their uneasy domesticity, long after the Trojan War.[186] And the more chaste woman is both more foolish and more unhappy: the clever Helen lives happily wherever she is—Troy, Sparta, Egypt; Sita suffers in separation from Rama, whether that separation takes place in Lanka or in another world (the realm of Fire). Sita is fooled by Ravana, fooled by the deer, and fooled by the demons who mimic Rama's voice; Helen fools others and successfully mimics the voices of the wives of the Greeks inside the Trojan horse.[187] Sita is fooled, and therefore innocent, where Helen fools, and is guilty.*

But in later tellings Helen becomes Sita, as it were, the chaste woman whose chastity is protected by her double (she even becomes Alcmena:

one late retelling imagines that Paris took the form of Menelaus to seduce Helen[188]), while Sita, when we look closer, has the shadow of Helen in her sexuality, especially in the Tamil tradition. In consonance with these moral contrasts, the religious roles of Sita and Helen are very different: Agni, a god, hides Sita in fire, the element of sacrifice, of religion; while Proteus, a man, simply guards Helen in a palace in Egypt, a real place (however symbolic of darkness, otherness, origins).

The Greek war against Troy was situated, and was recognized as being situated, in history; Schliemann really found Troy. And when history changed, the war had to be denied. By removing Helen, the Greeks problematized the Trojan war, emptied it of its superficial meaning as a war fought for a woman, and opened the way for a new discourse on the futility of war and/or the hollowness of female beauty. Stesichorus surely did not tell his story primarily to let Helen off the hook; she was, after all, one of the most famous adulteresses of antiquity. (Thersites repeatedly calls her a whore in Shakespeare's *Troilus and Cressida*.) Instead, Stesichorus extended Herodotus's cynical point about war, making Helen not merely absent from Troy but absent from the adulterous bed that was the excuse for the war. Euripides had represented an undoubled Helen in *The Trojan Women*, in which women explicitly called into question the values of war. The Helen in that play is hated, as she is in Euripides' *Iphigenia in Tauris* (c. 412 B.C.E.) and *Iphigenia at Aulis* (c. 405 B.C.E.), and she has no phantom double—though Iphigenia, who (especially in the former play) functions much like Helen, has one: she is saved (from being sacrificed by her father, Agamemnon) by a deer ex machina sent by Artemis to take her place. The device of the deer killed in place of the heroine comes to the story of Iphigenia from mythology and folklore, in which it was to become a cliché (Snow White, Brangane, etc.); we may also see here a shadow of Sita's illusory deer. By using this device in his telling of the play, Euripides was, like the Piraeus whore played by Melina Mercouri in the film *Never on Sunday* (1959), retelling the Greek tragedies to give them a happy ending—everyone goes to the seashore—like the comic book ending of the story of Saranyu.

Euripides' *Helen*, composed in 412 B.C.E., was produced after the disastrous defeat of the great Sicilian expedition, a time when the Greeks were again at war, now with Sparta (the home of Helen!), and were questioning the justice of that war (and arguing that it was an extension of the Trojan War). Aristophanes' *Lysistrata*, in 411 B.C.E., made the same point about the

Peloponnesian War; and when Lysistrata suggests that the women go on a sexual walkout (lie-out?) to force the men to make peace, Lampito, the Spartan woman, reminds her that Menelaus put up his sword when he saw Helen's naked breast (presumably when he was about to kill her, as he intended to do in *The Trojan Women*). The play ends with a hymn to Helen of Sparta—still undoubled and presumably willing to lend her erotic forces to the women's sexual strike for peace, a recasting with obvious heavy irony. Yet, on a deadly serious level, it also made sense for Euripides, in *Helen*, to use the image of the phantom Helen to problematize the paradigmatic Trojan War and, by implication, the present wars as well. And so, like Stesichorus, Euripides changed his story, and doubled Helen in his *Helen*.

Sarah B. Pomeroy suggests other reasons that the Greeks might have had for producing the phantom Helen at this time:

> Greek historians of the Classical period found it incredible that men would fight a protracted war over a woman—even if she were the most beautiful woman in the world. . . . We can be fairly certain—knowing the political stakes of a matrilineal marriage—that the Trojan War was provoked by more than Menelaus's personal jealousy. Since Menelaus was king by virtue of his position as Helen's husband, he might lose the throne if he lost her. Therefore he refused to accept the validity of her change in husbands and determined to recover her, as the essential prerequisite to his claim to the throne of Sparta. Thus Helen, who was responsible for the war, ironically suffered the least.[189]

Pomeroy cites Herodotus's idea that Helen was in Egypt and not in Troy; and, like Herodotus, she doesn't mention the phantom. Yet her remarks about Helen's political base in Sparta suggest a good reason for the myth of the phantom: to make sure that the real Helen, and the real money, remained at home.

In contrast, by removing Sita the Hindus deproblematized the war with Ravana, denying the demon any power at all over the wife of a hero who had become an unambiguously incarnate God, more significantly, a divine *king*. Sita became less of a goddess as Rama became more of an uppercase God. In the Valmiki *Ramayana*, Sita was the original excuse for the war against Lanka, as Helen was for Troy: but Sita was used in what we would nowadays call entrapment (as the phantom Hera was used in the myth of Ixion), set up precisely so that Ravana would fall in love with her and steal her, thus giving Rama an excuse to destroy him.

The Hindu war was quickly appropriated by religion; even when history changed, the religious texts argued that the war did not have to be denied. But as history (in the form of epigraphs and inscriptions, proclamations and panegyrics) claimed the epic for its paradigms, religious texts claimed it all the more for the ahistorical realms of eternity. In contrast with the Greeks, who took up the tale of the phantom Helen at the time of a war in which they were the aggressors, the Hindus developed the shadow Sita over centuries of occupation by an invasive foreign presence. For in the twelfth century the *Ramayana* became a paradigm for a certain sort of history in response to the Turkic presence in India;[190] it began to be used to demonize historical figures, to cast them as actors in the *Ramayana* battle, just as, in Greece, the *Iliad* was used to cast shadows upon the present wars. Hindus never asked whether that battle was futile, for it became a holy war invoked, even in our day (1992, to be more precise) to justify the destruction of the Babri mosque said to stand over Rama's birthplace—an act that triggered riots in which hundreds of Muslims and Hindus were killed.

Over the centuries, Sita's ordeal has proved problematic for different reasons to different South Asians, from pious apologists who were embarrassed by the God's cruelty to his wife, to feminists who saw in Sita's acceptance of the "cool" flames, in Tulsi's telling, and in the connection with Sati, an alarming precedent for suttee, the immolation of widows on their husbands' pyres. Sita and Helen are not real people, but Lanka and Troy are real places. Sita was "of Lanka" as Helen was "of Troy" (or, in the later tradition, "Not of Troy"), and each was caught up in the subsequent history of these cities and the cultures that claimed to have conquered them. North and South Indians identified Rama with the North and Ravana with the South; the North demonized the "Dravidian" Ravana, the South the "Aryan" Rama. Though both Sita and Helen are quasi-goddesses, recovering goddesses—one married to a kind of god, the other to a mortal—, they seem to lack the agency to produce their own doubles (in contrast with Samjna, who produces her own doubles in the post-Vedic texts), and what divine power they have to begin with is eroded in much the same way in the course of retellings. Like the two shadow women and the women whom they imitate, the two sets of texts not only look alike on the surface but share deeper resonances in their receptions as well.

Sita and Helen and Saranyu

I have suggested that, in a sense, Helen became Sita. One might argue that historically, both Helen and Sita became Saranyu, or, perhaps, that

Saranyu, Helen, and Sita are all reflections of the same shared story. One explanation for the similarity of the stories of Sita and Helen may be that the Vedic goddess Saranyu—or the subject of another, now lost story on which Saranyu herself was modeled—served as the model for both the Greek adulteress and the Hindu wife. Saranyu could have inspired both the myth of the Greek whore and the myth of the Hindu wife because Saranyu herself is sexually ambivalent—either more or less sexual than her husband, depending on how you calculate or who you ask. A link between Saranyu and Helen was first suspected by Sanskritists in the last century;[191] so too, Sita was compared to Helen by A. K. Krappe in 1931[192] and by Cristiano Grottanelli in 1982[193]—but on grounds other than their doubling. Now it is time to put these ideas together and to argue for a triple bond connecting Saranyu, Sita, and Helen. Let us begin with the bonds between Sita and Saranyu, since they come from the same tradition.

Sita still behaves very much like a goddess in Valmiki's text:[194] at the moment when she emerges from the fire, she is said to have garlands that do not wither,[195] which is a sign that she is an immortal.* Like a Swan Maiden,[196] like Urvashi and Saranyu, Sita comes out of the otherworld to marry a human king, bears him twins, and leaves him when he mistreats her. Technically parentless (she sprang out of a furrow), she is like an earth goddess, born from the earth and returning to it at her death. She does not, therefore, appear to share the solar symbolism of Saranyu, though it is striking that at the moment when Rama rejects Sita he says that she is as offensive to him as a lamp to a man whose eyes are diseased,[197] unwittingly invoking the metaphor for a mortal unable to gaze at a deity;* and then, when Sita emerges safe from her fire ordeal, Rama says, "Ravana could not even think of raping Sita, for she is as unattainable as a blazing flame of fire; nor could she have ruled over Ravana's bedroom, for she belongs only to me, just as light belongs only to the sun."[198] In addition to these rather vague solar tropes, we might also see an even vaguer link to Saranyu's equine nature in the fact that Sita's twins appear to their father on the occasion of his horse sacrifice.

Helen, by contrast, is stunningly solar: like Saranyu, she is associated with the seductive, ambivalent, and destructive Dawn;[199] indeed, Helen and Ushas (the Vedic dawn) have the same epithet, "daughter of the Sky/God."[200] The two aspects of the sun, often reflected in the equine twins of Indo-European theology, may also represent the day and the night, the solar aspect of the horse as morning star in contrast with the chthonic aspect of the horse as evening star. Linda Lee Clader argues that Dawn is replaced in the epic by Aphrodite, who is closely associated with Helen.[201] Helen is the daughter of the sky-god, Zeus; Otto Skutsch, apologetically reviving the solar mythology of F. Max Müller, notes that one late and admittedly rather dubious Greek source even asserts that Helen's father was not Zeus but the Sun.[202] An equally dubious,[203] but suggestive, etymology connects "Helen" with "Saranyu" (through the Sanskrit *sarana,* "swift").[204] (Yet another connects Saranyu with the Greek goddess Demeter Erinus and the Furies *[erinues],*[205] an etymology supported by another link between the Indian and Greek myths, for Demeter Erinus, like Saranyu, changed herself into a mare to avoid being raped—also in vain, for Poseidon changed himself into a stallion and covered her.)[206]

Helen is like Saranyu not only in having (in post-Homeric texts) a shadow double but in having as brothers the Dioscuri or Gemini, the half-equine twins who are the Greek counterpart of the Ashvins, Saranyu's twin equine sons—and who, through their half-immortality (Castor is mortal, Polydeuces/Pollux immortal) are also the counterpart of Saranyu's other twins, Manu and Yama. The equine imagery of Helen, which is also a sign of her transgressive sexuality, is maintained in a key Homeric episode in which Helen tempts the men trapped inside the Trojan horse, the horse pregnant with death for the Trojans, and almost succeeds in betraying the Greeks inside it, her countrymen, by impersonating the voices of their wives[207]—doubling, aurally, as their wives. The Trojan horse, closely associated with Helen, is, like Pandora's box, an image of the deceptive equine woman who is hollow inside and full of evils. (*Trojan horse* in our day is the name given to a kind of computer virus that masquerades as another sort of file, an electronic trickster.)

Skutsch remarks that it "can hardly be an accident" that Saranyu, the woman associated with the Ashvins, was replaced by an *eidolon,* just like Helen, the sister of the Dioscuri.[208] The Ashvins' Vedic epithet of *Nasatyas* may be related to the Greek verb *nes,* as in *nostos* (homecoming), with a general meaning of returning to life and light.[209] This would make the Nasatyas "retrievers," and indeed they are closely concerned with the recovery of Suryā, the daughter of the Sun (Surya) and wife of the Ashvins. (I have generally omitted diacriticals, in an effort to make this book more accessible to the general reader. In a few places, however, we need them. Here they point out that the Suryā in question is female, in contrast with the usual word for the sun, the masculine form, Surya.)

Clader suggests a Greek parallel to Suryā: "the only character who can possibly fit the loss-recovery motif with reference to the Dioskouroi is Helen."[210] She admits that "Homer never states explicitly that she is the Sun-princess and Indo-European consort of the Dioskouroi,"[211] but argues that the Atreidae, the brothers Menelaus and Agamemnon, take the place of the Dioscuri in the epic version of the myth, while the Dioscuri themselves seek Helen when she is raped by Theseus. I would add that the myth of Saranyu contains these same elements, but in a different configuration: the equine twins (the Ashvins) are born when Saranyu is sought and found—*and then raped*—by her husband. The order of the elements in one myth is inverted in the other; where the Greek myth tells of rape, then equine twins, then a search, the Hindu myth tells of a search, then a rape, then equine twins.

Clader's final argument suggests broader connections between Helen and the Sun-princess (or, I would say, between Helen and Saranyu—and, to some extent, Sita):

> The most convincing evidence in myth for the identification of Helen as a fertility goddess is the fact that she is consistently being raped. . . .[212] In legend and literature what Helen is best known for is rape, and secondarily, perhaps, marriage. . . . The mythology surrounding the Sun-princess involves continual rape and recovery, as she disappears and reappears again. The Twins are responsible for bringing her back each time, and the Dioskouroi-Helen-Theseus myth fits this pattern well.[213]

Helen as Sun-princess is thus assimilated to Persephone, the vegetation goddess who is raped and recovered: "Both types spend much of their time out of sight, under the earth, and reappear regularly." As the daughter of Demeter the mare, Persephone is connected with the equine shape-shifting goddess, the Greek parallel to Saranyu; but as the daughter of the earth, she resembles Sita, who returns to her earth mother. Helen herself is thus "a goddess who spends half her time in the dark—either under the earth or in the night sky." Thus she resembles both Sita ("under the earth") and Saranyu ("in the night sky"); and all three of them spend not half their time but half of their essence "in the dark"—in their shadow forms.

From these bits and pieces it seems likely that Homer may well have known about the phantom Helen, as Herodotus insisted, for the general theme of the shadow woman is pre-Homeric, at least on the evidence of related Vedic texts. And if even some of these speculations are valid, then an ancient story of a shadow double—perhaps the Vedic story of the goddess Saranyu—may have inspired, or at least been available to, the authors of the texts about both Sita and Helen.

Gazing at the Shadow of the Sun

Certain themes embedded in the myth of Saranyu also shed light, if I may use the term, upon the shared mythology of Sita and Helen. One retelling of the tale of Samjna turns upon a pun about eyes: "When the Sun looked at her Samjna used to shut her eyes, and so the Sun got angry and spoke sharply to her: 'Since you always restrain *(samyamam)* your eyes when you see me, therefore you will bring forth a twin *(yama)* who will restrain *(samyamanam)* creatures.'"[214] Samjna is punished for looking away from her husband's full sexual blazing, and a rather awkward pun on the actions of the mother's eyes (restraining) makes Yama a Restrainer (one of his famous epithets). We might expect the son to be cursed here to become blind, like the sons of other women in Hindu mythology who close their eyes against their husbands.[215] Yet there may be an implicit connection between blindness and justice (the judgment of the dead, or prophylactic "restraining" of sinful mortals, which is Yama's task) which would make some sense of the curse. In fact, another variant plays upon precisely this concept of blind justice: "Yama has the eye of justice *(dharma)* because of [the Sun's] boon. And because he has the eye of justice he is impartial to friend and foe."[216] Here we might recall that Stesichorus and Homer are blinded, as several texts suggest, in punishment for failing to see the phantom Helen. Being blind is sometimes a blessing: it keeps you from seeing things you don't want to see, sometimes things that can kill you. But blindness is more often a curse, as we will learn from Cyavana,* blinded when Sukanya pierces his eyes, and Teiresias,* blinded for saying that women enjoy sex more than men.

Eyes play a more important role in the Saranyu myth when the pun on "restraining" is translated in the contemporary comic book, which takes the solar phenomena very literally: Sanjna's father warns her that she may not be able to bear her husband's "brilliance in all seasons," and one of the women who dress her for her wedding remarks, "Let me darken your eyes. You will need protection from his glances." ("Darken" here can hardly mean sun-glasses, but may refer to kohl painted around the eyes, to beautify them—for the husband's gaze—as well as to protect them—from that same gaze.) Sure enough: "Then suddenly one summer Surya's rays beat down intense and oppressive. He was at his Zenith." At this moment, the Sun says to his wife, "Come Sanjna, sit by me."

> Sanjna: "My lord! Why do you glare at me so! Lord! I cannot open my eyes." The Sun: "Sanjna! Look at me! I am your husband! Sanjna! Will you repel me?" "I am sorry, my lord." The Sun: "Then listen carefully. Since you closed your eyes on me, the sustainer of all living beings, the son you bear now shall be Yama, the god of death."

The pun on *samyamanam* and Yama is lost on the voyage from Sanskrit to English and awkwardly replaced by a vague contrast between life and death. But the idea that Samjna is punished for being unable to gaze directly at the Sun (or, in the earlier version, that the gods may have hidden Saranyu in order to conceal her brilliance) draws upon a very ancient mythological mindset.

Saranyu's story is certainly not merely a solar myth, but the fact that her husband is the Sun is hardly irrelevant to the metaphysical concerns of the myth. The sun functions in these myths as a metaphor (for power, for mortality, for divinity, for a god or goddess, or truth) but also as a literal thing, the ball of fire in the sky. The idea that the sun itself is an eye, the eye of a god, looking at us,[217] is implied by a funeral hymn in the *Rig Veda*, which says to the dead man: "May your eye go to the sun."[218]

The related plain commonsense observation that staring at the sun makes one blind,[219] that one cannot return the Sun's gaze, is theologically expanded into the belief that one cannot look at God[220] without dying (or, for Saranyu, giving birth to death). This belief is reflected in the doomsday image in the *Bhagavad Gita*, when, at Arjuna's request, Krishna shows him his doomsday form, "brighter than a thousand suns" (the form that J. Robert Oppenheimer recalled when he saw the first explosion of an atomic bomb),[221] a sight that Arjuna cannot bear.[222] In the *Tibetan Book of the Dead*, too, the dead man loses his shot at easy, immediate release from the wheel of rebirth—which is to say, his shot at immortality—and slips down into rebirth simply because he cannot bear to gaze at the bright light of Enlightenment.

Similar ideas are attested in ancient Greece. Plato, in the *Republic*, remarked, "Sight is not the sun, neither itself nor that in which it occurs which we call the eye. . . . But I think it is the most sunlike of the organs of sense."[223] But in *The Sophist*, embedded in a comparison of the images made by artists and the natural images made by shadows and reflections in water,[224] he says that the philosopher is "difficult to see on account of the brilliant light of the place; for the eyes of the soul of the multitude are not strong enough to endure the sight of the divine."[225] Then there was Medusa, on whom Jason could only gaze in a reflection.[226] Gazing at such a demonic figure is courting death—just like gazing at the sun, or God. The idea also lives on in Europe, as in de la Rouchefoucald's maxim, "Neither death nor the sun can be stared at," echoed by Georges Bataille: "Human eyes tolerate neither sun, coitus, cadavers, nor obscurity, but with different reactions."[227]

Because of the unbearable lightness of the Sun's wife (Samjna), we can see only her "shadow." But does the Sun, or the Sun goddess, have a shadow? The gods, in general, do not have shadows; only humans have shadows. Shadows express a paradoxical condition: even though they are immaterial and insubstantial, their presence is essential to embodied, living creatures, who, without them, lose a crucial element in their defining character.[228] Thus, in ancient India, the lack of a shadow is the sign of an immortal; the mortal is the (only) one who has a shadow to lose. The shadow is one of the primary criteria that distinguishes humans from gods in the Hindu story of Nala and Damayanti.

It is presumably because gods are made of light that they cast no shadows. Charles Malamoud, in an article entitled "The Gods Have No Shadows," says:

> This is the weakness of the gods: they are altogether light/clear *(clairs)*. When they are forced to reveal their nature, they reveal their affinity with the light of the sun: It does not change them, it does not burn them, they don't have to shelter themselves against it, and the material of their bodies does not constitute an obstacle for it to engender (and be betrayed by) an attached shadow.[229]

Malamoud goes on to argue that the principle of light/clarity characterizes the speech of the gods. But a language without shadow is a language without ambiguity, and the gods are often said to love obscure speech, what is "out of sight" *(paroksham).*[230] (When, in one early text, Saranyu creates the female who looks like her, she does it "out of sight *[paroksham]* of her husband.")[231] This desire for ambiguity modified and limited the shadowless quality of the language of the gods: "The gods wished to create areas of shadow in their language, mysteries that only they would understand."[232] And so Samjna, "the name," must create Chaya, the shadow of the text—in a story first told in a riddle.

Thus gods in certain circumstances do have shadows after all; Valmiki's *Ramayana* describes the huge shadows (*chaya*s) of gods, demigods, and demons.[233] But what does it mean to say that the Sun has a shadow? In naturalistic terms, this cannot be so; neither the sun nor any other source of light has a shadow; they merely cause other solid objects to have shadows.[234] (Of course, the moon, during a solar eclipse, casts its shadow on the sun, and one Vedic commentary relates this phenomenon to the story of Tvashtri.)[235] But the Hindu Sun, theologically freed from naturalistic considerations, violates this rule because, unlike other gods, the Sun is *not* immortal. That is why his immortal wife gives him her shadow instead of her bright self. Indeed, she presumably confirms, or perhaps even preserves, her own immortality forever by shedding her shadow, leaving it for her mortal husband and her mortal children—us.

Shadows mean different things in different cultures. Even within India, the *Rig Veda* was composed in the mountains of the northwest, where it is cold and the sun is welcome. But the post-Vedic texts were composed in the Ganges valley, where it is hot and shade is welcome. This may well have contributed to the shift in the meaning of sun and shadow. In post-Vedic India, as Ann Gold reminds us, "[T]he term shadow has connotations of benevolence and protection (shelter from the sun)—not of frightening darkness."[236] More specifically, there is a Sanskrit saying that there is no shade like a mother, a natural metaphor that is unpacked, and inverted, in complex ways in the myth of Saranyu and her shadow. Perhaps, then, we are fortunate to have the shadow rather than Saranyu for our mother—though both she and Saranyu fail, disastrously, to "shade" or protect their children.

It is useful to distinguish the two rather different arguments given as to why we mortals might be able to see only a shadow of a god: first, because even if the gods were there for us to see, we could not bear to look directly into their brilliance; and second, because that is all that is left of them for us to see, to remember. The second idea, of the remainder, accounts for Samjna's shadow: she went away, and her shadow is all we have. But the first idea, of blinding brilliance, expresses the problem faced by the Sun in early texts and by Samjna in later texts: the spouse is too bright/hot for the direct gaze of the partner. It is more than an accident of language that her brilliance renders Samjna either unseeable or unrapable, depending upon the variation of a single letter in certain manuscripts (*dh* or *d*, between *adhrishya*—unable to be raped—and *adrishya*—unable to be looked at); the male's gaze is interchangeable with his sexual violence. The two basic ideas are often causally related: because the deity knows that we cannot look at him or her, he or she leaves us something else to look at. The shadow of a god who is also a lost lover appears when Giraudoux's Leda,* complaining that Jupiter never came to see her after his one-night stand, admits one exception: "Now and then, in the bath, the shadow of a swan settles on me, and no amount of soap can wash it off."[237] In the mythology of ancient India, and perhaps ancient Greece, we are forbidden access to the woman that the Sun loved—the Sun goddess, mother of the human race, Saranyu—and may only have access to her shadow. But the shadow is not the substance; in Shakespeare's *Merchant of Venice* (2.9), the inscription on the silver casket—the one of the three caskets that has neither the value of (solar) gold nor the value of the portrait of the beloved—reads: "Some there be that shadows kiss; / Such have but a shadow's bliss." For mirror images or shadows are not exactly the same as the figures that they double: mirror images are inverted and shadows are colorless, shape-changing, and often not there (this quality of discontinuous existence being what, according to Otto Rank,[238] made shadows natural metaphors for the soul).

The Sun Is a Whore

Freud connected the inability to stare at the sun with an abandoning parent, rather than lover or god, in one of his most famous cases, "The Case of Schreber." In the course of his analysis of this man who wanted to be a woman, Freud remarks, "Schreber has a quite peculiar relation to the sun. It speaks to him in human language. . . . he 'used to shout threats and abuse at it and positively bellow at it.'" And Freud tells us, in a footnote, what Schreber "used to exclaim": "The Sun is a whore."[239] In another footnote, Freud again quotes Schreber: "When I stand facing it [the sun] and speak aloud, its rays turn pale before me. I can gaze at it without any difficulty and without being more than slightly dazzled by it; whereas in my healthy days it would have been as impossible for me as for anyone else to gaze at it for a minute at a time." What does Freud make of this? He rounds up the usual suspect: "The sun, therefore, is nothing but another sublimated symbol for the father. . . . In this instance symbolism overrides grammatical gender—at least so far as German goes, for in most other languages the sun is masculine." (It is feminine in German grammar, *die Sonne* —and also, as we will soon see, in Japanese myth.*)

In assuming that the sun is a symbol of the father, Freud overlooks two vital clues that he himself records but misinterprets: Schreber's curse ("The Sun is a whore") and the fact that *sun* in German is feminine, not masculine. In keeping with the general pattern that we have observed in the case of Saranyu/Samjna, Freud transfers the solar power from the female to the male, ignoring the possibility that Schreber's relationship with his mother might have something to do with his belief that God wanted to turn him into a woman. Freud often gets things *almost* right.

Freud continued to shift agency from females to males when he discovered what he regarded as the mythological parallel to Schreber's solar fantasies. In his original publication of this case, he had confessed, "I can make no more than the barest allusion to the relation of all this to cosmic myths." But some years later he published a postscript in which he remarked on a Greek myth about an eagle who tested his young to find out if they were legitimate by making them look into the sun without blinking. Thus, he concluded, "[W]hen Schreber boasts that he can look into the sun unscathed and undazzled, he has rediscovered the mythological method of expressing his relation to the sun, and has confirmed us once again in our view that the sun is a symbol of the father."[240] Here Freud notes Schreber's claim to be a nobleman, "Adler," which is also the word for "eagle."

Following the paper trail that Freud leaves for us (citing Salomon Reinach,[241] who cites "Greco-Roman" sources cited by Otto Keller,[242] who cites Aristotle),[243] we find a revealing bit of slippage between the female and the male. Aristotle's text about the eagle also tells us that another bird, a *phene* (a kind of vulture), rears both its own young and those of the eagle, which it catches as they fall from the nest when the *mother* eagle ejects them from the nest. The first villain in this piece is therefore the mother eagle, and the heroine is the vulture (the *phene,* a feminine word in Greek, and the implicit female counterpart to the explicitly female eagle), who, like an inverted cuckoo, cheerfully adopts what she knows to be someone else's children. Indeed, it is presumably this very adoption that inspires the male sea eagle, by a kind of retroactive reasoning, to test his young *to make sure that they are eagles and not vultures,* apparently believing (as Aristotle believes) that "the *phene* has a film over its eyes and sees badly, but the sea-eagle is very keen-sighted."[244]

In Hindu mythology, the criterion of blinking distinguishes the true lineage not of eagles but of immortals, in contrast with mortals. In the story of Nala and Damayanti, the gods neither cast shadows nor blink; unlike us, they can keep their eyes open when looking at the light that would blind us. Appropriately, the (mortal) Sun alone among deities is said, in Vedic mythology, to blink its eye occasionally,[245] and the Sun is an eagle[246]—called Martanda, "dead in the egg," because he is a bird born of a dead egg and kicked out of the nest. The *Rig Veda* says that the gods do not experience the need to close their eyes, for they never sleep.[247] When Yama rejects the incestuous advances of his sister Yami, he says, "These spies of the gods who wander about here below do not stand still, nor do they blink their eyes," and she replies, "She would do what he wished in the nights and in the days; she would deceive the eye of the sun for the instant of the blink of an eye."[248] Sometimes the gods are said to lack eyelids altogether, like serpents.

Thus the issue of disputed parentage (of the fledglings, or Yama) is keyed to the belief in the child of a Sun-bird (the eagle, or the Sun) who is rejected by his mother (the female eagle, or Samjna) and adopted by a bird who cannot gaze at the Sun (the vulture, or shadow Samjna). *Female* parentage is what is at issue in the avian vignette cited by Aristotle—though here, as so often, doubts about the mother inspire the paranoid violence of the father. But Freud (following Keller) shifted the emphasis from the abandoning mother of the Sun-eagle to the threatening father, just as he shifted his attention from the mother to the father of the man, Schreber, who once had, but lost, the ability to gaze at the whore, the mother, the sun.

The Shadow of a Goddess, the Statue of a Woman

The mythologies of Sita and Helen (and Saranyu) share a number of assumptions about the symbolism of shadows and sculptures. The theme of the consoling statue that reifies the shadow is another link between Sita and Helen: when Sita vanishes, Rama puts in her place a golden image, just as the statue of Athena is stolen and duplicated when Helen is stolen and duplicated. But here again there is a distinction within the textual traditions: where Helen, the cunning and wicked woman, is replaced by an *eidolon,* an artistic image, Sita, the innocent and virtuous woman, is replaced by a *chaya,* a natural image of shadow or reflection. And where the Indian texts rest upon the metaphor of the shadow of a goddess, the

Greek texts rest on the metaphor of the artistic image of a woman. Saranyu/Samjna functions as a trope for verbal deception, the deception of texts; Helen by contrast becomes a trope for visual deception, the deception of statues.

Freud suggested that, "in the last analysis the 'spirit' of a person or thing is the faculty of remembering and representing the object, after he or it was withdrawn from conscious perception."[249] This spirit is the shadow, and its representation is the statue. Let us consider the two parts of this metaphor one by one, and then together: first the shadow of a goddess; then the statue or artistic image of a woman; and then the shadow of the statue.

We have seen that although immortal gods are not supposed to have shadows, mortal gods, like the Sun, do, and the immortal Saranyu sloughs her shadow in part to preserve her own immortality. As a result, Saranyu's shadow is all that we have of her to see, to remember: she went away, and her shadow is all that is left. The gods have no shadows because they gave them to us. Faith in shadows of a different sort is reflected in the viewpoint of certain Hindus who argue that since God is not so much absent as devoid of material qualities *(nirguna),* to love such a deity the worshipper must imagine him/her with material qualities *(saguna).*[250] The image or shadow is the essential, though false, representation of an unrepresentable deity.

Other goddesses too leave their shadows behind for us when they vanish, which makes it possible for us to see the divinity that we cannot otherwise see or look at directly. The goddess in the temple of Lepakshi is visible only through both a mask and a mirror (as well as a footprint*), as David Shulman has pointed out:

> The mirror offers accessibility, since the goddess is not truly visible. . . . The mirror makes her most available, and also shows her to herself. . . . The mask seduces her, as it were, into an accessible self, that is then reflected in still greater intensity and wholeness from the mirror. . . . The mirror thus offers the reflection of a mask of an image seen in a dream—and, as in so many Hindu contexts, we might expect that the more deeply embedded the form, the more whole and real it must be. This is the ontic advantage of the play within a play, the story within a story, the dream inside a dream.[251]

Just as there are two reasons why we must see the deity only in reflection (first because the deity is unavailable and second because it is too dangerous to look at), so there are two reasons to view Lepakshi through both a mirror and a mask: the double reflection is somehow deeper and truer, as well as safer and more accessible, than the direct gaze. The double distancing of mirror plus shadow is an expression of the logic of the principle of reduplicating duplication that we saw in the proliferation of Manus in reaction to the proliferation of his stepmothers (and in the proliferation of images of Athena); by that logic, in one form of Tantric yoga the adept reaches only "the shadow of the second shadow" of the Goddess *(pratichaya).*[252] Sometimes the deity uses shadow to erase the distance from the worshipper: in contemporary India, in Rajasthan, when a person is possessed by a deity it is said that the deity's shadow *(chaya),* representing the divine essence or presence *(bhav),* has come to that person so that the deity can speak and act through a human body.[253]

The shadow functions as a consoling remainder in an Indian Buddhist text that tells of an evil snake king who converted to Buddhism and prayed to the Buddha to help him keep from relapsing; the Buddha responded by agreeing to leave in the snake's cave his "shadow" or "reflection," whose power would keep the snake from committing further sins.[254] This shadow in the cave *was* the Buddha in his absence, as were the Buddha's footprints* and other symbols both of the Buddha's presence and of his absence, allowing devotees to see the Buddha while remembering that he was gone. A Chinese Buddhist text tells of a dragon whom the Buddha reformed in a cave and to whom he promised to leave his shadow after his death. The text continues:

> In old days there was a shadow of Buddha to be seen here, bright as the true form, with all its characteristic marks. In later days men have not seen it so much. What does appear is only a feeble likeness. But whoever prays with fervent faith, he is mysteriously endowed, and he sees it clearly before him, though not for long.[255]

The Buddha is in a sense absent and present from the start, for the shadow is associated with the absent presence of the hidden god, the abandoning deity whom the worshipers long to see and whose shadow is a tantalizing and unsatisfying taste of what has been lost. Blanchard regarded ruined Greek temples as temples dedicated to the absence of a god.[256] But in the Buddhist myth, all temples are monuments to the absence of a god.

There are obvious parallels between the parable of the Buddha in the cave and Plato's metaphor of the shadows in the cave (not to mention the shadow painting that Plato compared to the illusion of Helen of Troy).

The mythology of shadow women raises questions noted by the historian of science Lorraine Daston: "What if all of philosophy since Plato was crashingly wrong about the *ontos on,* the really real? What if it is really the shadows in Plato's cave that are true, the accidents rather than the substance, the phenomena rather than the noumena?" And she suggests that this might be seen as the revenge of the mythologist against Plato for condemning myths as lies.[257] Philostratus in the second century wrote that even an image made of nothing but shadow and light *(skia* and *phos),* lacking color and substance, can still convey not only likeness and form, but intelligence, modesty, and bravery.[258]

Just as the solar brilliance is theologized to a divine brilliance, so, too, the experience of the loss of the deity may be seen as a theological extrapolation from the experience of the loss of a lover or parent; the lost woman is hypertrophied into the lost the woman of the Sun, seen only through a shadow or mirror. Hindu texts often speak of the shadows of human beings that we long for. The *Kamasutra* suggests that the lover separated from his beloved should kiss the shadow or reflection *(chaya)* of the object of his attentions in a mirror, on a wall (cast by a lamp, the commentator explains), or in water, in order to express his emotion.[259] When the sage Vyasa grieved inconsolably for his beloved son, Shuka, who was gone forever, the god Shiva pitied Vyasa and said, "You will see a shadow that looks just like your son and that will never go away," and Vyasa was filled with joy when he saw the shadow.[260] Far beyond India, the solar metaphor has been used to express the lost love object; in Edmond Rostand's *Cyrano de Bergerac,* when Cyrano woos Roxane, he says, "You know how, after looking at the sun, / One sees red suns everywhere—so, for hours / After the flood of sunshine that you are, / My eyes are blinded by your burning hair." [261] Looking at the Sun makes one see multiple images, multiple shadows, of a woman one loves.

In ancient Greece too, the shadow or mirror reflection was sometimes regarded as the only way to see a lost loved one. In general, the shade *(eidolon* or *skia)* of a person remained in the underworld, while in the case of a hero, the person survived on Olympus, as Homer says, for instance, of the *eidolon* of Heracles.* But sometimes the process was reversed; thus Pindar speaks of us as "creatures of a day. What is a someone, what is a no one? Man is the dream of a shade."[262] Noting that in Homeric usage the word *skia* (shade) can designate a dead person, Gregory Nagy remarks: "I suggest that the shade of the dead person is literally dreaming—that is, realizing through its dreams—the living person. . . . It is as if we the living were the realization of the dreams dreamt by our dead ancestors."[263]

So much for shadows. As for statues, the concept of the dangerous solar or divine gaze is embedded in the belief, among contemporary Buddhists in Sri Lanka, that the artisan carving the statue of the Buddha must leave the eyes for last—and look at the statue only through a mirror as he paints them on.[264] The eyes of Greek statues, too, are dangerously alive. Strabo, writing at the very end of the first century B.C.E., tells us what he calls a myth about the much-stolen statue of Athena, the Palladion:*

> They say that wooden image *(xoanon)* of the Trojan Athena in Heracleia closed its eyes when suppliants were dragged away by the Ionians who had captured the city and taken it by force; even today the wooden image can be seen closing its eyes. . . . In just the same way they say that the image in Troy turned away when Cassandra was violated.[265]

The statue closes its eyes when the suppliants are violated and turns away when Cassandra (who is abducted *by* Agamemnon, just as Helen is abducted *from* Agamemnon's brother) is violated—responses to the very act from which the statue, or double, of Helen was intended to protect her. (Euripides' Iphigenia says, lying, that the wooden statue of Artemis at Tauris turned its head away and *shut its eyes* when the polluted Orestes approached it.)[266]

When these statues, eyes and all, proliferated, how could you tell if you had the real thing? Well, apparently the eyes of the genuine article would glow and its wooden body would sweat when it was made "genuine" by the presence of the goddess within it.[267] By Hindu logic, as we learn from the story of Nala, mortals sweat, though gods do not; the real statue of the Greek goddess, by that criterion, behaves like a human. But in fact, sweating means something else in ancient Greece: it distinguishes between a living creature, human or divine, and an inanimate one. By this criterion, the sweat proves that the statue of Athena is alive.

The statue, like the shadow, may represent not only an otiose god but an absent human lover. Pliny, in the first century B.C.E., relates the legend of a Corinthian girl who, as her lover was going abroad, traced the profile of the shadow of his face, thrown on the wall by the light of a lamp. Her father, the potter Butades, compressed clay on this surface and made a relief, which he hardened by fire with the rest of his pottery.[268] Thus the artist creates a shadow double to contain the memory of the lost lover, challenging the Platonic view of the shadow as unreal and negative. Butades' shadow-sculpting technique may have been what Plato meant by "painting with shadow." Helen, whom Plato connected with this shadow painting, argued in John Erskine's novel, speaking of her faded passion for Paris, that the way to maintain the illusion of the perfect lover would be never to see him again. In this view, the absent lover is the only one we can go on loving, by maintaining the image in the absence of the real person; but Helen mocked the other half of this syllogism, the preference for the illusion of art over the reality of love, when she accused Menelaus: "You didn't spare the woman you loved; you preserved me as an object of art."[269] Saranyu's father does what Butades does, and much more, to her lover: Tvashtri, who is the artisan of the gods, the Indian parallel to Hephaestus, puts the Sun on his lathe and turns him just as if he were a pot, fashioning out of the unbearable, excessive material of the Sun an artistically crafted, limited, controlled form that Saranyu accepts as a kind of surrogate for the rejected original.

The artisan of the gods, the blacksmith, in many mythologies is himself crippled and sometimes consequently abandoned by his wife or cuckolded. The divine Greek artisan, Hephaestus, was lamed as a child when he tried to intervene in a fight between his parents, Zeus and Hera, and was hurled down to Earth, a casualty of trouble in marital heaven.[270] His wife, Aphrodite, betrays him with Ares[271]—and, significantly, it is Helios, the Sun, who observes the guilty couple "mingling in love" and tattles to the cuckolded husband; Hephaestus then uses his craft not to trim but to trap Ares, to paralyze him. The Greek parallel assigns the roles differently from the Hindu: the lameness of the Greek artisan drives his wife away, while in Hinduism it is the artisan's son-in-law (the Sun) and his grandson (Yama) who are crippled and abandoned by their wife/mother.

The Greek myth of Butades speaks of a statue that comes from a shadow, a kind of meta-image, like Lepakshi's mirror of a mask; and this too has an Indian (Buddhist) parallel. In one of the variants of the tale of the shadow of the Buddha in a cave, King Rudrayana summoned his court painters to produce a portrait of the Buddha. The painters, however, were unable to portray his image until the Buddha, using a lantern, projected his shadow onto a screen and instructed the painters to color it in.[272] Hindu mythology also makes the connection in the other direction, so that the *absence* of a shadow coming from a statue reveals the *presence* of the deity. The criterion of shadowless divinity was used obliquely by the Bengali Tantric saint Ramakrishna to establish the fact that the goddess had entered into his stone image of her: "In the lamplight at night, although I looked very closely, I could never see the shadows of Mother's divine limbs on the temple wall."[273] Jeffrey Kripal's comment on this passage is very much to the point:

> It would seem that the Goddess is real *precisely* because the stone image casts no shadow. The fact that She is a stone image and not a living form, in other words, complicates the argument. When a human form casts no shadow, it is not really human: shadowlessness is equivalent to being unreal. But when a stone casts no shadow, it is not really a stone, but a deity: shadowlessness is equivalent to being real.[274]

We have seen that the sweating statue of the Greek goddess proves that some living creature, whether human or (in this case) deity, is present, whereas in India it distinguishes mortal from immortal. The statue of Ramakrishna's goddess plays upon another Hindu criterion of mortality from the story of Nala—the shadow, whose *absence* reveals the *presence* of a deity in an apparently human body (for Nala) or a statue (for Ramakrishna). The shadow, by its presence or absence, is thus, like sweating, a consistent index of mortality, on the one hand, or of life (mortal or immortal), on the other. By this logic too, the "real" Sita and Helen, who lose their shadows, do not experience the event, do not suffer like humans who keep their shadows; the unreal shadows of Helen and Sita are the ones who really commit adultery (or are suspected of committing adultery). This is a paradox to which we will return when we consider the greater reality of humans in comparison with gods who become the doubles of humans.*

There is another paradox here, too. What we noted of shadows is also true of statues: the worshipers have the image, not the original, both because they cannot have the original and because they couldn't bear the original if they had it. And so, when the original breaks through—when the statue sweats, or casts a shadow—on the one hand, they rejoice, because it erases their longing for the original, but, on the other hand, they are afraid, for the very reasons that made them prefer the statue in the first place.

The statues of shadows in these myths are a manifestation of the power of projection, the power that love and desire have to produce the image of the beloved when someone else, or no one else, is there. Mourners trace shadows in the attempt to create soul-catching doubles, preserving the memory of loved ones who have died or gone away; in the myth of Butades, art itself originates in the need to comfort the lonely. Marina Warner speaks of "the love motif in Dibutades' story and the increasingly romantic appeal of the later retellings." And she explains why this romanticism is essential to the illusion of art:

> The record of a face needs emotional engagement as a stimulus to accuracy, to likeness. Some of the earliest ideas about portraiture assume, first, that the relationship between the subject or model and the artist is intimate and loving, even erotic, because the fantasy or the memory of the maker can play on the gaps, and fill in what is missing, like color.[275]

E. H. Gombrich has illuminated the way in which this sort of projection (which he likens to our habit of seeing, wrongly, the bus we are waiting for in the rain) plays a role in our perception of works of art;[276] it is even more effective in our perception of those we love. As François Flahault has argued of written texts, the lost object, the lost lover, the lost deity, is retrieved through art.[277] Thus Helen of Troy becomes the phantom image that is projected onto, and onto which are projected, the images of actual women, loved and lost. Her projection also works so that when she drinks a magic drug, someone else (Menelaus) sees the illusion that she is young.

Many cultures assume that the eye is able to project itself, or at least to project light waves that reflect off the object of vision and bring information back to the eye. The word *cakshus* in Vedic texts means the gaze, the power that the eye has to send out light in search of an object. The ancient Hindu magic ointment of invisibility was something that you placed on *your* eyes in order to prevent *others* from seeing you—or your shadow. Thus the *Kamasutra* tells us that if a man makes an ointment out of the heart of a mongoose, the eyes of a snake, and certain other substances, and smears it on his own eyelids like eye shadow, his form *and his shadow* become invisible.[278] This ointment resurfaced in an American advertisement that promises to "Make Your Shadows Vanish":

> New *Illusion* is a break-through. It works by the same technique employed by Hollywood directors to make actresses look younger using LIGHT to flatter your face. Wrinkles can be seen because they cast shadows

on your skin. No cream will remove wrinkles. But *Illusion* actually "bends light" to make your shadows vanish.[279]

Saranyu had no need of this cream.

Saranyu in Japan

Hindu, Buddhist, and Greek texts might be related by the sorts of historical factors suggested either by Georges Dumézil, on the one hand, or Sheldon Pollock, on the other. But the argument for a broader cross-cultural distribution of the Saranyu story is supported by a myth in a Japanese text, the *Kojiki* (composed in 712 C.E.), a work of imperialist Japanese mythology. If this text is historically related to India (perhaps through Buddhism), it is certainly a far, far distant cousin:

AMATERASU AND THE MIRROR

The demiurges Izanami (female) and Izanagi (male) had intercourse. But since she invited him before he invited her, the child born of them was a failure (a leech). Then the man invited her first, and she gave birth to fire, but the fire burnt her genitals and she died; in anger Izanagi killed fire. He went to retrieve his wife from the dark realm, but she made him promise not to look at her while they left that realm. Impatient, he produced some light and saw her corpse oozing with maggots; he ran away and blocked her path with a boulder. She said she would kill a thousand of his offspring each day, and he replied that he would produce fifteen hundred each day. From his left eye he produced the deity *[kami]* named Amaterasu, a female, solar deity; from his right eye, Tukuyomi, a male, lunar deity; and from his nose he produced the stormy Susanowo.

Susanowo and his sister Amaterasu produced children; he then went wild with victory and dropped through the roof of the sacred weaving hall a dappled pony, which he had skinned backwards; it alarmed the heavenly maiden who was weaving there, so that she struck her genitals against the shuttle and died. In fear, Amaterasu concealed herself in a cave and shut the opening with a boulder; this caused darkness to spread throughout the world. To lure her back out, the gods asked the smith to make a mirror; they summoned Ame-no-Uzume, who danced, became possessed, and exposed her breasts and genitals, so that all the gods laughed. Amaterasu, curious, came out of the cave and asked why Ame-no-Uzume was dancing and why they were laughing. Ame-no-Uzume told Amaterasu that they had a deity more beautiful than her; and they placed a mirror in front of her. Even more curious, Amaterasu moved forward, and the gods went behind her and prevented her from going back into the cave. Later, when Ama-

terasu sent her grandson to rule the land in her name, she gave him the
mirror and said, "Keep this mirror with you as my spirit, and worship it
just as you would worship in my very presence."[280]

This is my stripped-down summary of a long and highly detailed text—a
text that is, moreover, like the Greek and Hindu texts we have considered,
just one of a number of different retellings of this story, each of which incorporates different details. I have summarized only those elements that
correspond to the myth of Saranyu; much that I have omitted, therefore, is
entirely different from the Hindu story. The statement that "the demiurges
Izanami (female) and Izanagi (male) have intercourse," for instance, col-
lapses a thoroughly Lacanian conversation: He: "How is your body
formed?" She: "My body has one place which is formed insufficiently." He:
"My body has one place which is formed to excess. Therefore I would like
to take that place in my body which is formed to excess and insert it into
that place in your body which is formed insufficiently, and give birth to
the land." But a striking number of the basic themes overlap between both
texts, as becomes evident if we outline the elements shared by the Saranyu
myth and the Amaterasu myth in the order that they occur in the Japanese
text (which is often different from their order in the Hindu myth), with
the Hindu variants in brackets:

> A solar mother, Izanami [Aditi] who violated correct procedure produced
> a deformed child, a leech [the Sun]; fire [the Sun] burnt the genitals [the
> eyes] of the solar mother, Izanami [Saranyu], who hid her light. She [her
> husband] issued a command not to look [a command to look] at her
> [him], which the other disobeyed. The corpse of Izanami [Yama] decom-
> posed and was eaten by worms. She cursed her offspring to die, and her
> husband, Izanagi [the Sun] limited the curse to keep them alive. A female
> solar deity, Amaterasu [Saranyu], was created, intimately associated with
> the eye. A child [children], Susanowo [the Ashvins], appeared from the
> nose of the parent, Izanagi [Saranyu].
>
> The brother and sister, Susanowo and Amaterasu [Yama and Yami][281]
> were incestuously attracted. A horse mutilated the genitals of [raped the
> mouth of] a woman [a mare]. The solar goddess, Amaterasu [Saranyu], hid
> herself. The smith fashioned a mirror [the form of the husband]. She saw
> her mirror image and took it for [made it into] a separate person. She was
> caught. She left the mirror [mirror image] as a substitute for herself.

This is of course an even more brutal summary, but it does suggest that
certain elements of the Saranyu myth have an internal connection that

survives, in recombination and retransformation—most notably, assigning the same themes in different combinations to different characters—, in a very different text, composed by a very different culture, for a very different purpose. This overlap casts serious doubt on the wisdom of limiting the Saranyu pattern to Greece and India, as the Dumézilian agenda would demand.

Most striking, perhaps, is the fact that the Sun is sexually female in Japan, as it is gramatically in German, and, in a sense, as it is in the Veda, where Saranyu has a power and status later transferred to the male solar deity.[282] By contrast, the majority of cultures make a natural connection between the monthly phases of the Moon and of women; this pattern even begins to exert its influence over Japan, where Amaterasu came to be identified with the male solar deity Vairocana and was sometimes treated as a male. Another significant resemblance-in-difference is in the contrasting emphasis upon eyes in the Vedic myth and genitals in the Japanese; as we shall see, eyes* and genitals* often function as minimal pairs in Hindu myths; and even in this Japanese myth, the eyes and genitals combine in the episode in which looking at the genitals causes the sun (light) to return. Amaterasu's curiosity about the mirror is glossed with significant ambiguity by the translator: "Either she saw her reflection in the mirror and thought that the reflected image was another deity; or seeing the mirror, a symbol of the sun-deity, she thought that there was another sun-deity besides herself."[283] In the case of Saranyu, both of these ideas are true.

CONCLUSION: ABUSE AND FLIGHT

In the stories we have considered here, the abuse of goddesses and mortal women generates fantasies of splitting and dissociation. The women who split can sometimes choose how to split, and we may hear women's voices in these texts alongside the voice of the official male narrator, even though these stories were, by and large, composed by men.[284] Women may see in these stories the fantasy of splitting in flight from rape, the woman's reaction to sexual violence; the woman's revulsion against the rapist is also expressed in the fantasy of a violent punishment of the man by another man. Many of these stories turn out to be about rape, from which the shadow serves to exonerate the woman, distancing her from any possible defilement at the hands of the demonic rapist or unwanted husband. Stories such as these may express a kind of dissociation in reaction to a rape: "This happened to some other woman, not to me." The double implies

that the "real self" did not experience the event.[285] These are stories of denial, and of the asymmetry even in many less violent sexual acts, where
one partner is "there" and the other is not; on this register, they may express the fantasies of a marriage in which the woman does not want to
sleep with the man who will merely give her children or who will merely
take his pleasure from her in the dark, so that she splits away the part of
herself that is being used in this way. (A recovering stripper named Sherry
Britton has said: "I experienced what I now know was a dissociative
episode. There seemed to be two of me. One, onstage undressing. The
other saying 'What are you doing, taking your clothes off for those mo-
rons?'")[286] The meaning of the splitting as perceived by the person who is
split is not merely "I am one, but I am also two," but "This is happening to
me and this is not happening to me," and "I am here and I am not here."
Elaine Scarry writes movingly about the similar effects of torture:

> What the process of torture does is to split the human being into two, to
> make emphatic the ever present but, except in the extremity of sickness and
> death, only latent distinction between a self and a body, between a "me" and
> "my body."[287]

It takes an extraordinary combination of courage and self-understanding
to continue to say, in the midst of great suffering or humiliation, "I am
(still) me."

Many of these stories represent syndromes that seem to mirror multiple-
personality disorders, or what is still referred to in popular culture
(though not by psychiatrists) as "schizophrenia." When the wife of the
man who produces three identical clones in the film *Multiplicity* (1996)
begins to notice the inconsistencies in his behavior and memory, she suggests that he might be suffering from a "bipolar disorder" or "multiple
personalities." The mind-body separation experienced by victims of rape
is often invoked in contemporary discussions of sexual violence.[288] Much
has been written in psychological circles about the role of abuse in generating multiple-personality disorders or, sometimes, in generating repression, a less manifest (and less pathological) splitting. Let us consider a few
dramatic instances.

The Rape of Maria Dyce

Cases of what was called "double consciousness" in nineteenth-century
Britain often cited pain, usually psychic pain, as a precipitating factor. As Ian

Hacking comments, "This idea is consistent with current views on the asso-ciation of childhood MPD [multiple-personality disorder] with trauma and abuse." Hacking cites the famous nineteenth-century case of Maria Dyce:

> Maria was sixteen. . . . In one respect Dyce's case is unique in the British lit-erature. There is a frankly sexual episode. A fellow serving-woman allowed a young man into their quarters, who then raped Maria while she was in her alter state. The assault was said to be forcible. In her normal state next day Maria had no recollection of this, but she told everything to her mother when next she was in the alter state.[289]

Since Maria was *already* split in two when the rape took place, the rapist in a sense raped her shadow. Or was the shadow created—on this occasion, and perhaps on others—in retrospect? Maria became doubled in litera-ture as well as in life, for hers was almost certainly the same as the case of Mary Reynolds reported in 1817 as "[a] double consciousness, or a duality of person in the same individual."[290] (If, as usual, the report protected her by giving her a pseudonym, *Dyce* is certainly an appropriate name for a double personality.) Therefore, as Ian Hacking points out, the failure to recognize that Mary Reynolds and Maria Dyce were the same woman "led to the notorious doubling of Mary Reynolds, for in France she became the quite distinct 'la dame de Mac-Nish' [Maria Dyce was the patient of Mac-Nish], with 'similar' symptoms. As late as his Harvard lectures, Pierre Janet spoke of them as two individuals."[291] Or, in another sense, four.

The Two Faces of Eve

A notorious case of multiple personalities in our day involved not four women but three, made famous by the film *The Three Faces of Eve* (1957) based upon a true case reported in a book by the same title. The therapists who documented the case gave the three women fictitious names high-ly evocative of the contrast between the bright goddess and her dark shadow: Eve White was a rather dull, meek woman who had two more personalities—the flamboyant and sexy Eve Black and the thoughtful, in-telligent Jane—who "came out" (a phrase that takes on new, and surely relevant, meaning in our time) during periods of which Eve White re-membered nothing. This presented her husband, Ralph, with the problem of telling the three women apart:

> Perhaps because of the easy laxness of [Eve Black's] posture and her more vigorous movements, the lines of her body seemed somehow a little more

voluptuously rounded. A thousand minute alterations of manner, gesture, expression, posture, of nuances in reflex or instinctive reaction, of glance, of eyebrow tilting, and eye movements—all argued that this could only be another woman. . . . It would not be difficult for a man to distinguish his wife (or perhaps even his secretary) if she were placed among a hundred other women carefully chosen from millions because of their close resemblance to her, and all dressed identically.[292]

Here the problem is analogized to the "lineup"—the myth of many identical doubles.* Ralph had trouble at first, but finally figured it out:

He had lived with his wife for almost seven years. Certainly he should be able to recognize her through any disguise, be it of play-acting, hysteria, or psychosis. No matter what changes might have occurred in this woman, he should be able to discern features inaccessible to another that would establish for him her inimitable identity as Eve White. . . . The recognition is probably achieved through thousands, perhaps millions, of small items of perception, data from the dim periphery of awareness, through subliminal minute elements never consciously recognized or clearly labeled, by indescribable distinctions vaguely sensed in nonlogical reactions, by some loosely called *intuitive.*[293]

This is a fine argument, but it didn't work:

Contradicting all this came the brash, unfamiliar voice in which Eve Black said that she had never married him, that she was no wife of his. Anatomically this face was the face he knew, but all that it expressed was alien. The physiological functions, the small involuntary movements through which a countenance reflects feeling were not those he had ever seen in the face of his wife. . . . "The longer I looked at her," said Mr. White, ". . . the stranger she seemed to me. I got to feeling after a while that I didn't know her at all. It's no different from the way it would be if I'd never seen her before in my whole life."[294]

Sometimes Eve Black masqueraded as Eve White to escape from men she had flirted with,[295] but Eve White always became Eve Black to escape from "Mr. White." Her male doctors, and the film (in keeping with the reductive Hollywood Freudianism of the era), insisted that husband and marriage "didn't matter" to her and blamed her fragmentation on her childhood trauma; the three Eves, too, later testified that as a child Eve was traumatized by the sight of a man who had been sawed in half* in an accident at the mill. But even the film depicted her husband as a brute whom Eve

Black urged her to leave, and the later books insisted that an equal, if not greater, factor in the re-emergence of Eve Black in adult life was Eve White's desire to escape from her abusive husband. Both Eves, even the flirtatious Eve Black, were frigid and submitted with disgust to his sexual embraces; the tension between their desire to leave him and their fear of the stigma of divorce precipitated the literal crack-up. But all four books, their multiplicity further compounded by two ghost writers, bear unmistakable signs of mythologization.

On one occasion, Eve Black consummated a sexual act that Eve White did not desire. When her husband, Ralph, asked Eve White to come with him on a trip and she refused, Eve Black—who wanted to go on the trip to buy some pretty clothes—came to him in his room:

> *Was* it his wife? Eve for a moment tried to pretend that this was so, saying that she had thought the matter over and had changed her mind. Though she had practiced such impersonation of her alternate before, Eve Black did not deceive Ralph. He made this known to her at once. "All right," she said, "so what of it? She don't want to go with you, but maybe I do. She don't like you. But . . . well, I'm beginning to think you're right cute." . . . The amazing differences between this girl and the unhappy, frigid woman he had known as his wife must have made it possible for him not to feel, however illogically, that the intimate relations she offered might constitute an act of marital infidelity. If anything like this became clear in his thought, would it not have been challenged by the absurdity that arose as he reminded himself that he was married to this woman and that, for the first time in so long, perhaps for the first time ever, she welcomed him fully and cordially as a mate? Here, one might say, even if nothing more valuable or abiding came of it, beckoned an enticing adventure, something with all the allure of stolen fruit. And yet it remained free from penalty and from wrong.[296]

Apparently this time the act was consummated (despite Eve Black's general disclaimers), and Ralph (and, on his behalf, the male authors) felt that he had to justify falling for her. His justifications failed to persuade Eve White, however, for she regarded Eve Black as the Other Woman, and decided to divorce him.

The subsequent history of *The Three Faces of Eve* raises still other questions of myth and reality. In 1958, 1977, and 1989, the woman on whose life the book was based, Chris Costner Sizemore, wrote three books about her life, with titles that proved unduly optimistic: *The Final Face of Eve*, *I'm Eve*, and *A Mind of My Own*. She related how, after eighteen more years of mental illness and twenty-two personalities, all her identities merged and she was cured. Sissy Spacek (who had played the voice of the brain in *The Man with Two Brains**** in 1983) wanted to coproduce and star in a new movie of the sequel of Sizemore's life (to be called *In Sickness and in Health*),[297] and Sizemore began to negotiate with Spacek. But a lawsuit was brought by Twentieth Century Fox, the studio that had made *Three Faces,* which argued that it owned the story of Sizemore's life—her *whole* life, "even the 32 years she had lived since Joanne Woodward walked away with an Oscar for portraying her on the screen." Fox claimed that it had owned those rights since 1956, when one of Sizemore's personalities signed over to Fox, for $7,000, "forever," the film rights to "all versions of my life story heretofore published or hereafter published." Sizemore filed suit, arguing "that the contract she signed in 1956 was meant to cover only the material in *The Three Faces of Eve,* a book written by her doctor, Dr. Corbett Thigpen, and his colleague, Dr. Hervey Cleckley." Moreover, Sizemore's attorney contended that the original contract proved that Fox knew Sizemore was still mentally unbalanced—since it was signed by all three of them, Eve White, Eve Black, and Jane. The case was settled out of court,[298] and, as far as I know, the film was never made. An article entitled "Whose Life Is It, Anyway?" quotes Chris Sizemore's explanation of her commitment to the fight: "I was prepared from the beginning, even if I lost the movie with Sissy, to pursue this till I had my life back."[299] Apparently *all* of a woman's fragmented personalities in this litigious age must read the fine print on their ontological contracts.

"My God! There's Two of Her!"

The mirror image of Maria Dyce and Chris Costner Sizemore appears in all the twin sisters, identical in body but not in mind, who are mistaken for a single, schizophrenic woman in films like *Dark Mirror* (Olivia de Havilland, 1946), *A Stolen Life* (1946), and *Dead Ringer* (1964)—the last two played by Bette Davis, making a total of four of her. Jeanine Basinger calls the good-and-evil-twin genre the "My God! There's two of her!" theme (from the poster for *Dark Mirror*).[300] (Less frequently, men double up, like the twin brothers in *Dead Ringers* [1988], the title doubling that of the second Bette Davis movie. "There's two of them!" says the villain who first sees the two Jean-Claude Van Dammes together in *Double Impact* [1991].) Special effects allowed the grande dame to play two parts simultaneously on the screen, resulting in all of those melodramatic tours de force such as *The Divorce of Lady X* (1938, Merle Oberon) and *Two-Faced Woman* (1941, Greta Garbo in her last film—written by S. N. Behrman* just three years after his stage version of the Amphitryon* myth). So widespread is the film scenario that when a real woman impersonated her real (and murdered) sister in 1997, the police chief remarked, "I don't know if bizarre quite describes it; this is the stuff of a Hollywood movie."[301] The film critic Richard Winnington, commenting on *A Stolen Life,* remarked, "What I'm waiting for is a film about beautiful identical quintuplets who all love the same man."[302] Well, he would have loved Saranyu, or better yet, the multiple mistresses of Heracles* and Krishna.*

Women continue to be the victims either of assaults that precipitate multiple personalities, or of psychiatrists who diagnose them as having multiple personalities, or both. Elaine Showalter comments on this double pattern:

> The Jekyll-Hyde story, however, has taken a weird realistic turn in the United States where, in the last few decades, there has been an epidemic among women of what is now called Multiple Personality Disorder. [Most of the women were] "sexually or physically abused as children." The theory is that the sexually abused child shuts off a part of itself in denial, which then undergoes further splitting. . . . We might say that as the roles demanded of American women increase, female personalities do as well: by 1975, for example, when her identity became public, "Eve's" selves [in *The Three Faces of Eve*] had "multiplied like rabbits," reaching a grand total of twenty-two.[303]

The sexual metaphor of rabbits is well taken; here again we may recall the proliferation of Manus and Athenas.

The film of *The Three Faces of Eve,* reflecting the reductionist Freudian scenario that Hollywood was playing at that time, attributed the splitting of Eve to a shock of death* that she had received in her childhood (being forced to kiss her grandmother's corpse). But other stories, and even other versions of that story, speak more of adult sexual abuse than of childhood trauma; rather than enduring personality disorders, they tell of specific situations in which women split in order to survive an assault. A depth psychologist might argue that our texts repress childhood memories and present only the adult manifestation, or projections, of symptoms; and so it may be. But mature women are abused too, and our stories certainly make perfectly good sense on this level.

This sort of splitting has its comic aspects even in real life. The promiscuous Siamese twins Violet and Daisy Hilton were joined at the hip:

> The story goes that they were in a restaurant once when they got into an argument about whether they had slept with a certain man who was sitting on the other side of the room. Daisy was convinced they had had him. Violet denied all knowledge of the man. To settle the argument, they decided to get up and go over and ask him to his face. They crossed the restaurant and began, "You may not remember us, but . . . "[304]

In a grotesque literalization of the myth, these twins indulged in an embodied ambivalence, here not with multiple personalities but, as it were, with multiple heads*—the apotheosis of the split woman who does and does not experience the sexual encounter. There are times when life outdoes mythology in its lack of subtlety.

Myths in which a woman splits herself or produces a double in order to avoid rape are closely linked with myths in which the woman simply becomes her own double, in a sense, by changing herself into something else. Thus Saranyu not only produces a double but changes into a mare (as Daphne changes into a laurel tree to avoid Apollo) in reaction to a sexual assault. Men can also force women to metamorphose *after* they have raped them: Ahalya is a vivid instance of this, changed into a stone by her husband (who curses her) as a result of the actions of Indra (who rapes her). Women too may change men into animals after raping them: this is what Circe does to everyone but Odysseus, making them all (presumably male chauvinist) pigs.[305] Tales of splitting also offer an alternative, opposite way of accommodating (or failing to accommodate) evil: possession, in which moral responsibility or intolerable pain is avoided by the statement not that the self was absent but that another self—the possessing self of a demon or ghost or another person—was present.

But not all of these accretive transformations are negative; a desired deity—often, as we have noted, called a shadow—may also possess a person. Indeed, we might view the taking on of a second personality not as, or not merely as, an escape from pain or an unbearable self but as a creative movement toward another self. The women's voices in these stories may also express a woman's need to regard herself as two separate adults in a positive erotic encounter, simply as a way of experiencing her own sexual ambivalence, her own conflicting desires. In the 1948 film of *Anna Karenina,* Anna says to her husband, speaking of her adulterous love for another man, "I am still the same as I used to be. The other woman in me—*she* fell in love." And when the hero of a contemporary novel accuses his mistress of being complex, she retorts, "I'm not complex; I'm just a combination of two very simple women."[306] Helen or Sita (or, for that matter, Renuka/Mariatale or Scylla) could have said the same thing.

Women as well as men can use doubles—even doubles foisted upon them—to achieve, rather than to avoid, sexuality. When King Arthur suspects that his wife, Guenevere, is committing adultery with Lancelot, he subjects her to an ordeal, as Rama did to Sita; but Guenevere, like Helen, is in fact guilty, and she survives the ordeal only by subterfuge.[307] A late medieval tradition about King Arthur states that Guenevere had a bastard half-sister who happened to look like her and was also, conveniently, named Guenevere. But this double replaced Guenevere in the bed not of the adulterous lover but of the husband, Arthur, while the real Guenevere, though agonized at the loss of her royal status, was able to console herself by remaining in the care of her lover. Indeed, Guenevere knew that Arthur accepted the impostor, and banished her, the true queen, precisely in order to punish her for her adultery; but Arthur also greatly preferred the impostor to the real queen. On her deathbed, the false Guenevere confessed the hoax and the real Guenevere was restored to Arthur.[308] Thus the true queen is adulterous, and is replaced by the double only after, and because of, the adultery that the double inadvertently facilitates.

William Butler Yeats expresses the essence of the positive aspect of the split self through the metaphor that lies at the heart of this mythology:

> I think that all happiness depends on the energy to assume the mask of some other self; that all joyous or creative life is a re-birth as something not oneself, something which has no memory and is created in a moment and perpetually renewed. . . . a game like that of a child, where one loses the infinite pain of self-realisation. Perhaps all the sins and energies of the world are but its flights from an infinite blinding beam.[309]

The flight from the blinding god, the blinding sun, here becomes conflated with the flight from the unbearable self. The two—god *(brahman)* and the self *(atman)*—are equated in the Upanishads (texts that Yeats knew well). But Yeats sees that flight not in the sense of fleeing but in the sense of flying, not, or not just, *from* the self but *to* something else. This is the masquerading rather than splitting aspect of doubling, to which we will now turn.

Indra and Ahalya,
Zeus and Alcmena

~~✦~~

Let us consider two stories about a woman who is not doubled herself but who is, rather, tested by a god who doubles (as) her husband. And let us again begin with India and move to Greece.

INDRA AS GAUTAMA WITH AHALYA

The story of Ahalya is one of a number in which Indra, king of the gods, impersonates a human husband in order to gain sexual access to a human woman, assuming the form of a particular man in order to commit adultery with the man's wife. Indra shares this propensity with Zeus and Wotan, his Greek and German cousins and counterparts (through the historical links that I have discussed in the introduction). On one occasion, Indra took the place of the stallion in the horse sacrifice in order to sleep with the sacrificer's queen, a transformation that further connects him with the corpus of Saranyu the mare.[1] In some myths of this type, such as the story of Damayanti, the human woman succeeds in seeing through the illusion in order to remain faithful to her husband. But in the myth of Ahalya, this point is debated: some variants insist that she couldn't tell the difference between them, while other variants imply that she merely pretended not to see through the illusion in order to sleep with the god.

The question of whether or not the woman chooses to commit adultery is closely related to the question of guilt: Who is responsible? Who is punished? In classical Hinduism, these two questions received two different answers. The jurist Medhatithi says that the punishment for a man who has slept with his guru's wife—the ultimate incest in Hinduism—is abrogated or mitigated if it was done "without premeditation, because he mistook her for his own wife."[2] Medhatithi does not, however, contemplate the possibility that a wife might be forgiven for making the same mistake about her husband. In *The Laws of Manu*, it is primarily the man who is punished for adultery; yet in the myths, adulterous women as well as men are often mutilated or killed. The woman is regarded as naturally responsible, on the assumption that all women are seductive, just as all snakes bite; but the man is culturally responsible: knowing that all women are seductive, the male adulterer is at fault when he allows a woman to do what she is naturally inclined to do. In keeping with this pattern, the texts describe the punishments of both Ahalya and her lover Indra at some length, and these punishments, in some variants, have implications for the future history of humankind tantamount to the implications of the sin of Adam and Eve in Eden.

One of the earliest references to the tale of Ahalya and Indra is in a formula used to call Indra to be present at the Vedic sacrifice, an important and much-repeated text, in which Indra is addressed as "The lover of Ahalya . . . who said he was Gautama."[3] If we read these phrases together, as I think we should, we have the essence of Indra's masquerade: he pretends to be Gautama in order to seduce Gautama's wife Ahalya. But the rape, rather than the seduction, of Ahalya is described at some length in one of its earliest full tellings, in the Valmiki *Ramayana,* when the Creator reminds Indra of his (Indra's) past sins:

INDRA RAPES AHALYA

King of the gods, once upon a time I emitted many creatures, but they were all of a single kind *(ekavarna),* of the same speech, and entirely of one form. There was no distinction among them in appearance or in characteristic mark *(lakshana).* Then in order to make a distinction among them, I fashioned one single woman, and limb by limb I drew out each part of the (former) creatures. Because of her beauty and qualities, this woman was "Not To Be Plowed" *[ahalya],* and so I called her Ahalya and she became known by that name. But then, I began to worry: "Whose will she be?" And you, Indra, came to know in your heart and mind about this woman, and you said, "This woman should be my wife, because of the preeminence of my position." But I kept her in trust for the great-souled Gautama, and after many years he took her away. I gave her to him for a wife because of his stability and his achievements in asceticism. The great sage Gautama, who was the soul of dharma, took his sexual pleasure with her, but the gods lost hope when she was given to him.

And you, who are the soul of lust, became angry and went to the sage's hermitage, and saw the woman, blazing like the flame of a fire. You raped her, Indra, when you were tortured by lust and full of anger, but when Gautama saw you in his hermitage, he became angry and cursed you for

having raped his wife so recklessly. And he added: "This emotion which
you have set in motion, you fool, will surely now exist among all mortals."

Then Gautama, who had such great inner heat of asceticism, reviled his
wife and said, "You evil woman, get out of my presence and my hermitage.
Since you who are gifted with youth and beauty have been loose, therefore
you will not be the only one with beauty in the world. All creatures will
have that beauty, so hard to get, which led you astray when you relied upon
it." And from that time forth, most creatures have had beauty, because of
the curse emitted by the sage.[4]

What is striking about this version of the story of Ahalya is that, in contrast with the many, many variants that follow it, there seems to be no
doubling at all: Indra simply takes Ahalya by force. Though Gautama
curses her for being loose, or unsteady, and led astray by her beauty,
the text gives no evidence of this. The fact that she was raped *(dharshita)*
should, we might assume, absolve Ahalya of any misdoing: she was helpless. (And it is truly a rape: the text tells us, twice, that Indra was driven as
much by anger—presumably against Gautama and Brahma for giving the
woman to someone other than him—as by lust.) But this argument is
never made; perhaps these ancient texts already assumed, like modern sex-
ists (and Herodotus*), that any woman who is raped is asking for it. When
Ravana rapes Rambha he is referred to as a "demonic Indra,"[5] and the *Kamasutra* singles out Indra with Ahalya and Ravana with Sita as examples
of men who were destroyed by uncontrolled desire.[6] Clearly Indra is be-
having in a demonic manner.

Here the problem of creating woman is in itself a problem of doubles:
all the original creatures, presumably male, are indistinguishable, and it is
in order to make someone of a different kind that woman is created in the
first place; she is the only creature who is *not* a double. (This paradigm
strongly resembles the "one-sex" model of medieval Europe as laid out by
Thomas Laqueur, a model in which women are merely inferior variants of
the basic unisex human form.)[7] Ahalya is then distinguished by her youth
and beauty, but this distinction is her downfall, and Gautama punishes
her by assuring her that she will no longer be unique in these qualities that
have led to her fall: femininity in general, and youth and beauty in particular, will be as common (presumably among all women) as, previously,
the "one kind" was common among all men: all women will be alike. This
also has the indirect effect of reinforcing the other curse, upon Indra, ex-
tending his sin of adultery to other men and women, just as Indra had, in

earlier, Vedic texts, bequeathed other evils to women on other occasions.[8]

Subsequent texts argue that Indra masqueraded as Ahalya's husband, an argument that might—but in fact does not—absolve Ahalya of guilt. This change is made when the Valmiki *Ramayana* tells the story again in the context of the coming of Rama (whose miraculous power identifies this passage as a later layer of the *Ramayana*). It is an innovation, building upon earlier Vedic texts in which Indra plays the role of a sexual trickster.[9] Yet, even now that Indra halfheartedly masquerades as Gautama, Ahalya is even more deeply implicated than she was when she was raped by Indra in his own form:

INDRA DOESN'T FOOL AHALYA

The thousand-eyed Indra, the husband of Indrani, knowing that Gautama was absent, put on the sage's garments and said to Ahalya, "Well-made woman, with a beautiful waist, men who want it do not wait for a woman's fertile period. I want to make love with you." Knowing that it was the thousand-eyed god in the garments of the sage, the foolish woman consented, because she was sexually curious about the king of the gods. Then, when her inner heart had gotten what it wanted, she said to the best of the gods, "You have gotten what you wanted; now you must go away quickly. Lord of the gods, my lover, you must always protect yourself and me."

Indra laughed and said to Ahalya, "You have wonderful hips, and I am fully satisfied. I will go back where I came from." And so, after he had made love with her he came out of the hut, hastening in some confusion, worrying about Gautama. But the great sage Gautama entered, saw the wicked thousand-eyed god wearing the garments of the sage, and cursed him. Then he cursed Ahalya: "You will live here for many thousands of years, eating wind, without any food, lying on ashes and generating inner heat. Invisible to all creatures, you will live in this hermitage. And when Rama, who is unassailable, comes to this terrible forest, then you will be purified. By receiving him as a guest you will become free of greed and delusion, you evil woman, and you will take on your own form in my presence, full of joy."[10]

The fact that Indra really just dresses up as Gautama (assuming his *vesha*, his garments, which does not necessarily imply a change of form, just a change of costume) makes Ahalya's sin all the more obvious. The text explicitly tells us that Ahalya (and Gautama) knew who Indra was, that she desired him precisely because she knew who he was. Her curse of invisibility is, in a sense, merely a variant of the curse in the first text: to have the same beauty as other women is to become invisible. (Sita too was rendered invisible when she was merely vulnerable to a rape.) When Indra did, at least, try to disguise himself, Ahalya was cursed to become invisible, for a while; when he simply used brute force, she was cursed to share her beauty with other women. It doesn't really make much difference at all; Indra might have saved himself the bother.

Several of the manuscripts of the first *Ramayana* text, about the rape and the origin of adultery, insert a brief paragraph (probably folded back in from this second *Ramayana* version) in which Ahalya herself insists on her innocence because she was raped:

> Ahalya begged Gautama, the great sage, to forgive her, saying, "I was raped, great sage, by the god who had taken your form, because I did not know (who it was). I did not do it out of desire, great sage; you should forgive me." When Ahalya had said this to Gautama, he replied, "When Rama is born and comes to the forest, and you see him, then you will be purified. When you receive him as a guest you may come back into my presence, and you will live with me."[11]

Gautama may or may not believe her; he modifies her curse in the same terms that he uses in the second text, but the modification doesn't make a great deal of sense in either case: since the curse was the loss of her unique beauty (text 1) or invisibility (text 2), being purified and permitted the luxury of living with Gautama (text 3) hardly seems an adequate compensation.

In a Sanskrit text composed in about 750 C.E., one of a genre known as Puranas, compendia of myths, Indra does more than just change his clothes; he fools Ahalya, and Gautama forgives her:

INDRA TAKES THE BLAME

> All the four World-Protectors, including Indra, lusted for Ahalya. One day, when Gautama had gone to bathe and Ahalya was cleaning the house, preparing to make the offering to the gods, Indra took the corporeal *[gatrena]* form of Gautama and entered the house, excited. Wearing the garments of the sage, he said to Ahalya, "I am overwhelmed by Kama, the god of erotic love. Give me a kiss and so forth." But Ahalya replied, "My lord, you should not tell me to abandon the worship of the gods and so forth. This is not the right time for such things." Indra said, "Enough of this talk. What should and should not be done is decided by a husband's words. You should obey your husband's command, especially in matters of sex. Give me an embrace and so forth." Then he embraced her and fulfilled his desire.

[When Gautama returned, Indra entered the body of a cat, but Gautama recognized him and cursed him. Then,] Ahalya, his chaste wife, said, through her tears, "You should forgive this act, since it was committed in ignorance." But he replied, "You have done a bad thing and become impure by having intercourse with another man. For a long time you will stand alone, made of nothing but skin and bones, with no flesh and no nails, and let all the men and women look at you." In misery, she asked him to set an end to the curse, and even the sage was flooded by pity, and he said, "When Rama comes to the forest and sees you standing by the path, dried out and bodiless, he will laugh and ask, 'Who is this female with the dried up form, a mere image (of a woman) made of bones?' And when he hears what happened in former times, he will say, 'This woman is not at all at fault; it is Indra's fault.' And when he says this, you will lose your disgusting form and take on a divine form and come to my house." And so she dwells with Gautama in heaven even today.[12]

Ahalya in this text believes that she is with her husband. Since, at the time of the seduction, she is preparing to worship the gods, presumably the Vedic gods (including the World-Protectors or guardians of the four directions, Indra, Agni, Varuna, and Yama), the ritual is fulfilled more literally than she might ordinarily expect, or indeed hope, and Indra comes to her in person (albeit in disguise). Her protest that this is not the right time for sex (the South Asian equivalent of "I have a headache"), which is also expressed in the Nepalese retelling of the story of Sita, is an inversion of the amorous male's (or female's) argument, voiced in many versions of the Ahalya myth, that a woman's fertile season *is* the right time, whether or not she has a headache. She protests not against Indra but, as she thinks, against her own husband; she is fooled; she really does not know it is Indra.

Most unusually, Gautama admits (through a projection into Rama's words) that it was all Indra's fault, and even acknowledges that Ahalya's mind was pure—though he himself still curses her for being the helpless victim, for having been physically polluted, or, as usual, unconsciously asking for it by being beautiful. His curse makes her not invisible but hideously old, which comes to the same thing: her youth and beauty vanish. Yet Ahalya is also cursed to have people look at her, or rather to look at her invisibility, the final humiliation. Gautama recognizes Indra even in the form of a cat, for Indra uses his shape-changing powers here not only ahead of time, to take Gautama's form in order to protect Ahalya's virtue, but also after the fact, to attempt to get out of the bedroom when he is caught with his pants down. The cat has supplied alibis in the dark for lovers (and thieves) throughout the world; in R. K. Narayan's retelling of this story, Indra becomes a cat because a cat is "the most facile animal form for sneaking in or out."[13]

Ahalya is also fooled in a Purana composed some time after 750 C.E., in which Indra appears to her both in his own form and in disguise:

INDRA TRIES AGAIN

Indra saw Ahalya bathing and fell in love with her. He approached her in his own form, praised her beauty, and boasted that only he, an expert in love and the *Kamasutra,* could do justice to her, not a dried up old ascetic like Gautama. She refused him, went home, and told Gautama everything, to which he reacted with amusement. Indra then returned one day when Gautama was absent, this time taking Gautama's form; he made love to Ahalya, but Gautama caught them and cursed Ahalya to be a stone. When she pleaded with him he said, "I know that you are pure in mind-and-heart, a woman who has kept her vow of chastity and fidelity *(pativrata).* But nevertheless I will reject you, for you have another man's semen in you. And a woman who has been sexually enjoyed by another man is rendered impure for all rituals. A woman who unwillingly makes love with a lover is not defiled, but a good woman is certainly defiled if she makes love (with a lover) willingly. Since you thought that Indra was your husband, you happily enjoyed sex with him in the house; only afterwards, when you saw me, did you realize who had deceived you in the night. Go to the forest and take the form of a stone, and when the big toe of the foot of Rama touches you, you will be purified and come back to me."[14]

Indra's warning about the loss of youth bears a strong resemblance to Ravana's proposition to Vedavati*—who, like Ahalya here, refuses it. But this time Indra returns in disguise; he makes no speeches, and she accepts him. Gautama argues that because she was fooled, she made love willingly; the implication is that had she just been raped against her will, she would not have been cursed. But Ahalya is still cursed in other texts when she is raped, and even here she is defiled (if not cursed) simply by the presence of another man's sperm. In another retelling from the same approximate period, Ahalya remains silent after Indra's erotic boasts, and Indra takes this for acquiescence; yet this time too he approaches her a second time in the shape of Gautama, with the usual results: Ahalya is turned to stone.[15]

In contemporary Hindu wedding ceremonies in Sri Lanka, Ahalya appears as a black stone that the bride touches with her foot (just as Rama touches the stone Ahalya with his foot) while she promises never never to be like Ahalya but to be a good wife.[16] The logic of the curse that turned Ahalya to stone may also be at work in the practice of depicting voluptuous women in the stone sculptures on Hindu temples: it is the best way to capture and control them. Closer to the bone of our inquiry, the concept of an oversexual woman captured in stone may lie behind the stories of Helen and other lost, highly sexual women who remain only in the form of statues. When the Arabian theologian Ibn Battuta first visited India and saw the scattered ruins of stone carvings of "contorted" human figures, presumably images of divine women carved on Hindu temples in elaborate erotic poses, he interpreted them as the remains of the citizens of an old city turned to stone for their depravity.[17]

Ahalya continues to be fooled in another Purana in which Indra appears only once, but Gautama seems to appear twice:

THE TWO GAUTAMAS MEET

The Creator made many beautiful women, of whom Ahalya was the best; he gave her to Gautama to raise, and then, when she had come of age, and Indra and all the gods desired her, he gave her to Gautama for his wife, and Gautama took his pleasure with her.

One day, Indra took the form of Gautama, approached Ahalya, told her that he had been overcome by desire for her, and led her inside. She did not recognize him; she took her lover (jara) to be Gautama, and made love with him according to her pleasure. When Gautama returned, Ahalya failed to meet him and greet him as she always did. But when the servants guarding the front door saw him they were amazed and frightened. They said, "Master, what is this strange thing? You are visible inside and outside. You went inside with your beloved wife, and here you are outside. My, what ascetic power you have, to assume various forms." When he heard this, Gautama was amazed, wondering, "Who is there inside?" He called to Ahalya: "My dear Ahalya, why don't you answer me?" When she heard this, Ahalya said to her lover, "Who are you in the sage's form? You have done a bad thing." And she jumped out of the bed in terror. Indra turned into a cat but resumed his true form when Gautama threatened otherwise to burn him to ashes. Indra blamed the arrows of the god of erotic love (Kama) and asked Gautama to forgive him, but Gautama cursed him; and then he cursed Ahalya to become a dried up river. She said to him, "Evil women who desire another man even in their mind and heart suffer in unbearable hells. But he came to me in your form; these servants will bear witness." "Yes," said the servants, "Ahalya is telling the truth." And Gautama knew the truth by meditation, too. So he calmed down and said to his faithful wife *(pativrata),* "When you meet Gautami, the river goddess, by my favor you will get back your own beautiful form."[18]

The masquerade is clearly exposed when the two men appear side by side, like the two Sitas in the nineteenth-century Tamil text or the multiple Nalas, and Ahalya has witnesses to support her defense. But she herself, as soon as she realizes that there are two Gautamas (as there are, in another sense, in her life normally, for he is both her stepfather and her husband), knows which is the real Gautama. And she knows this even before Indra betrays his identity (at least as a superhuman creature, if not as the particular god Indra) by taking the usual feline escape route. Unlike most other variants, in which Gautama comes home expressly because he knows supernaturally that Indra is in bed with his wife, this time Gautama innocently returns and is astonished to meet his double; only after he questions human witnesses does he use his magic vision to find out what happened, and thus to learn that his wife is innocent. As usual, however, that innocence can only limit, not rescind, the curse, a new variant of the usual theme: instead of a stone, an equally moribund and antierotic form, a dried-up river, matched by her redeemer: she will be released not by Rama but by the river goddess Gautami, in whose praise this particular text was composed.

In yet another, far more elaborate Puranic version of the story, Ahalya both does and does not recognize Indra:

INDRA'S ODOR OF IMMORTALITY

One day the sage Narada described Ahalya to Indra, saying, "Once upon a time in the world of death I saw Gautama with Ahalya. No one has beauty like hers, not even the Shadow Samjna, the wife of the Sun." Indra resolved to have her. He became Gautama and came to the sage's hermitage and saw Ahalya at a time when Gautama had gone to bathe. He went inside and said, "Wife, prepare a lovely bed for us!" Then she said, "Why have you stopped reciting [the Vedas] and come home now? How did you conceive this most despicable desire to make love during the day?" Gautama [*sic*] said, "As soon as I began to bathe, a lovely nymph came there to bathe alone and appeared naked within my sight. Her lower lip was like the bilva fruit, her body was exquisite, and she had superb big breasts. Lovely lady, my heart was oppressed by the arrows of the god of erotic love, and I could not stick to my recitations. So I came back to the hermitage. Make love with me now, my darling! Or else you will see me dead, burnt by the fire of desire, or I will curse you and go away." Ahalya said, "I will obey your command, because a woman has no duty but to obey her husband."

Believing that he was her own husband because of his voice, body, and unconscious gestures, Ahalya got into the bed to make love with Indra, the god who bears the thunderbolt. Without hesitation, Indra, in the shape of Gautama, played with her, kissing and embracing her, unfastening her waistband, and so forth. But when she smelled his celestial fragrances she became startled and very doubtful. In her mind she reasoned, "Is this a man who has taken on a deceptive form?" And in anger she asked that rogue, "Who are you in this deceptive form? I was convinced it was my husband's form. Speak, or I will curse you."

When he heard this, Indra displayed his own shape *[vapus]*, because he was frightened of a curse; he said, "Know that I am Indra, the husband of Indrani," and he wondered, "Whatever am I going to say to my wife?" When she heard this, the sage's wife became furious; seeming to vomit a flame from her mouth, she said, "Because your shape was his, you fool, you idiot, you evil wretch—I don't know what will happen when my husband arrives. You have shattered my fidelity to my husband. What will happen to me when I am cursed by Gautama's voice?"

Gautama came home and called to her to bring him water. She came and told him what had happened: "The depraved Indra, lord of the gods, assumed your form. Mistakenly thinking that it was certainly you, I obeyed your command exactly. But when I smelled those celestial fragrances, I became uncertain once again and said, 'Evil man, tell me who you are.' . . . Forgive me this transgression. It is not a fault when one declares it oneself, but only when someone else declares it." The sage cursed his wife: "Since you behave like a rolling stone, you will become a stone. You will not recognize my own form, my own unconscious gestures, or my movements, because your lustful heart has been fixed on another man." And he promised that she would be released when the foot of Rama touched her. Meanwhile Indra, terrified, had taken the form of a cat, but the sage perceived him through meditation and cursed him.[19]

Narada compares Ahalya with the shadow Samjna, a rather casual reference (and why to the shadow rather than to the real thing?) that links Indra's doubling with Samjna's. This time there is no ambiguity about Ahalya's deception, for Indra is actually said to become Gautama *[Gautamo 'bhut]*, with Gautama's body, as usual, but now also with his voice and his unconscious gestures *[bhavas]*, more intimate details that Indra does not usually take the trouble to copy. It is Gautama's voice too that

Ahalya fears when she anticipates his curse; in this telling Gautama's voice precedes him, when he comes home by chance and calls out the South Asian equivalent of "Honey, I'm home"—requesting water to wash his feet.

What Indra fails to mimic, however, is the smell of mortality: the clue that makes Ahalya realize her mistake is Indra's celestial fragrance, a perfume produced by the absence of putrefying flesh. For Gautama's form *(rupa)* and shape *(vapus)* are visual qualities that would not include evidence for the other senses. Indra sounds like Gautama (he has Gautama's voice), and he looks like Gautama, but he doesn't smell like Gautama. Actually, Indra doesn't really act like Gautama, either: Ahalya remarks on his uncharacteristic lust, but she goes along with it; she doesn't even notice the smell until he has kissed her, embraced her, untied her waistband, "and so forth"—the "so forth" apparently including enough to constitute a stain on her fidelity. Nor does Indra talk like Gautama, even though he has Gautama's voice: Ahalya could probably have guessed it was Indra by the fact that he threatens to curse and abandon her if she *doesn't* make love, the reverse of Gautama's predictable position. She might also have noted that, with a tactlessness characteristic of his cousin Zeus,[20] Indra propositions her by telling her how he has desired another woman; exposed, he identifies himself to Ahalya as "Indra, the husband of Indrani," and worries about his jealous wife.

The curse of becoming a stone is now explicitly glossed as the appropriate punishment for the crime of nonrecognition: now Ahalya won't be expected to recognize anyone's form or gestures (or movements, *ceshtitani*), all of which she herself will henceforth lack; in particular, she won't be able to recognize her husband, a petrification of the very flaw for which she is being petrified. This text is equally specific about the release from the curse: as in other texts, it is the touch of Rama's foot, not the mere sight of Rama or the words of Rama, that will release Ahalya.

In several retellings, Ahalya knows from the start that she is committing adultery, and Indra, as in the first *Ramayana* text, does not even bother to change into the form, or even the wardrobe, of Gautama. One such variant is found in a text of a different genre, *The Ocean of the Rivers of Story* (the *Kathasaritsagara*), a long Sanskrit romance that shares many stories with *The Arabian Nights* and was composed in about 1000 C.E.:

INDRA SEDUCES AHALYA

Once upon a time, there was a great sage named Gautama who knew the past, present, and future. His wife, Ahalya, surpassed the celestial courtesans in her beauty. One day, Indra, lusting for her beauty, secretly propositioned her, and she, the idiot, bulling (lusting for the bull like a cow in heat, *vrishasyati*), gave in to [Indra] the husband of Shaci. But the sage Gautama, realizing what had happened because of his special powers, came there. Indra, in terror, at that very moment took the form of a cat. Then Gautama asked Ahalya, "Who is here?" "It's just the tomcat," she replied, in the Prakrit dialect. And in that way, she replied to her husband without deviating from the truth in her actual words. "Truly, it's *your* tomcat," the sage said, laughing, and he brought down upon her a curse that had a set limit, because she had not deviated from the truth: "Since you behave like a rolling stone [literally, since you have an evil nature (*shīla*)], you will become a stone (*shilā*) for a long time, until Rama comes into this forest and you see him." And at the same time Gautama cursed Indra, saying, "You will be branded with a thousand of the sexual organ of a woman, which is what you lust for, but when the artisan of the gods makes a heavenly woman named Tilottama and you see her, the marks will become a thousand eyes." When Gautama had given the curses he desired, he returned to his asceticism. Ahalya became terribly transformed, into a stone.[21]

In this text, as usual, Indra becomes a cat, and Ahalya is likened to an animal in heat. But she is an animal gifted with speech. She replies to her husband's awkward question in a Prakrit dialect, since, being a woman, she is forbidden to speak Sanskrit, but she uses this disability as a weapon, playing upon the cliché motif of the cat in such a way as to produce an ambiguity that saves her. For *"majjao"* ("the tomcat") may be a dialect version of either of two Sanskrit words: *"mad-jaro,"* meaning, "my lover," or *"marjaro,"* meaning, "the cat" (from the verb *mrij,* to wash, because the cat constantly washes itself). But since Ahalya both lied and did not lie (it was her lover, but in the form of a cat), she is given a modified curse—appropriately, another pun, on "stone." As in the tale of Saranyu, the double meaning of a word masks the doubling of a human being. The half-lie of Ahalya's recognition or nonrecognition of the god is masked by the liminality of her access to Sanskrit.

In several South Indian variants too Ahalya is not fooled for long. In Kamban's Tamil *Ramayana,* it is said that Indra "sneaked into the her-

mitage wearing the exact body of Gautama, whose heart knew no false-
hoods. Sneaking in, he joined Ahalya; coupled, they drank deep of the
clear new wine of first-night weddings, and she knew. Yet unable to put
aside what was not hers, she dallied in her joy, but the sage did not tarry,
he came back, a very Shiva with three eyes in his head."[22] R. K. Narayan's
retelling fills in some of the psychological details:

INDRA CROWS LIKE A ROOSTER

Indra, however, never got over his infatuation for Ahalya, and often came
in different guise near to Gautama's *asram* . . . One day, hardly able to wait
for the sage to leave at his usual hour, Indra assumed the voice of a rooster,
and woke up the sage, who, thinking that the morning had come, left for
the river. Now Indra assumed the sage's form, entered the hut, and made
love to Ahalya. She surrendered herself, but at some stage realized that the
man enjoying her was an impostor; but she could do nothing about it.
Gautama came back at this moment, having intuitively felt that something
was wrong, and surprised the couple in bed. Ahalya stood aside filled with
shame and remorse; Indra assumed the form of a cat (the most facile animal form for sneaking in or out) and tried to slip away. The sage looked
from the cat to the woman and was not to be deceived. . . . After Indra had
slunk away, back to his world, Gautama looked at his wife and said, "You
have sinned with your body. May that body harden into a shapeless piece
of granite. . . ."[23]

Indra here assumes one of his many theriomorphic forms, becoming not a
cat but a rooster, manipulating the coming of dawn to extend the night
just as Zeus does in precisely the same situation with Alcmena. Ahalya
continues to make love with Indra after she has recognized him "at some
stage"; she carries on through the unstoppable momentum of either her
passion or his (Narayan is not entirely clear about this). The ambiguity of
her guilt is mirrored, as usual, in the ambiguity of her curse: because she
has perhaps sinned only with her body, not her mind, only her body is
cursed. A. K. Ramanujan remarks: "In Kampan, Ahalya realizes she is doing wrong but cannot let go of the forbidden joy; the poem has also suggested earlier that her sage-husband is all spirit, details which together add
a certain psychological subtlety to the seduction."[24]

Ahalya's complicity and Gautama's inadequacies are developed in far
greater detail in a highly sophisticated Telugu rendering composed in
Madurai in the early eighteenth century, which retells the story of Ahalya
and Gautama without even bothering to pay lip service, as it were, to the

idea of female fidelity; instead, it paints Indra and Ahalya as Romantic adulterers:

AHALYA DREAMS OF INDRA

Brahma created Ahalya to be the model of perfect female beauty, since all the courtesans of heaven were flawed. No sooner was Ahalya created than Indra fell in love with her and she with him, but Brahma gave her to the wizened old sage, Gautama, for a wife. She kept thinking about Indra; she especially liked listening to his praises as they were sung during sacrificial rituals, and she offered the oblation to him with all her heart. Daydreaming about him, she wished for a sophisticated lover who would know how to make love at the proper time and could satisfy her and make her heart melt with all the arts of sexual delight. Indra too was longing for Ahalya. Soon he took to visiting Gautama's hermitage simply in order to see her; he spoke with her when her husband was out, flirted with her, praised her in oblique and punning ways. After a while, he began to commute between heaven and the hermitage, like a shuttle on a loom. He lost his taste for his consort, Indrani, because of his passion for Ahalya.

One day, Indra sent a messenger, a female yogi who told Ahalya that Indra spent his days gazing at a picture of Ahalya that he had painted, kissing it, embracing it, sighing in pain when it failed to respond. The messenger made fun of husbands who don't know how to make a woman moan with pleasure, who make love silently and quickly, head covered, face turned away in disgust, just to pay their debt to the ancestors, who keep refusing to make love, saying, "Today is new moon." "Today is full moon." "I'm fasting." "Your fertile season is past." "Control yourself." She continued: "To be born a human being is the best result of many good deeds. And to be born as a woman is luckier still, for women have the ultimate desire and pleasure in sex."

Ahalya protested that so skilled a lover could not possibly love her, a sage's wife on earth, when he had all the accomplished courtesans of heaven at his disposal. But the messenger said, "Don't you know that the sacred texts refer to Indra as 'Ahalya's lover'?" Then Ahalya protested, "A woman should turn herself to stone, and give up all thought of pleasure. . . . When once in a while my old husband makes love to me, I close my eyes and pretend he is Indra." The messenger returned to heaven with this message.

At nightfall, Gautama, exhausted by his studies, lay down under a tree. Ahalya began to massage his feet amorously, but he pushed her away, reminding her that her fertile time was past. "If only Indra were here," she thought, "he would know my mood, and satisfy me." But she said to the sage, "Don't worry. I'm not thinking of *that*." She was angry, and turned her face away. He, on the other hand, sank at once into an ocean of deep serenity.

Indra knew this through his yoga. He became a cock and crowed long before the dawn; Gautama awoke and went off to bathe in the Ganges. Taking Gautama's form, Indra appeared before Ahalya and wanted to make love. She had her doubts: "This must be Indra or someone like him, in the guise of the sage, who has come to take me. This is not my husband." He said, "The fool who fails to enjoy pleasure every day before his youth slips away will regret it later; it is like building a dam for water that has long since flowed past. No sin will comes to a person who has vowed to make love every day, or any day, no matter what, in season or not." She understood him, knew he was Indra, come to embrace her. She wanted to talk to him and see him. "The sage has never shown me so much love. You're not my husband. I don't know who you are. I won't stand for it if you force me in desire, without showing me your real form." He revealed himself and pleaded with her: "Let me kiss you now, to wash away the insipid aftertaste of ambrosia. . . ." He bowed at her feet, and Ahalya, overcome with shyness and love, raised him up, pressing against him with her breasts. They embraced and made love joyously. When Indra reluctantly got up to go, Gautama returned. In terrible anger, he cursed Indra, and he cursed his wife to become a stone.

After many years, Rama came to that spot and his feet touched the stone. Slowly, it softened, grew round, melted into the charming form of Ahalya. Gautama arrived and was reconciled to Ahalya. From that time on, Gautama and Ahalya spent their days in bed, happily inventing new ways of making love. Their passion unabated, they lived forever in immeasurable pleasure.[25]

The image of passion as dammed-up water resonates with the basic image of the woman turned into a stone, which Ahalya herself predicts when she comments, as she contemplates succumbing to Indra, "A woman should turn herself to stone, and give up all thought of pleasure." Yet just as Ahalya knows that her heart would melt at Indra's touch, so the stone Ahalya melts at Rama's touch. As David Shulman remarks, "Ahalya's confession . . . reveals that Indra's assumption of Gautama's form is already present as an inner reality, a doubling within Ahalya's mind."[26] Ahalya has the fantasy, and Indra makes it happen. There is a similar reflexivity in Indra's use of artistic forms, visual and narrative: he kisses a painting as a substitute for her—a theme we know from Sita and Helen. Moreover, he points out to Ahalya that they have already become a living legend, as it were—a story that is being told by the text that we are reading—, and he uses that epithet to persuade Ahalya to make it true. (Another example of this thinking occurs when Sita, in one telling of the *Ramayana,* insists that, in all tellings of the *Ramayana,* Sita is allowed to accompany Rama to the forest.)[27]

Shulman comments on "the striking innovation of the ending, which—perhaps not surprisingly, in the milieu of the Nayaka courts—awakens lust in the cantankerous and aged Gautama and transforms the mismatched couple into a harmonious and vigorous pair of lovers." But this text produces another, even more surprising inversion of the point of the first *Ramayana* text: where Ahalya (with Indra) is there said to have invented adultery, here Ahalya (with Gautama) is said to have invented legitimate variations of the connubial embrace.

The preference for the human is a strong undercurrent of this variant of the myth, which belongs to a pattern that Shulman calls "reverse hierarchies." Thus the messenger speaks of the possibilities of human sensuality, greater than that of the gods, but Ahalya inverts this possibility, speaking of the total negation of the value of human life if a woman is married to an unfeeling or inhibited husband. As Shulman remarks, this part of the argument "completely reverses the normative denigration of feminine status and simultaneously provides another rationale for erotic violation—not to realize the woman's priceless potential is a kind of suicide, *atmahatya.* Standard dharma terminology is again appropriated for an antinomian end."[28] The final choice of a mortal husband, despite Ahalya's earlier preference for the god, is foreshadowed by the very premise of the plot: Indra prefers Ahalya over the courtesans of heaven, just as he finds the taste of the ambrosia of immortality insipid, and just as Narada (in "Indra's Odor of Immortality") tells Indra that he has found, in the world of death, a woman more beautiful than any goddess. This pattern—that the male god prefers the human woman, while the human woman prefers the god—is one to which we will return.

This Ahalya knows that someone else might have taken the form of Gautama, someone who is "like" not only Gautama but Indra, and, unlike the Ahalya whom Rama declared free of blame, she recognizes Indra when (like the *undisguised* Indra who boasts of his erotic skills) he expounds a hedonistic doctrine, reminiscent of Fitzgerald's Omar Khayyam, or John Donne to his Coy Mistress, a speech that Gautama never would have uttered. She recognizes the impostor because he desires her and her husband does not. She recognizes Indra not by any particular sense, not because he looks or smells like Indra, but because he makes use of all of his senses in bed, unlike her husband, who refuses to make love to her when it is not her fertile season. Yet, precisely because Indra says he loves her, she insists on knowing who he really is; otherwise, she says, it would be rape.

Another retelling, from a philosophical text composed in tenth-century Kashmir, adds yet another twist to the contrast between adulterous and married love:

QUEEN AHALYA AND THE PIMP INDRA

A queen named Ahalya lived in a city where there was a pimp named Indra. Because of all the stories of Indra and Ahalya, the queen Ahalya fell passionately in love with the pimp Indra, sent for him, and made love with him night after night. The king found out about the affair and had the couple tortured; but they laughed and continued to delight in one another. They died and were reborn as a married couple.[29]

Here again the text jumps out of its frame to refer, reflexively, to its own story. Ahalya is guiltier than ever—she sends for Indra—and is punished not by being turned to stone but, it seems to me, near enough, by being made to marry her lover.

The Eyes of Indra

To highlight the question of Ahalya's innocence or guilt, I have concentrated on her curses without discussing Indra's, though these too are an essential part of the pattern that concerns us. In our first *Ramayana* text, Gautama curses Indra to fall into his enemy's hands in battle and to be insecure in his reign;[30] in a brief passage in the *Mahabharata*, Gautama curses Indra to have a green beard.[31] But in several Vedic texts from the eighth century B.C.E.,[32] in the same *Mahabharata* passage,[33] and in the second *Ramayana* telling,[34] as well as in many subsequent texts, including the Telugu version cited above, Indra is castrated and eventually restored with the testicles of a ram. This sexual curse is then transformed into another sort of sexual curse, again beginning in the *Mahabharata*:[35] Indra is marked all over with vaginas (which, in one manuscript of this verse, are further transformed into eyes). And this is the curse in most of the Puranic retellings: vaginas, commuted into eyes.

Indra is branded, like Cain, with the mark of his sin, a common punishment in the *Laws of Manu*,[36] which recommends that an adulterer be branded—with a vagina if the woman in question is his guru's wife, and Gautama is very like a guru, though not Indra's guru. Nor is the image of Indra covered with vaginas a singular or perverse occurrence in a few obscure texts; it is a famous story that is even satirized in a Sanskrit farce, where a whore says, "I wish I had as many vaginas (*bhaga*s) as Indra; I could make a thousand times as much money as I'm making now."[37] Thus the Vedic myth is eventually transformed into secular literature and ends up in a pornographic farce.

Indra's brand of a thousand vaginas on his body literally emasculates him, or at least enfeminizes him, and may therefore be roughly equivalent to the castration that he receives in other versions of the myth. R. K. Narayan psychologizes the brand, for Gautama says that he has given it "so that in all the worlds, people may understand what really goes on in your mind all the time."[38] Gautama's curse is here regarded as a displacement from the mind to the body: Indra's "obsession," "what really goes on in your mind all the time," is transformed into a physical organ. But the vaginas function quite vividly and literally as vaginas (before they are turned into eyes) in the version of the story in which Ahalya recognizes Indra by his divine smell:

> The sage cursed him to have a thousand vaginas. Indra wondered, "Whatever am I going to say to my wife?" And he took the form of the beetle called Indragopa ("Guardian of Indra") and went inside a lotus. Gautama told the gods to go to Ganesha to get a sacred verse [*mantra*] that would turn Indra's vaginas into eyes like lotuses. When the gods found Indra, his limbs were covered with pus and blood, he was filthy, and he had a terrible smell. The gods covered his stinking holes with bits of cloth and taught him the *mantra* from Ganesha, and Indra obtained his celestial body again, with a thousand eyes, like another Sun.[39]

Indra's celestial smell is inverted in the curse described in this ingenious text: he doesn't merely get marks that look like vaginas, he gets real vaginas, even menstruating vaginas, which smell terrible and are bandaged with the ancient Indian equivalent of sanitary napkins. In another retelling, after Indra gets the vaginas he remains "in darkness and seclusion," which probably implies that here, too, the vaginas menstruate.[40] The idea of menstruation may have entered this myth, along with the theme of hiding in a lotus, from another well-known corpus in which Indra, afflicted with the sin of Brahminicide, hides in a lotus until his sin is distributed to four recipients, one of which is menstruating women.[41] But the lotus in which Indra hides is also a kind of eye (for Indian poetry uses the cliché of "eyes like lotuses" much as American songwriters use "eyes like stars") as well as a common symbol for the womb (as when Brahma is born out of a lotus); when the Indra beetle hides inside a lotus, therefore, he is returning to the womb (becoming not only feminized but infan-tilized) or committing a sexual act, as well as validating in yet another way the equation of eyes and vaginas. The lotus enhances this equation, since it symbolizes both an eye and a womb.

Whenever Indra is cursed with vaginas, they are turned into eyes. In one of the folk *Ramayana*s, after Indra has been cursed to have a thousand vaginas as a result of being caught with Ahalya, Rama turns Indra into a peacock with a thousand "eyes" in his tail[42]—a transformation that may have been inspired by tellings in which Indra becomes a cock. In the vari-ant of the story in which Indra gets the blame, he gets the vaginas *and* the eyes *and* the castration:

> Gautama cursed Indra, saying, "Since you have committed this false and violent act for the sake of a vagina, let there be a thousand of them on your body, and let your penis *[linga]* fall." Indra was so ashamed that he hid in the water for a long time. There he praised the goddess in her aspect of In-drakshi ("[She Who Granted the] Eyes of Indra"), and when she offered him a boon he asked her to cure his deformity. But she said, "I cannot de-stroy the evil created by a sage's curse; only gods like Brahma can do that. But I can do something so that people will not notice it: you will have a thousand eyes in the middle of the female organs, and you will have the pe-nis and testicles of a ram."[43]

Appropriate to this woman-and-goddess-oriented text, it is a goddess, rather than the sage himself, who modifies Indra's curse, though male su-premacy still rears its ugly head when the goddess acknowledges that she has less power than the male gods to alter a curse. She cannot, therefore, turn the vaginas into eyes, as Gautama often does when he modifies the curse; the best she can do is to decorate the vaginas, superficially, with eyes, "so that people will not notice it."

In *The Ocean of the Rivers of Story*, the transformation takes place in yet another way. Gautama curses Indra, saying, "You will be branded with a thousand vaginas, which is what you lust for, but when the artisan of the gods makes a heavenly woman named Tilottama and you see her, the marks will become a thousand eyes." Indra's curse is ended when Tvashtri (the father of Saranyu), here called Vishvakarman ("All-Maker"), makes a literally eye-catching celestial courtesan, Tilottama, for Indra to look at.[44] Indra is elsewhere said to have sprouted his thousand eyes in the first place in order to see Tilottama as she danced to seduce a group of demons;[45] here he is freed when he wants to see Tilottama so much that his vaginas become eyes. Tilottama's participation in this story is most appropriate, since in our first version of the myth, Ahalya herself, the first adulteress, is said to be more beautiful than the celestial courtesans; her beauty causes the problem solved in this text by Tilottama. The condition under which Indra is released from his curse is also a neat inversion of the condition under which Ahalya is released from *her* curse: where Ahalya is freed by the sight of a good/chaste man, Rama, Indra is freed by the sight of a courtesan; the *sight*, the *darshan*, of the husband of the chaste woman frees Ahalya just as the sight of the promiscuous woman frees Indra.

There is a mythological lineage for both Indra's eyes and his vaginas. Indra is called "Thousand-eyed" in many early myths (as are several other Vedic gods);[46] the text that likens Indra to the thousand-eyed Sun is another link back to the paradigm of Saranyu, where doubling and the solar gaze are connected in a rather different way. In most versions of the story of Ahalya, however, Indra gets those thousand eyes only as a result of having seduced Ahalya, and so he is not, narratively speaking, thousand-eyed until the end of the story. Yet he is often called "Thousand-eyed" proleptically at the beginning of the story; one text even says at the start that he has "eye-vaginas."[47] This is a kind of logical riddle, the word preceding the thing it represents, like the reflexivity in the text in which Indra is said to have had his epithet of "Ahalya's lover" before the story in which he becomes Ahalya's lover. It is also a stunning example of what Freud would have called upward displacement. But in terms of the history of the story, we can see that the myth is displacing not space but time, reversing the course of time through a kind of mythological backward displacement or back-formation (to borrow a term from linguistics). Indra's ancient feature of a thousand eyes was the source of a myth that gave him (through downward displacement?) thousands of vaginas that were immediately turned (back) into eyes. More precisely, to the ancient mytheme of Indra's thousand eyes was grafted another corpus that we are about to consider, the almost equally ancient mytheme of the multivaginated demoness, to yield the new mytheme of Indra with a thousand vaginas all over his body—before it reverted back to the original, Indra with a thousand eyes.

The transformations of Indra's sexual organs into eyes is made possible because the eyes themselves are sexual organs. If the curse of a thousand vaginas on his body literally emasculates him, like the curse of castration, then the transformation of the vaginas into eyes remasculates him, as it were, just as the ram's testicles cure the castration. The eyes are not vaginas but un-vaginas or ex-vaginas or even anti-vaginas: in this sense, at least, they are penises. This corpus of myths seems to confirm Freud's hypothesis about the connection between castration and blindness;[48] the cure for castration is to be covered with eyes.

Where darkness makes incest possible, blindness punishes it; Oedipus blinded himself when he realized that he had slept with his mother. The cause of blindness is the inability to see whom one is in bed with, the madness of being blinded by lust, wrong seeing—seeing too much, or too little—, excessive sexual voyeurism, or inadequate sexual discrimination by eye, judging by appearances or being taken in by a visual trick. The curse of blinding generally occurs in myths in the same places (usually after sexual sins have been committed) as the curse of castration. The structural method here validates Freud: two mythemes that replace one another like minimal pairs are structurally the same. But the myths also suggest that the concept of upward (or downward or backward) displacement can, and must, be extended from its original androcentric formulation (beheading = castration, eyes = penis) to include the rest of the human race (eyes = penis or vagina) as well as a more ambivalent attitude to sexuality in general (beheading = the termination or the release of sexuality). These ideas are all connected, but not in any simple, causal way.

Further complexities arise when we realize that some myths make blindness both a cause and a result of sexual sin, and that blinding can be regarded as not only punitive, but compensatory. Whereas in ancient Greece blinding occurs as punishment for a sexual sin, in ancient India the sexual sin of a man may result in giving him more eyes. The Greeks blind the male child in punishment for the sexual sins of the male, while the Hindus blind the male child in situations where the mother has sinned. The thousand eyes of Argos are a boon, not a curse, and the thousand eyes of Indra were useful to him long before a myth was invented to give them to him as a sexual punishment for the seduction of Ahalya. Teiresias,* blinded for sexual tactlessness, has greater power by virtue of the compensatory opening of the inner eye; the myths tell us that we often see better without our eyes. Some texts view blinding as a kind of welcome castration that leads to enlightenment, turning the gaze away from sex to what is really important. For this same reason, blindness is what is wished upon people whom one wishes to make free of all further sexual impulse; where there is no sight, there is no desire.

The Tongue of the Demoness

The vagina may be analogized not only to a male or female eye, but to a female mouth. In the Brahmanas, c. 800 B.C.E., Indra tangles with a demoness named Long-tongue *(dirghajihva),* who licks up the oblations with her long tongue; since she also happens to have vaginas on every limb, Indra equips his grandson with penises on every limb and sends him to subdue her. As soon as he has had his way with her, he remains firmly stuck in her, and Indra then appears in person to finish her off with his phallic thunderbolt.[49] Long-tongue, a bitch who threatens to lick up the oblations elsewhere in this same text, is a grotesque nightmare image of the devouring sexual woman, her mouth a second sexual organ. But gross as she may be, she is subtle in comparison with the Roman goddess Baubo, as described by Maurice Olender: "This lady is a kind of gastropod, a head showing a womb, the upper mouth mixed with the lower one. Her mouth and lips that help articulate speech are merged together with the mute genital mouth."[50]

Long-tongue is not unique in her excessive genitalia. In a related myth, to subdue another demoness who has vaginas on every joint Indra makes penises at every joint, and so he is called "Penis-joint" *(parucchepa).* When the demoness enchants him with the illusion *(maya)* of the demons, he conjures up Vedic verses that have repeated feet *(pada*s, quarters of the verses), and they set him free from every limb, from every joint, from all evil.[51] Here Indra himself matches the demoness organ for organ (his name, "Penis-joint," is unusual but not unprecedented),[52] but she still seems to overpower him intellectually. He then reverts to the organ of culture, rather than nature, his mind and voice: he repeats not his penises but the feet of a Vedic verse, conquering one articulate organ (the joint/genitals—*parvan,* the word for "joint" also comes to designate a section or book of a text, particularly the *Mahabharata*) with another (the tongue). This sets him free, presumably both from the demoness and from his own multiple organs. Feet* are here implicitly equated with genitals, another cross-culturally attested instance of downward displacement. Where this text refers only to a particular illusion that the demon woman used once she and Indra had united, the commentary states that the whole sexual nightmare was an illusion: "Indra reasoned, 'One who uses illusion must be conquered by illusion.' Otherwise, why would he have taken on such a disgusting [*jugupsitam*] form?"[53] The means of attack is justified by the doctrine of the trickster tricked: illusion against the illusory.

Thus, Indra has multiple vaginas in one myth and multiple penises in another; faced with a goddess with excessive genitals, correlated with her excessive tongue, he uses his tongue to free himself from her (and his) multiple organs. The excessive sexual organs of both demonesses are referred to euphemistically, an unusual move in Sanskrit mythology, which usually calls a spade a spade, and a vagina a *yoni*. The vaginas are called "mice," a word that, in the dual, is more often used to designate the two testicles of a man; this may indicate that these demonesses are "male" women, women with penises (or, more precisely, balls).[54] We may also see a conceptual, or even historical, connection between the many vaginal eyes of Indra, the many vaginas of the bitch Long-tongue, and the many eyes of the dog Cerberus in Greek mythology (who is etymologically related to Sarama, the bitch who goes hunting with Indra in the *Rig Veda*).[55]

In many of these myths, the tongue, like the eyes, functions as both a vagina and a phallus. And the tongue itself is, like the eyes, an organ of sexual aggression. Long-tongue set the precedent for the long (phallic?) tongue of the destructive Hindu goddess Kali, who is depicted in many icons sticking out her tongue, and who is doubled, in one myth, both by a demon in the form of a woman with teeth in her vagina—the *vagina dentata*—and by a lion with a mouth full of teeth. The theme of the fatal female tongue also reappears in later Hindu mythology in the tale of the demon "Blood-seed" *(raktabija),* from every drop of whose blood (or, if you prefer, semen) a new demon appears; to conquer him, the Goddess emits multiforms of herself who extend their tongues (or, if you prefer, vaginas) to lick up each drop of the semen-blood before it can fall to the ground.[56] The long tongue of Kali, like that of the demoness Long-tongue, is in a certain sense a phallus, the (male) organ of the (female) demoness; but it is also an antiphallus, a vagina, the upward displacement of her excessive vaginas. Here, as in the variants of "unseeable" and "unrapable" in the myth of Saranyu, the male gaze is interchangeable with male sexual violence and the female gaze with the devouring vagina.

Where Long-tongue has vaginas that are tongues, Indra has vaginas that are penises and eyes. Both Ahalya's curse—to become invisible, or to become a statue—and Indra's curse—to be covered with vaginas—reverse the sexuality of the sexual offenders. As a statue, Ahalya is, like Helen, the consoling artistic token of the lost sexual woman (in the Telugu text, Indra actually takes comfort in a painting of Ahalya), evading the male gaze, and when Indra is branded with vaginas he becomes himself the object of the gaze. The restorations are even more closely connected: she is made visible, and he is given exaggerated powers of vision, the male gaze hypostasized. The statue is turned back into a woman, and the man can once again gaze at her.

ZEUS AS AMPHITRYON WITH ALCMENA

The Greek and Roman myth of the seduction of Alcmena by Zeus (or, in Rome, Jupiter) in the form of her husband, Amphitryon, has given its name to one variant of the double; Otto Rank, for instance, refers to it as "the Amphitryon motif,"[57] though a better title might be "the Alcmena motif," since her dilemma rather than her husband's is regarded as the focal problem in most tellings. The story has been reinterpreted through-out Western literature—notably by Plautus (in the early second century B.C.E.), Molière (1668), Heinrich von Kleist (1807), Jean Giraudoux (1929, who called it "Amphitryon 38" because there had been, according to the title page of Roger Gellert's translation, thirty-seven versions before his), and S. N. Behrman (1938, a translation and adaptation of the Giraudoux version that he too called *Amphitryon 38,* fixing Giraudoux's joke in a new pun on the date of his own version), and each generation has found new meanings in it. Charles Passage, in his preface to his and James H. Man-tinband's book about Amphitryon, cautions against venturing "into the unsure field of Oriental analogues."[58] But this is a gauntlet that I have already taken up; indeed, I regard the story of Alcmena as an Occidental analogue to the story of Ahalya.

Like his cousin Indra, Zeus is a trickster and a doubler; we have seen him put a shadow Hera in the bed of Ixion.* The myth of Amphitryon is mentioned in enough Greek sources to make it clear that it was well known in Greece,[59] and the seduction of Alcmena by Zeus was the subject of plays by Sophocles and Euripides that have perished,[60] but the story is never actually narrated by any of the extant older Greek sources. Homer refers to "Amphitryon's wife, Alcmena, who, after lying in love in the em-braces of great Zeus, brought forth Heracles,"[61] and Zeus lists Alcmena among the women he seduced in his own person;[62] but there is no talk here of fooling her with a double of Amphitryon. Herodotus, on the other hand, simply refers to Amphitryon and Alcmena as the parents of Heracles, with no mention of Zeus.[63]

The earliest Greek text to tell the story in any detail, Apollodorus in the first century C.E., is much later than the earliest Latin source, a play by Plautus (early second century B.C.E.), and largely agrees with it. Ovid (at the end of the first century B.C.E.) says that Jupiter, as Amphitryon, "took" Alcmena,[64] an ambiguous verb which we could take to mean either "tricked" or "had" sexually, but Ovid gives no further details. Let us therefore begin with a summary of the earliest full Greek version of the story of Amphitryon, as retold by Apollodorus:

The Seduction of Alcmena

Alcmena's brothers had been killed by the Teleboans; her father, Electryon, set off to avenge their deaths, leaving his kingdom and his daughter Alcmena with Amphitryon, from whom he exacted a promise to keep her a virgin until he returned. But before Electryon had succeeded in his mission, Amphitryon killed Electryon [by mistake, says Apollodorus, though Hesiod says he killed him in a quarrel][65] and was banished from Argos; he took Alcmena with him to Thebes. Alcmena said she would marry him when he had avenged her brothers' deaths; and so Amphitryon made war against the Teleboans.

Before Amphitryon could return to Thebes, Zeus came by night and, stretching the night to three times its usual length, took a form like that of Amphitryon and lay in bed with Alcmena, and told her what had happened to the Teleboans. But when Amphitryon arrived and saw that he was not welcomed by his wife, he asked why, and when she told him that he had come the night before and slept with her, he learned from the seer Teiresias how Zeus had slept with her. Alcmena bore twin sons: Heracles by Zeus and Iphicles, one night younger, by Amphitryon. When the child [Heracles] was eight months old, Hera sent two serpents to destroy him; Alcmena called Amphitryon to help her, but Heracles strangled the serpents with his hands. Pherecydes says that Amphitryon put the serpents into the bed to find out which of the two was his, and that when Iphicles fled and Heracles stood his ground, he knew that Iphicles was born of him.[66]

The myth of Alcmena is in many ways a gendered reversal (and hence a reversal in other ways) of the myth of Saranyu: both Alcmena and Saranyu give birth to twins who have doubled parents (a doubled mother for

Saranyu's twins, a doubled father for Alcmena's—another example of the shift from female to male deities*). Double-fathered twins recur in both Indian and Greek lineages: when Leda, the wife of Tyndareus, was seduced by Zeus she gave birth to two eggs from which four children were born from two fathers, Pollux/Polydeuces and Helen fathered by Zeus, Castor and Clytaemnestra by Tyndareus,[67] just as Heracles and Iphicles were fathered by Zeus and Amphitryon. As Roberto Calasso tells this story, "Zeus spent half a night of love with Leda, leaving the other half to her husband, Tyndareos."[68] (Similarly, in ancient India, Mammata simultaneously bore Dirghatamas to her husband Utathya and Bharadvaja to his brother Brihaspati.)[69] This configuration proved too much for family viewing, apparently; the Disney animated film of *Hercules* regards Zeus *and Hera* as the parents of Hercules; Alcmena and Amphitryon merely adopt him when he falls to earth, just as Ma and Pa Kent adopt Superman.

Alcmena's twins are the object of an ancient paternity suit in which the question of mortality or immortality is applied not to the father, as in the story of Saranyu, but to the child. There are double versions of the test: some say Hera sent the serpents—presumably to kill Heracles, the illegitimate son of her womanizing husband, though perhaps to kill Iphicles, to eliminate a possible rival of the son of Zeus (who is, after all, called "Glory of Hera")—, while others say Amphitryon—presumably to find Iphicles, his son and heir.

The terror of the infant Iphicles revealed that he was the mortal offspring—and therefore the one that Amphitryon claimed as his own; we will return to this motif of the choice of the weaker of two doubles.* In Apollodorus's telling, Heracles is just one night older than his twin brother; in Plautus, "One of them, you see, will be a ten-month baby, the other will be a premature child of seven months. Amphitryon's the former's father, Jove's the latter's. So that the younger baby has the greater father, and vice versa."[70] Unlike their fathers, the children are distinguished by their actions: the one who fights the serpent is the son of Zeus. In Jean Giraudoux's witty retelling, when Jupiter tries to entice Alcmena by promising to beget in her a superhuman baby, "A son who would grow to be the greatest of heroes, and even in his infancy would be capable of fighting with lions and monsters," she says, "In his infancy! In his infancy he will have a spaniel and a tortoise." And when he adds, "He'd kill huge serpents that had come to strangle him in his cradle," she retorts: "He'll never be left alone. That sort of accident only happens to working class babies. No, I want him to be a weak whimperer who is frightened of flies."[71]

To seduce Alcmena, Zeus eschews both rape (his usual modus operandi) and bestiality (his second favorite). Where doubling as a woman's husband might often be regarded as an insult to her intelligence, here, at least, it is intended *not* to insult her fidelity, and not to defile her but, on the contrary, to protect her from defilement: Alcmena's chastity was so great that the god was obliged to impersonate her husband. In Apollodorus's telling, Zeus even takes the trouble to fool her with words as well as with his form: he narrates the events that the real Amphitryon has experienced since Alcmena last saw him, saying what she might expect the real Amphitryon to say.

She has no basis for comparison in bed: she has never slept with Amphitryon. In the surviving fragments of Euripides' variant too, Alcmena presumably denied herself to Amphitryon until he avenged the death of her brothers in war, and since he returned from the war to find her pregnant by Zeus, he never slept with her at all, even after that.[72] But in almost all tellings after the Greek fragments, beginning with Plautus and Apollodorus, both Amphitryon and Zeus sleep with Alcmena, and in those later variants in which she sleeps with Amphitryon *before* she sleeps with Zeus, questions of comparison, recognition, and discernment do arise. It is essential for the later, psychological variants of Molière and Kleist that she sleep with both the god and the mortal, in order to raise the twin problems of knowledge (if she had not slept with Amphitryon, it is more likely that she would not have been able to tell him from Jupiter in bed) and jealousy ("Which night did you like best?" Jupiter keeps asking).

Plautus assumes that Alcmena did not knowingly sleep with anyone other than her husband Amphitryon, but Molière snags the thread of Alcmena's unknowing, and Kleist gradually unravels the web of innocence that the myth had spun around the character of Alcmena.[73] Molière says that Alcmena was not seduced but actually initiated the whole affair herself, bringing Jupiter down from the skies "in the semblance that she cherished most in love,"[74] just as Ahalya, in the Telugu telling, summons Indra. But Kleist's Alcmena seems, at first, entirely innocent. The question of her knowledge is debated at some length in the fourth and fifth scenes of the second act. There, Alcmena sees the god as a mortal who is like a god: she tells her servant, Charis, that on the night when she slept with the man whom we know to be Jupiter, though she thought it was Amphitryon, she felt "an ineffable awareness of / My happiness, such as I never knew"; she thought Amphitryon was like a god (to which Charis simply comments, "Imagination, Princess Love's conception"). When she notices a difference between the two forms of Amphitryon, she interprets this as nothing but a heightening of Amphitryon himself, as if in a dream, larger than life, "more beautiful than ever / Last night," or as if he were "his own picture, / A painting of him by an artist's hand, / Quite true to life, yet heightened to the godlike."

This imagery, however, which we have already encountered with reference to Helen, applies as well to Jupiter as to Amphitryon: the form heightened by art corresponds to the painted image of the god that Alcmena needs to imagine him. Kleist's Alcmena defends this use of art in her worship of Jupiter: "Must I pray to white marble walls? To think of him, I need some form and features." She wants the god to appear to her in a form less powerful than full godhead but more detailed than white marble. Kleist's Alcmena experiences great ambivalence between her feelings, which respond differently to Jupiter than they did to Amphitryon, and her mind, which is befogged by the arguments that they are the same person (arguments also reinforced by cognitive dissonance: if they aren't the same person, she's an adulteress). Jupiter confuses Alcmena even more by asking her how she would feel if she were in bed with Jupiter but thought he was Amphitryon, and just then Amphitryon were to appear. Alcmena hedges: "Yes—I would then be sad, and I would wish / That he were the god, and that you would / Remain Amphitryon, as you surely are."

And so she objects when, after the seduction, Jupiter tells her that she has been in bed with the king of the gods, not her mortal husband. It could not have been a god, she argues, or else she would "perish in such radiance" and there would be no life coursing through her "warm heart" at that moment. We recognize this argument: a god (or goddess) may be too hot to handle.* When Alcmena finally realizes her mistake, she pleads with Jupiter, "Leave me forever in my error if / Your light is not to shade my soul forever."[75] The imagery of light and shade and soul implies that the error in which Alcmena wishes to remain consists in believing, wrongly, that the man she has made love with was just her husband; she is asking to be protected from looking on the face of godhead—and truth—directly.

She is also arguing that, since she could not gaze upon a god, she must gaze upon his shadow. In Giraudoux's telling, when Jupiter masquerades as Amphitryon, the person describing him says, "He glows. . . . Really, the sun's quite pale in comparison. He's like a block of light with a man's shadow."[76] The gods, who can bear to look at that light, have eyes different from ours, as Mercury reminds Jupiter when they are preparing for the masquerade:

> Your eyes—let's see, now. . . . Oh no, much too brilliant. They're all iris, no cornea, and not a trace of tear-gland—you may easily need to cry, you know. . . . Earthly light corresponds to what we in heaven would call total darkness. . . . I can still see the pupils through your eyelids when you blink. . . . The main thing that strikes me about a man, a living flesh-and-blood man, is that he's continually changing, he's getting a fraction older every second. I can even see the light in his eyes aging.[77]

Our inability to gaze at the sun is the clue to our mortality, to the aging light in our eyes.

If Helen is the negative of a negative, as Sita was the illusion of an illusion, Alcmena is the shadow of a shadow. For Giraudoux goes on to invert the idea of the deity whom we cannot bear to look at directly and to combine that idea with the image of the sexually rejecting woman. The god cannot bear to look at anything but the shadow of the mortal woman he desires and cannot possess. As Jupiter and Mercury are watching Alcmena through a window at night, Jupiter speaks:

> J: "You may see her shadow pass over it."
> M: "The shadow will be plenty for me."
> J: "It's the shadow of her shadow."

But when Mercury realizes that it is the shadow of Alcmena embracing her husband, he remarks, "I begin to see why you do without your divine vision, Jupiter. It's obviously a good deal less painful to watch the husband's shadow hugging the shadow of his wife than to see the whole performance in flesh-and-blood detail."[78] But here it is the god who is blinded by the mortal and is grateful to be able to look at her shadow alone. In the end, Giraudoux moves back from the solar symbolism to simple human psychology; instead of closing her eyes, Alcmena closes her mind: she asks explicitly to be allowed to forget "today": "Oh, master of the gods, can you bestow forgetfulness?"[79]

Like Ahalya, Alcmena thinks of the god as lover when she worships him, and yet is surprised when he comes to her. Kleist's Jupiter argues, with supreme casuistry, that it was because she had used the sexual image of Amphitryon as an idol in the temple that Jupiter came to her in bed, to get even, sexually, with Amphitryon for the religious betrayal.[80] He goes on to advise her to reverse the process by meditating upon the god, not upon her husband, "Recalling each detail of that occurrence," and to dismiss her husband if he interrupts her. And he concludes with an even more convoluted version of the idolatry argument, by warning her that if, at the altar, she thinks of Amphitryon instead of Jupiter, Jupiter may come back to her again. Previously, Alcmena worshipped Amphitryon at the altar of Jupiter; now, she will worship Jupiter in the bed of Amphitryon. Idolatry must be transformed into fantasy.

Kleist's Jupiter wants to be loved both as a human and as a god. He is a jealous lover in both the theological and the human senses of the word: he does not want her to worship other gods, or to prefer sleeping with other men. His jealousy of Amphitryon takes on a double meaning, when as Amphitryon he tells Alcmena about "the envy of Jupiter"— those who envy him and those whom he envies. Tactlessly, he tells Alcmena about other human women with whom Jupiter has slept, repeating (in a kind of inversion) his tactlessness to Hera in the *Iliad,* when, as he takes her to bed, he insists that he desires her more than any of his other women, several of whom he lists—including Alcmena.[81] And when he is talking to Alcmena as Jupiter, he insists that Juno had never pleased him so much in bed, and that he lives on the nectar of Alcmena's love—just as Indra asks Ahalya to kiss away the taste of ambrosia. This passage also expresses the god's genuine envy of the fidelity that only a mortal woman can feel for a mortal man. Thus Kleist argues for the superiority of mortals over immortals through the idea of a god humanized by his love for a mortal woman. When Behrman's Mercury asks Jupiter why he does it the hard way, he replies: "I have a nostalgia for mortality. I would like to experience the same difficulties human beings do—and the same delights."[82] He wants to win the fight with his supernatural hand tied behind his back.

Kleist also tackles other theological implications of the masquerade: Why does the god become incarnate? Does he do it for love of the woman? Or in order to produce the child? Or because he wants to verify his *own* existence by being loved, just as mere mortals do? This last reason is central to Kleist's strange mixture of Christian and pagan theology. Jupiter curses the "illusion"—that is, the illusion that he might be loved for himself—that brought him down from the skies, driven by a combination of celestial loneliness and ardor:

> O Alcmena, Olympus too is empty without love . . . / [The god] wants their love, not their illusion of him. / Enshrouded in eternal veils, / He craves to mirror himself in a soul / And be reflected in a tear of rapture.

The metaphors of illusion, veils, mirrors, and reflections suggest the doubles that haunt all relationships between gods and humans.

Molière and Kleist combine the erotic dynamics of the typical Jovian rape (wham-bam, thank you ma'am) and a modern, Alan Alda–type sensibility about sex (did I please her more than anyone has ever pleased her?). It is because Jupiter takes on a *human* form, rather than an animal form (let alone a shower of gold, as he did for one seduction: could a shower of gold be jealous?), that the problem of his jealousy arises. Molière's great innovation lies in attributing to Jupiter the desire to be accepted by Alcmena not simply out of marital duty but for his own sake.[83]

Kleist's Jupiter as Amphitryon continually uses theological double-talk to confuse Alcmena as he impersonates himself, "pretending" to be Jupiter, and when he finally confesses, "It was no mortal man that came to you / Last night, but Jupiter himself, the god of thunder,"[84] Alcmena is too confused to recognize the truth when she sees it, and she berates Jupiter as Amphitryon ("you godless Man") for blaming the gods for his own sacrilege. She also tells the real Amphitryon, "You said playfully . . . you were a god."[85]

Kleist paints Alcmena as a woman who, faced with a man who says he is her husband, is fragmented in herself: she no longer knows who she is, since she does not know who he is. Amphitryon too loses his sense of who he is when she does not know who he is: "If she can recognize her husband in him, / I will inquire no further who I *am*, / But I will hail him as Amphitryon."[86] The identity crisis is doubled, for Mercury assumes the form of Amphitryon's servant Sosia when Jupiter takes the form of Amphitryon, and the name *Sosia* comes to mean "a double" in both French and Italian.[87] The French dictionary summarizes this character: "Sosie finds himself face to face with another Sosie . . . He comes to doubt his own identity."[88]

Molière's Amphitryon expresses rational French doubts about the whole Greek mess:

> Nature does sometimes produce resemblances / And some impostors have abused them on occasion; / But that a man as husband finds acceptance is, /

I find, incredible in such a situation. / On every count there are a thousand differences, / Each bound to strike a woman's shrewd evaluation. / The magic spells of Thessaly / Are credited with strange effects since times of old, / But all the famous tales about them ever told / Have always struck my mind as sheer inanity.[89]

Common sense rejects coincidence, and a wife should be able to recognize her husband.

Kleist too puts a sensible argument into the mouth of Charis, Alcmena's maid, who protests with down-to-earth German common sense: "How could a woman err in such a case? Wrong clothes, wrong household items one might take, But / husbands are known in the dark."[90] And Amphitryon later objects:

In rooms where candlelight was shining fair / No one who had five healthy senses has / Mistaken friends until today. Mere eyes/ Wrenched from their sockets and laid on the table, / Mere limbs, ears, fingers, severed from the body / And packed in boxes, would have been enough / To recognize a husband by.[91]

Thus, without actually condemning Alcmena, the later European tellings cast what our courts call "reasonable doubt" upon her statement that she thought Jupiter was her husband.

Even when the double is immortal, certain individual traits prevail, over and above the generic distinctions between humans and superhumans.* Both Molière and Kleist explain how Amphitryon might or might not prove his identity through detailed material proofs, each of which ultimately fails. In Plautus, echoed in the others, the most elaborate argument turns upon a goblet, a signet ring, a jewel inscribed with a name, and a sealed casket. The sealed box is a metaphor for Alcmena's chastity (indeed, in those variants where she has not yet slept with Amphitryon, her virginity). Something has gotten out of it (or into it), yet it remains sealed; her body has been violated, but not her mind. In a satire on these material proofs, in both Molière[92] and Kleist,[93] Sosia suggests that the person who has invited them to dinner must be the real Amphitryon. These rational views of jewelry and dining out do not prevail, however, and so the real Amphitryon proposes a simple, indeed simpleminded solution:

Now when that son of Darkness comes in sight, / That monster of a man upon whose head / Each individual hair curls just like mine, / . . . . Be sure then to remember *I'm* Amphitryon, / You citizens of Thebes, / The one that bent his helmet crest like this.[94]

This is a desperately silly way to tell two men apart: bend your hat. For this "proof" depends upon our belief that the one making this speech, and bending his hat, already *is* Amphitryon. Wisely, the First Colonel objects: "What good now is the bent-down helmet crest? . . . The one his wife accepts must be the real one." Sexual intimacy is the ultimate test.[95]

Finally, Alcmena chooses the *wrong one,* despite the fact that she has slept with them both. Does Alcmena *knowingly* select the false Amphitryon, hoping that he will remain with her as her husband? We know, though she may not, that she prefers Jupiter (in contrast with Giraudoux's Alcmena, who steadfastly insists that her night with Jupiter as Amphitryon was *not* the best). Amphitryon cries out in horror, "Alcmena!" and "Beloved!", but to no avail. Finally, he gives in, acknowledging the force of the sexual test: "He is Amphitryon to her."[96] At this point, knowing that he has won and can afford to be generous, Jupiter says to Amphitryon, "You are Amphitryon."

Alcmena and Amphitryon, Jupiter and Leda

Giraudoux's Alcmena is, as usual, fooled in bed, but the plot doesn't stop there. When she then sees the real Amphitryon, she mistakes him for Jupiter, thus completing the round-trip mistake of taking husband for god and god for husband. This time, however, her error makes her create a counterdouble, as Giraudoux (followed by Behrman) introduces a new twist. After Jupiter has slept with Alcmena as Amphitryon, at dusk, he has it widely announced that Jupiter will soon visit Alcmena to beget Heracles upon her. Leda, the woman who had previously been impregnated by Zeus in the form of a swan and given birth to Helen, hears that Jupiter intends to seduce Alcmena (though, like Alcmena, she doesn't know that he has already done so), and she visits Alcmena. When Alcmena says to Leda: "Save me and get your revenge on Jupiter for only making love to you once,"[97] Leda asks, "How does one revenge oneself on a white swan?" Then Alcmena replies: "With a black one. Now listen to me: you take my place! . . . Look: this door leads to a darkened room where everything is ready for tonight. Put on my veils, spray my perfume around. It'll fool Jupiter, and much to his advantage." Leda agrees: "Your swan will be an Amphitryon. The very next time your husband is away for the night, Jupiter will enter your palace and deceive you.[98] . . . Between now and tonight, then, Alcmena, Jupiter will burst through those doors in your husband's shape and you will give yourself to him in perfect trust." Which is, of course, what has already happened.

Plautus plunges into Swan Lake, and the "black swan," the deceptive double to counter Alcmena's presumably white swan, Jupiter, is none other than Leda herself. Alcmena thinks she will avoid Jupiter in the traditional way: by sending a shadow double to a man she doesn't want to sleep with. But now the real Amphitryon arrives, at dawn, and Leda assumes he must be "Jupiter . . . the false Amphitryon," to which Alcmena replies, "In that case, he's going to find a false Alcmena." He insists on making love to Alcmena, who sends him into the darkened room where she promises to join him, and into which Leda goes instead; Amphitryon makes love to Leda as Alcmena.

The denouement is treated very differently by Giraudoux and Behrman. In both plays, Jupiter's desire to be loved for himself leads him to reveal his true identity to Alcmena (after he has seduced her as Amphitryon) and to attempt to get her to sleep with him for what we know would be the second time and she thinks would be the first time—but in any case, for the first time as Jupiter rather than Amphitryon. Giraudoux's Jupiter refrains from his usual policy of announcing his true identity as he leaves the bedroom, because Alcmena tells him that she would kill herself rather than commit adultery, and he fears she might do so if she knew, in retrospect, that she had.

In Giraudoux's third act, Alcmena and Amphitryon debate their response to the announcement that Jupiter will come to Alcmena that night. They waver between refusing (a decision which, Jupiter has made clear, will mean not only their deaths but the destruction of Thebes) and resigning themselves to his will; in the end, they decide to die. But in recalling their moments of happiness together, Amphitryon says, "Do you remember, Alcmena, the morning I came back from the war to embrace you in the shadows of dawn?" To which she replies, "Dawn? Don't you mean dusk?" And he, "Dawn or dusk, what does it matter now?" She insists: "Please, Amphitryon, I beg you, tell me if you came at dusk or dawn! . . . . It was night, wasn't it?" "Oh, in our room, utter night," he replies, humoring her. So, then, she knows, from Amphitryon's reference to dawn rather dusk, that she has inadvertently engineered a kind of double play: she realizes that she let Leda sleep with Amphitryon (though she still does not allow herself to realize that she herself slept with Jupiter).

When Jupiter arrives at last in his own form, he dismisses Amphitryon and tries in vain to persuade Alcmena to sleep with him. But when,
at her request, he takes her in his arms, she says, "I have the feeling that
it's not the first time you've fingered that lock of hair, or bent over me as
you are now." Thus she begins to suspect from certain physical details of
his lovemaking that he was her lover. She persists: "Was it at dawn or
dusk you came and took me?" And he replies, "You know very well it was
dawn. Do you think I didn't see through that trick with Leda? I took
Leda to please you." That is, he lies both about dusk (when Alcmena
thinks, wrongly, she was with Amphitryon) and about dawn (when Alcmena thinks, wrongly, that Leda was with Jupiter). The familiar theme of
the ambivalent sun is here expressed in the two liminal solar moments,
dawn and dusk, once again assimilated to the theme of the ambivalent
sexual partner.

INTERLUDE: PANDORA

Ahalya in the first *Ramayana* telling is the first woman, intended as the
solution to the problem of the doubleness of men and women. In this
she provides a parallel not to Alcmena but to Helen, who is both unique
and double in her beauty, and an even closer parallel to the Greek Pandora, who is created as the first woman and is herself merely a "likeness."
Pandora is constructed by the gods in punishment for the rebellion of
Prometheus, in order to bring sex and death into the world—sex on the
outside, death on the inside; she proves that beauty is not truth. She is not
explicit or obvious in her doubling, but like Saranyu she is responsible for
the origin of the human race, and she is, in ways rather different from
Saranyu's ways, a double woman.

Hesiod tells the story in some detail:

PANDORA

Zeus told Prometheus that he would give to humankind an evil in which
they would all find joy. And he told Hephaestus to fuse earth with water
and set a human voice in it, to make her a face like that of an immortal
goddess, the figure of a desirable maiden. Athena taught her to weave a
web, and Aphrodite gave her grace and painful lust and anxious desire; and
Hermes gave her the cunning mind of a bitch. Hephaestus shaped the likeness of a chaste virgin, and Hermes put in her heart lies and dissimulation
in words, and a voice, and he named her Pandora, because each of the gods
gave her a gift. She took the lid of her jar and scattered diseases and suffer-

ings; all that she kept inside the jar was hope. These diseases come to men in silence, for Zeus has stolen their voice.[99]

Pandora is not *a* likeness, but, rather, she *is* likeness, an *ikelon* of women, like the image *(samjna)* of woman that Saranyu represents even before she produces the likeness or shadow *(chaya)* of that image. Where Helen is an image, an *eidolon,* of one particular woman, Pandora is a likeness, an *ikelon,* of all women.[100] Pandora is the principle of doubling, the archetype of the woman who is her own double, good on the outside ("just like a chaste virgin"), bad on the inside. As Nicole Loraux remarks, "In this semblance lies all the truth about woman: woman resembles a virgin; woman resembles a woman; it is the same as saying that she is entirely and essentially *a simulacrum. . . .* The 'false woman' is not a man disguised but woman herself."[101]

The creation of the woman is the beginning of the human race: "If the creation of woman is the ultimate consequence of the separation of men and gods, the paradox consists in the fact that 'men' are really born into the human condition only by becoming *andres,* or one half of humanity. . . . In her and through her, therefore, duality is reintroduced into humanity."[102] When Zeus gives humans Pandora he gives them the doubleness that the gods have always had.[103] Pandora cuts the human species in two; and she herself is cut in two in more than the basic contrast between inside and outside, for she is made of both earth and water, with a human voice in the image of an immortal goddess, a virginal body and the mind of a bitch. More than that, she subsumes in herself the most basic of human doubles: life and death, together with beauty and ugliness, good and evil. She is truly what Rudolf Otto called the *mysterium fascinans et tremendum.*[104]

Through Pandora, Zeus tricks and abandons the human race, just as Saranyu does; but Zeus himself has been tricked by Prometheus—or tricked him. For Zeus gives Pandora to mankind in revenge for Prometheus's attempt to fool Zeus by concealing the bones of the sacrificial ox within a layer of fat and skin. This punishment is yet another substitution and concealment, for the hiddenness of Pandora is connected with the hiddenness of god, as Jean-Paul Vernant has argued:

> The Woman was man's double and his opposite. . . . a *kakon kalon,* the kind of evil one can neither do without nor endure. If you marry her, her belly eats you out of house and home and lands you in poverty in your own life-

time. But if you do not marry and lack a female belly to receive your seed
and nurture the embryo, you have no children to carry on your line.[105]

The double woman, Pandora, is the concealing woman, curious about
what is locked up (like Bluebeard's bride), but herself the source of what is
mysteriously locked up: the child in her womb. This image was given a
positive inversion in the medieval *vierge ouverte et fermée*, the Virgin Mary
whose belly can be opened up to reveal inside not disease and horror but
salvation: the infant Jesus, for she is the (virtuous) woman who conceals
(good) things. The *vierge ouverte* then gives way to the medieval anatomi-
cal drawings of the woman displaying her womb,[106] an image that is in
turn reinverted back into the Pandora paradigm in the Iron Maiden, a medieval torture instrument consisting of a hollow iron statue of a woman,
hinged to open so that the victim could be inserted; and when she was
closed up again, long spikes projecting from her inner surfaces would im-
pale the victim. This is a nightmare inversion of the comforting statue as
afterimage: a smooth statue on the surface, it opens to expose the long
teeth of the *vagina dentata*.

COMPARISON: AHALYA AND ALCMENA

Ahalya is innocent in the earliest telling but guilty in later tellings, when
she clearly recognizes Indra and sleeps with him anyway. Alcmena is also
assumed to be innocent at first, in Plautus and Apollodorus; she only realizes what's happening when the two Amphitryons confront one another,
as the double Sitas and Helens, and Ahalya's husband and Indra, do in
some texts. Although later texts begin to cast doubt on Alcmena's innocence (Molière openly, Kleist more subtly), she is never really accused
of adultery or punished; the point of the Greek myth is to justify the
divine parentage of the son (Heracles) that results from the seduction of
Alcmena—like similar tales that explain the divine parentage of Achilles,
Sarpedon, and so forth. By contrast, the fact that no child results from the
seduction of Ahalya makes the point of the myth purely erotic, particularly since so many Hindu stories of divine seductions are designed, like
the Greek parallels just cited, precisely to justify the divine parentage of
sons, such as the Pandavas in the *Mahabharata,* or the entire human race
in the story of Saranyu. This distinction too makes Alcmena the good
woman, Ahalya the evil woman.

Heracles (who resembles the Hindu god Krishna in various ways),[107] born of a double, is a womanizer. In Giraudoux's play, a voice from heaven predicts that the son Alcmena conceives by Jupiter will know all women to be faithless: "He shall seduce them, suck them dry, discard them, jeer at their outraged husbands, and die at last at women's hands."[108] In fact, Heracles is the victim of multiple doubles, in a story told by Apollodorus:

HERACLES AND THE DAUGHTERS OF KING THESPIUS

King Thespius entertained Heracles for fifty days, and each night, as Heracles went out to hunt, the king put one of his fifty daughters in his bed, because he was eager to have each of them bear a child to Heracles. Heracles, thinking that only one woman was in his bed always, slept with all of them.[109]

This is a striking parallel to the myth of Krishna and the cowherd women, but an even closer parallel to the myth of Agni and the sages' wives. For where Krishna fooled a group of women, Fire was fooled by successive impersonations of a group of women by one woman and Heracles was fooled by a group of women pretending to be one woman.

Heracles in this myth is fooled, like his mother, by doubles; though he thinks himself monogamous like his human father, he is in fact promiscuous like his divine father. Apollodorus here is surely satirical, and probably skeptical. Moreover, the post-Homeric Greek tradition soon began to debate the divine ancestry of heroes. Herodotus, who refused to consider the presence at Troy of either a real Helen or a phantom Helen, also satirized the theme of the phantom husband in his tale of Demaratus, born to Ariston's wife less than ten months after she slept with Ariston; accused of adultery, she told this tale to Demaratus:

THE PHANTOM ARISTON

When Ariston brought me home, on the third night after that first, there came to me a phantom in the likeness of Ariston and lay with me and put upon me the garlands that he had when he came. The phantom vanished, and then came Ariston. When he saw the garlands, he asked me who had given them to me. I told him that he had given them himself, and he would not believe me. . . . It turned out that the garlands came from the hero's shrine by the door of the palace, and this hero was called Astrabacus; and, moreover, the prophets said that it was the hero himself who had fathered the child. . . . Either you are the son of that hero and your father is Astrabacus, or it is Ariston; for it was in that night that I became pregnant with you. . . . Women give birth at nine months and seven months; not all of them complete the full ten; I bore you, my son, at seven months.[110]

Herodotus does not think much of this overdetermined series of excuses; the phantom Ariston, like the phantom Helen, is too obviously convenient.[111] So too Semele's story about the divine birth of Dionysus is challenged (though ultimately affirmed).[112]

The idea of a god impregnating a mortal woman was a matter for mockery in Hellenistic Greece, as we learn from a tale in the *Great Alexander Romance,* in about the third century of the Common Era, which is said to have reached India and Indonesia through Arabic retellings.[113] This alternative tale of the birth of Alexander the Great begins with the statement: "People generally are under the misapprehension that [Alexander] was the son of King Philip. This is quite wrong. He was not the child of Philip but, rather, as the wisest Egyptians assert, the son of Nektanebos, conceived after he had been driven from his throne."[114] This is the story:

NEKTANEBOS, AS AMMON, AND OLYMPIAS

Nektanebos was a magician who desired Philip's Queen, Olympias. The queen had heard a rumor that Philip was going to divorce her and marry someone else; she called in Nektanebos, who confirmed the prophecy but advised a way to avoid it: "You must have intercourse with a god on earth, conceive by him, bear a son and rear him, and have him to avenge the wrongs Philip has done you." He recommended the god Ammon, and described him. He made her dream that night: she saw the god Ammon embracing her and as he arose from her saying to her, "Woman, you have a male child in your womb to be your avenger." She told Nektanebos, and asked him to bring her together with the god again. He agreed, saying, "Cover your face and do not look directly at the god you saw coming to you in your dreams."

Nektanebos put on a ram's fleece, complete with horns on its temples, and an ebony scepter and a snake-colored cloak, and went into the bedroom where Olympias was lying covered up on the bed. But she was looking out of the corner of her eye: she saw him coming and was not afraid, since she was expecting him to be as he had appeared in the dream. The lamps lit up, and Olympias covered her face. Nektanebos, setting down his scepter, got into her bed and lay with her.

In the morning she asked him, "Will this god be coming back to me? I had such pleasure from him." He went to her as often as Olympias wanted—with her thinking he was the god Ammon. After a while she became pregnant, and Nektanebos sent Philip a dream; Philip told the interpreter, "I saw a god in a dream. He was very handsome, and he had horns on his temples, both like gold; and in his hand he held a scepter. It was night, and he was going to my wife, Olympias, lying down, and having intercourse with her. Then, as he rose, he said to her: 'Woman, you have conceived a male child who shall tend you and shall avenge the death of his father.'" The interpreter identified the god as Ammon.

Philip did not like what he heard. When he returned home, he said to Olympias, "You have deceived me, wife: you were made pregnant not by a god, but by someone else—and he is going to fall into my hands." Nektanebos heard this. There was a great banquet in the palace, and everyone was feasting with King Philip to celebrate his return. King Philip alone was downcast—because Olympias, his wife, was pregnant. So, in front of everyone, Nektanebos turned himself into a serpent. Olympias, however, recognized her bridegroom and reached out her right hand to him. And the serpent stirred himself to rest his head in her hand and coiled down to Olympias's knees and, putting out his forked tongue, kissed her—a token of his love for the benefit of the onlookers.

Philip counted himself lucky at what he had seen: the child his wife bore was going to be known as the seed of a god. When the child, Alexander, became a man, his appearance was not like Philip's and, indeed, not even like his mother Olympias's or his real father's—he was a type all of his own. Indeed, he had the shape of a man, but he had the mane of a lion and eyes of different colors—the right eye black, the left gray—and teeth as sharp as a serpent's. One day, Alexander killed Nektanebos by pushing him into a pit; as he died, Nektanebos told Alexander the story of his birth, how he had gone to Olympias as the god Ammon and had had intercourse with her. With these words, he breathed out his spirit. Alexander heard him say this and, being convinced that he had killed his father, was heartbroken. He went home and told Olympias in detail everything he had learned from Nektanebos. She was astonished and blamed herself for having been deceived into adultery by him and his evil magical skills. But she buried him as befitted the father of Alexander.[115]

The folk motif of the serpent lover who saves his mistress from justified accusations of adultery[116] appears in the middle of this story, but it is not entirely clear that Philip is taken in by it: he says that the child will be "*known* as the seed of a god," but not that he believes that he is in fact the seed of a god. The theological lie does serve, in any case, to keep the queen alive, and the secret apparently died with her—for we all believe that Alexander was the son of Philip. He does not resemble either of his fathers—he has his human father's shape, and the sharp teeth of his serpent father—, nor does he treat either of his fathers well (he kills Nektanebos and he avenges, but does not prevent, Philip's death); his ambivalence is captured in the image of his two eyes of two different colors.

CONCLUSION: DID SHE FALL, OR WAS SHE PUSHED?

Though I chose, for my primary purposes, to look first at the women, Ahalya and Alcmena (and Sita and Helen), the texts devote more time to the men than to the women, in particular to the quandary of Zeus/Jupiter in wanting to be loved for himself and to the quandary of Indra, whose various mutilations we have noted. Zeus gets away with it, mostly; Indra does not. Zeus suffers inner torment, while Indra is physically mutilated (as is Ahalya, who also suffers inner torment in some texts). The Hindu tradition regards Indra's suffering and restoration as a ritual problem, involving, first, the sacrifice of a ram and, later, visits to various Hindu shrines. The Greek tradition, divorced from any ritual specific to the text, treats the theme of Zeus's suffering in the realm of theology.

At the start, we should note a difference in the status of these myths as they survive over the centuries. At the time of the composition of most of these texts, Indra was no longer worshipped and had been supplanted by other gods, but he was still regarded as a god; Zeus, however, after the beginning of the tradition was no longer God, and texts composed within European traditions treated him with less and less reverence. So too Ahalya remains a part of the Hindu wedding ritual tradition to this day, where she is literally the touch-*stone* of wifely fidelity, while Alcmena, and even Amphitryon, survive only as literary tropes.

Certain patterns emerge if we go on (or back) to compare Ahalya and Alcmena with the women we considered in chapter 1, Sita and Helen. Ahalya is to Alcmena not as Sita is to Helen, but as Helen is to Sita; that is, Ahalya is, like Helen, the paradigmatic beauty and adulteress in Hindu civilization, directly contrasted (even in her name) with Sita, the paradigmatic Good Wife: Ahalya, whose name means "Not to Be Plowed," is the field that is plowed by one man too many, a significant designation, given the importance in Hinduism of the agricultural metaphor of the legitimate wife as the field that belongs to her husband;[117] by contrast, Sita, whose name means "The Furrow," was born from a furrow that her father was plowing, and she was plowed by only one man, Rama. Ahalya and Sita

meet, indirectly, within the text; when Ahalya meets Rama, the paradigmatic faithful husband of the paradigmatic faithful wife, Sita, she will be
purified and her curse will be fulfilled. But Rama, like Gautama, wrongly
doubts his wife's chastity and rejects her, in the very same book of the *Ramayana* that tells the story of Ahalya.

Alcmena, on the other hand, becomes a paragon and paradigm of
virtue in Greek and European mythology, like Sita in Hindu mythology.
Where Indra, in some texts, first tries in vain to seduce Ahalya in his own
form and only then resorts to the device of impersonating her husband,
Jupiter succeeds first in seducing Alcmena when he impersonates her husband and only afterwards tries, in vain, to seduce her in his own form. Together, the two sets of myths provide double paradigms for two cultures,
one virtuous woman and one whore per culture. Yet they assign different
sorts of stories to the two women: the whore is given the shadow double in
Greece and falls for the god in Hinduism, while the chaste wife is given the
shadow double in Hinduism and falls for the god in Greece.

On the surface, the texts seem to be saying that the woman who is
fooled is innocent:[118] the innocent Sita is fooled by Ravana, while the
guilty Helen fools the other Greeks; the innocent Alcmena is fooled by the
divine impostor, while the guilty Ahalya is not. But the woman who is
fooled is often said to be guilty too, guilty at the very least of not recognizing her own husband.[119] Moreover, in general, women and goddesses in
these stories are fooled less often than men and gods; they are regarded as
more duping than duped. There are exceptions to this trend, stories in
which men fail to be fooled or make the right choice, or women are fooled
or make the wrong choice; for example, when the man is God, he is not
fooled (Tulsi's Rama with Shurpanakha or Sati); indeed, when he is
fooled, as in the Nepalese tellings, we may assume that this means that he
is no longer (or not yet) God. Another important exception to the rule
that good women are fooled is offered by the cycle about the good Arundhati, who is *not* fooled. But in general our texts focus more often on the
ways in which women see through the ruses of gods than on men who
recognize goddesses.

When a man is the victim of a double, the text generally assumes that
he was fooled. The texts relatively seldom ask: "How does the man succeed
in telling his true wife from the impostor?" When a woman is the victim,
however, the text more often asks: "Was she really fooled?" Or "How did

the woman succeed in telling her husband from the impostor?" It is as if
the texts assume that women are always the tricksters, never the victims,
and therefore that any apparent counterinstance must be justified by arguing that the woman was not in fact victimized, that even when she appears
to be the victim her trick consists in pretending to be tricked by the trickster, or indeed in tricking the trickster. Whether the man or the woman
produces the double, the stories assume that the men are fooled (by Sita
and Helen) and that the women (Ahalya and Alcmena) are not. The argument that "she really knew" plays precisely the role in myths in which men
trick women as the argument that "she asked for it" plays in sexist discussions of rape: it shifts the blame from the perpetrator to the victim.

Although we might read these stories as indications that women are
more perceptive than men, smarter, the narrators of these stories do not
regard the women who are not fooled as morally superior to men. On the
contrary. For, in addition to distinguishing between women who are, like
men, fooled (Alcmena, usually) and women who are not (Ahalya, sometimes), we must further subdivide this second group into women (like
Damayanti) who are not fooled and therefore resist the god, and women
(like Ahalya in other versions) who, still not fooled, nevertheless go ahead
and sleep with the god. In this latter variant, though the end result is the
same as that of the woman who is fooled, the woman is far worse than
foolish: she is a knowing and complicitous pseudovictim, a category for
which I know no male counterpart within this corpus. The accusation that
the woman pretends to be fooled when in fact she is not fooled floats just
under the surface of the long history of the myths of Alcmena and Ahalya.
Thus, when women are not being blamed for being so stupid that they can
be tricked, they are blamed for being too cunning to be tricked; heads she
loses, tails she loses.

Yet we do not have to read these stories solely through the surface voice
of the male narrator. When Ahalya pretends to be fooled, the version
or vision of women's identity that she projects is not necessarily entirely
negative. The "bad" women—Helen and Ahalya, not to mention Pandora
and Saranyu—often demonstrate initiative, spunk, and agency in
ways that even the male narrator occasionally seems to admire despite
himself and that female audiences must have appreciated. Our texts
assume that women fool men far more than men fool women, not just
because of the (usually male) author's assumption that women are dis-

honest, but because women must resort to trickery when they cannot resort to force, because they are forced to use their wits, the weapons of the weak (to use James Scott's phrase), to subvert a scenario that they lack the physical or political power to change. Both Hindu and Greek societies were (and are) patriarchal. What kinds of tricks, powers, sexualities, and viewpoints are female beings allowed to have in mythic narratives? Our stories tell us that women trick men, outmaneuver them, a fact that may be interpreted from a man's point of view ("Women are dishonest and always manage to get their way through secret manipulations") but also from a woman's point of view ("We are forced to trick them and we can do it").

The "appreciation" of women's cunning can be sexist too. Thus Schopenhauer characterized women: "As the weaker sex, they are driven to rely not on force but on cunning; hence their instinctive subtlety and their irradicable tendency to tell lies."[120] A character remarks of an actress who plays a spy double in a John Le Carré novel, "For a woman, lying is a protection. She protects the truth, so she protects her chastity. For a woman, lying is a proof of virtue."[121] But a more sympathetic view would argue that it is a privilege to be able to play straight when you don't have to fear brutal power.

Moreover, it is worth recalling that the relationship between gods and humans is conceived, by humans, as one between the powerful and the weak. In this light, the entire corpus of myths in which humans trick the gods, as well as the much larger corpus of myths in which gods try in vain to trick humans, are mythological examples of wit used as the weapon of the weak. When a male god uses his power (including his power of illusion, the "woman's" weapon) against a human woman, she is doubly overpowered, as a woman and as a human, and doubly called upon to use her wits. In the case of Giraudoux's Alcmena, when Jupiter threatens not only to kill Alcmena and Amphitryon but to destroy Thebes if she does not sleep with him—a spectacular example of divine sexual harassment—, the trick that she works with Leda is a brilliant stratagem designed to save not only her life (and the lives of her husband and countrymen) but her honor. As Ann Gold has remarked of this corpus of stories, "Often females are limited, bound, and generally dis-ed (disallowed, disrespected, dismissed, objects of disgust). Yet female sexual, and even political, exuberance often shines through these tales."[122]

There are, moreover, women who are neither fooled by doubles nor doubled themselves, in both India and Greece: Damayanti and Penelope. The innocent Damayanti is not fooled by the gods' disguise, and the innocent Penelope sees through Odysseus's disguise. They offer us the hope of an image of women with both more moral stature and more agency than the women we have encountered so far.

Nala and Damayanti, Odysseus and Penelope

~~✦~~

A single god impersonates a single mortal in the myths of Indra and
Ahalya and of Amphitryon and Alcmena. The human husband and the divine impersonator may never appear together, and the emphasis may shift
from the problem of telling the two men apart to other themes, such as
the semidivine parentage of children. But among those myths in which the
central problem is telling one male from another is a subcorpus in which a
number of gods present themselves in forms identical to that of the human lover and the victim must choose between them all. In this subgroup
the issue of individualism, already made generic by the contrast between
one entire species and another (human and nonhuman), is made even
more generic by the existence of a whole group of gods, and the criteria of
choice are correspondingly even more sharply focused on the properties
of immortals in contrast with mortals. This more extreme, more dramatic
form of the identity crisis is the lineup.

Within this extreme of the genre, divine lineups prevail; there are relatively few myths in which the human impostor, who is often an identical
twin, proliferates into triplets or larger groups. Multiplicity, in contrast
with mere doubling, seems to be primarily a divine prerogative (with
a few notable exceptions, such as the film about multiple clones actually
entitled *Multiplicity* [1996]). Indra, who goes it alone when he seduces
Ahalya, becomes one of a group of gods who try to seduce Damayanti. But
before we consider that story we should look at another, earlier story on
which it depends, a story about the paradigmatic doublers in Vedic
mythology, the Ashvins.

SUKANYA AND THE ASHVINS

The tale of the Ashvins (the half-horse twin sons of Saranyu) and Sukanya (whose name means "Beautiful Girl") has a cryptic Vedic source[1] and is told in some detail in the *Jaiminiya Brahmana*, c. 900 B.C.E.:

SUKANYA'S CHOICE

The aged sage Cyavana said to his sons, "Put me down on the sacrificial place and go away." They said, "We cannot do that, for people will cry out against us and revile us, saying, 'They are abandoning their father.'" "No," he said, "by this means you will be better off, and by this I hope to become young again. Leave me and go forth." As he gave them this command, they placed him at the fountain of youth on the Sarasvati River and went away. As he was left behind, he wished, "Let me become young again, and find a young girl for a wife, and sacrifice with a thousand (cows)."

Just then Sharyata the descendant of Manu settled down with his clan near him. The young boys who were cowherds and shepherds smeared Cyavana with mud and balls of dust and cowshit and ashes. Cyavana then produced a condition among the Sharyatis so that no one recognized anyone else: a mother did not know her son, nor a son his mother. Sharyata said, "Have you seen anything around here that could have caused this state of affairs?" They said to him, "Nothing but this: there is an old man on his last legs lying there. The boys who are cowherds and shepherds smeared him today with mud and balls of shit and dust and ashes. This has happened because of that."

Sharyata said, "That was Cyavana, the son of Bhrigu. His sons have left him in the sacrificial place and gone away." Then Sharyata ran up to Cyavana and said, "Honor to you, great sage; have mercy, sir, on the Sharyatis." Now, Sharyata had a beautiful daughter named Sukanya. Cyavana said, "Give me Sukanya." ... They gave her to him, but they said to her, "My dear girl, this is a worn-out old man, who will not be able to run after you. As soon as we have harnessed the horses, run after us right away."

And so, when they had harnessed the horses, she stood up and was about to run after the clan, but Cyavana said, "Serpent, come and help your friend to save his life." And a black snake rose up right against her as she was about to go. When she saw it, she sat down again.

The two Ashvins, who have no share in the Soma offerings, happened to be wandering about there. They came to Sukanya and said, "My dear girl, this is an old man, not whole, not fit to be a husband. Be our wife." "No," she said, "I will be the wife of the man to whom my father gave me." Then they went away, but Cyavana had overheard them, and he said to

Sukanya, "My dear girl, what was all that noise about?" She told him what they had said.

Cyavana was very pleased about that. He told her, "Those were the two Ashvins; they will come tomorrow and speak to you in the same way. Now, you say to them, '*You* are the ones who are not whole, for though you are gods, you do not drink the Soma.' Then they will ask you, 'Who can see to it that we may share in the Soma?' 'My husband,' you say. This is my hope of becoming young again."

The next day, the two Ashvins came and said the same thing, and she said what Cyavana had told her to say. Then they said to him, "Sage, sir, make us share the Soma." "All right," said he, "and you make me young again." They drew him down into the fountain of youth of the Sarasvati River.

He said, "My dear girl, we will all come out looking the same; by this characteristic mark [lakshana], you will know me." They did all come out looking the same, the handsomest men in the world; but she recognized him and could tell them apart. "This is my husband," she said, and they said to him, "Sage, we have granted your desire: you have become young again. Now teach us so that we may share the Soma." Now, Indra had threatened to cut off the head of Dadhyanc if he told anyone the secret of the sacrifice: how the sacrifice is made whole when the head is cut off. The Ashvins gave Dadhyanc the head of a horse, through which he told them the secret of the sacrifice. Indra cut off that head, and then the Ashvins replaced Dadhyanc's head. Thus the Ashvins became sharers in the Soma.[2]

The old man is abandoned by his sons (a theme doubled when the young sons of King Sharyata too mistreat him), though the text goes out of its way to tell us that this was his own wish. His wife too plans to abandon him, but she changes her mind when she sees his magical phallic powers incarnate in the big black snake that rises up right against her; and finally she makes him young, indirectly accomplishing his initial goal.

The problem of recognition is foreshadowed by the young boys' failure to recognize the great sage; when the king recognizes who it is, he remedies the initial insult. That insult was appropriately avenged by a curse of nonrecognition: a mother did not know her son nor a son his mother (a common basis for incest); a parallel variant in another Brahmana merely says that fathers fought with sons, and brothers with brothers.[3] A later variant, in the *Mahabharata,* perhaps recalling the shit with which Cyavana was pelted, says that Cyavana stopped up the piss and shit of Sharyata's army;[4] in a still later variant, he also stops up the piss and shit of the elephants, camels, and horses;[5] and in a contemporary, rather bowdlerized comic book version, there is just a "strange ailment."[6] Sukanya then fails to recognize the Ashvins; Cyavana has to explain to her who they are. These failures are resolved in the final recognition, Sukanya's recognition of Cyavana, made possible because he teaches her a characteristic mark *(lakshana)* by which she can know him. What is the mark? We are never told.

The conflict between Cyavana and his sons is expressly denied in the opening verses of this story (and is even further muted in a parallel text, which merely says, "When the Bhrigus reached the world of heaven, Cyavana, the son of Bhrigu, was left behind, worn out and like a witch"). The young boys mock the old man, and he becomes young again, but he does not become immortal. The Ashvins reconstitute him in the water, but they cannot give him the watery boon that he gives them: the elixir of immortality, the Soma. Thus the Ashvins further "twin" themselves by giving the sage Cyavana a form identical with their own. Though they remain somewhat déclassé because of their continuing affection for human beings, they alone of all of Saranyu's children escape death.

The *Mahabharata* adds an interesting prelude, explaining how Cyavana and Sukanya first met and came to marry:

THE BLINDING OF CYAVANA

Cyavana was meditating in an anthill when the beautiful young princess Sukanya came along and saw his two eyes gleaming red out of the hill. He desired her and called to her, but his throat was dry and she did not hear him. Then, seeing the two eyes and wondering, "What is this?," in confusion and curiosity she pierced the eyes of the old man with a thorn. The old sage became furious, and the king gave Sukanya to him in order to appease his fury.[7]

In this version, Sukanya herself commits the sin, blinding the sage (perhaps in unconscious punishment for his desire for her, his sexual gaze). She is therefore the appropriate person to make up for the problem that she herself has now caused. After she has married Cyavana, the Ashvins come to her and say, "How could your father have given such a beautiful girl to an old man beyond the pleasures of sex?" and they offer to make Cyavana young and handsome. Again youth is the issue, and we are told even less about how it is that she can distinguish her mortal husband from the gods, for they come up out of the lake "all young and divinely handsome, wearing the same outward appearance." The text simply says,

"Sukanya decided with mind and heart, and chose her own husband."

In the *Bhagavata Purana* (c. 900 C.E.), again Sukanya pricks the sage's eyes with a thorn, and when it comes to the restoration by the Ashvins again there is no sign or mark, and all three look alike, but this time the gods themselves assist her:

SUKANYA'S FATHER'S SUSPICIONS

Seeing them all of the same form, with the glory of the Sun, not knowing her own husband, she took refuge in the two Ashvins. They were so satisfied with her fidelity to her husband that they pointed out her husband to her and went off to heaven. But then her father came there and saw a man with the glory of the Sun by her side. He was not very pleased in his mind, and he said, "What is this you have desired? You have deceived and abandoned your husband, whom all the world honored, a sage swallowed by old age, and you have taken a lover who just came along on the road." Smiling at her father as he talked like this, she said, "Daddy, this is your son-in-law, Cyavana the son of Bhrigu." And when she told him all that had happened, he was amazed and pleased and embraced his daughter.[8]

The gods intervene in this text to help Sukanya identify her husband, but they are not available when Sukanya's father comes by and fails to identify him, so that Sukanya herself must help him to recognize Cyavana. The assumption, and accusation, that if a woman's transformed husband does not look like her husband he must be her lover, is a frequent leitmotiv in this corpus. Sukanya's father, like Saranyu's, is concerned that she not dishonor her husband.

Divine intervention is the key to the recognition when the *Devi Purana* retells the story, c. 1200 C.E. But before that happens, the prelude is retold in a way that expands upon Sukanya's father's suspicion that she might have a lover, which he expresses here even before Cyavana is transformed:

SUKANYA'S FATHER'S DOUBTS

Sukanya saw Cyavana in an anthill. He did not desire her, but rather pleaded with her, "Go away and don't stick that thorn into the anthill!" When she nevertheless blinded him, Cyavana said to the king, "What shall I do, your majesty? I have lost my eyes and am overcome with old age. Who will serve a blind man? I am blind and alone. Give me your daughter who has lotus eyes." The king thought to himself, "How could I be happy if I gave my own daughter, who is like a daughter of the gods, to a blind, old, deformed man? If she, who has lovely brows and is tormented by the five arrows of the god of erotic love, marries Cyavana, who is blind and old, how will she pass the time? Desire is hard to conquer when one is young, especially for a woman who is very beautiful, even when she has a husband who is her equal; how much more so if she has a husband who is old and has no eyes? When Ahalya, who had beauty and youth, married Gautama the ascetic, that lovely woman was seduced by Indra very quickly, and afterwards her husband cursed her when he found out that dharma had been transgressed. Therefore I will endure my misery, but I will not give my lovely daughter (to him)." Sukanya, however, volunteered to be given to the sage and insisted that she would be faithful to her husband, and her father gave her to Cyavana.[9]

The father's argument seems to be that Sukanya will be unfaithful to her husband because he is blind—blind both in the sense that he is deformed and unattractive and in the sense that he cannot keep an eye on her to guard against her sexual restlessness. The reference to Ahalya is well chosen, since Ahalya faced the same problem that Sukanya is about to face: choosing between her husband and a god who looks just like him (Indra). But Ahalya differs from Sukanya in two significant ways: where Cyavana was made to resemble a god, Ahalya's lover changed himself to resemble the mortal husband; and Ahalya made the wrong choice—she mistook the god for her husband.

The theme of sight and blindness continues to be important as the *Devi Purana* goes on to narrate the scene with the Ashvins:

THE RESTORATION OF CYAVANA'S SIGHT

One day the Ashvins came playfully to Cyavana's hermitage. When they saw Sukanya bathing, they were completely enchanted by her and asked her who she was and who was her husband. She said, "King Sharyata, my father, gave me, through a kind of accident, to be the good wife of Cyavana. My husband is blind and a very old ascetic. I serve him night and day, which gives me pleasure." The Ashvins said to Sukanya, "Why should a beautiful young girl waste her life with a blind old man? Choose another husband, one of us." When Sukanya took umbrage and threatened to curse them, they said, "Calm down. Know that we are the physicians of the gods; let us make your husband young and handsome. Then choose as your husband one from among the three of us when we have the same form and bodies, O you who are so smart and clever." She was amazed and went to Cyavana and said, "My lord, the two sons of the Sun came to your hermitage and saw me, lovely in all of my body parts, and were overcome by lust. They said, 'We will make your husband an adolescent with a divine body, and sight. We will give him the same limbs and form that we have, and you must choose your husband from the three of us.' So I came to ask you. The magic illusion *[maya]* of the gods is hard to recognize; I don't know if this is some trick that those two are playing." He replied, "Let us do what they say quickly, without hesitation."

They went into the pond and all came out similar. She prayed to the Goddess, who put into her heart the knowledge of which was her husband, and she chose him. Thus they gave her a boon when they saw her fidelity to her husband, and by the grace of the Goddess the two gods were satisfied. And so Cyavana obtained beauty, his two eyes, his wife, and youth. And he was so happy that he offered the Ashvins a boon, and they asked him to make them Soma drinkers.[10]

Since the Ashvins do not help her make her choice, as they do in the *Bhagavata Purana*, she invokes the Goddess for this purpose. We are still not told the mark by which Sukanya recognizes her husband. But whereas in the other versions, Cyavana gets his youth by promising to make the Ashvins immortal (by giving them the Soma), in this version Sukanya gets Cyavana his youth all by herself, through her fidelity to her husband (her *sati-dharma* or *pati-vratya*), and Cyavana just throws in the Soma at the end as an extra bonus for the Ashvins. And there is another way in which Sukanya has more agency in this text: the Ashvins offer Cyavana youth and beauty, but when Sukanya repeats the offer she adds "and sight," and at the end we are told that he did in fact get his eyes back. Thus Sukanya's ability to see her husband when he is physically identical with the Ashvins transforms Cyavana's original inability to see her or anyone else.

The tension between different forms of seeing and blindness, knowing and ignorance, is what drives this myth. Sukanya always knows who Cyavana is: she recognizes his worth when her father and her brothers mock his superficial appearance, and she defends him again when the Ashvins mock him. As usual in these stories, the woman sees more than the man; she is not fooled, but this time the story regards her intelligence as a Good Thing—because she uses it in the service of her husband. Cyavana, however, suffers a mental transformation as profound as his physical transformation. The true sight, the true knowledge, is present from the start, but it is hidden and has to be uncovered, discovered—or, rather, rediscovered. This preexisting latent knowledge is actualized through the myth; Cyavana needs Sukanya to recognize him in order for him to become what he already is. Sukanya blinds Cyavana so that he can see, pokes out his eyes so that he can be given new young eyes, to see himself as she has always seen him, young and virile[11]—powers that he demonstrates to Sukanya's satisfaction by showing her his snake.

A similar activation of latent knowledge characterizes the Ashvins' access to immortality through the head of a horse (the mythical counterpart of Cyavana's snake),[12] which is the sequel to the story of Cyavana's rejuvenation. Dadhyanc has the equine secret of immortality, but he needs a horse head to tell it to the Ashvins, who must actually already know the secret (with their own horse's heads) but have no access to it except by giving (their own) horse head to someone else to use to tell it to them.

The comic book version of the Sukanya story follows the *Devi Purana* (though it claims that its version is "adapted mainly from the Mahabharata") in emphasizing the blindness of Cyavana. King Sharyata says to Cyavana, "My daughter . . . blinded you," and Cyavana also says "She has . . . blinded me," and, when he asks for her in marriage, "I will need someone to look after me, blinded and helpless as I am." When Sukanya meets the Ashvins, and they tell her they are "physicians to the gods," she wonders, "Will they be able to restore my husband's sight?" And she says, "I am Sukanya, the wife of sage Chyavana. But alas! He is blind." The Ashvins say, "Surely your father must be a cruel man to have given you in marriage to a blind, old sage." In this they imply not merely that she doesn't enjoy looking at an old man but also that he does not enjoy looking at (and therefore making love to) her. The Ashvins therefore offer first of all to restore his vision and then also to give him back his youth, on condition that she can spot him when he looks like them. They emerge from the pond looking alike, and she prays to the Goddess, who appears to her and says, "Look carefully. Only the eyes of mortals blink." This is the mark by which she recognizes her mortal husband, Cyavana.

NALA AND DAMAYANTI

The criterion of blinking eyes probably migrated into the comic book version of the Sukanya story from another myth that closely resembles it—and was evidently perceived as closely resembling it—, the story of Nala and Damayanti, which like the story of Cyavana and Sukanya turns upon the problem of telling the god from the mortal and the preference for the mortal. But now at last we learn what mark or sign there might be to tell your husband from a resembling immortal. This story, first told in the *Mahabharata* and retold throughout Indian history with many interesting variations, is also a paradigmatic text for Western Indologists, in part because the standard Sanskrit primer (by Charles Lanman) begins with it, so that the opening lines (*asid raja nalo nama,* "There was a king named Nala") plays the same role in Indology that the opening lines of Caesar (*gallia omnis divisa est in partes tres,* "All Gaul is divided in three"—another tale of splitting) played for earlier generations of classicists. (How appropriate that the prototypical Roman text is about politics, the prototypical Hindu text about sex—and politics.)

There are two episodes of recognition in the story of Nala and Damayanti; let us postpone the second for the moment and here consider the first, in which Damayanti must recognize Nala among four gods who have taken his form on the day of her wedding self-choice (*svayamvara,* a ceremony in which a princess puts a garland over the head of the man she chooses to marry):

DAMAYANTI'S DILEMMA

Nala and Damayanti fell in love merely from hearing about one another from a swan. But four gods—Indra, Yama, Agni, and Varuna, the four "World-Protectors"—heard that Damayanti was going to hold a self-choice, and they made Nala promise to go to her to plead for them; they gave him the power to enter the well-guarded harem. As soon as he saw Damayanti, Nala desired her, but he mastered his heart to keep his promise to the gods. When Damayanti's companions saw Nala's beauty they exclaimed, "Who is he? Is he a god?" And Damayanti asked him, "Who are you, handsome? You have come like an immortal. How did you get in here unobserved?" He said, "I am Nala, and I have come here as the messenger of the gods. It is by their power that I have entered here unobserved." She bowed to the gods and said to Nala, smiling, "I am yours. If you refuse me who love you, I will kill myself." Nala said to her, "How can you want a mortal man, when the gods, the World-Protectors, await you? I am not worthy of the dust from their feet. Set your heart on them, for a mortal man who displeases the gods dies. Save me; choose the gods." She told him she had a plan by which no fault would attach to him: she would choose him from among the gods at the self-choice ceremony. Nala reported to the gods, "By your power, no one saw me enter except Damayanti. I told her about you but she has set her heart on me, and she will choose me."

On the day of the self-choice, Damayanti saw five men standing there, entirely identical in appearance; any one of them she looked at seemed to her to be Nala. She wondered, "How can I know which are the gods, and which is Nala?" She remembered that she had heard, from old people, of the identifying signs *[lingani]* of the gods, but still she saw none of them on the men standing before her. Then she prayed to the gods, by her faithfulness to Nala, begging them to point Nala out to her and to display their own forms so that she could recognize him. The gods were moved by her pitiful request, and demonstrated their divine identifying signs. She saw all the gods without sweat, with unblinking eyes, with unwithered garlands, without dust, and standing without touching the ground, and she saw Nala revealed by his shadow, his withered garland, his dustiness and sweatiness, his blinking eyes, and his feet on the ground. She chose Nala for her husband.[13]

Conventional hyperbole explicitly likens Nala, like most heroes and heroines of classical Sanskrit literature, to the various gods; in a Telugu version of the story, he is "just like Indra, brilliant as the Sun, gentle as the Moon, remarkably similar to Varuna, akin to Kubera, equal to the Ashvins."[14] He is so godlike that the women in the harem mistake him for a god, and even Damayanti at first wonders at his godlike powers of invisibility, though she soon finds out that he is human. So the gods return the compliment by imitating him, making the cliché come true. The guardians of the quarters, or World-Protectors (who also desire Ahalya in one late text, perhaps influenced by the tale of Damayanti),[15] are often invoked together in the Vedic sacrifice. Three of them—Indra, Yama, and Agni—are, as we have seen, involved in other myths of doubling.

Like Sukanya, who recognized her husband because of a characteristic mark *[lakshana]* that he taught her, Damayanti recognizes her lover by the identifying signs *[lingani]* of his mortality, the normal human flaws that all of us share with him; and she recognizes the divine impersonators by their (abnormal) lack of those signs.[16] (The fact that *linga* also comes to mean "penis" may also be relevant here.) These criteria—a shadow, withered garland, dust, sweat, blinking eyes, and feet on the ground—are also, with some minor variations, the characteristics of Buddhist angels about to fall from heaven: their garlands wither, their clothes get dirty, perspiration pours from their armpits, they become ugly, and they no longer enjoy the world of the angels.[17] Thus lack of beauty is the Buddhist equivalent of the lack of a shadow, and distaste for heaven the equivalent of feet that touch the earth.

What is the meaning of the signs by which Damayanti recognizes the gods? Some (such as the faded garlands and the dust) are particularly Indian; others (such as the shadow, the blinking, and the feet) occur as criteria in other cultures as well. Sweating, in an ancient Greek or Indian statue* of a deity or a human, is a sign of life. Sweating is also the crucial criterion in a very different sort of text, the film *Total Recall* (1990): when the hero is told that he is merely a dream double of his true self, he sees through the illusion by noting a drop of sweat on the man making the argument—a man who also claims to be an illusion; the hero apparently (and rightly, in this case) assumes that illusory doubles, like gods, don't sweat.

Setting aside, for a moment, the feet, we might note that two other signs—blinking and the presence of shadows—are closely related: both are phenomena of sunlight and vision, and they are the only two criteria of mortality in the version of the story of Nala and Damayanti told in *The Ocean of the Rivers of Story*.[18] It is significant that Damayanti falls in love with Nala before she ever *sees* him; vision does not rank high in her criteria of identification. There is a minor lapse in the *Mahabharata* text: though Nala is expressly said to have a shadow, the gods are not said to lack them.[19] That gods have no shadows may have been such a truism even at this early period that shadowlessness didn't have to be listed among their defining criteria.

We have noted some of the meanings of blinking.* Other meanings more directly pertinent to Damayanti's dilemma are captured in the story of the nymph Varuthini, who falls in love with a mortal who does not love her; a demigod takes the form of the mortal to seduce her, first making her promise to keep her eyes closed as he makes love to her.[20] In the Telugu version of this story, when Varuthini is pining for her rejecting lover she says she wishes she were a human woman and could die; being so unhappy she is sorry to be immortal.[21] Her envy of mortals, who can die, resonates with her choice of a mortal lover, and the association of blinking eyes with mortality is crucial to the verse describing Varuthini "as she is beginning to fall in love with the hapless mortal who has strayed onto her path":

> Fluttering glances healed / her inability to blink, / and for the first time / she was sweating. / Even her surpassing understanding / was healed by the new / confusion of desire. / Like the beetle that, from ever concentrating / on its enemy, the bee, / itself *becomes* a bee, / by studying that human being / she achieved humanity / with her own body.[22]

The erotic passion that makes women's eyes flutter and makes their bodies sweat here makes the goddess mortal. The Telugu verse implies that,

by loving a mortal, she herself took on his mortality in some ways—
"achiev[ing] humanity with her own body" being a reversal of the usual
goal for a holy man in Hindu mythology, which is to reach heaven with his
own body. The verse thus plays on the corpus of stories in which people
are reborn as whatever they have been obsessed with, particularly at the
moment of death.[23] In this case, the obsession is mortality itself. Or, as
Shulman puts it, "This is a portrait of ontic transformation, which makes
a goddess—who, like all her species, has no eyelids and therefore cannot
blink, just as she cannot sweat or even properly touch the ground—into a
mortal woman."[24] The blinking of the eyes is a symbol of the fact that we
mortals cannot always see straight—especially in matters of the heart or
groin—as well as a reference to the eyes of Brahma, each blink of which
represents a night for mortals. It is also a prefiguration of that moment in
which, unlike the gods, we will close our eyes forever.

But like other criteria of immortality and identity, these are not fool-
proof. The gods, as we have just seen, can manipulate them: sometimes
they have them, sometimes they do not. For Damayanti, at first they do
not, and Damayanti is ultimately able to identify her husband not by her
powers of recognition, dwelling within herself, but by her faithfulness to
him, the ultimate power of a woman in Hinduism, which compels the
gods (or at least persuades them) to reveal themselves to her. She is defined only by reference to her man. Or to take a less feminist tack, she
knows him because she knows herself. Her steadfastness and faithfulness
to her husband are not what reveal her to him but what reveal him to her.

The story was elaborately retold in the *Naishadiyacarita* of Shri
Harsha, in the twelfth century C.E. The scene in which Damayanti must
choose Nala from among the gods who resemble him (the scene of the five
Nalas, called the *pancanaliya*) is given a lovely poetic twist: the goddess
Sarasvati (goddess of Speech), fearing the wrath of the gods but sympathetic to Damayanti, simultaneously describes the gods (for Damayanti)
and Nala (to please the gods). She does this through a series of riddling
verses that can be read with two different meanings:

DAMAYANTI'S CONFUSION

Sarasvati described Indra without revealing his disguise as Nala, and her
whole speech applied so equally well to Indra and Nala, and Agni [Fire]
and Nala, that Damayanti could derive no conclusive evidence from her
ears or her eyes and was unable to perceive any difference between them.
Her mind said of the same one, "He is Nala" and "He is Fire/not Nala

[anala/a-nala]." She thought, "How can there be any mark [cihna] of a descendant of Manu [i.e., a mortal human] to distinguish my lord from among this group of five who have cast this delusion over my mind? Why don't the gods bear their signs [lakshanas]—with no dust on their bodies, and so forth?" [Then she worshipped the gods, and with their help she figured out the double meanings of Sarasvati's verses. Only then,] at that moment Damayanti saw that the gods did not touch the earth, but Nala did; that the gods didn't blink their eyes, but the king [Nala] seemed to be winking at her, as if to say, "Come and be with me." The gods had no dust on them, but Nala did; and he, but not they, perspired, as if he was heated by his separation from her. The garlands of the gods were fresh, but Nala's was faded.[25]

The doubling of words masks the doubling of people, and the visual criteria, as usual, fail, even though some of them are now glossed as revelations of psychological states rather than ontological status.

Even before Harsha gets to the self-choice, he inserts into the previous episodes of the story a series of images of illusion and doubling that prefigure the climactic scene of impersonation:

THE PHANTOM NALA AND THE PHANTOM DAMAYANTI

Nala was so handsome that every woman saw him in her dreams, uttered his name by mistake, and aroused her erotic feelings in sexual play by imagining her husband in the form of Nala. Damayanti had artists paint herself and Nala on the wall, and Nala drank in her portrait on a wall with eyes unblinking because of his eagerness, so that "lack of blinking" and "love at first sight" each claimed to have caused his tears.[26]

When the gods summoned Nala to employ him as their messenger, they recognized him because the features of his beauty corresponded to what they had heard of him before. Indra made Nala invisible so that he moved freely among the women in the inner apartments, seeing everything, but, perhaps because of the illusions worked by the god of erotic love (Kama), Nala saw Damayanti everywhere. Since he saw the other women along with the illusory Damayantis, he did not like them or mistake them for Damayanti, and when he recovered from the illusion, he grieved to see her no longer. The women bumped into him and thrilled at his touch, as they thrilled to see his reflection. They saw their own reflections in the air on his invisible jewels, and when they threw a ball, it hit him and bounced back reflected from him. They saw his reflection on the floor and his shadow and his footprints in the flowers that they had scattered on the floor. But though his reflection was clearly visible on the jeweled floor, no one noticed it among the portraits of him that had been painted by Damayanti's friends to divert her.[27]

Then Damayanti came upon him, but he could not distinguish her among the false Damayantis he saw, and she couldn't see him because he was invisible. She threw a garland at the neck of an illusory Nala [whom she imagined], but it fell on the neck of Nala, who was standing there. Nala was astonished to find the real garland from the woman he was imagining, and she was surprised to see it disappear. They were in the same place, thinking that they were in different places, and they actually embraced in the midst of their illusory selves. She felt his touch but thought it was an illusion; he saw her but could not bring himself to hold her since he was paralyzed. Corresponding as they did in every way to their real selves, they rejoiced to embrace, even when each discovered that the other was unreal.[28]

[Then Nala made himself visible and told Damayanti that he was the messenger of the gods—though he did not say that he was Nala.] But just as she could not keep silent when she had the illusion of seeing Nala, so she could not keep from speaking in the presence of the real Nala. In those who are bewitched, is there any power to tell real from false? Thinking him to be a god as beautiful as Nala, and remarking upon his resemblance to the portrait of Nala that others had (verbally) painted, she praised the beauty of her beloved in him. She said to him, "You aren't Kama, because he has no body [Shiva had burnt him to ashes]; nor one of the Ashvins, because there are always two together. What is the use of any other distinctive marks? Your beauty is the distinctive feature that makes you superior to them. Nala is your reflection in this ocean of the world. For the Creator never made two things completely alike, except for an object and its reflection. And a mortal woman can never be worthy of a god."[29]

When she asked him to stay, Nala revealed that he was Nala. And Damayanti, who had blamed herself for her attraction to the messenger of the gods, was now relieved to find that it was in fact Nala.[30]

The gods had one last hope: "Damayanti might, by chance, mistake us for Nala and accept us." And so the four gods, Indra and the others, became a miraculous group of four false Nalas. But none succeeded in achieving similarity to Nala; for the artificial is indeed different from the natural. They kept looking at their faces in the mirror and breaking it. Indeed, when the Creator brought those "kings" to Damayanti, she could see the difference between them and Nala. But there was no difference between gods and kings, because the breeze of the yak-tail fans kept everyone from sweating, the wonders of each object kept everyone from blinking, and the parasols kept all the garlands from fading. Moreover, the people couldn't tell the difference between gods and kings because both spoke Sanskrit, since the kings feared they might not understand one another's dialects.[31]

Damayanti fulfilled their wishes, for she gave them the illusion of winning her when she appeared to them in their dreams. But the kings said among themselves, referring to the magic Nalas, "Well, there are many like him." The envious, when inferior to a rival, take comfort in likening him to others. Finally, Damayanti worshipped the gods, who revealed their signs. She chose Nala, and the gods revealed their own forms. The disappointed suitors were consoled by being given Damayanti's companions, to whom she had taught all her arts, for their wives.[32]

This passage, which I have constructed by stringing together verses from a much, much longer poem, is exhibit A for the case for sexual fantasy;[33] Nala and Damayanti are so dazzling in their beauty that they delude everyone (the women fantasize about him, the men about her), including one another. Nala and Damayanti almost miss one another in the darkness of their erotic fantasies; the illusions of love are reflected in the illusions of art: verbal portraits and visual portraits* are mistaken for the real thing. Nala appears as a kind of reverse vampire:* mirrors and portraits reflect his image, but he himself, like a god who leaves nothing but his shadow, cannot be seen. (In this he is like Bhavabhuti's Sita, who comes invisible into Rama's presence.) People who aren't there are mistaken for those who are, and the reverse; gods are mistaken for mortals, and mortals for gods. Gods are jealous of mortal men, and the other human kings are jealous of Nala. The traditional distinctions between gods and mortals are constantly undercut and satirized: people fail to blink not because they are immortal but because they are in love or dazzled by royal splendor (a trope that we have already encountered in Varuthini, who stopped blinking as she stared at the Brahmin and yearned to be mortal). Yet true love does have a kind of discernment: though Nala cannot tell the difference between the real Damayanti and his illusion of her, he does know the difference between her and all other (real) women. The gods, on the other hand, are satisfied in the end with illusory Damayantis and the human kings with other women trained to imitate her. They settle for the doubles, where Damayanti would not. If the story of Nala is a story about what it means to be human, and about the schizoid nightmare of having two of everything,[34] this theme reaches its ultimate expression in this text. But it has a happy ending, when the sense of touch comes into play: the poet tells us that later, on the night after they had made love, Nala went to Damayanti and crept up behind her and put his hands over his eyes; but she felt the difference in his touch and said, "Darling, I recognize you. . . ."[35]

The folk traditions rang many changes in their retellings of Damayanti's dilemma. The singers of a version from the contemporary Dhola epic of Braj Kshetra, in eastern Rajasthan and western Uttar Pradesh, sometimes call it the *Nal Purana* or even "our *Mahabharata*":

NAL AND VASUKI'S DAUGHTER

Nal met the daughter of the great Naga serpent Vasuki. She wished to marry him, but he regarded her as his daughter because of his close friendship with her father, and he told her that he could marry her only if she would be reborn again as a human. She was reborn as a human princess named Damayanti, and when she was of age her father sent an invitation to Indra to come to her self-choice, but the swan carrying the invitation fell into Nal's hands instead. The king sent a second message to Indra, and both Indra and Nal arrived to claim Damayanti. Because Nal was human, Damayanti was able to identify him despite Indra's tricks.[36]

Here the contest between multiple gods and Nala is reduced to a single combat between Nal and Indra, rather like the conflict between Gautama* (Ahalya's husband) and Indra.* Susan S. Wadley, who recorded the story, does not here specify what the tricks or the telltale "human" qualities are, but her 1996 essay reproduces a delightful picture of the self-choice, with characters labeled "Indra" and "Nal" looking absolutely identical. Moreover, in the second part of the story, which we will soon consider, when Nal and Damayanti are united after a long absence Nal's shadow is the clue to his humanity, revealed to Damayanti (who is repeatedly called a *pativrat*, faithful to her husband) by the Goddess, and this recognized sign of mortality is augmented by other, more particular signs that identify Nal as not merely a generic mortal but an individual mortal.

A Kannada folktale collected by A. K. Ramanujan again narrows the field of gods to one (Indra), but also reverses the gender. Now the choice must be made by the youngest of four princes, who marries four goddesses, including the daughters of Indra and Agni (two of the four gods who tried to bamboozle Damayanti). Eventually, Indra sets the young prince four tasks that he must accomplish in order to keep his each of his four wives, and the last test, to keep Indra's daughter, is this:

THE PRINCE AND THE FOUR LOOK-ALIKES

He was faced with four look-alikes that he could not tell apart, though he looked at them closely. Suddenly he remembered the *bharani* worm [whom he had saved from a spider's web], which arrived from nowhere, now a winged insect. It touched the sari of Indra's daughter and flew in circles around her head. At once the prince said, "There, that's my wife!" and seized her hand. He had won her, too.[37]

Here the usual criteria of immortality are replaced by a well-known folk theme: the animal helper who appears at the moment of crisis to repay the hero or heroine for an earlier good deed. The good deed in this text functions as the equivalent of the good character, the steadfast fidelity, by which Sukanya and Damayanti persuaded the gods to reveal themselves. But in this myth the man who must select his wife from among four women also gets to keep four women in the end (though not the four look-alikes). Moreover, the mortal man wants, and successfully chooses, an immortal wife, not a mortal one. We will return to that choice in our conclusion to this chapter.

DAMAYANTI AND NALA

Let us turn now to the second half of the story of Nala and Damayanti. Years after Damayanti had to distinguish Nala from four look-alike gods, she must do the opposite: she must recognize Nala within the form of a dwarf that does not look like him at all:

DAMAYANTI'S TESTS

Nala and Damayanti married and she gave birth to twins, a boy and a girl. But the demon of gambling and bad luck (Kali) entered Nala when he neglected to wash his feet; he gambled away his kingdom, and he and Damayanti were forced to go to the forest. When birds, incarnations of the dice, stole the clothes he had been wearing, Damayanti wrapped him in the other half of the single cloth that she was wearing. One night, in despair, he cut the piece of cloth in half as she slept, leaving her with one half, and he abandoned her there. The Kali in him wanted to leave her, but the husband wanted to stay with her; he was like a swing that goes back and forth. After a while, a snake magically transformed Nala into a dwarf named Bahuka ["Short-armed," or "Dwarf"] by biting him when he had taken ten steps, and Nala became the charioteer of a king, for Nala had been an expert horseman.

Damayanti became the servant of a queen. Her parents searched for her and a messenger recognized her by a tiny birthmark, a mole, between her eyebrows; it was hidden by dust, but he recognized the mark *(cihna)* and her and brought her home. They washed the dust off the mole, and her parents embraced her. For years Damayanti searched for Nala, sending out a messenger to recite the words, "Gambler, where did you go when you cut our cloth in half and abandoned me?" One day, she learned that Bahuka had said, in reply, "Faithful wives should never get angry, even if their husbands desert them—especially if birds stole the husband's clothes." To bring Nala to her, Damayanti sent a message to the king whom Nala served, announcing that she would hold a second ceremony of self-choice on the very next day, "Since she does not know whether Nala is dead or alive."

When Nala in the form of Bahuka heard this announcement, he thought, "Maybe she is doing this as a scheme for my sake. But women in this world are fickle by nature, and I did do a terrible thing. Still, how could she do such a thing, when she has had (my) children? I will go there to find out if this is true or not." He drove the king's chariot so swiftly that they were able to cover the hundred leagues in a single day, and the king began to suspect that, despite his appearance, the charioteer might be Nala; for who else could drive horses so well? "And great men, driven by the gods, sometimes live in disguise, so that it is hard to recognize them." As Bahuka drove the horses into the city, the chariot roared in a way that Nala's old horses, in the palace stables, recognized; they became excited, and so did Damayanti. But when she saw the deformed charioteer, she did not recognize him and thought that Nala must have taught him to make the chariot roar like that.

Still she had him questioned by her woman, Keshini, who asked him about Nala. Bahuka said, "King Nala left his two children here and went where he wanted. No one knows where Nala is; he is disguised and deformed. Only he himself knows Nala—and she who is closest to him. For Nala never announces his identifying signs *[lingani]* anywhere." Then Keshini said, "When Damayanti's messenger said, 'Gambler, where did you go when you cut our cloth in half and abandoned me?' you made a reply. Damayanti wants to hear what you said then." And Bahuka wept and replied, " 'Faithful wives should never get angry, even if their husbands desert them—especially if birds stole the husband's clothes.' " Keshini told Damayanti what he had said and how he had wept and revealed his emotional transformation *[vikara]*.

Then Damayanti suspected that this must be Nala, and she sent Keshini to observe him, and especially to note any divine clue or sign [*nimitta*, cause or omen] that she saw in him. Keshini went and noted the charioteer's identifying signs and the divine sign that she had seen while he was cooking the king's meat: low doorways grew tall as he approached them, and narrow openings opened wide; when he looked at an empty pot, it became full of water; when he held up a handful of grass, it burst into flame; when he touched fire, he was not burnt; and when he held flowers in his hands and pressed them, they blossomed and smelled sweet.

Damayanti suspected that he must be her husband Nala, revealed by his actions and behavior though he had taken the form of Bahuka. She sent Keshini to bring her some of the meat that Bahuka had cooked, and as soon as she tasted it she knew that the cook was Nala, for in the old days she had often tasted meat cooked by Nala. Then she sent Keshini to him with the twins, and Bahuka recognized them and took them on his lap and wept and said to Keshini, "They look just like my own pair of twins; that is why I am crying. But if you keep coming to meet me, people will get the wrong idea, for we are foreigners here. So you had better go."

Then Damayanti told her mother, "Suspecting that Bahuka was Nala, I tested him in various ways. The one remaining doubt is about his appearance." And with the permission of her father and mother, she had him brought to her room; she was wearing a red garment and her hair was matted and she was covered with mud and dirt. When he saw her he burst into tears, and she said to him, "Bahuka, did you ever see a righteous man who abandoned his sleeping wife in the forest? Who but Nala? And how had I offended him, to deserve this? How could he abandon me who had chosen him, rejecting the gods who stood before me? Me, his faithful and passionate wife, who bore his children?" She wept, and he wept again, and told her all that had happened to him, concluding, "But how could a wife ever abandon a devoted and loving husband and choose another, as you are doing?" Then she told him that she had proclaimed the self-choice only as a scheme to bring him there, purposely announcing it only in Nala's city and stating that it would take place in a day's time. "Who but you," she asked Nala, "could travel a hundred leagues in a single day?" Still Nala hesitated, but she called the elements to witness that she had done nothing wrong, even in her mind, and the Wind spoke from the sky, so that everyone could hear, affirming that Damayanti had been faithful to him even in her mind.[38]

There are important symbolic bonds between this part of the story and the earlier episode; the second self-choice is the mirror image of the first, and the disguises and recognitions in this part of the story balance those in the first part. Where, for instance, Nala's feet were one of the things that revealed his humanity, here again his feet prove the weak spot through

which disaster enters him. That disaster divides him against himself, someone vividly described as swinging back and forth like what we used to call
a schizophrenic, now a person with a multiple-personality disorder.* And
where in the earlier episode Nala speaks with the gods' voice but they look
like him, here it is the voice (more precisely, the voice of his horses and
chariot) that reveals him to Damayanti even when he does not look like
himself. (The horses are the first to recognize him; and both the king and
Damayanti recognize him by his skill with horses.) In their final con-
frontation, Damayanti wears the red garment, matted hair, and mud and
dirt that characterize the renunciant and exile, symbolizing the form she
had when he abandoned her.

Damayanti herself is hidden under ashes, like Cinderella, but is quickly
recognized by a partially obscured birthmark (an auspicious mark on the
forehead that other Hindu women paint on with collyrium). Then it is her
turn to recognize him. Where Nala in the first episode was mistaken for
someone higher (which Damayanti throws back in his face at the end, in
her final accusation: I rejected gods for you, and then you rejected me),
here he is mistaken for someone lower, literally smaller, a dwarf, as his
name indicates. The dwarf, however, is also the most famous disguise of
the god Vishnu, who took three expanding steps to trick the demons into
giving him (back) the triple universe;[39] the dwarf Nala, like the dwarf
Vishnu, has powers of expansion: low doorways rise before him. And like
the dwarf Vishnu, Nala takes numbered magic steps to become transformed through the magic of wordplay: on the tenth step, the snake bites
him, in a pun on the number ten *(dasha)* and the imperative of the verb
"bite" *(dasha)*.

There are several sorts of signs by which Damayanti recognizes Nala,
tests by which he proves who he is, and there are two different terms for
them in the Sanskrit text: there are the identifying signs *(lingani)* of Nala
as an individual, the same term that was used for the signs that identify
the gods as a class (the related term, *cihna,* is used for Damayanti's identifying mole); and there are the divine omens *(nimittani)* that identify Nala
as a human who is not merely a human. The identifying signs are intended
specifically for Damayanti to unravel, for, as Nala tells Keshini, only "she
who is closest to him" will know the identifying signs that he never makes
public. They are multiple, a chain of tests.

First is the riddle of abandonment, the riddle of memory, the words
that refer to something that only the two of them knew about. The riddle

is broken in half like the two halves of the cloth that Nala split when he left her, the cloth that the riddle is made of: her message is the first half, the accusation ("Gambler, you cut the cloth in half and abandoned me"), and his reply is the exactly parallel second half, the excuse ("Forgive me for abandoning you; the birds/dice stole my clothes"). The riddle occurs three times, twice in the exact same words and, at the end, in paraphrase, without the cloth or birds/dice: "Why did you abandon me?" "Why did *you* abandon *me*, by deciding to remarry?"

Then Damayanti recognizes Nala by a series of his actions and skills, beginning with his horsemanship and his cooking. Though Nala as Bahuka passes both tests (horsemanship, equated with nonremarriage, and cooking, a sign of intimacy), neither is definitive: he might have learnt the horsemanship from the real Nala, and even after she recognizes his cooking she worries about his changed appearance. But the twenty-four hour limit on the remarriage ceremony limits the field of possible suitors to Nala alone, by calling upon his unique horsemanship, and this sign then rebounds back for Damayanti, when she uses it to prove not her own identity (which he does not doubt) but her fidelity (which he does). It proves simultaneously who he is (a unique horseman) and that she has been true to him in bed (because she worded the wedding invitation to limit the field to the unique horseman).

(Jean Giraudoux's Alcmena too thinks that she can identify her husband by his horsemanship, but she is wrong. When horses' hoofs are heard offstage, she says to Amphitryon, "Here are your horses. Kiss me." And he replies, "My horses jog along easier than that; but I don't mind kissing you all the same." Later, Mercury refers to "the same gentle jog-trot by which Amphitryon recognizes his horses and Alcmena her husband's heart."[40] In this case, of course, she has *not* recognized the heartbeats—or the hoofbeats. Later, when Amphitryon returns, she mistakes him for Jupiter, in part because of his superhuman horsemanship; the nurse says, "I saw him from the ramparts, galloping his horse straight at the moat. . . . He took it in one leap," and Alcmena says, "But no one's ever done that!" When Amphitryon arrives and says, "Oh, damn my horses. I'll be off again in a moment," she remarks, "Damn his horses? That's certainly not Amphitryon."[41] Damayanti did not make those mistakes about Nala's horsemanship.)

Another aspect of Nala's behavior is also suggestive, though not finally persuasive: the emotional transformation that comes over him when he weeps, the *vikara* that simultaneously indicates his momentary change of mood (sudden sadness) and his apparently permanent change of form (from a prince into a dwarf). And finally Damayanti recognizes Nala through his own recognition of their resembling children, the inevitable twins of doubling parents, who look just like one another even as they "look just like" Bahuka's own twins. On this final occasion, Nala relaxes enough to tease Keshini about her repeated visits to him ("We can't go on meeting like this"), implying that she will be accused of being a messenger who woos for herself—just as he was when he first wooed Damayanti for the gods. Now at last, when he is in disguise, he can woo for himself.

Another version of the story was recently recorded in Rajasthan by Ann Grodzins Gold and Lindsey Harlan,[42] an entirely realistic version in which Damayanti must choose Nal from among kings, rather than gods, and he is made unrecognizable not by magic (as in the *Mahabharata*) but simply by misfortune. In the end, there are two queens, for Damayanti, too, is doubled, and when both the mother and the stepmother claim the child, there is a test to discover who is the real mother: the stepmother puts on a silk blouse, and Damayanti puts on a wooden breastplate, but Damayanti's milk squirts through the wood. As usual, Damayanti recognizes Nala by his good cooking (in this case, by its smell), and as usual, she must find Nala in order for him to find himself.

Damayanti is also doubled in the second part of the Dhola epic of Braj Kshetra (of which we have seen the first part, about Nal and Vasuki's daughter, now born as Damayanti):

NAL AND DAMAYANTI

In envious fury, Indra cursed Nal to have bad luck for twelve years; one day Nal and Damayanti became separated in the forest. After a while, Damayanti arranged another self-choice and invited the kings of fifty-two kingdoms. When the invitation came to the king whom Nal was serving in disguise, he asked Nal to drive the chariot to the self-choice in six days. Nal (who had received, in a previous adventure, Jaldariya, Indra's magical horse) wasted much time buying the most decrepit horses imaginable, and they had to make the journey in only an hour and a half. Damayanti knew that Nal could come in an hour, so she sent a servant to ask how long it took each king to arrive. Then she asked each to cook, but there was no fire anywhere in the kingdom and only Nal could light the dung for cooking. Finally, she adorned him with the garland, only to have Indra protest (again) and force her once again to identify Nal while he was disguised by Indra. Instructed by the goddess whom she worshipped at her home shrine, she recognized him as human by his shadow and as Nal by his ability to cook without coals.[43]

Here the episode of the self-choice is repeated, together with the criterion of the shadow, in combination with the tests that occur only in the second episode in the *Mahabharata:* the cooking (now reduced to the simple ability to light dung without fire) and the horses who are magically swift (now reduced to an hour and a half instead of twenty-four hours).[44]

The Dhola epic prefaces these two episodes with an entirely new story, about Nal and yet another woman, the goddess Motini, which involves other tests of identity that also occur in the second half of the *Mahabharata* story:

NAL AND THE GODDESS MOTINI

When Nal's mother was pregnant with him, her cowives plotted against her and persuaded the king that the child, when born, would kill his father. With great sorrow, the king sent a servant to kill the queen, but the servant killed a deer instead, and took back the deer's eyes to prove that she was dead. She gave birth to Nal, and a merchant adopted her as his daughter and raised Nal as his grandchild.

A goddess named Motini fell in love with Nal. Since she was worried about his caste when he said he was a merchant, she invited him to play dice in order to discover his identity. He declined at first, saying that it was a game only for those who wear turbans (i.e., kings); but when he won, it was clear that he must be of royal blood.

Motini and Nal married, but she said, "I may bring you only unhappiness. I am a devi's [goddess's] daughter and your kingdom will be destroyed because I cannot carry a child in my womb. Your lineage will be destroyed. If you marry a human, you will have children and your throne will survive." Motini came to the court of Nal's father, who fell in love with her, but she refused to marry anyone unless the *Nal Katha* [the story of Nal] were told.

Now, Vasuki's daughter had given Nal a flower that transformed him into a man a hundred years old. So transformed he had said, "O brother, I don't think that I'll be recognized by my love. . . . She will say, 'Where has this old man come from, almost dead.' She will kill me." Vasuki's daughter then gave him a second flower to restore him to his form as a handsome young man and told him to keep both flowers. Now Nal, as an old man, came to the court and told the *Nal Katha* [i.e., his own story up to that point]. The people of the court recognized Nal and reunited him with his

wife Motini. They sent for his mother too. He was himself again. But since
Motini could not bear children because of her nonhuman birth, she departed for Indra's heavenly kingdom so that Nal could marry again, returning to earth to intercede when he got into trouble.

[Then Nal married Damayanti. . . .]

The character of Damayanti has been split into two nonhuman women,
Motini and Vasuki's daughter, a goddess and a serpent woman, who devise
new solutions to new variants of the old problems. Several clues to Nal's
identity are expansions of themes that we know from the Sanskrit epic:
where he identified himself there by half of a riddle, here he identifies
himself by telling his entire life story (as Odysseus tells his in the *Odyssey*,
to *conceal* his identity), reciting an already existing text in a kind of frame-
jumping self-reference that we encountered when Indra called himself
"Ahalya's lover" in order to seduce Ahalya. Other clues are inversions of
themes from the Sanskrit epic: now dice are no longer the problem, but
part of the solution, part of his identification; and the male snake who
helps Nala in the Sanskrit epic becomes the daughter of the serpent king,
who gives him the gift of transformation into someone first old, then
young (and who apparently does not mind when his first concern is that
his other woman might not love him so transformed).

This telling introduces a new episode about Nal's birth and his abandonment by his parents, and a significant metaphor: commenting on Nal's
many troubles, the poet says, "When destruction comes to a man, / First
lightning falls on the brain, / One's own mother is as ferocious as a lion, /
And father seems like Yamraj." Yamraj, king Yama,* appears here in a
metaphor for the cruel father—an irony given the history of Yama's suf-
ferings at the hands of his own parents. Nal experiences what Freud called
the Family Romance: the noble child raised in disguise by people of lower
status.[45] His first, unconscious disguise comes when he presents himself to
the world as a merchant; he himself doesn't know who he is, doesn't know
that he is of royal blood.

The Family Romance often involves incest, as in the paradigmatic case
of Oedipus and in this very text in the episode of Nal and Vasuki's daughter, when the daughter of Nal's friend/brother wants him. Here, his father
wants his wife. The threat of incest, the danger of marrying someone too
close, is balanced by double incidents of the immortal-mortal romance
that presents the opposite danger of marrying someone too distant. This
theme occurs in both gender variants: a goddess (Motini) falls in love with

Nal, and then a god, Indra, falls in love with Vasuki's daughter. When Vasuki's daughter disregards the incest barrier, he tells her to be reborn as a (presumably unrelated) human, cleverly solving two class problems at once: that she is a goddess and that she is incestuously related to him.

But it is Nal's other wife, Motini, who explicitly raises the problem of class *(varna)*, a problem that we know from Saranyu and her husband, and raises it on two parallel levels: the tension between mortal and immortal and between low caste and high caste. At first Motini fears she is too distant from Nal, of a higher class than he, until Nal's skill at dice reveals his true social class (to her at least, if not to himself); his knowledge is his identity. This apparent conflict between Nal's apparent and real castes causes Motini to experience the dramatic ambivalence that Nal experiences in the *Mahabharata:* where he was torn in half, pulled and pushed, she is caught between cold and hot: "When she sees his beauty, she is like water; when she thinks of his caste, her body burns." And the Dhola epic jokes about one of the occasions when Motini descended to earth to help Nal: "Motini disguised herself as a young soldier and joined the army; she convinced Nal that the young soldier's hand was so soft because 'he' was a banya, a wealthy merchant." Here both gender difference and species difference (immortal versus mortal) are translated into and masked by caste difference: where Nal, a prince, says he is a merchant, Motini, a goddess, pretends to be a human, a male, and a merchant. The conflict between the larger classes of mortal and immortal, however, proves the more serious problem. Damayanti's preference for a mortal husband is here transformed into Nal's preference for a mortal wife, and the reasons for this are spelt out in this text: a goddess can't bear children.

PENELOPE

The second half of Damayanti's story tells of a man who returns to his wife after a long absence and must prove to her that he is her husband, despite the changes wrought by time and suffering. Homer tells the paradigmatic Greek instance of this theme in the *Odyssey:*

THE SIGN OF THE BED

When Odysseus returned to Ithaca after twenty years, disguised as a beggar who claimed to have known Odysseus, his old dog recognized him, and with his dying strength wagged his tail but had no strength to move toward his master, who gave no sign of recognition but secretly wept; and then the dog died. When Odysseus's wife, Penelope, first saw him, she gave no sign of recognizing him but said to him, "I think I will give you a test, to see if you really knew my husband. Tell me what he was wearing when he was your guest." And Odysseus replied, "Well, it was twenty years ago, but he was wearing a purple woolen cloak, and it was pinned with a clasp of gold, depicting a hound killing a fawn. None of the women could tear their eyes away from it [or him, *auton*]." And she recognized the sure signs that Odysseus had shown her.

Then Penelope instructed the old nurse Eurycleia to wash the stranger's feet, remarking to her, "Your master Odysseus was the same age, and probably has such hands and feet now, for mortals grow old quite suddenly in misfortune." And Eurycleia remarked, "I never saw anyone so like Odysseus in form and voice and feet," to which Odysseus replied, "Yes, old woman, that's just what people who have seen both of us with their own eyes always say, that we look just like one another." As she touched him, he turned away from the fire toward the darkness, for he thought she might recognize his scar. And indeed as soon as she washed him she recognized the scar that the white tusk of a boar had made in his leg above the knee when he was a young man, at the home of his mother's father, who had given him his name, Odysseus. She knew it by the touch, "by the feel," and she dropped the foot and said, "I didn't know you until I had touched all of my lord." Eurycleia wanted to tell Penelope right away, but Athena and Odysseus forbade her to do so.

After "the stranger" had killed all the suitors, Penelope told him to sleep in the hall or to let the maids make him a bed. But later, Eurycleia told Penelope that the stranger was Odysseus, insisting, "I will quote you a clear sign, that scar from the boar's white tusk long years ago." Penelope went downstairs, but she hesitated; she did not know him because he was wearing such wretched clothes; yet, as she said to her son, "If he really is Odysseus, then we will find other, better ways to know one another, for we two have signs, hidden from others, that we know." And Odysseus smiled and said to his son, "Let your mother test me, and she will understand sooner and better. But now, because I'm wearing such wretched clothes, she won't *say* who I am."

Finally, Odysseus said to Penelope, "You strange woman, the most stubborn of all women. What other woman would hold back like you from her husband when he had come home after twenty years of suffering! Come, then, nurse, make up a bed for me here, for this woman has a heart of iron." Then Penelope replied, "You strange man. I know very well what you were like when you left Ithaca. Come, then, Eurycleia, make up a bed for him here, outside the bedroom; move out the bed that he built himself." Then Odysseus replied in fury, "Woman, who has moved my bed somewhere else? That would be very hard to do, unless a god came to move it. But no mortal man alive, no matter how strong, could move it easily. For a great sign is built into it; I myself made it, no one else. I took a living olive tree and built the bedroom around it, and roofed it, and added close-fitting doors, and trimmed the trunk to make a bedpost, and built the bed and decorated it with gold and silver and ivory. Thus I declare this sign to you. But I don't know, woman, if the bed is still in its proper place, or if some other man has moved it somewhere else, cutting under the roots of the olive tree." That is what he said, and she recognized the clear signs and burst into tears and ran to him and kissed his head and said, "Don't be angry with me or blame me. I was afraid that some mortal man would come and deceive me with words. Helen would never have gone to bed and made love with a foreigner if a god had not inspired her to do the shameful thing she did; before that, she did not place the ruinous folly in her heart. But now, since you have told me the clear signs of our bed, which no other mortal man has seen, no one but you and I and the maid who kept the doors of the bedroom—you have persuaded my heart, stubborn though it is." And finally Odysseus said, "Come, woman, let's go to bed."[46]

I have selected and strung together passages, mainly from books 19 and 23, that reveal a pattern of approaches to the recognition of signs. The so-called Homeric formulae themselves highlight these patterns; Odysseus and Penelope (and Homer) recycle the same phrases, teasing one another and joining together in the very phrases that are ostensibly keeping them apart. Thus, even when Homer says that the stranger's "wretched clothes" kept Penelope from recognizing him (like Nala, Odysseus is *polumetis,* a man of many tricks, many disguises), the fact that the stranger uses the very same phrase to reassure their son indicates that he does indeed understand her, and understands that she knows more than she is saying. They call one another "strange" *(daimoni/e)* and agree that her heart is stubborn—an agreement that makes her anything but strange and shows that her heart, however firm, is soft. Most of all, both of them keep talking about signs, realistic signs that play a different role than they play in the less realistic corresponding scenes in the story of Damayanti and Nala, involving tests that are a match for the gamut that Damayanti and Nala make one another run in the parallel situation.

The word "sign" (*sema,* pl. *semata;* cf. our "semantic," "semiotic," "semaphor," etc.) is said to be cognate with the Sanskrit *dhyama,* "thoughts"; more particularly, it may be connected, in Sanskrit, with the idea of reminding the Sun* to rise.[47] *Sema* is used again and again in the episode of the sign of the bed in a range of related meanings, principally as an exceptional mark in its own right (the extraordinary bed) or a sign or token of something else (in this case, Odysseus's true identity). *Sema* refers to the details of the golden clasp proving that the stranger did know Odysseus, the hound on the clasp echoing the dog that recognized Odysseus (just as Nala's horses recognized Nala); and to tease Penelope Odysseus adds the bit about the women admiring Odysseus when he was wearing it (just as Nala teased Damayanti by pretending to flirt with her messenger, Keshini). It refers to the scar made by the boar, which the nurse calls a *sema* to prove to Penelope that the stranger *is* Odysseus. It refers to the ways that, Penelope assures her son, the two of them have of knowing one another.

And finally it refers to the marriage bed, whose *sema* is both a "unique characteristic" (as Richmond Lattimore translates) and a way that Odysseus has of proving that he is the only man who has the right to sleep with Penelope in it. Odysseus refers to the bed twice as a sign, and so does Penelope, four references within forty lines. He says "a great sign is built into it" (which Lattimore renders, obscuring the pattern, "one particular feature") and Penelope speaks of "the clear signs of our bed" (Lattimore, again missing the echo, "these authentic details of our bed"). The bed is a riddle: "When is a marriage bed impossible to move?" Answer: "When it is a living tree." The bed carved from a living tree and then carefully roofed and gated and bound in gold and silver is a magnificent metaphor for marriage, which cages and codifies the living force of sexual passion but keeps it alive. Aristotle, perhaps with this scene in mind, quotes Antiphon's statement that if a man buried a bedstead *[kline;* though Homer called it a *lechos]* and the sap in it took force and threw out a shoot, a tree and not a bedstead would grow.[48] Odysseus knows that if the tree in the bed is still alive, his bond with Penelope is still alive, keeping her from sleeping with anyone else in that bed, and so he himself is still alive. This is why he loses control of his temper when she even attempts to trick him about the bed; he is angry both about being subjected to a trick and about the very idea that she might have moved the bed. She has to beg him not to be angry, pointing out that the gods are jealous of human happiness and have already robbed them of twenty years of marriage. By citing the case of Helen, Penelope implies that she worried that he might be a god in disguise. That is, she suspects that Zeus might be appearing as the *eidolon* of Odysseus, just as he appeared as Amphitryon (and the Hindu gods appeared as Nala). Only the endurance of marital bonding can prevail over divine treachery. Only after the bed has been tested can Homer give us what Froma Zeitlin has nicely characterized as "that most satisfying of romantic closures: 'and so to bed.' "[49]

Physical, visual evidence does not bear as much weight as words, knowledge, memory. Despite his superficial filth and the fact that Athena has transformed him, the stranger resembles Odysseus first in his feet, then in his "form and voice," then in the scar on his thigh, and finally in his memory of the bed. The nurse recognizes the scar "by the feel" and believes it over the evidence of vision. Later, in the final book, Odysseus's father asks for a sign *[sema]* that Odysseus is really Odysseus, and Odysseus tells him about the scar and the boar, signs that he has offered to others (in addition to the nurse and his father) to aid their recognition of him. But this time he adds something that he didn't add for the nurse or Penelope: he names the trees in the orchard when he was a boy: thirteen pear trees, ten apple trees, forty fig trees, and like the partridge in a pear tree, the ripening of things in their season, the seasons sent by Zeus. These living trees function symbolically as offshoots, shadows, of the living tree from which the marriage bed was made. And Odysseus's father recognizes the sure signs; indeed, as he hears them he sees them, for he is standing there right then in the orchard, probably the very orchard that Odysseus is talking about, just as Odysseus ends up with Penelope in the same bed with which he had proved himself to her. Thus the bed test in book 23 is framed by the signs in books 19 (the cloak and brooch, the scar) and 24 (the trees in the orchard).

It is also supported by yet another sign, one that is not explicitly called a *sema* and is not a thing but an ability, an event: the sign of the bending of the bow. In book 21, after the conversation about the cloak, Athena inspires Penelope to set the wooers a contest with the bow of Odysseus: "whoever strings the bow most easily and shoots an arrow through all twelve axes, I will go with him and leave this home, which I will remember even in my dreams." Telemachus, ignoring the Oedipal implications, tries to do it and then, at a sign from Odysseus, says that he will let his mother go off with one of the suitors—he'll keep the house (that she will remember in her dreams, those dreams of the return of Odysseus that she always doubts . . .). Telemachus would have succeeded had Odysseus not signaled with those eloquent brows for him to stop. Penelope then asks that the bow be given to "the stranger" to try—does she know who he is?—but

Telemachus again interferes: he sends her up to her room, saying that *he* is the one to say to whom the bow should be given. Penelope, astounded, goes to her room, weeps, and goes to sleep. Odysseus strings the bow and begins the slaughter.

Now, there are significant Hindu parallels with this scene. In the *Mahabharata*, the text in which Nala appears, the hero Arjuna* wins his bride Draupadi* through a contest with a bow: Drupada, Draupadi's father, says that the man who can string the bow and use it to shoot arrows through the hole in a wheel and hit the mark will win Draupadi. Arjuna strings the bow, takes five arrows, pierces the target and knocks it down entirely; after that, he takes Draupadi for his wife.[50] And in the other great Sanskrit epic, the *Ramayana*, Rama wins Sita by stringing a bow—indeed, he not only strings it but breaks it in half.[51]

The symbolism of the Hindu bow contests is primarily erotic: the blatant sexual metaphor of the arrow moving through the hole to pierce the target needs no Freudian to gloss it, and Rama's cruelty to Sita is foreshadowed when instead of merely bending and stringing the bow that symbolizes his right to Sita, he breaks it in half as he will break her by rejecting her. Violence is implicit in the image: in the other epics too, *Mahabharata* as well as *Odyssey*, a fight breaks out right after the contest as the defeated suitors attack the victor. But the *Ramayana* is unique among the three in a way most significant for our central theme: the hero is not in disguise. The *Mahabharata*, by contrast, makes explicit what seems at first to be implicit in the *Odyssey:* the bow contest proves the identity of the disguised hero. Arjuna and his brothers, the Pandavas, are disguised as Brahmins at the time of the contest; after Arjuna has strung the bow, people begin to whisper, "They must be the Pandavas." So too even before the riddle of the bed, the bow trick suggests to Penelope that the stranger might be Odysseus.[52] Technically, it does not: Telemachus could have passed the test (though this might simply prove that he is his father's son, part of the broader agenda of the homecoming), and perhaps some of the other suitors (they never get to try). But the dramatic effect is striking: the stranger has bent and strung Odysseus's bow. Who could he be?

Odysseus's unfounded suspicions of Penelope may be projections of the fact that he himself has been jumping in and out of bed with Calypso and Circe. But Penelope, who knows about Calypso (the spiteful

Telemachus told her that Odysseus was with Calypso when it was no longer true),[53] and has good reason to be jealous, has fears about herself as well as about him. In her final speech of recognition and acceptance, she argues that she tested Odysseus because of her fear of being tricked like Helen of Troy. Odysseus's nightmare is that Penelope will turn out to be Clytaemnestra (about whom both Odysseus and Telemachus have taken great pains *not* to inform Penelope, perhaps in order not to put a bad example in her head), but Penelope's own nightmare is that she will turn out to be another phantom of Helen—who believed her dream sent by the gods, while Penelope, in the famous piece about gates of horn and ivory (a dream about the return of her husband), did not.[54]

In fact, in Euripides' revisionist history, Helen turns out to be very much like Homer's Penelope, the heroine of "another 'faithful wife' story, of a woman's unflagging fidelity to her knight-errant."[55] Like Penelope, Euripides' Helen fears that her husband, gone so long, is dead, and when Helen says, "If my husband were alive, we would recognize one another by symbols that would be clear to us alone,"[56] she could be quoting Homer's Penelope. Like Penelope, Helen hears the news that her husband is "in this country, near at hand, a shipwrecked castaway with few friends left."[57] Norman Austin comments, "Here begins what we would expect to be the great recognition scene of all time.... Can her secret tokens better Penelope's? The reunion of Odysseus and Penelope pales beside this reunion, since Penelope was never called upon to play a ghost of herself, as Helen is."[58]

Like Damayanti, Penelope knows that her steadfastness and faithfulness to her husband are not what reveal her to him but what reveal *him* to *her*. Zeitlin describes the bed as "a double-sided sign—of identity for him, fidelity for her.... Yet a certain paradox remains in the unequal symmetry between identity and fidelity that dictates to each sex its defining terms.... But the ruse works in two directions, because in raising the awful possibility that his bed has been moved, her testing of *his* identity raises the far more important question of *her* sexual fidelity to him."[59] More than that; the trick proves that she is worthy of him not only in fidelity, but in trickiness: "in tricking Odysseus into revealing the secret of the bed, she proves herself to be his match in the same qualities that characterize him (and that therefore identify her as a suitable wife for him, his 'other half')."[60]

In Edmond Rostand's *Cyrano de Bergerac*, when Roxane tells Christian how she loved his letters from the war, she says,

> Do you suppose / The prim Penelope had stayed at home / Embroidering,— / if Ulysses wrote like you? / She would have fallen like another Helen—/ Tucked up those linen petticoats of hers / And followed him to Troy![61]

This was Odysseus's fear. But there was to be no phantom Penelope. She made sure of that by testing him.

A story that has been called "one of the best known ballads in modern Greece"[62] combines the two episodes in which Odysseus is recognized first by Penelope and then by his father. The singer tells the story in the first person: he says he met a maiden who was waiting for her husband, gone "these ten long years." He told her he had buried her husband with his own hands and asked for a kiss in payment. When she refused, the following conversation took place:

THE RETURN OF THE LONG-ABSENT HUSBAND

"My good girl, I am your husband, I am your beloved man."

"My good stranger, if you are my husband, my beloved man, tell me of marks in the courtyard, and then I will believe you." [He tells her of an apple tree and a vine].

"These are marks in my courtyard and everybody knows them; a passer-by you were and passed, you tell me what you saw. Tell me of marks inside the house, and then I will believe you."

"Right in the midst of the bedroom there burns a golden lamp; it gives you light while you undress and while you plait your tresses; it gives you light at sweet daybreak, as you dress in your best."

"A wicked neighbour it must be, who told you what you know. Tell me of marks on my body, give me tokens of love."

"You have a dark spot in your armpit, and between your breasts you wear your husband's amulet."

"Good stranger, you are my husband, and you are my beloved man."[63]

The most significant difference from the *Odyssey* is that the woman does *not* recognize her husband; and now it is the woman, not the man, who is recognized by a scar on her body (just as Damayanti, rather than Nala, is recognized by her mole). Kakridis notes that "[i]n some variants, among the marks on the body of his wife is also a scar from a bite, but on a different part of the body"; the singer says, "You have a dark spot on your cheek, a dark spot in your armpit, and on your right breast a little scar from a bite."[64] But this text, like the *Odyssey,* constantly repeats "the identical terms, *semata/semadia,* as a proof of the recognition."[65] And in yet other variants of the song, the wife is explicitly tested with what is implicitly at stake in the *Odyssey,* as in the tale of Damayanti: she is told that her husband is dead and that his last wish was that she marry the stranger. "When she categorically refuses to, the man is assured about her faithfulness, and he reveals his identity."[66] As in both the *Odyssey* and the tale of Damayanti, "[t]he formula of the motif of the home-coming husband's recognition requires a double test: on the one hand, the test of the man to prove his identity; on the other, the test of the woman to prove that she has been faithful all these years."[67] As the signs move in sequence from the external to the most intimate, the final test is invisible: her faithful heart, symbolized by her husband's amulet between her breasts.

In addition to the fairly close correspondence between these testing scenes at the end of the stories of Damayanti and Penelope, there is also a less obvious correspondence between the testing scene at the beginning of the Damayanti story, the scene in which she chooses Nala and rejects the gods who resemble him, and another scene at the very beginning of the *Odyssey,* in which Odysseus rejects Calypso. When we first meet Odysseus he is longing for his homecoming and his wife, but the powerful nymph Calypso, the bright goddess, keeps him back in her hollow caves, longing to make him her husband.[68] Later, when Calypso expresses her disbelief that he should prefer his mortal wife to her, an immortal woman, he replies:

THE REJECTION OF CALYPSO

Mighty goddess, don't be angry with me because of this. I know perfectly well that the thoughtful Penelope is not as good as you are to look at, in appearance or stature, for she is a mortal and you are not merely immortal, but ageless. Yet even so I wish and hope every day to come home and to see the day of my homecoming.[69]

And with that, he goes to bed with Calypso. Nothing is said in Penelope's favor other than the fact that she is a part of a home. All else is against her: she lacks beauty, size, immortality, and youth. Setting aside the fact that the man of many wiles would not make the mistake of praising other women to the woman he is sleeping with at the moment, as Zeus does to both Hera and Alcmena[70] and as Indra does to Ahalya,[71] what endears Penelope to Odysseus is her *lack* of divine characteristics. Had Homer spoken Sanskrit, he would have said that she is a woman whose feet touch the ground and who casts a shadow.

COMPARISON: DAMAYANTI AND PENELOPE

There are interesting correspondences and differences between these two texts. Some of the tests that Damayanti and Nala use on one another are of a different order from those that Odysseus and Penelope use in the parallel situation. Telemachus's resemblance to his father, Odysseus, plays an important, though very different, role from that of the twins of Damayanti and Nala in the mutual recognition of Odysseus and Penelope: where Nala's recognition of his twins helps Damayanti to recognize him, Telemachus announces that although his mother says he is Odysseus's child, no one knows his own father for sure.[72] Yet Damayanti's children (like the children of Sita and Helen) play a minor role in the story as a whole in comparison with the role played by Telemachus.

Supernatural signs are far less important in the more realistic corresponding scenes in the *Odyssey*, but natural signs abound. Where Nala's feet identify him to Damayanti, Odysseus's telltale feet, together with the scar on his leg, identify him—not to Penelope, whom he does not yet trust, but to his old nurse, whom he does trust. And just as the folk tradition in India changed the force of the sign of the second marriage by having Nala marry some other woman, so the folk tradition in modern Greece reversed the force of the sign of the scar by having Odysseus recognize Penelope by the telltale marks on *her* body.

Zeitlin likens the two mutual bed tests set by Penelope and Odysseus to the two once divided and now reunited halves of a literal symbol, the *sumbolon*[73] that was broken in half (like the two pieces of a thousand-dollar bill in a melodramatic espionage contract) to be re-joined as proof of identity (she is his "other half"); but Nala literally tears the two halves of the bed in half when he leaves Damayanti, since her cloth that covers them both is all the bed they have that night. In the *Odyssey*, it is Penelope who unilaterally fits the broken symbol back together with the riddle of the bed that is a tree.

Like Penelope, Damayanti uses the ruse of a proposed remarriage to smoke her husband out; as Zeitlin points out, "To accept a second marriage is not, after all, equivalent to adultery. . . . There is a distinction between acquiescence to courtship, no matter how unwelcome, and actually sleeping with the enemy."[74] Like Damayanti, Penelope is apparently free to choose as her husband any man she desires. Both of them use the proposed marriage to force their husbands to reveal themselves by appealing to their pride and vanity, tempting them to reveal their skills—Nala his horsemanship, Odysseus his carpentry (he is a fine raft builder, as we know). The twenty-four-hour test that Damayanti sets is like the bed test that Penelope sets for Odysseus, forcing his hand, forcing him to show his sign of identity even if he wishes to remain in disguise. (This too is a more widely distributed trope in both ancient India and ancient Greece: Arjuna,* in hiding, reveals himself when he cannot resist bending the bow and shooting the targets in the contest to win Draupadi; Achilles, hiding in drag on Skyros, is tricked by Odysseus into revealing himself when he cannot resist reaching out for shining weapons.)[75]

And this sign then in both cases—horsemanship and bed carpentry—rebounds back for the woman, when she uses it to prove not her own identity (which he does not doubt) but her fidelity (which he does). Both tricks prove simultaneously who the man is and that his wife has been true to him in bed—his identity and her fidelity, the two qualities that are implicitly equated and essentialized: where he must prove who he is, she must prove that she is his. Damayanti does this twice: before they are married she forces the gods to reveal their (and Nala's) identities when she swears by her fidelity to him, and then years later she proves her fidelity to him when she has successfully tested his identity.

Thus the two texts are arguing simultaneously for the choice of the mortal over the immortal and for the ability to see the true husband through the disguises of age—of mortality. Yet again, as with the images of the adulteress and the chaste wife, the two cultures reverse the genders of those who choose mortals over immortals. It is the Hindu woman (Damayanti) and the Greek man (Odysseus) who choose the mortal spouse over the immortal surrogate, though in both cases it is the wife who must recognize her changed husband. Though Nala and Penelope recognize their spouses, who return the compliment by recognizing them, Damayanti and Odysseus in this sense choose their spouses twice: over against both divinity and youth. The Hindu text thus doubly affirms the virtue of the woman, while the Greek text doubly affirms the man.

In both epics it is the woman, not the man, who has the more serious doubts—not about chastity, but about identity. Yet the women have far better cause than the men to doubt the chastity of their spouses: Penelope has good reason to be jealous, and though Nala suspects Damayanti of infidelity (which he regards as implicit in her desire to remarry), he is the one who has been to blame for their separation, as she well knows; his unfounded suspicions of her are projections of his own abandonment of her. And though Nala in the Sanskrit version is not explicitly unfaithful to Damayanti, in the Dhola epic, Nal does take a second wife.

Both of the women manipulate the signs themselves; truly they have agency. Mihoko Suzuki has pointed this out with reference to Penelope, taking Claude Lévi-Strauss's formulation that men exchange women like words or signs,[76] and remarking that Penelope (and, I would add, Damayanti) "insists upon her status as a [speaking] subject, a generator of signs,"[77] especially the sign of the bed. The Hindu woman has a power over her husband that the Greek woman lacks, and takes a more active role in planning the recognition scene: Damayanti sends messengers to seek Nala while Penelope treads water, unweaving what she has woven. Penelope is far from her home, alone, and under pressure by the people around her (the suitors) to remarry, while Damayanti is in her base of political power, with the support of her parents, and presumably under strong pressure *not* to remarry. Yet despite the fact that Damayanti is more active than Penelope, even Damayanti is still defined, like Penelope, by her fidelity to her husband.

An interesting inversion of the story of Damayanti (and in other ways of the story of Ahalya) occurs in an Irish text related to the Hindu and Greek myths of Damayanti and Penelope if one accepts the hypothesis of an Indo-European* cultural system, but in any case strongly analogous to it. That is, this is another story in which a god doubles as a mortal, but this time in order not to destroy but, on the contrary, to protect the chastity of a human woman, Etain:

THE WOOING OF ETAIN

[King Echu Airem married Etain, but his brother Ailill Angubae fell in love with her. He pined away for his secret love of her, and when he told her she agreed to meet him secretly the next night, on the hill above the house.] Ailill remained awake all night, but at the hour of the meeting he fell asleep, and he did not wake until the third hour of the following day. Etain went to the hill, and the man she saw there waiting for her was like Ailill in appearance; he lamented the weakness his ailment had brought about, and the words he spoke were the words Ailill would have used. . . .

[But then the man, who was Mider, said, "In a previous life], I was your husband. . . . It is I who made Ailill fall in love with you, so that his flesh and his blood fell from him; and it is I who quelled his desire to sleep with you, lest you be dishonoured. Will you come to my land with me if Echu bids you?" "I will," said Etain. [He told her of his country: "A wonderful land that I describe: youth does not precede age." Mider won her from Echu by gambling, but when he came for her,] Etain was serving the chieftains, for serving drink was a special talent of hers . . . He bore her up through the skylight of the house. Ashamed, the hosts rose up round the light, and they saw two swans.

[Echu and his men came after her and found Mider, with the aid of blind dogs and cats. Mider promised that Etain would return to him.] They saw fifty women, all of the same appearance as Etain and all dressed alike. At that, the hosts fell silent. A grey hag came before them and said to Echu, "It is time for us to return home. Choose your wife now, or tell one of these women to remain with you." . . . "My wife is the best at serving in Eriu, and that is how I will know her," said Echu. . . . It came down to the last two women: the first began to pour, and Echu said, "This is Etain, but she is not herself." He and his men held a council, and they decided, "This is Etain, though it is not her serving." The other women left, then.

[One day, later, Mider said to Echu,] "Your wife was pregnant when I took her from you, and she bore a daughter, and it is that daughter who is with you now. Your wife is with me, and you have let her go a second time." With these words, Mider departed. Echu . . . was distressed that his wife had escaped and that he had slept with his own daughter; his daughter, moreover, became pregnant and bore a daughter. "O gods," he said, "never will I look upon the daughter of my daughter." [He ordered the child to be thrown into a pit with wild beasts; the men threw her to a bitch and its pups in the hounds' kennel, but the herdsman took her from the kennel and reared her. She grew up to excel at embroidery, and she married a king and became the mother of Conare.][78]

At first, this story seems to bear a stunning resemblance to the story of Nala and Damayanti. It begins with a scene in which a god masquerades as a mortal, just as Indra and the other gods masqueraded as Nala; but unlike Damayanti, Etain cannot tell the difference. Yet she has only two men to choose between, where Damayanti had five in the Sanskrit text (though only two in some of the folk retellings); and she prefers the god to her lover (not to mention her husband). Then Echu gambles Etain away, which is essentially what Nala does to Damayanti in the second half of the story; and finally there is, as in that second half, another scene of disguise and recognition, with the numbers (and genders) reversed so as neatly to balance out the first reversal: where Damayanti had to recognize only one husband, Echu must choose among fifty wives.

But herein lies the essential difference: Etain and Echu cannot tell the difference. Indeed, Etain not only wishes to commit adultery (from which only the intervention of the god saves her) but chooses to remain in the other world, with the gods, the land where "youth does not precede age"; it is precisely this quality of the magic land that skews linear time so that the daughter born there looks just like her, instead of much younger. As in the Nal saga, the theme of incest is introduced through the doubling of parent and child. And this preference for the adulterous lover and for the immortal makes Etain finally the narrative parallel not of Damayanti but of Ahalya.

Differences between the true husband and his impersonator or between two forms of the same person are often accounted for by the passage of time, the aging that produces natural changes. (Here we may recall that Hofmannsthal's Menelaus was inclined to regard the real Helen as an impostor precisely because she had no lines on her face, because her face was "too untouched by life," since she had apparently not aged a day since she left Sparta.) Nathalie Zemon Davis's reconstruction of *The Return of Martin Guerre* tells of a man who, like Odysseus and Nala, but in recorded history, returned to his wife after a long absence in a war and had to prove to her that he was her husband, despite the changes wrought by time and suffering.[79] (In the American film version of that story, *Sommersby* [1993], the hero returns from the American Civil War.)[80] In those stories, the man is an impostor who pretends to be the man who left for the war long ago. But in the tales of Damayanti and Penelope, the true husband is pretending to be someone else; in the context of our expectation of the other tale, the tale of the impostor, the true husband is in a sense tempting his wife to commit adultery with her own husband.[81] How do we recognize one another, and ourselves, despite the ravages of time? Ask Penelope. Ask Damayanti.

INTERLUDE: HOW TO TELL A HUMAN FROM A GOD

We began chapter 2 with the virtuous, faithful, but gullible Ahalya, and moved on (through the knowing, sinful, and complicitous Ahalya) to the wise, virtuous, and faithful Damayanti (together with her predecessor, Sukanya). So too in Greece, we moved from the virtuous, faithful, but gullible Alcmena (through the possibly complicitous Alcmena) to the wise, virtuous, and faithful Penelope. These two groups of myths differ not only in their opinions about discernment but in their attitude to preference. The group in which the woman prefers her mortal husband (the Damayanti-Penelope genre) argues that the human woman can tell the difference; the group in which she prefers a god (Etain, and some variants of the Ahalya and Alcmena genre) argues that the woman cannot always tell the difference. Let us begin with the issue of telling the difference and conclude with the issue of preference.

How do the wise women (and occasionally wise men) tell their spouses from the divine impersonators? This was a problem for Ahalya and Alcmena, as we have seen, and the authors of our texts made various suggestions (the smell of Indra, the glow of Zeus, etc.) The most basic sign of mortality is, of course, death, but this seldom provides a useful rule of thumb in the situations we have encountered; the signs of aging and death appear to normal mortals only in the course of time, and the protagonists of our myths must look for more immediate and generally more subtle signs. In the case of Alcmena, as in the story of Damayanti, telling the god from the mortal means seeing the flaws in an otherwise perfect magical replication—flaws both in the sense of an imperfect replication and in the sense of the failure to reproduce those human shortcomings (like sweating, blinking, and casting a shadow) that are the clue to human identity. Alcmena is mildly troubled by these discrepancies, but fails to conclude from them that she is in the presence of a god; Damayanti reads the clues correctly. In the contrasting paradigm of Ahalya, perfection is exalted: Ahalya herself is created in order that there should be one flawless human woman (an oxymoron, in terms of the Damayanti paradigm: to be flawless is to be inhuman), and it is therefore not so surprising that such a woman often prefers a (physically flawless) god to a human. But whether or not the human woman prefers the god (a question that we will take up below), she recognizes him sometimes by the signs of his immortality (as Ahalya recognizes Indra from his smell) but often simply by the ways in which his personality differs from her husband's just as any other man's would (the way he makes love, or talks, or cooks, or desires her). Here, as throughout this study, we must also be alert to differences in genre: the Greek texts are more realistic, in contrast with the Indian, and therefore depict the heroine as exercising a relatively hard logic, where the more mythical Hindu texts give the heroine an advantage that proves more useful in her situation: the readier expectation that the man in front of her might be a god in disguise.

The problem of telling a mortal from a divine double raises questions of recognition different from that of telling a mortal from a mortal double or an immortal from an immortal double. While specific criteria distinguish one human being (or one immortal) from another, they are often literally outclassed by generic criteria that distinguish any mortal from any immortal. These are the criteria of mortality and class *(varna)* that we encountered in the story of Saranyu, Yama, and Manu and continued to find in the tales of Ahalya, Alcmena, and Damayanti. And these generic criteria often descend from the divine to the banal, suggesting most down-to-earth ways out of dilemmas such as Damayanti's and Ahalya's, ways far less dramatic than divine intervention. Greek and Hindu traditions weight these theological, sociological, and psychological criteria in different ways, and individual storytellers express different perceptions of the human dimensions of the dilemma.

Greek gods can recognize one another behind the mortal veil: Jean Giraudoux's Mercury sees through Jupiter as Amphitryon and announces: "You can't fool me. Divinity is clearly visible at twenty paces."[82] But when Giraudoux's Alcmena mistakes the real Amphitryon for Jupiter, she scrutinizes him and says she sees on his face "some bird's footprint—Jupiter's eagle, no doubt?" When Amphitryon protests, "A crow, darling—that's my crow's foot," she ignores him,[83] mistaking the crow's feet, the signs of mortality around her husband's eyes, for the eagle's* feet that, especially near the eyes, the unblinking eyes, are the sign of immortality (the ability to gaze at the sun).* Thus Giraudoux's Alcmena thinks that she would know, and reject, the god by his perfection and nobility, but she misreads the feet.

Feet again prove the crucial criterion in a Bengali story:

THE WOMAN WHO COOKED WITH HER FEET

[A ghost seized a woman and hid her in the trunk of a tree. She put on the clothes of the woman and returned to the home of her husband, a Brahmin who lived with his mother.] The Brahman thought his wife returned from the tank. . . . Next morning the mother-in-law discovered some change in her daughter-in-law. Her daughter-in-law, she knew, was constitutionally weak and languid, and took a long time to do the work of the house. But she had apparently become quite a different person. All of a sudden she had become very active. She now did the work of the house in an incredibly short time. Suspecting nothing, the mother-in-law said nothing either to her son or to her daughter-in-law; on the contrary, she only rejoiced that her daughter-in-law had turned over a new leaf.

[But one day she observed her daughter-in-law stretching her arm from one room to another to get something.] The old woman was struck with wonder at the sight. She said nothing to her, but spoke to her son. Both mother and son began to watch the ghost more narrowly. One day. . . . she went in, and, to her infinite surprise, found that her daughter-in-law was not using any fuel for cooking, but had thrust into the oven her foot, which was blazing brightly. The old mother told her son what she had seen, and they both concluded that the young woman in the house was not his real wife but a she-ghost. The son witnessed those very acts of the ghost which his mother had seen. An *Ojha* [exorciser] was therefore sent for. . . . He lighted a piece of turmeric and set it below the nose of the supposed woman. Now this was an infallible test, as no ghost, whether male or female, can put up with the smell of burnt turmeric. The moment the lighted turmeric was taken near her, she screamed aloud and ran away from the room. It was now plain that she was either a ghost or a woman possessed by a ghost. The woman was caught hold of by main force and asked who she was. At first she refused to make disclosures, on which the *Ojha* took up his slippers and began belabouring her with them. [The ghost confessed and was released, and the wife was retrieved.] After which the Brahman and his wife lived many years happily together and begat many sons and daughters.[84]

The demonic impostor does housework dramatically better than the mortal woman—but the mother-in-law is so pleased by this that she does not question its implications; she allows herself to be fooled. (Ondine* too, in the Giraudoux telling, does the housework wonderfully well, but her adoptive father complains, "I've never *seen* her washing or cleaning anything—nor have you, come to that.")[85] The abnormal stretching of limbs, however, is not such an attractive sign (though surely it is equally useful in housekeeping—those hard-to-reach places), and thus begins the process of exposure.

Often the criteria for gods who impersonate human men turn, as do the criteria for women, on the qualities that are regarded as the essence of that gender; where woman should be good seamstresses, men should be strong. This is the crux of a South Indian text about Mariyatai-Raman, who functions in the folk literature as a Solomon type:

THE GOD AND THE STONE

A man, known for his great strength, abandoned his wife in a fit of rage. A god then took his form and moved in with the wife. In a few months the

real husband, his anger cooled, returned, and the case presented to Mariyatai-raman (whom the king called in when his own jurists found themselves stymied) was to decide who was who. Mindful of the real husband's
great strength, he commanded each man to lift an enormous stone. The
real husband heaved and hauled and lifted it but a few inches. The false
one lifted it over his head as though it were a feather, and the crowd cried
out, "There is no doubt, this one is the real husband." The judge, however,
decided in favor of the first, saying that he had done what was possible to
humans, even those with extraordinary strength, while what the second
had done only a god could do.[86]

Apparently the judge is called in because the wife cannot recognize her
husband. Here, as in the story of Damayanti, the sign of weakness, of mortality, is what wins the human woman. The paradoxical logic of this genre
argues that the masquerading god will sometimes helplessly betray his immortality by failing to pull his divine punches, as it were, by forgetting to
pretend that he has no more power than a mortal would have. This story
puts a new twist on the old Christian theological riddle, "Can God make a
stone so heavy that he cannot lift it?" We have already encountered a variant of this in the story of Alcmena and Zeus, whose problem is that the
perfect mortal woman whom God created is so chaste that she will not go
to bed with him.

In many tellings of the story of Alcmena, Zeus's very perfection is paradoxically his flaw; his total knowledge and perfect memory make Alcmena
suspect him. (The criterion of divine memory stands in contrast with one
operative in most *human* masquerades, in which the double is unmasked
because he does *not* remember what the original—and the victim—
remembers.) We have encountered a variant of this paradigm in the
Nepalese version of the story of Sita, in which the test is to bring a *parijata*
flower from Indra's heaven; the ogress can do it and is too stupid to refrain
from doing it, while Sita simply faints. So too in Ann Gold's version of the
tale of Nal, Damayanti's milk squirts through the wooden breastplate,
proving that she has supernatural milk, supernatural powers of motherhood—but this is, after all, just a supernatural version of the most common, basic human (indeed, mammalian) talent.

One variant of the story of Ahalya also involves a contest of this sort.
In this telling, after Indra is unmasked (he had taken the form of a cat,
as usual), Indra and Gautama end up side by side (like the two Gautamas
in another telling, or Zeus and Amphitryon in most tellings of that story),

and each of them demands to have Ahalya as his wife. But since Indra resumes his own form, Ahalya is not required to tell them apart, nor is she allowed to choose for herself in a self-choice ceremony. Instead, there is a contest, and Narada sets the terms (which echo those of the story of Sukanya, in which Cyavana and the Ashvins emerged together from a pond): this time, whichever of the two, Gautama and Indra, stays underwater longer will win Ahalya. Gautama, the great yogi, remains underwater for a thousand years, but Indra cannot bear to be away from Ahalya and shoots up through the water; Narada announces that Indra has lost Ahalya, though he has proved himself the greater lover.[87] (Indra is sometimes condemned to remain underwater as punishment for the seduction of Ahalya.) This telling subverts the conventional values of the story of the contest between a god and a mortal. The god has, one assumes, greater physical powers than the mortal, but the mortal has greater self-control and uses his powers where the god refuses to use his. The mortal thus wins the contest of strength (more precisely, a contest of weakness), and thus wins the woman. But the irony lies in the fact that the god—having the more endearing weakness, in this case the most endearing of all weaknesses: he loses the woman because he loves her more—is the one who proves, in a sense, more human than the human. Had Narada had the wisdom of Mariyatai-Raman, surely he would have given Ahalya to Indra.

The Mortal Foot

Why should the foot that touches the ground be a sign of mortality, in contrast with the gods' feet, which float ever so slightly above the ground like hovercraft? Perhaps, through the literal-minded play of the imagination, because the point of the body where we are earthbound is what binds us to the grave, and the foot is in touch with Earth as opposed to the heavens.[88] "Both feet on the ground" is what we say of a particularly "down-to-earth" or realistic person, but it is what our myths say of one who is doomed to mortality.[89] (Walking on water, another gravity-defying, hence death-defying, act, is also an old Indian trick.)[90] Antaeus, in Greek myth, is said to have remained victorious in combat while his feet touched the ground because the god of the earth endowed him with power (like Bram Stoker's Dracula, who had to sleep every night on a coffin filled with Transylvanian soil). On the other hand, the Irish hero Ossian remained immortal as long as his feet did *not* touch the ground on his visit back to our world from Tir-na-Nog; when he slipped from the saddle to the ground he dissolved into dust. Therefore, to prefer the mortal is to prefer the person who is grounded, so to speak: as Shakespeare complains, with tongue in cheek (in sonnet 130), "I grant I never saw a goddess go; / My mistress when she walks treads on the ground. . . ." And this is the poem that begins with the line, "My mistress' eyes are nothing like the sun. . . ."

It is perhaps with some sense of irony that Nala protests that he is not worthy of the dust on the gods' feet,[91] since the very fact that the gods have no dust, especially on their feet, is what will win Damayanti for him instead of for them[92]—though it is through his feet that disaster will later enter him. And when Nala becomes invisible in order to penetrate into Damayanti's harem, he is noticed when the women there see his shadow and his footprints in the flowers that they have scattered on the floor[93]—evidence, in this case, that someone whose feet touched the ground, a human, was present.

Despite this criterion, supernatural creatures often reveal themselves to us precisely by treading upon the earth and leaving footprints, just as they leave shadows or statues.* The footprint of Jesus is said to be preserved in the Church of the Ascension in Jerusalem. The serpent-woman Mélusine leaves her footprint in stone, along with her ghostly form, when she abandons her husband and children.[94] The Upanishads tell us that "the Self is the footprint [padaniya] of the All, for by it one knows this All, just as one might find [an animal] by a footprint."[95] Ravana* follows the footprints of Parvati when she has been taken from him,[96] and Shurpanakha* falls in love with Rama when she sees his footprints in the earth[97] and, in one telling, tricks Sita into drawing a picture of Ravana's "big toe"; Shurpanakha completes the sketch, and Ravana comes to life—just as Rama comes into the bedroom. (This is said to explain why Rama accused Sita of being unfaithful to him and threw her out.)[98] In the temple of Lepakshi* in India, the footprint and the shadow join to keep the goddess Durga simultaneously near and far: outside the shrine is a footprint, regarded as the mark left when the goddess jumped off a swing: "A footprint, a dream, a stone, a mask, a mirror: such is the presence of the Lepaksi goddess."[99] Where the mirror or reflection interposes itself between the worshiper and this present goddess to make her safely distant, the footprint brings back the absent goddess to make her safely present.

A king in a Sanskrit play, who forgot his wife and remembered her only when he saw a certain ring, muses: "Just as a man in doubt might say, 'There is no elephant,' even as it walks past him before his very eyes, but then, seeing its footprints, he might be satisfied—my mind underwent changes just like that."[100] Clifford Geertz uses this story as a metaphor for the imaginative work of the anthropologist: "For me at least . . . anthropology, ethnographical anthropology, is like that: trying to reconstruct elusive, rather ethereal, and by now wholly departed elephants from the footprints they have left on my mind."[101] Footprints on the mind are the signs of the mortality of the object of the imagination, all that is left when the foot (like Yama's* foot) decays, just as when the body decays all that is left is the shadow, the soul. But how can the gods leave these footprints when their feet do not touch the ground? I think these are stories in which, as in the paradigm of the Bodhisattva, the gods compassionately suspend their infallibility, as it were, in order to give the worshiper something to grasp (a statue, a footprint) when they are out of reach.

Carlo Ginzburg has argued persuasively that the human experience underlying our most basic classificatory system is that of the hunter tracking an animal by its footprints. He sees the foot as a sign, the great metonymy: the hunter knows the animal by its footprints, tracks, traces.[102] This technique, eventually transferred from the realm of prehistoric hunters and gatherers to that of scientists, remains the basis of many of our taxonomies. Cuvier in 1834 argued that

> [t]oday, someone who sees the print of a cloven hoof can conclude that the animal which left the print was a ruminative one, and this conclusion is as certain as any that can be made in physics or moral philosophy. This single track therefore tells the observer about the kind of teeth, the kind of jaws, the haunches, the shoulder, and the pelvis of the animal which has passed.[103]

As humankind began to stand upright, we moved from footprints to fingerprints. But it may well be that the memory of the more ancient and enduring way of knowing the identity of a creature operates, subconsciously, to bring footprints into so many of our myths in which identity is in question.

Our feet symbolize our separation not only from the gods above us but from the animals below us (or, by some calculations, also above us). That our feet are the sign of our human condition is confirmed by our basic way (derived from Aristotle) of classifying the animal orders: bipeds, quadrupeds, and six-legged insects.[104] In ancient India, too, the *Rig Veda* divides living creatures into two groups: "those of us on two feet and on four."[105] This classification was satirized by George Orwell in *Animal Farm,* when the old prize boar, the Major, taught the animals, "Whatever goes upon two legs is an enemy. Whatever goes upon four legs ... is a friend." After the Major's death, the clever, wicked pig Snowball reduced these sentences to the slogan, "Four legs good, two legs bad." Years later, when the pigs had thoroughly betrayed the revolution, the animals saw a whole row of pigs walking on their hind legs. The animals were about to protest when the sheep bleated out, "Four legs good, two legs *better!* Four legs good, two legs *better!*" To walk upright is the final betrayal, the final denial of the real barrier, the final lie.[106]

By walking upright, we gain the use of the opposable thumb, what Orwell's pig, Snowball, calls "the organ with which [man] does all the mischief," the source of our "manipulation," a word derived from *manus,* hand. Erect posture is a specifically, though not exclusively, human characteristic; "hence," notes Ginzburg, "the ambiguous reactions aroused in humans by other species capable of erect posture, such as monkeys and bears."[107] Gulliver, in *Gulliver's Travels,* finding himself in a place where the horses (Houyhnhnms) are the rulers while the humanoid Yahoos are the beasts of burden, pretended to be a horse; his shoes and stockings concealed his Yahoo-like feet from the horses. But, he confesses, his equine master saw through his masquerade through "my Affectation of walking continually on my two hinder feet."[108] The crucial distinction is as usual walking upright.

Not just *where* the feet are, or have been, or *how* we use them, but *what* they are may be the sign that distinguishes humans from animals or gods— or devils. When Giraudoux's Alcmena greets Mercury and says, "Mercury, to judge from your face?" he replies, "Thank you. Most humans recognize me by my feet, my winged heels. You are either cleverer or better at flattery."[109] The devil often has the cloven hoof of a goat, sometimes together with birds' claws or webbed toes. A one-eyed devil in a medieval miracle play tells the heroine: "It's not in our power, we devils from hell / To incarnate ourselves ... / Without some little defect here or there, / Be it in the head or the hands or the feet."[110] In the Babylonian Talmud, the devil is revealed by his backward-pointing feet. European witches' feet, too, are backward, a sign that often betrays them; and a particular sort of Hindu demoness "appears as a seductively beautiful woman, recognizable from the fact that her feet point backward."[111] The ogress who replaced a Brahmin's wife who was about to be raped and killed pointed out to the rapist that she had hair on the bottoms of her feet, a clue that he failed to understand and that cost him his life.[112]

Since women in these mythologies partake of both the bestial and the demonic, and since these two species are often distinguished by their feet, women are doubly likely to have bestial/demonic feet. When we become bestial, the first thing to go are the feet; therefore, though female devils *still* have animal feet—they are not yet fully transformed—, bestial women *already* have animal feet—they are beginning to be transformed. The sexist equation of the feet of uppity women and upright animals gave rise to Samuel Johnson's notorious remark that "a woman preaching is like a dog's walking on his hind legs. It is not done well; but you are surprised to find it done at all."[113]

Women on trial for witchcraft in Italy confessed to night-flying with mysterious "women from outside, who were beautifully dressed but had cat's paws or horses' hooves"; others had "webbed feet, a recurrent sign of contrariness, and, in women, of deviancy." The very range of possibilities was significant:

> the exact form of the bestial nether limbs is mutable: webbed, clawed, gnarled, three-toed, five-toed, encurled, club-footed, not to forget cloven, the appendage itself partakes of polymorphous perversity within the range of the base, not-human possibilities. Indeed, this very mutability informs the character of the heterodox and the dangerous.[114]

Heterodox and dangerous male humans too, defined as nonhumans, may be associated with the foot. In Hinduism, the Shudra, the servant, the lowest of the four classes of society, is born from the foot of the primeval man,[115] and this is often cited to justify the fact that Shudras are outside the social system, condemned to the service of the other classes.

The Jews, in later European history, were similarly stigmatized by their feet, a prejudice that Clive Sinclair mocks in his "Bulgarian Notes":

> "Tell me," he says. "I've often wondered how you know . . . how you recognize one another. I mean, how did you know that [he] was a Jew? Did you give each other signals, or are there secret signs, or what? I mean, what do you do when you are introduced?" . . . I raise my trouser leg. "That's what we do," I say, "we show each other our cloven hooves."[116]

Jews are also said to have naturally deformed feet, an aspect of another criterion, the wounded foot, that is, over and above the foot *tout court*, a distinguishing sign of mortal beings. What is the meaning of mutilated feet in these stories? The devil limps, "walking *pede claudo,* listing to the left."[117] By the turn of the century the images of the limping devil and the limping Jew had become interchangeable.[118] Oskar Panizza's *The Council of Love* (1895) imagines a conversation between Mary and a Jewish devil: "Mary: By the way how is your foot? The Devil: Oh, so-so! No better! . . . Mary (in a lower voice): Your fall did that?"[119] The Nazi caricaturist Walter Hofmann argued that Jews had flat feet because the body of the archetypal Jew was literally constructed from wet clay, but since the Jew disobeyed the divine order and arose while the clay was still damp and soft, "the smarty developed after the first few steps extraordinarily bandy legs, but also flat feet—literally feet of clay."[120] And Hermann Schaaffhausen, in the late nineteenth century, maintained that Jews walked with "the dragging gait of a lower-class individual."[121]

Bruce Lincoln has illuminated a more general Indo-European paradigm in which the sovereign (the first of Georges Dumézil's three functions) loses an eye or his head, the representative of martial force (the second function) loses a hand or arm, and the one responsible for production, consumption, and reproduction (the last function) loses a foot or leg or is wounded in the lower body.[122] Within this third category, the one that concerns us here, in Norse sagas and Roman sources the ravening Fenris wolf is bound by its leg, Egil's feet are fettered, and Guntharius, the greedy king, loses his leg.[123] In our own troubled times, those whom society has discarded often reveal themselves to the more fortunate by their feet: lacking proper shoes or medical care, they often limp. This too is the revelation of a "class" through the foot. The "well-heeled" shy away from those who are "down at the heel," the homeless with their telltale shuffle.

The myths tell us that we suffer injuries to our legs when we try, hubristically, to separate ourselves from the animals by standing upright. E. M. Cioran suggests that we lost a metaphysical as well as physical advantage when we made this transition: "One can only think horizontally. It is almost impossible to conceive of eternity from a vertical position. Animals may well have evolved to the rank of men when they started to walk upright, but *consciousness* was born in moments of freedom and laziness."[124] The injured foot symbolizes the hobbling of uprightness and the inauthenticity of our relationship with the earth. It symbolizes the deal that we made with the (limping) devil: the use of our hands, for the loss of the power of our (four) legs.

The locus classicus for the mutilated and identifying female foot is the tale of Cinderella, who is in many variants turned into an animal and called Catskin or Donkeyskin, with a shoe of fur rather than of glass.[125] The foot of the Bengali demoness, which does *not* become injured in a fire, is the sign of her nonhuman nature. Oedipus's foot (in Sophocles' *Oedipus Rex*) is the key to the Sphinx's riddle: the creature that goes on four feet, then two feet, then three feet is the human being who crawls as a child (or an animal), walks upright as a man (or a human), walks with a cane as he ages—and then, we might add, dies. Oedipus himself is that man; his name means "Swollen Foot," and his feet are pierced when, at his birth, he is exposed on the hillside—among the animals. (Why, we might ask, didn't Jocasta recognize Oedipus from his feet?) In some tellings of the myth, Oedipus's father, Laius, runs the chariot wheels over Oedipus's feet,[126] or Laius's horses bloody Oedipus's ankles with their hooves.[127] Oedipus's mutilated feet further connect him, especially in Claude Lévi-Strauss's analysis,[128] with other mortals who are paradoxically born from the earth (the place where our feet make contact) and born from their mothers; they remind us that we too were born of the earth, not of the gods. Jesus is like Oedipus in that he is threatened at his birth, exposed among animals, has multiple parents,[129] and finally has pierced feet. The medieval tradition depicts Jesus as a hunted stag whose hoof is stained with blood.

The riddle of Oedipus and the Sphinx is a variant of the metaphor of the Four Ages: once we were united with goodness, with the Gods, and now we are not. Hinduism also imagined four Ages of diminishing goodness (as did Buddhism), but visualized them as feet. Thus the Hindu law book says: "In the First Age, religion *(dharma)* is entire, standing on all four feet, and so is truth. . . . But in the other (Ages), religion is brought down foot by foot; and because of theft, lying, and deceit, religion goes away foot by foot."[130] That is, religion in the First Age stands firm, four-square, like a four-footed cow, but loses half of its power when it goes on two legs like a human; a quarter of religion departs in each age.[131] Here, as elsewhere, the foot is associated with the loss of immortality (for the creatures in the First Age live a very long time, and life spans diminish gradually from then on). We may hear an echo of this concept in Euripides' remark that the four feet of the Trojan horse* bring disaster.[132]

In Hindu cosmogony, Yama* becomes the first mortal when a part of his foot is taken down to the earth, away from immortality; his foot is both the cause and the object of his injury. The corruption of the flesh

symbolized by the wounded foot is embellished in one text with particularly gory details:

> The Shadow cursed Yama: "This one leg of yours, wounded, full of worms,
> will drip with pus and blood."... The god [the Sun] said to Yama, "What
> more can I do? Who doesn't get into trouble as a result of foolishness, or
> the workings of *karma*, which cannot be deflected even from Shiva; so how
> much more from other creatures? But I will give you a rooster[133] that will
> eat your worms and take away your pus and blood, my little calf." When he
> heard this, Yama generated ascetic heat until Shiva gave him a boon and
> made him lord of the underworld.[134]

Yama is dissatisfied with his father's halfhearted assistance (made all the
more unpalatable by his snide remarks about fools getting into trouble):
what good is a bird to eat up a pustulating wound? He seeks better help
from a higher source; it is Shiva who makes him lord of the dead. (In later
mythology, the charioteer of the dawn has no legs; all the solar family are
notoriously at odds with their own feet.)

The Sanskrit curse and countercurse turn upon a double pun, a riddle,
for *pada* (foot) (cognate with Latin *pes, pedes,* French *pied,* and English
foot) has two other meanings that are relevant here. It also means "a quarter, a part" (one of the four feet of the paradigmatic quadruped that represents wholeness), so that the countercurse invokes a kind of synecdoche,
pars pro toto: Yama will lose not his whole body, but only part of it (or
even just a part of the part, a part of the foot), the part that the worms will
take away. And *pada* also means a word or a line or measure of poetry
(that is, one of the four quarters of a paradigmatic verse), a meaning that
"foot" also has in English (and Greek). Thus the trick of the word *(pada)*
is what saves Yama's foot *(pada).* (In the same way, the metrical "feet" of
verses spoken by Indra* match the multiple genitals on every joint—or
literary section, *parvan*—of a demoness who has trapped him, and thus
set him free.)[135] The foot of Yama, like the foot of Oedipus, is the clue to
the riddle of old age and death.

Yama inherits his lameness as well as his mortality from his father, the
Sun. For in implying that Samjna left her husband because he had an un-
satisfactory form, these texts also seem to imply that he became properly
formed after she left him, indeed as a direct result of that leaving—when
her father trimmed him. But sometimes that operation injures, or at least
neglects, the Sun's feet: "Tvashtri made his form one without peer [or

without reflection, *apratima*], all except for his feet. For he could not look at the form of the feet of the Sun."[136] The excess brilliance of the Sun* now explains his apparent lameness: his feet were the brightest part of him, too bright to look at or trim. Other texts state that the Sun's legs are not absent but merely invisible: the only part of the Sun's body not pared away by Tvashtri, the feet are so blindingly radiant that they must be always be covered.[137] Mortal artisans, therefore, are instructed to make images of the Sun without feet, because the primeval artisan was unable to trim them and thus to bring them within the compass of an artist.

The mutilated foot may function as a synecdoche for the mortality of the human body as a whole; the image of the worms eating Yama's foot is surely suggestive of this. We speak of the Achilles heel, and point to our own Achilles tendons as the sign of our mortality, the place where Achilles' mother, the goddess Thetis, held him when she dipped him into the waters that made the rest of him immortal, the place where—because she forgot to dip it—he remained vulnerable and through which death entered him. (As anyone over fifty will testify, we might more properly refer to our fatal weakness as the Achilles knee: whoever had arthroscopic surgery on a heel? Woody Allen, in *Mighty Aphrodite* [1996], remarks that his whole body is an Achilles heel.) The Greek myth of Achilles' heel is matched, in India, by the myth of the incarnate god Krishna, who is killed when a hunter named, surely significantly, "Old-age," mistakes him for an animal and shoots him in the foot.[138] Since the foot is precisely what is used to distinguish humans from animals in many myths, the foot is the mythological (if not logical) place to shoot a human that one has mistaken for an animal. We continue to speak of feet of clay (that is, of earth) as a metaphor for the weak spot, the mortal spot. The very word for human in Arabic *(rajal)* means foot.

And, on the other border of the human, we suffer the mutilation of our feet when we cease to be gods and become real human beings. The heels of Eve's descendants are cursed to bruise and be bruised by the head of the serpent (which sloughs its skin in immortality) as she is banished from Eden for her transgression (Genesis 3:15). The meaning of the juxtaposition of Eve's heel and the serpent's head is inverted when Mary is said to have trodden on the serpent because she had been immaculately conceived; as the new Eve she is pure and hence is not wounded, as Eve is, when her foot touches the serpent. Thus Mary is depicted barefoot with her heel on a serpent in many medieval sculptures. The mermaid in Hans

Christian Andersen's story has no feet and hence is immortal, but she cannot dance (surely a euphemism for the sexual act); she tortures herself to disguise herself by cleaving her tail in two and creating feet that bleed and cause her constant agony.[139] The mermaid's lover, in Oscar Wilde's telling, cuts his own shadow—his immortal soul—away from his feet,[140] the place where the soul is attached, where death is attached. (So too Peter Pan, the boy who will never die or age, loses his shadow* and when he finds it asks Wendy to attach it to his foot.) Through the fatal link between sexuality and death, when the mermaid gets feet, she can dance, and love, and bleed (menstruate?), and suffer—and finally die.

The wounded foot may stand as a metaphor for someone higher instead of (or as well as) lower, than the rest of us: the godlike artist. Indeed, lameness may literally signal the touch of the gods: when Jacob wrestles with the angel his thigh is touched and wounded so that he limps forever after, and Hephaestus,* the lame artisan of the Greek gods, becomes lame when he is hurled from Heaven to Earth—like the devil. The putrefying foot, like the festering foot of Philoctetes in Sophocles' play, is the mark of the artist, who pays with the wound in his foot for his skill with his hands in art or archery, as Edmund Wilson argued in his book entitled *The Wound and the Bow.* We use our hands to write, and by writing we extend our individual memories into the future, a kind of immortality. Saul Bellow saw the opposite causal pattern at play: "It was probably no accident that it was the cripple Hephaestus who made ingenious machines; a normal man didn't have to hoist or jack himself over hindrances by means of cranks, chains, and metal parts."[141] The privilege of being artisans is balanced by the loss of the swift and secure movements of quadrupeds; the mythological sacrifice of the lame artisan leads, in real life, to chronic lower-back pain. The power, as well as the deformity, of the lame artisan often inspires fear and distrust. As Otto Fenichel put it, "The deep feelings of uneasiness entertained toward the devil and the cripple-god ... increases when any physical disadvantage is combined with superiority in certain mental spheres (think of the uncanny, skillful, lame blacksmith of the sages)."[142] The wounded foot is often coupled, in anti-Semitic literature, with the presumed intelligence (it's usually called cunning) of the Jew. Alberich the dwarf in Richard Wagner's *Ring of the Nibelung* is another (perhaps Indo-European) lame artisan—with anti-Semitic overtones of the lame Jewish artisan as well. Wagner argues, in his story of Wieland the Smith, that the artisan smith was crippled as a result of his art: King Envy severed the sinews of Wieland the Smith's feet, "For he rightly guessed that the Smith had only need of hands, and not of feet, to do his work." So Wieland is "crippled. . . . limping, lamed, and loathly" until he forges wings with which he escapes.[143]

Finally, we should note (though not necessarily accept) Freud's suggestion that Oedipus's blinding was a euphemism for castration;* but his wounded foot may also foreshadow a kind of castration, since the feet may stand for the genitals (as they often do in the Hebrew Bible). This reading is not inconsistent with the one that I am about to make for the connection between immortality and sterility on the one hand and mortality/humanity and progeny on the other. The wounded foot of the human artist would symbolize a kind of castration, a kind of substitution of the artistic creations of the human imagination in compensation for the loss of the animal creation of somatic offspring.

Conclusion: Why Prefer a Human to a God?

So much for the criterion of the foot. Now let us return to the more general problem of distinguishing mortals from immortals and to the closely related topic of choice. For in considering the criteria for telling a god from a human, we have already from time to time slipped across the border into the closely related topic of the reasons why one might prefer a mortal lover or spouse.

Ancient Hindu and Greek mythologies generally agree that gods and goddesses usually prefer human lovers, but they differ in their attitude to preference among human men and women. These myths of choice send several different messages, for humans are double in this respect too: some prefer their own kind, but others prefer creatures from another world. Although our earliest example is an immortal woman (Saranyu) who rejected a mortal man, we have encountered various counterinstances: the wise, virtuous, and faithful Sukanya and Damayanti prefer their human husbands, and the Dhola epic of Nal applies this to both genders: the woman (Damayanti) rejects her immortal suitors, and the man (Nal) rejects the love of a goddess. But the virtuous (but not wise) Ahalya gives way to the knowing, sinful, and complicitous Ahalya, who preferred the god (while Indra preferred the mortal). Within the Greek texts, we encountered both Alcmena, who chose the mortal (as did Zeus) but knowingly or unknowingly enjoyed the god, and Odysseus, who preferred the human woman (but also knowingly enjoyed the goddess).

The Permutations of Preference

Certain patterns prevail in one culture, others in others. But statistical generalizations are never very sound and seldom even interesting. Let us consider the quality, rather than the quantity, of the two alternatives, noting the implications of three basic variables within these myths of choice: the protagonist may be human or nonhuman (a better category than immortal for this taxonomy, since the gods in many traditions do die, and some humans become immortal), male or female, and may prefer (or implicitly prefer, by rejecting the other category) someone the same as or of a different kind from the protagonist. These three factors yield eight possible permutations of choice (2^3):

1. A human woman prefers a human man (Damayanti)
2. A human man prefers a human woman (Odysseus)
3. A nonhuman woman prefers a human man (Calypso)
4. A nonhuman man prefers a human woman (Indra)
5. A human woman prefers a nonhuman man (Etain; Ahalya often)
6. A human man prefers a nonhuman woman (Pururavas)
7. A nonhuman woman prefers a nonhuman man (Hera)
8. A nonhuman man prefers a nonhuman woman (Ares)

Categories 7 and 8, gods and goddesses choosing one another, are built into all the classical theogonies and need not concern us here, since they involve no divine/human miscegenation. Saranyu and Vivasvant do not really fit this pattern: although the immortal Saranyu rejects the mortal Vivasvant, he is not a human, she does take him back again, and she never chooses an unambiguously immortal partner.

Categories 5 and 6, humans who choose deities, are what we might expect, and we might quickly summarize the relatively short (perhaps because so obvious) arguments of those who prefer nonhuman lovers, beginning first with general considerations and then comparing texts about women (category 5) and men (category 6).

David Shulman regards the prevalent pattern in Hindu tales as one in which "the self-transcending human being marries an immortal, usually with tragic consequences."[144] In general, humans choose nonhuman sexual partners for the eroticism that is part of the sexual fantasy, the thrill of making love with a strange person, epitomized by a superhuman creature. But the eroticism of a nonhuman lover of either gender is a mixed blessing. Often the lovers of gods and goddesses die because they violate a contract (like the contract that Pururavas violates with Urvashi), which may amount to: "Don't ask my name or look at me," i.e., don't unmask me or break through my masquerade. Sometimes the human doesn't make the choice knowingly; his/her companions (jealous sisters, etc.) trick him/her into violating the contract; sometimes the nonhuman's companions do this. But often the human violates the pact of secrecy because he/she is literally "dying to know" the true nature of his/her mysterious companion. The eroticism, therefore, though intense is literally short-lived. Within the texts, gods always seem to assume that mortals will prefer them as lovers but in fact mortals usually do not, and with good reason.

Yet there is also a gendered asymmetry, a double standard that informs these comparisons: the mating of gods with human women (categories 4 and 5, the Indra/Etain/Superman scenario), no matter who chooses whom, is depicted as less harmful to the human than is the mating of goddesses with human men (categories 3 and 6, the Calypso/Pururavas scenario), again, no matter who chooses whom. This syndrome results in part from transferring to the interspecific world the pattern that prevails in the interclass (or, in Hinduism, intercaste) world: hypergamy—the groom should be higher than the bride. Or in simple sexist terms, men should be more powerful than their women.

With this in mind, let us consider the case of a human woman who chooses a nonhuman man (typified by Etain, and Ahalya in some variants), category 5. Some reasons for this preference are erotic, some are procreative, and some are both. Is the gods' sexuality different from that of human men? In most cultures it is (Shiva can make love for as many years as he likes without releasing his seed), though in other cultures the gods are entirely anthropomorphic in this respect; Homer makes no special claims for Zeus, nor does Hera, though Zeus himself occasionally does. Yet Alcmena in some tellings seems to prefer Zeus to Amphitryon, however much she may insist that she *wants* Amphitryon. Giraudoux's Alcmena fancies Jupiter in the abstract (though, unlike Ahalya, she does not actually plan to do anything about it): she says that, just as she has a favorite man, she has a favorite god—Jupiter. "He's handsome, and melancholy, and serene." And she admits to envying Leda and the other women he has seduced.[145] Moreover, she regards Jupiter's immortality as a sexual plus: when Jupiter, as Amphitryon, urges her to say that this past night was better than any other, she says, "For once I didn't have that sort of divine misgiving I always have that you'll suddenly die in my arms."[146] Thus the one advantage of an immortal lover is precisely that: his immortality. And this is just what Jupiter doesn't want to hear. So too in Garrison Keillor's satire on this story, when Zeus becomes a Lutheran minister to seduce a woman from Pennsylvania, it is precisely because of his divinity that he is encouraged to seduce her: "She refused to look at him, but, being a god, he could read her thoughts. She was interested."[147] And there is always the chance that the immortal lover will make the human immortal too, and unaging; this is apparently Etain's hope.

Fertility is a more telling factor, for the god who impregnates a human woman often begets an important child, like Heracles from Zeus and Alcmena. When a human woman is impregnated by a male god, she may make either (or both) of two separate but closely related claims: (1) I didn't commit adultery (because my lover was a god, who doesn't count, legally speaking), and (2) my child should be a king, or even a god (because my lover was a god, who produces extraordinary children). According to Seneca, Alcmena was responsible for her son's deification: when Heracles was dying, she failed at first to recognize him (an irony, given the circumstances of his birth); after his death, she took his ashes to Thebes to establish the cult of his worship.[148] Like the children of Greek deities, the children of Hindu gods and human women often call upon their parents for help. This happens even though the offspring of gods in Hinduism are often raised as if they were in fact the children of their human parents, the doublets of the gods.[149] Clearly, divine liaisons do have their uses for human women. And stepping out of the text, we may assume that human women choose nonhuman lovers because the human men who write the stories want to be able to say that their dynasty was founded by a god.

So much for the women; now for the human man who chooses a nonhuman woman (category 6, Pururavas). In addition to the general reasons why liaisons with nonhumans are bad for humans, our texts give us far more reasons why a man should not desire a woman from the other world than reasons why he should: the goddess usually brings the man nothing but trouble—or, indeed, death.[150] The human man who is desired by a woman from the other world—animal, goddess, or demoness—is likely to die, whether he rejects her or accepts her: once the goddess fancies him, he is, quite literally, damned if he does and damned if he doesn't. Aphrodite manages to save the life of one of her mortal lovers (Anchises, father of Aeneas) by leaving him in time, and quenching his ardor with two cautionary erotic tales: Ganymede, whom Zeus loved and made immortal, but whose father never saw him again (a tale with parallels to the myth of Shuka* and Vyasa); and Tithonoos, whom Dawn loved and whom she persuaded Zeus to make immortal—but forgot to ask to make him unaging too. . . .[151] (The connections between Dawn and Saranyu are significant in this context.) Calypso offers Odysseus an immortal body, but it is death-in-life; for Calypso is, as her name tells us, the one who veils, resonant with the black cloud of death that veils mortals.[152] Hell certainly hath no fury like a goddess scorned, and the maneuvers that mortals make to dodge the divine pass utilize all the weapons of the weak.[153]

Given the fatal track record of the mortal lovers of goddesses, why do some men choose death and the goddess? The men who do not kick goddesses out of bed are often enchanted by the extraordinary beauty of the nonhuman women and (1) do not know or (2) do not care that their partners are goddesses, or (3) do not know or (4) do not care that their brief life with the goddess must be purchased at the cost of death. Yet, though desire is clearly an important part of this fatal paradigm, fertility more often justifies it, at least explicitly, just as it justifies the mating of human women with male gods. Yama and Manu—the founders of the human race—are born from the immortal Saranyu and the mortal Sun. Men who mate with goddesses, like women with gods, often produce heroic children on earth: the goddesses Thetis, Venus, and Ganga give birth to Achilles, Aeneas, and Bhishma in Greek, Roman, and Hindu mythology; and like certain heroes born of powerful human women, the children of goddesses often bear matronymics (Gangeya for Bhishma in the *Mahabharata*, for instance). Here too the hope may be that the immortality of the divine lover may rub off on the mortal through intimate physical contact. The paradigm is confirmed by Helen of Troy, not really a goddess but (according to Marlowe) an immortal woman whose immortality Marlowe's Faust hopes will be contagious; right after he makes that notorious remark about launching a fleet, he adds, "Sweet Helen, make me immortal with a kiss. Her lips suck forth my soul; see where it flies." But of course she does not make him immortal after all. She may well suck forth his soul, but it does not fly to heaven; on the contrary.

The other four categories, 1 through 4, contain people, male and female, human and nonhuman, who prefer the human (and/or reject nonhuman lovers). Again we must note from the start how differently the texts treat the different genders and how differently Hindu and Greek texts, as well as other cultures, tackle the problem. Let us begin with human women who choose human men (category 1, typified by Damayanti).

As with goddesses as lovers for human men, the reasons for human women not to prefer gods work in favor of human men, reasons over and above the general considerations noted above. Why does the human woman prefer her human lover? Not, presumably, for sexual reasons. The question of the gods' performance in bed recurs in our day in the movie *Superman* (1978), when Lois Lane (Margot Kidder) asks Superman (Christopher Reeve), "Are *all* your powers super?" But as all fans of the real Superman, the comic book Superman, know, Superman never never goes to bed with (which is to say, in the moral world of early comic books, marries) Lois Lane. Ostensibly, this is to protect his secret identity, which he might reveal in the intimacy of pillow talk; in this sense, it is dangerous for a god to sleep with a human. But Larry Niven has made hilariously explicit the other side of the coin, the danger for Lois:

> Assume a mating between Superman and a human woman, designated LL for convenience. . . . The problem is this: Electroencephalograms taken of men and women during sexual intercourse show that orgasm resembles "a kind of pleasurable epileptic attack." One loses control over one's muscles. Superman has been known to leave his fingerprints in steel and in hardened concrete, accidentally. What would he do to the woman in his arms during what amounts to an epileptic fit? Consider the driving urge between a man and a woman, the monomaniacal urge to achieve greater and greater penetration. Remember also that we are dealing with kryptonian muscles. Superman would literally crush LL's body in his arms, while simultaneously ripping her open from crotch to sternum, gutting her like a trout. Lastly, he'd blow off the top of her head.
>
> . . . With kryptonian muscles behind it, Kal-El's semen would emerge with the muzzle velocity of a machine gun bullet. In view of the foregoing, normal sex is impossible between LL and Superman. [Niven adds a footnote:] One can imagine that the Kent home in Smallville was riddled with holes during Superboy's puberty. And why didn't Lana Lang ever notice *that?*[154]

Kryptonian semen, like the sperm/energy of Vivasvant or the radiance of Jupiter that Alcmena fears would make her perish, is too hot to handle. This is one reason why mortal women prefer mortal lovers.

The argument that a human can't bear to *look** at a god is part of the broader argument against taking a god for a lover. Giraudoux's Alcmena cannot bear even the memory of her partial realization that she might have slept with the god without knowing it. She begs him for forgetfulness, not only of her possible adultery but of her glimpse of immortality. Still he tries to tempt her with Faustian visions:

> "Don't you want to know, as you're about to forget it all, what semblances your happiness is built on, what illusions sustain your virtue?" "No." "Nor what I really am to you, Alcmena? Nor what's inside this dear, dear belly?" [i.e., the fact that he rather than Amphitryon is the father of Heracles]. "Oh, hurry!"[155]

He allows her to forget what she knows, what she guesses.

Stepping back outside the text again for a moment, we might suggest that since on the one hand our texts were composed by human men and on the other the superiority of human men over gods is by no means obvious, it is hardly surprising that the preference for human men inspires a great deal of fancy ideological footwork of justification in our myths. One of the many functions of a myth is to affirm the status quo (or more precisely, what David Tracy has called the fluxus quo.)[156] For instance, in addition to those myths that we will soon consider, which explain why we chose death (knowingly or accidentally), some myths imagine what the world was like when there was no death, in order to affirm either that we must settle for what we have (since it is our own fault that death came into the world),[157] or that we really would not be happy if there were no death (there would be overcrowding, no moral law, etc.)[158] And there are many stories about a man and woman who exchange roles for a day, the woman working in the fields, the man in the house, with hilarious and disastrous results, confirming that a woman's place is in fact in the home. The myths in which the woman chooses a mortal husband combine the choice of her own role with the choice of her own mortality and thus doubly affirm the fluxus quo. When our stories imagine that a woman might be able to make love with a god, they do so in order to encourage the female reader or hearer to imagine that she would rather keep the human husband she has. As Mercury says of Giraudoux's Alcmena, "She simply lacks imagination."[159]

How unimaginative can it get? Jungian, that's how. In Robert Johnson's Jungian analysis of Damayanti:

> She chooses—that is, she maintains a realistic human perspective when she is offered a god as a husband. . . . She avoids the romantic fantasy of a god as a lover. . . . She is aware of limits and chooses the limited human,

who needs to blink his eyes, over the divine, which would be timeless and immortal. She is capable of seeing that the human condition is preferable to the divine at a particular point in her life. . . . Women in their relationships with men often feel that the men disappear psychologically and emotionally. This ability to identify one small sign of a man's true nature and connect with it can help him toward wholeness.[160]

Yes, well, though there is little to disagree with in this analysis, it hardly does justice to the issues raised in the myth. So much for the human woman who prefers her human man.

Let us turn now to human men who prefer human women, category 2 (Odysseus), noting that as with men versus gods, the reasons that we have seen not to prefer goddesses work in favor of human women. Odysseus is not alone. To select just three famous instances, Enkidu in the *Gilgamesh* epic rejects Ishthar; the human hero Arjuna* in the *Mahabharata* rejects the immortal nymph Urvashi[161] (a story that may actually have historical connections with the tale of Odysseus's rejection of Calypso);[162] and Ovid's Cephalus rejects Aurora.[163] Men often reject goddesses, though usually when the goddess is depicted as a whore. Many texts depict this rejection, though few actually give positive reasons for the human man's preference for human women in contrast with the reasons given for gods to prefer human women (4) and for human women to prefer human men (1).

The paradox of the mortal man who wins not immortality but death from his encounter with the nonhuman woman is just half of a broader paradox, of which the other half is supplied by the nonhuman woman who wins not death but immortality from her encounter with the mortal man. This brings us to the other side of the question: Why do nonhuman women, like Calypso—for a while—choose human men (category 3)? Different cultures suggest different reasons. In Christian mythology it is the mortals who are ultimately immortal—for they have immortal souls, which is what the nonhuman women want.[164] These women do not always take the men's souls away in order to get their own souls (though some do); it usually suffices just to seduce them. Undine, the water nymph (the European equivalent of an *apsaras* or celestial water nymph and courtesan like Urvashi) is such an otherworldly, mortal creature. She is best known from Friedrich de la Motte Fouqué's German novella, *Undine*, which later inspired an opera by E. T. A. Hoffmann and many plays (one by Jean Giraudoux) and movies (one with Audrey Hepburn), as well as Hans Christian Andersen's story "The Little Mermaid." Fouqué stressed not the bestiality but the otherworldliness of the heroine; the hero is the one who proves to be morally bestial as he abandons Undine and destroys her. The human lover of Giraudoux's *Ondine* betrays her with the lost (human) daughter of the human parents who had adopted her, the woman for whom Ondine is in a sense a changeling; and though she tries to save him, he dies for betraying her, in keeping with the inexorable contract enforced by her father. The issue of the soul is given a nice twist in a discussion between Ondine and a human queen about her likely betrayal by her human lover. Queen: "He has a small soul." Ondine: "I haven't got any soul, that's much worse." Queen: "The question doesn't arise for you, or for any creatures except humans. The world's soul breathes in and out through every bird and fish and animal; but man wanted his soul to himself. So, like a fool, he chopped up the human spirit into bits so that every man could have one. . . ."[165] This Ondine has no soul but apparently does very well without one, while her human lover, who presumably has one, dies.

The idea that the woman from the otherworld seeks not the body of her mortal lover but her own soul from him can be traced back to Paracelsus's treatise on the four nature spirits. One of these is an Undine, who resembles a human woman in every way except the possession of a soul, which she obtains only if she unites with a man. And so, Paracelsus tells us, she seduces a man in secret, just as a heathen seeks baptism in order to get a soul and to find eternal life as a Christian.[166] Paracelsus went on to condemn Mélusine, a serpent woman who masqueraded as a human woman, though never on Saturday; when her husband violated his promise and intruded upon her in her Saturday bath, he discovered Mélusine, "her lower extremities changed into the tail of a monstrous fish or serpent." He cursed her: "Away, hateful serpent, contaminator of my honorable race!" She kissed him and embraced him for the last time, then swept from the room, "leaving the impression of her foot on the stone she last touched." She returned in a ghostly form at night to nurse at her breast the two babies that she had left behind.[167] Her ghostly form, like Samjna's shadow, nourishes her children, the usual twins; her present absence is also captured in her footprint on the stone—a particularly poignant symbol of a snake-woman who, like the closely related mermaid, has no feet until she marries the mortal who will betray her.

Paracelsus called Mélusine a "nightmare" and condemned her not for being a serpent but for being the devil's minion—not only a serpent, but a Catholic serpent to boot:

> Such is the devil that he transforms these beings into different shapes, as he also does with the witches, transforming them into cats and werewolves, dogs, and so forth. This happened to her also, for she never was free of witchcraft but had a part in it. A superstitious belief resulted, that on Saturdays she had to be a serpent. This was her pledge to the devil for helping her in getting a man. . . . Yet there are more superstitions in the Roman Church than in all these women and witches. And so it may be a warning that if superstition turns a man into a serpent, it also turns him into a devil. That is, if it happens to nymphs, it also happens to you in the Roman Church. That is, you too will be transformed into such serpents, you who now are pretty and handsome, adorned with large diadems and jewels. In the end you will be a serpent and dragon, like Mélusine and others of her kind.[168]

Thus Mélusine, who was, Paracelsus insisted, originally a nymph, was transformed into a serpent not by her mother or father or unfaithful husband but by Satan himself (or perhaps the pope). She is a devil masquerading as a Christian. (Heinrich Heine is said to have remarked that Mélusine's husband was a relatively happy man, since his wife was only *half* a snake.)[169]

Later Christian mythology, polluted by the twin forces of racism and sexism, assimilated the soulless pagans to both women and Jews. And Otto Weininger, a Jew who committed suicide in 1903, "set out to prove that all Jews were, essentially, women. 'Those who have no soul can have no craving for immortality, and so it is with the woman and the Jew.' "[170] Were mermaids Jews longing to be Christians, or just women longing to have what men had?

In the corresponding other gender paradigm, the story of the nonhuman man who prefers a human woman (our final category, 4, typified by Zeus and Indra) is one of the dominant themes of worldwide mythology. Thus the messenger in the Telugu variant of the myth of Ahalya speaks of the possibilities of human sensuality, greater than that of the gods. The consideration of a child fathered by a god often comes into play, as in the myth of Amphitryon, but eroticism is also a factor here; Giraudoux's Jupiter says, "I'm not concerned with Hercules any more. Happily, the Hercules business is over. I'm concerned about myself now."[171] And

Behrman's Jupiter pleads, "I beg you, Alkmena, do not abandon me; do not leave me with nothing on my hands but my divinity."

But the mating of a god with a human woman was a popular Christian theme as well (think for instance of the Holy Spirit and Mary), in part because of the arguments just cited for the superiority of the human soul. Kierkegaard, in his analysis of the Danish tale of Agnete and the merman, perhaps under the influence of the paradigm of Undine, merely switched the genders and suggested that the winning of a human soul was the reason for the merman's desire for Agnete: "The merman does not want to seduce Agnete although he has seduced many others. He is no merman any more. . . . Yet he knows . . . that he can be saved by the love of an innocent maiden. . . . Soon he was tired of Agnete, yet her body was never found."[172]

But the non-Christian texts themselves give a nongendered reason for the nonhumans' preference for humans, one rather different from the reason constructed for them by Christian texts: they desire a child rather than a soul. In the Scandinavian myths of the seal-men, "the essential plot concerns the desire of the seal for contact with the human world and for a son."[173] We noted in the story of Saranyu that immortals do not have children because if you don't die there is no need to reproduce yourself. This explains why gods seduce and impregnate mortal women rather than just desiring them or seeking their sexual pleasure among them. (But this applies far more to gods than to goddesses: Motini explicitly cautions Nal that, being a goddess, she can never have children, even with him.) The Chinese fox wife wants a mortal lover because she wants children;[174] in her world, where no one dies, no one can be born. The story of the loss of Eden in the Hebrew Bible presents the causal sequence in the opposite order: because there is sex there will be death.

Gregory Nagy stated the case very well for the Greek gods: "As we see clearly from the Hesiodic *Theogony,* the lineage of purebred Olympian gods comes to a halt, for all practical purposes, at the third generation. . . . The Olympian gods of the third generation propagate by mating with mortals, not with each other. Mortal genes, as it were, are dominant, while immortal ones are recessive, in that any element of mortality in a lineage produces mortal offspring."[175] Is the choice of a mortal lover a move from Eros to Thanatos? I think not; on the contrary, as we have just seen, death, or rather mortality, is what makes sex possible. The otherworldly woman chooses life when she chooses her mortal lover. After Giraudoux's Ondine falls head over heels in love with a mortal man, her father remarks: "She was the most human being that ever lived, because she was human by choice."[176]

The Romance of the Stone (and the Banana)

I have argued for a gendered asymmetry in these myths—something that might better be designated by its old name, the double standard, a term that takes on new meaning in the context of these myths of doubling. But in some ways, when it comes to the reasons for choosing a mortal man or woman over a goddess or a god, gender does not seem to matter very much, since many reasons for choosing a mortal partner transcend gender: an immortal soul, children, sexual ecstasy. Barbara Fass Leavy has speculated on the reasons why women in folklore and myth "spurn the advances of demon lovers, preferring reality to the imagined pleasures of the otherworld,"[177] but her remarks also apply to men who reject goddesses:

> Of primary importance is the nature of the otherworld itself, a land of dreams-come-true, where man is forever young and pleasures forever available. It is a static realm, lacking the earthly cycles of birth and death, a point worth stressing, for if the otherworld is, as the Irish put it, the Land of the Living, that is, a world in which no one dies, it also appears that it is a world in which no one is born. . . . La Belle Dame sans Merci and the land in which she dwells are not creative. What they supply instead is perpetual bliss, and bliss, when it is its own end, inevitably palls.[178]

Endless light and clarity is exhausting (as we learn from those who have experienced the White Nights of summer in Stockholm or Saint Petersburg). Damayanti knew this. She loves her human husband with all his imperfections and recognizes him by the imperfections that she loves: sweaty, blinking, earthbound, dusty, shadowy old Nala. In Hindu mythology, the gods are twenty-five years old forever.[179] To some of us over fifty, this might appear an attractive alternative; but to most of us, it would not.

Angela Carter, in her retelling of "Beauty and the Beast," has imagined the heroine's reasons for rejecting divine perfection when she contemplates her beast:

> I never saw a man so big look so two-dimensional . . . He throws our human aspirations to the godlike sadly awry, poor fellow; only from a distance would you think The Beast not much different from any other man, although he wears a mask with a man's face painted most beautifully on it.

> Oh, yes, a beautiful face; but one with too much formal symmetry of feature
> to be entirely human: one profile of his mask is the mirror image of the
> other, too perfect, uncanny.[180]

The god who may become the mirror image of the human whom he impersonates is himself his own mirror image, too perfect and symmetrical to be real. The mirror here makes possible a symmetry and perfection that is inhuman. Here we may recall that the makers of Persian carpets deliberately introduce a flaw into each carpet as a sign of humility and in order to avoid the hubris of attempted perfection. Giraudoux's Mercury points out to Jupiter the flaws in his disguise: "Your garments are frankly eternal. I'm quite sure they're water-proof, non-fading, and unstainable even with lamp-oil. To a good housewife like Alcmena, those are real miracles, and you needn't suppose she'll miss them."[181] Alcmena herself says (wrongly, as it turns out), of Jupiter: "I shall recognize him. . . . He'll be a much more perfect, intelligent, noble Amphitryon. I shall loathe him the moment I set eyes on him."[182]

Roberto Calasso suggests a rather different reason for the (Greek) gods' preference for human women, a reason also highly meaningful in our broader context:

> When it came to his amorous adventures, Zeus found mortal women far
> more attractive. He wasn't interested in bothering those figures of fate; they
> were too similar to one another, disturbing the way twins can be, too ancient, and, in the end, hostile.[183]

Unlike human women with their asymmetrical flaws, all goddesses in their perfection look alike.[184]

In a story from the ninth-century Chinese *Sequel to the Record of Dark Mysteries,* an old man tells Du Zichun to remain silent and unmoved through illusions of pain and suffering, as he brews an elixir of immortality in a cauldron. Du Zichun experiences the illusion that he is reborn as a woman and gives birth to a son, but when her husband dashes their two-year-old child to the ground and kills him, Zichun, full of love and attachment, forgets his vow and cries out involuntarily, "Ah!," thus losing his chance for immortality. As Wei-yi Li points out, this story confronts the reader with the problem of inhuman immortality, an enlightenment that implies the denial of being human. We empathize with Du Zichun's failure, because had he not cried out, had he successfully divested himself of all forms of attachment, he would have behaved inhumanly.[185] A close

Greek parallel to this Chinese story is offered by the story of Demeter, who, after the descent into the underworld of her own child, Persephone, came in disguise as a nurse in order to make the child of a human king and queen immortal; but the child's mother entered just when Demeter was dipping the child in fire; she cried out, making Demeter stop before the job was finished. She could not stand the inhumanity it takes to become immortal.[186]

The choice made in these stories is the choice of real life, however brief, in preference to infinite nonlife, misleadingly referred to as immortality. The logic behind these apparently "wrong" choices is one that opts for a kind of continuous connectedness,[187] which is our symbolic immortality, the fragile, ephemeral, conditional, dependent intensity of real life, the emotional chiaroscuro,[188] the sense of impending loss that makes what we have so precious while we have it, more precious than the security of an eternity without that immediacy and intensity. To choose the imperfect mortal instead of the perfect immortal is to accept and even affirm one's own mortality and insufficiency, rejecting the vain goal of attaching one's perishable self to some seemingly perfect and unchanging unearthly form. Goddesses often desire mortal men, and gods mortal women, because of the heightened sexuality and excitement of those who change and suffer. Immortality in this view is not an expansion of being human, but a diminution or denial of being human; gods are less rather than more than human.

A closely related theme is that of the apparently *inadvertent* choice of mortality, a choice often made as the result of a trick or a riddle. This is the point of an Indonesian myth:

THE STONE AND THE BANANA

The natives of Poso, a district of Central Celebes, say that in the beginning the sky was very near the earth, and that the Creator, who lived in it, used to let down his gifts to men at the end of a rope. One day he thus lowered a stone; but our first father and mother would have none of it and they called out to their Maker, "What have we to do with this stone? Give us something else." The Creator complied and hauled away at the rope; the stone mounted up and up until it vanished from sight. Presently the rope was seen coming down from heaven again, and this time there was a banana at the end of it instead of a stone. Our first parents ran at the banana and took it. Then there came a voice from heaven saying, "Because ye have chosen the banana, your life shall be like its life. When the banana-tree has offspring, the parent stem dies; so shall ye die and your children shall step into your place. Had ye chosen the stone, your life would have been like the life of the stone changeless and immortal." The man and his wife mourned over their fatal choice, but it was too late; that is how through the eating of a banana death came into the world.[189]

They chose the banana because it was luscious (and perhaps phallic), a symbol of life, while the stone was a symbol of death. But in making this choice they foolishly and unwittingly threw away their chance of being immortal, never changing, like the stone. The stone is the touchstone, as it were, in contests between gods pretending to be human (who can lift the heavier stone?), contests in which the stone (in implicit contrast with flesh or a banana) represents the deity.

But were the humans in fact so foolish in choosing, instead of the sterility of an eternity of stone, the luscious, phallic banana of death? Did they really make the "wrong" choice? They made the same choice that Prometheus* made for mankind: the flesh, instead of the smoke. Operating on behalf of humans, Prometheus thinks that he tricks Zeus into choosing bones wrapped in skin, while mortals get the meat of the sacrificial animal; Zeus, however, thinks that he has tricked Prometheus into choosing meat, which rots and dies, while the gods live on the smoke of the oblation, which lasts forever. We might think that Prometheus outsmarts himself by engineering the choice that makes humans mortal and gods immortal. On the other hand, we might think that Prometheus had the last word after all, tricking the trickster: for he procured for us mortals a life of change and the delicious taste of food, a life in the flesh, rather than the shadowy existence of smoke that drove Zeus to find his sexual pleasures among mortal women. (Giraudoux's Jupiter says of Alcmena, "She is the true Prometheus.")[190] Here we may also recall that Zeus himself was replaced by a stone in the belly of his mother in order to foil the filicidal impulses of his father, Chronos;[191] here too there was a choice between a stone that fooled the god (like the bones that did or did not fool Zeus) and the flesh, or the banana, that survived: Zeus himself. That Chronos is Time, the force that turns flesh into dust, is surely not irrelevant here: to foil Time, one must be a stone.

When Giraudoux's Jupiter offers Alcmena immortality for herself, she refuses it and says, "It's a sort of betrayal for a human to become immortal. Besides, when I think of the perfect rest death will give us from all our little tirednesses and third-rate sorrows, I'm grateful to it for its fullness, its bounty even."[192] Damayanti too eloquently states the reasons a mortal might spurn a god:

> "Indra's merits, though attractive, do not make me give up a man who pleases me. People are unwilling to give up the three worldly goals of life—pleasure, religion, and profit—inferior though they are to [the fourth, transcendent goal,] Release. I will marry the immortal Indra—in his mortal form as King Nala. Even a virtuous man must come down from heaven [when he uses up his karma], but when he departs from here [at death], he goes to heaven. The two types of future are like gravel and sugar."[193]

To prefer Nala over Indra is to prefer sugar over gravel (that is, banana over stone). The stone is the curse inflicted on women who have been too much alive, like Ahalya.

Plato, in the *Gorgias* (494b), writes of the contrast between a stone and a certain bird, the *charadria*, who constantly eats and pisses. To compare the life of pleasure to the life of happiness, he says, is like comparing the *charadria* to a stone; is happiness just scratching an itch? The ridiculous bird through whom water (and presumably food) passes constantly takes the place of the banana in the Indonesian myth, or, closer to home, the flesh in the myth of Prometheus (or the child Zeus in the myth of the foiling of Chronos). (Lévi-Strauss wrote of similar myths about the goatsucker, a South American bird that shits constantly.)[194] Is Plato here making fun of these mythologies of choice and contrast, even making fun of the myth of Prometheus and Zeus? I wonder.

Carlo Ginzburg cites another variant of the Indonesian story of the banana from the island of Ceram (Molucca):

> The stone wanted men to have only one arm, one leg, one eye, and be immortal; the banana tree wanted them to have two arms, two legs, two eyes and to be able to procreate. The banana tree won the dispute: but the stone insisted that men be subject to death. The myth invites us to recognize symmetry as a characteristic of human beings.[195]

Yet most of these stories are arguing for just the opposite, for *asymmetry*, imperfection, as the defining human characteristic. And the two legs, regarded as standing in opposition not to one leg but to four, function as the sign not of symmetry but rather of nonanimal mortality.

The paradox that underlies these myths is the belief that to choose a mortal lover is to choose life (either in the form of an immortal soul or in the form of truly vivid existence), while to choose an immortal is not, as one might think, to choose life, let alone immortality, but to choose death, for the man who falls in love with a goddess often dies as a consequence. That is, by choosing death (the banana, the mortal), you choose life (rather than sterility), and by choosing immortality (life with a goddess), you end up choosing death (she kills you). Thus the myth of death meets itself coming in at the door: women choose mortal husbands and death, while men who choose immortal wives also inadvertently choose death. To put it differently, goddesses bring death to mortal men, while human women choose death (for themselves and also for mortal men). In either case, it is the female who appears to be responsible for death. (A female—not his lover but his mother—was responsible for the Achilles heel of Achilles.)

Yet these stories too are sometimes symmetrically gendered; in some, men (Prometheus, for instance) make the wrong choice. More important, the wrong choice that the women make turns out to be the right choice after all—the *felix culpa,* the fortunate error that makes human life possible. A beautiful Aynu variant of this myth contrasts the stone with wood rather than fruit, blames a presumably male animal rather than a human woman, and elaborates upon a whole series of fortunate errors:

THE STONE AND THE OTTER

When Kotankarukamui set out to make humans, he sent a sparrow to ask the heavenly deities what they thought he should use to make them. They replied that wood/trees would be good [and sent back the sparrow]. Later they thought that stone would in fact be a more durable material and summoned the otter and dispatched him with great urgency to the lower world to pass on this [new] command to Kotankarukamui. However, on his way Otter was distracted by a large school of fish and concentrating his whole attention on catching the fish completely forgot his mission, thus delivering his message far too late. Thus it was that humans were made of trees and not a single person is saved from aging and perishing. Yet, humans are also born one after another, they grow and develop and multiply. This too occurs because of the otter's forgetfulness. The deity was angry at Otter for this and stamped on his head; that is why it is so flat even today. Others say that the tree used to make humans was a willow and thus it is that humans, like the willow, bend and quiver as they age.[196]

Humans do not have a choice here: their fate is decided through the mistakes of two other actors, the gods (who choose the wrong substance at first, and wait too long to correct their error) and the otter (who miscarries his message, a common theme in cosmogonies). The stone is contrasted explicitly with the wood but also implicitly with the otter, whose playfulness and forgetfulness are eminently human. This text also makes explicit what was won as well as what was lost: the pleasures of growing and multiplying (that is, the pleasures of the otter); even old age is depicted by an image of grace and beauty, the willow.

The choice of death is not conscious in these myths; it is the result of a trick or a mistake, usually associated with food (but not always: the Aynu story of the otter imagines the choice as between building materials). The food itself may be what causes the unwitting mortal to make the unconscious choice of mortality; recall how Persephone ate the pomegranate and was doomed to remain half the year in the world of the dead and half the year among the living.[197] There is also a widespread folk belief that the human who eats fairy food must remain in the other world. A corollary of this belief occurs in the story of Naciketas, who did *not* eat anything in the underworld and thereby forced Death to tell him the secret of mortality and immortality.[198] And then there was that business in Eden, when Eve too chose the fruit (an apple? a banana?), and sex, and death.

Yet another Indonesian myth connects the inadvertent choice of death not with a stone or nonstone but with another index of mortality, the excessive heat of the Sun:*

THE ORIGIN OF DEATH

The wise and ancient Ndangi Lawo lived a long life amidst plenty by following the "word" or teachings of the Mother and Father Creator. Like all people back then, he would never die, because every time he would get old, he would shed his skin like a snake, be "renewed," and become young again. The Sun and Moon, however, would never set, and as a result, the earth would get very hot. So a young man named Mbora Pyaku went to the Creator to request that the Sun and Moon be permitted to set from time to time to cool things off. The creator agreed to let the Sun and Moon "live and die and live again," as Mbora Pyaku requested, but in exchange, "when humans die, they will die forever." As soon as Mbora Pyaku thus changed the "word" of the ancestors, Ndangi Lawo died, and people first began to cry and weep. Children began to be born, and people began to reckon time, counting the "months and years" until they died.[199]

Thus, death came into the world—from the confusion of the idea that the Sun is too hot and must have periodic times off (temporary death), with the idea that mortals made the mistaken choice to have nonperiodic time off (permanent death). Although this text is far distant from the Vedas in time and space, its culture has historical connections with India and it contains analogies with elements of the story of Saranyu, chiefly the link between the excessive heat of the Sun and his mortality (more precisely, the mortality that he bequeaths to us, through his son Yama). A footnote to the Indonesian myth points out that, "According to one version of this tale, the earth was too hot because there were two suns"—one too many, reflecting both the Sun's own excess and his unknowing possession of two wives.

But a *conscious* preference for the human is what we find in the myth of Damayanti, a preference that explains one of the enduring mysteries of the American cinema: Why did Dorothy want to leave Oz and return to Kansas? This decision always bothered me (I am a New Yorker, with a New Yorker's scorn for everything west of the Hudson), and I was not surprised to learn that it bothered the author himself, who later reworked the story. For in subsequent Oz books by L. Frank Baum, as Salman Rushdie tells us,

> Dorothy, ignoring the "lessons" of the ruby slippers, went back to Oz, in spite of the efforts of Kansas folk, including Auntie Em and Uncle Henry, to have her dreams brainwashed out of her . . . ; and, in the sixth book of the series, she took Auntie Em and Uncle Henry with her, and they all settled down in Oz, where Dorothy became a Princess. So Oz finally *became* home; the imagined world became the actual world.[200]

But mythology all over the word offers many precedents for Dorothy's original preference for a real home over the seductive world of fantasy, the world of immortality.

Mariatale / Renuka and Scylla / Charybdis

~~*~~

MARIATALE/RENUKA

The first chapters of this book have been about doubling: there were two Helens and Sitas, two Saranyus, two Amphitryons and Gautamas, and too many Nalas. Now let us consider the complementary aspect of this mythology, splitting—more precisely, doubling that also involves splitting. There is a well-known Hindu myth in which a high-caste woman, tricked into marrying an Outcaste man masquerading as a Brahmin, is transformed into a fierce goddess.[1] In a closely related corpus, the high-caste woman, abused by her husband (who is usually of a caste different from, but not necessarily lower than, hers), splits not into two separate women but into the head and body of a goddess. In some variants of this myth, two women split and then go on to combine: the head and body of the high-caste woman join with the supplementary parts of her Outcaste shadow "double" to form two other women (or two other goddesses), each consisting of two vividly contrasting halves.

The importance of this story as an origin myth about a goddess is confirmed by the existence of many variants told about the transformation of a human woman into the Kannada or Telugu goddess variously known as Ellamma or Yellamma or Allamma or Mariamma:

THE BRAHMIN WOMAN AND THE OUTCASTE WOMAN

A sage's wife, Mariamma, was sentenced by her husband to death. At the moment of execution she embraced an outcaste woman, Ellamma, for her sympathy. In the fray both the outcaste woman and the brahmin lost their heads. Later, the husband relented, granted them pardon, and restored their heads by his spiritual powers. But the heads were transposed by mistake. To Mariamma (with a brahmin head and outcaste body) goats and cocks but not buffaloes were sacrificed; to Ellamma (outcaste head and brahmin body) buffaloes instead of goats and cocks.[2]

Mariamma and Ellamma get mixed up in the course of the magical restoration, like the people on *Star Trek* who get scrambled when the transporter room malfunctions: "Beam me up, Mariamma." This version of the story ends up with two sets of mixed women and makes use of both sets of heads and torsos, splitting the women into two contrasting goddesses, who are named after their heads, not their bodies.

To discover some of the expanded meanings of this brief retelling, let us turn to a version of the story that Pierre Sonnerat retold in the eighteenth century, recorded from an oral Tamil tale. The following text is several times removed from the original telling: it is my translation of the eighteenth-century Frenchman's translation from the oral Tamil. But despite its mixed provenance as a kind of multicultural document in itself, it is valuable because of the ingenuity with which it presents an image that is meaningful to all three cultures, the image of the women with transposed heads. And since this central image is, as we have just seen, attested in other Hindu texts whose provenance is not sullied by the French connection, I think we may take the central points, at least, as evidence of Hindu thinking:

THE GODDESS AND THE OUTCASTE WOMAN

Mariatale was the wife of the ascetic Jamadagni and mother of Parashurama. This goddess ruled over the elements but she could keep this empire only as long as her heart remained pure. One day she was fetching water from a pool and following her usual custom was rolling it up in a ball to carry it home. She happened to see on the surface of the water several male demigods (Gandharvas), who were sporting gymnastically [here one suspects a French euphemism] right under her head. She was taken by their charms, and desire entered her heart. The water that she had already collected immediately turned to liquid and mingled back with the water of the pool. She could no longer carry it home without the help of a bowl. This impotence revealed to Jamadagni that his wife had ceased to be pure, and in the excess of his anger he commanded his son to drag her off to the place set aside for executions and to cut off her head. This order was executed; but Parashurama was so afflicted by the loss of his mother that Jamadagni told him to go and get her body, to join to it the head that he had cut off, and to whisper in its ear a prayer that he taught him, which would immediately revive her. The son ran in haste, but by a singular oversight he joined the head of his mother to the body of an Outcaste woman who had been executed for her crimes—a monstrous assemblage, which gave to this woman the virtues of a goddess and the vices of an unfortunate wretch. The goddess, having become impure through this mix, was chased out of her house and committed all sorts of cruelties; the gods, seeing the ravages that she was causing, appeased her by giving her the power to cure small-pox and promising her that she would be supplicated for this disease. . . . Only her head was placed in the inner sanctuary of the temple, to be worshipped by Indians of good caste; while her [Outcaste] body was placed at the door of the temple, to be worshipped by Outcastes. . . . Mariatale, having become impure through the mixing of her head with the body of an Outcaste, and fearing that she would no longer be adored by her son Parashurama, begged the gods to grant her another child. They gave her Kartavirya; the Outcastes divide their worship between his mother and him. This is the only one of all the gods to whom are offered cooked meats, salted fish, tobacco, and so forth, because he came from the body of an Outcaste.[3]

Like the goddess in other tellings, named Mariamma, from *mari* (a fierce goddess) and *amma* (mother), Maria-tale's name combines *mari* with *tale,* another synonym for "mother": thus, "The Fierce Mother Goddess." In this version of the myth, there is only one mixed woman, created by the fusion of Mariatale's head and the body of the Outcaste woman, like Mariamma in the first text. This text does not tell us what happened to the left-over pieces, Mariatale's body and the Outcaste woman's head, which became Ellamma in the text cited above; instead, her (disembodied) head and her (headless and presumably now Outcaste) body are worshipped as separate entities.

This story, retold in many versions, has a great deal to teach us about the dichotomizing of women and of goddesses. It juggles the different aspects of a human woman, on two levels: on the literal level, there is an interaction between a goddess and a woman; on the symbolic level, an implicit parallelism between the structure of a goddess and the structure of a woman. Let us therefore ask what the story tells us about the split between aspects of a goddess, classes of human society, and facets of a human woman.

There is a complex interaction between the high-born goddess, the Outcaste woman, and their two sons. Sonnerat's text doubles the ritual presence both by splitting the compound goddess and by introducing the second son, Kartavirya. The fused woman is a monster, impure and destructive, disease incarnate—ambivalent disease, whose Outcaste human body brings the fever of smallpox (as does the goddess who is tricked into marrying the Outcaste), a fever that is cooled by the grace of the divine head. This is the most basic of all theological doubles: she is the goddess who both brings disease and removes disease,[4] the deity who giveth and taketh away, the *mysterium fascinans et tremendum* that Rudolf Otto describes as the essence of the holy;[5]—in this case, a creature with a head that is *fascinans* and a body that is *tremendum*. (A variant of this coincidence of opposite supernatural powers may be seen in the ability of Jamadagni, the husband of Mariatale, both to remove heads and to restore them to life.)

So great is the tension within her that she does not remain integrated in ritual; she is split up once again, the divine head at last purified by being divorced from its polluting body, and the Outcaste body made literally liminal, placed on the doorstep, forever marking the pale of the Hindu society that sees woman as a divine-headed and Outcaste-bodied monster. Yet this is just one view, to be contrasted with another in which women also have positive relations not only with men but with doorsteps; in South India, for instance, Tamil women create beautiful, auspicious designs every morning in courtyards and on doorsteps.

The Outcastes further split their worship between the impure body of the goddess and the son born of her impure *body*—that is, not born of the divine part of her at all. For the son of the divine head and body (Parashurama) is pure, while the son of the divine head and the Outcaste body (Kartavirya) is impure; in this one case, where the head remains the same while the body changes, the son's quality is determined not by his mother's head but by her body (though it is always the father's head that gives the son his social status). Mariatale's head remains divine (and hence relatively pure) while her body becomes lower caste (and hence relatively impure); though her class is not specified, she is said to be pure in contrast with the Outcaste, and as a goddess she is high, if not necessarily pure, in contrast with a mortal. One South Indian variant implies that the anonymous woman is both low caste and menstruating (which makes her even more impure as well as sexualized): when the son went to behead his mother, the mother ran into the menstrual hut of a low-caste Cakkilicci woman "who had just reached puberty. Parasurama also ran inside and, thinking that he was cutting off the head of his mother, he cut off the head of the Cakkilicci woman—it was dark inside the hut. Then his mother ran out of the house, and Parasurama ran after her and cut off her head."[6] The opposition between the upper- and lower-caste woman, as between the chaste and the erotic woman, is expressed in the myth through a series of oppositions between the head and the body.

How is Mariatale's sexual ambivalence related to the mixture of castes in her head and body? Since higher castes often regard lower caste women as erotic, and her body ends up lower caste, we might assume that it is the site of her eroticism. There is an ambivalence of caste parallel to the ambivalence of sexuality. But in either case, the head is the source of a woman's identity and her legal status: if she has a divine head, she is a pure goddess. (An exception is posed by the contrast between two women, each of whom has the same, divine head; then the body, the only variable, determines the status.) And her impure bottom half, the half that lusts for the demigod, is the *human* woman, the denied woman, the passionate woman, as polluting and despised as the Outcaste. This half becomes the body of the finally integrated Mariatale, who is identified with the divine head but functions with an Outcaste body.

The theological level of the myth of Mariatale is thus inextricably intertwined with the question of class. Indeed, one can read this theodicy from several points of view: from the standpoint of Hindu society, the Outcaste woman pollutes the goddess, and the purpose of this myth is to explain the relationship between certain high-caste and low-caste goddesses. But from the point of view of a woman, certainly that of a Western woman and perhaps of the woman inside the story, Mariatale is unjustly treated by various men and driven to become a fierce goddess. (The other, related corpus of myths in which a Brahmin woman, tricked into marrying an Outcaste man, becomes a fierce goddess reinforces this pattern.)[7]

Mariatale's divine half reflects the unreasonable image of the entirely pure wife, symbolized by the impossible ability to roll water up, solid and dry, with nothing to sustain it. This is itself an image that cannot be sustained; the woman's natural emotion is expressed in the vision of the water that melts back into its natural liquidity and mingles again with the waters of the pool from which it was unnaturally frozen. The image of frozen and melting water, which recurs in other, related South Indian texts,[8] may be an expansion of a simpler image that occurs in a much earlier recorded version of this myth, in the *Mahabharata*, about a human woman, Renuka, who is beheaded and restored: "One day as she bathed in the river she caught sight of a king playing in the water with his queen, and she desired him. As a result of this unchaste thought, she lost her senses and became wet in the water."[9] This is a statement not only about her physical response but also about melting into her natural element.

We have encountered a similar metaphor in the tale of Ahalya, with the double image of passion as dammed-up water or a dried-up river and as a melting rock; indeed, in one text, Ahalya is cursed, like Amba,* to become a dried-up river.[10] The sin of making love in the water (which the Hindu lawmaker Manu, with uncharacteristic imagination, takes the trouble to prohibit)[11] may reflect the more general fear of the loss of sexual fluids:[12] in the water, you begin to leak. In the Tamil text, the image of the rolled-up water leaking back into the river is the image of a pure woman who feels passion, an ice maiden who is melted by lust; and such a woman can exist in Hindu India (and elsewhere?) only when she is physically split. Moreover, the water is the venue of the seductive celestial courtesans, the *apsaras*es, literally "sliding through the water," those sirens who siphon off the sexual fluids of unwitting sages.

We might note the male gaze in these myths, but there is also a powerful female gaze: it is by gazing, not by being gazed at, that Renuka discovers and reveals her eroticism. That is, the male gaze, as illuminated by early feminist discourse, assumes that the author of a text is male and that the women in it are just objects to be looked at, with no gaze of their own. But there are texts, and the tale of Renuka is certainly such a text, in which the woman certainly does have a gaze and is a subject, not merely the object or victim of a male subject (though she may be that too, and here she clearly is). And that female gaze, still perhaps seen through male eyes, is problematic and destructive. Thus, it is precisely because the male author of the text deems the female gaze unacceptable that Mariatale/Renuka must be beheaded, her gaze silenced, as it were.

Yet we may also read Renuka's gaze as the indication of a female voice surviving in this text, a voice that says that Renuka is an innocent woman with perfectly understandable feelings and that Jamadagni is an insane monster. I sometimes feel that even the Sanskrit text is meant to be read precisely in this way, as a subversion of the idea that women must never experience desire and that men have the right to destroy them if they do. Surely the Tamil retelling that we will soon encounter, in which "matricide is not such a good thing," must be read as an indictment of Jamadagni. We should also be aware of the possibility, though it is always dangerous to make this judgment of a text from a culture other than one's own, that these texts are satires, intended to make the people within the culture laugh at their own cultural stereotypes.

Mariatale is schizophrenic not only in her class but in her motherhood; her son Parashurama expresses his ambivalence toward her by first beheading her and then reviving her.[13] Parashurama, "Rama with the Ax" (the Lizzie Borden of Hindu mythology), is torn between obedience to his two warring parents, a personal problem (known to many a child of divorce) that escalates into a class problem in the *Mahabharata,* where Renuka is a Kshatriya princess, the daughter of a king, while her husband Jamadagni is a great Brahmin sage. Their son Parashurama is an awkward interclass mix who later lashes out against his mother's class (the whole race of Kshatriyas) even as he lashes out at his mother by beheading her.[14]

But beheading is seldom fatal in a Hindu myth. In the *Mahabharata* story, nothing really happens; at the end, all wrongs are righted. All that is lost when the head has been restored is memory—perhaps not merely the memory of the murder, but also the memory of the sexual *vision* that threatened Renuka's integrity as a chaste wife by threatening to unveil in her the conflicting image of the erotic woman. Parashurama requests as a boon, in addition to the revival of his mother, "that no one would remember her murder, that no one would be touched by the evil."[15] It is not entirely clear whether the evil consists in the murder or in the original lapse of chastity—nor, therefore, whether Parashurama is asking that his mother, or he himself, or everyone else, should never again experience lust. The ambiguity is removed in a South Indian retelling in which the boon, in addition to the revival of the mother, consists in the reversal of her lapse of chastity; the boy says to his father, "You had said that my mother had lost her chastity while she looked at a fish; give me the boon that she, in fact, did not lose her faithfulness."[16] Once again, as in the myths of Damayanti and Penelope, a woman's fidelity to her husband *is* her identity.

In the Tamil text, Mariatale becomes ritually impure through her son's error, but this impurity is said to be the reason why *he* rejects *her.* She then creates another son, entirely impure; this son is Kartavirya, worshipped by Outcastes and presumably himself an Outcaste. Kartavirya, however, in the *Mahabharata* version is not Renuka's son at all, but a man of her class (Kshatriya) who murders her husband Jamadagni.[17] This transformation says a great deal about the role of hate and revenge in the splitting of

Mariatale; but it also provides an ingenious link between the story of the war between the classes in the Sanskrit epic (Brahmins against Kshatriyas) and in the folk variant (upper classes against Outcastes), and the Oedipal war between fathers and sons: the father-killer in the Sanskrit text becomes the son in the Tamil text.

The violence that King Kartavirya perpetrates against Jamadagni is combined with the theme of Renuka's illicit sexual contact with another man in a Tamil text roughly contemporaneous with Sonnerat, the *Kancippuranam,* a text in which, as in the *Mahabharata,* the heroine is named not Mariatale but Renuka, and Kartavirya is not the son but the father-killer. Here, however, he is also the Other Man:

THE BEHEADING OF RENUKA

Renuka, the daughter of King Varma, married Jamadagni and lived a flawless, chaste, domestic life with him. One day she was seen by Kartavirya—by the power of karma—when she went to fetch water. He was immediately seized by desire, but she had her eyes fastened on the ground and thus failed to notice him. He then hovered in the sky above the lake, and Renuka at last caught sight of him. Then Kama, the god of erotic love, revealed his power to a slight extent: but the good lady at once forced her mind back to the way of truth, filled her pot with water, and headed home.

But her husband in his wisdom had divined the reason for her delay—the action of that cruel idiot, Kartavirya. Angry as the mare's-head fire, he turned to his son: "O glorious Rama, that poisonous Kartavirya has approached your mother lustfully, desiring her beauty, which is as great as the sea. With his youth, his kingly power, and his incurable foolishness, he will now come to take her, thinking nothing of us. Go and quickly cut off her head!"

Rama obeyed the word of his *guru* and went out, taking his mother. Sorrow it is to be born a woman; even greater sorrow, to be young; even greater, to be endowed with beauty; even greater, to be the refuge of those who seek boons!

Rama cut off his mother's head with his sharp sword and returned to bow at the sage's feet. Said Jamadagni in his grief, "Today I have seen that you are indeed the son of a Ksatriya princess, and that you love me. You have accomplished my command. Matricide, however, is not a good thing; the world will condemn it. So now follow this order: go there and join her head to her body; worship her golden feet, praise her, and say, 'Mother, go wherever you may wish.' Remove her thus from that place, and return."

While Parasurama was doing this, Kartavirya cut off Jamadagni's head and went away; Renuka, restored to life but widowed, prayed to Siva and Parvati: "I have been disgraced; now you must protect me. They say a husband is sweeter than anyone else, and that he is master of his wife's body. Siva is husband, father, and mother to all living beings. . . . Now that I have fallen from high caste to innumerable sorrows, let me flourish as a deity worshipped by the people." She became a goddess who grants desires to low-caste people. Parasurama also worshipped Siva, who came down to earth as an outcaste Pulaiayan, a slaughterer of cows, and fought with Parasurama; when Parasurama prayed to Siva, Siva revealed his true form and granted Parasurama what he asked: to have the power to slaughter the race of the Ksatriyas.[18]

This episode in retrospect seems inevitable or even veiled in other versions: Kartavirya, who is Renuka/Mariatale's son in Sonnerat's text and the murderer of her husband in the *Mahabharata,* here plays the role of the man who sullies her chastity. Only when we see it as a whole does this complex perhaps offer support for Freud's three-point Oedipal pattern: that the son (1, Sonnerat) would like to murder his father (2, *Mahabharata*) and sleep with his mother (3, *Kancippuranam*). Thus the Kshatriyas who are the object of Parashurama's insane hatred in all variants become, in this one variant, the social class not only of the man who murdered his father but of the man who adulterously desired his mother.

Jamadagni seems to resemble most closely the Red Queen in Alice in Wonderland; his reaction to a crisis is to say, "Off with her head!" (not even, as would seem more appropriate when he sees a man about to rape his wife, "Off with *his* head!"). Renuka, like Sita, and like Ahalya in the early tellings, is polluted through no fault of her own but merely through Kartavirya's sexual harassment of her; indeed, he does not even touch her at all, but is merely suspected by Jamadagni of *intending* to do it—though he does succeed in capturing her gaze, that all-powerful female gaze. The sin of Renuka is thus reduced to the absurd, and the text is correspondingly hard pressed to atone for the unjustified matricide. This is done through an elaborate encounter between Parashurama and the god Shiva in his not unusual form of an Outcaste[19]—a transformation of the episode in Sonnerat in which Renuka herself encounters an Outcaste. Renuka too retains her link with this theme when she herself becomes a goddess of Outcastes. She is, moreover, a widow, in this one text, and even when Jamadagni revives her (which he does here of his own accord, not at

Parashurama's prompting), he kicks her out. Shulman contrasts this situation with the ending in the Sanskrit texts:

> Renuka—revived already as a *widow*, a unique development of the myth and one that links her immediately to the Tamil village goddesses—goes on to consolidate her newly won divinity. The irony deepens mercilessly: they say, remarks Renuka, that a husband is sweeter than anyone else; no doubt she is thinking of her own sweet-tempered spouse. She is still burning with humiliation.... Her divinity expresses but cannot assuage her personal tragedy.[20]

Kartavirya in this text is indirectly responsible for the beheading of Renuka and directly responsible for the beheading of her husband. The neat parallelism between the two beheadings, in its turn parallel to the double beheadings of the goddess and the Outcaste woman in Sonnerat's text, prompts me to wonder if some text might not have constructed an androgyne, by switching the heads and bodies of Renuka and her husband. (We will soon encounter several people who split and recombine androgynously.) I have yet to find a text in which this happens, but I am still looking.

The closest I have come so far is a Hindu myth in which the soul of a yogi enters the body of a whore, and her soul enters his body; the resulting confusion is the subject of a Sanskrit farce (the *Bhagavadajjuka**), in which the whore thinks and acts like a yogi, and vice versa. Another possible androgynous analogue occurs in a text collected by the anthropologist Bo Sax, a contemporary Himalayan telling of the story of a beheaded goddess, Maya, who has little in common with the tale of Mariatale or Renuka except for her beheading:

> Now Maya's one body has become two; / Maya's head flew up to high Mount Kailash, / and her trunk, it fell down into Rishasau town. The goddess's head became Bhola Sambhu Nath [Shiva], / Bhola Shambhu Nath on high Mount Kailash. / In Rishasau town was old Hemant the sage / In that sage's home, Gauradevi was born.[21]

Thus Maya (whose name means illusion) splits into male and female, more precisely into the god Shiva (her head) and his wife Gauri (presumably her body)—a divine couple who often appear in the form of an androgyne.* Sax points out other relevant aspects of this myth:

> Maya makes a marital *re*-union possible in one fell stroke (!) by dividing her head from her body. The head is reborn as Shiva on Mount Kailash, and

the body as Gaura [=Gauri] in Rishasau. He is superior, high and cool relative to her, while she is subordinate, low and hot relative to him. In this way, asymmetries in the earlier relationship of Maya to her offspring are reversed, and a once disbalanced pair is balanced. . . . It is nothing more than a second asymmetry, but this time one that mirrors, rather than inverts, the dominant or hegemonic paradigms of the culture; now it is men, rather than women, who are on top. In this respect the songs of Nandadevi, even though they are sung by women, serve male interests more than female ones by representing male dominance as desirable and natural.[22]

Here we may also note that the beheaded (i.e., horizontally bifurcated) woman becomes a new form of the vertically bifurcated androgyne: the head functions like the right side, the male side, the good side.

Another hint of such an androgynous merging in the tale of Renuka is embedded in a Reuters report from Bangalore, March 7, 1995, that I would entitle

RENUKAMBA'S REVENGE

More than 1,500 policemen stood guard in a southern Indian village on Tuesday to prevent Hindu pilgrims from carrying out a centuries-old tradition of trekking to a hill-top temple in the nude. Police sealed entry to the village of Chandragutti, 400 km (240 miles) northwest of Bangalore, where a week-long festival dedicated to the Hindu goddess Renukamba began on Tuesday, District Police Chief Chandrashekhar said. Every year for centuries, thousands of low-caste Hindus would strip for a holy dip in the Varada River, then climb four km (2½ miles) with their clothes off to offer prayers to the goddess at the hill-top temple.

But police banned the nude pilgrimage in 1987 after devotees clashed with members of the Dalit Sangharsha Samiti (DSS), a group advocating the uplifting of lower castes. "It is all quiet here," Chandrashekhar told Reuters by telephone. "The ban is being implemented strictly. There is no ban on worship at the temple, but strictly with clothes on."

The Chandragutti Jathra festival has its origin in a legend that claims sage Jamadagni ordered his wife, Renukamba, beheaded after discovering she had fallen in love with a man she glimpsed bathing in the river. Renukamba's clothes dropped off as she fled for her life and took refuge in a nearby cave where devotees believe she merged with a god. Pilgrims trek to the cave temple in sympathy with the woman.

In 1986, DSS volunteers claiming the ritual was degrading were beaten when they tried to prevent pilgrims from undressing. The worshippers then attacked police and paraded 10 police officials including two women constables naked along the banks of the river. Until 1986, more than 100,000 women, men and children used to make the pilgrimage every year. Chandrashekhar said 3,000 were expected this year.

Renukamba (a combination of Renuka and Ellamma? of Renuka and the androgynous Amba*?) merges here not with an Outcaste woman but with a male god, simultaneously changing the image from one of assimilation to one of heterosexual union and from lowering status to raising status. Her nakedness is not a cause of Jamadagni's aggression, as in the earlier texts, but a result of it. Indeed, her nakedness, allowing her to be seen, is a transformation from the earlier text in which she did the seeing—thus making her a mere sexual object where she had been a subject.

The *Times of London* (March 15, 1986) told the story of the original clash with the police, under the headline

Naked Worshippers Lay Bare Dignity of Police and Press

Each year devotees of the Hindu goddess, Renuka Devi, gather on the banks of the Varada River in Karnataka, strip and parade naked for two and a half miles to an ancient temple. They have been doing it for centuries, but recently the festival has become the centre of unenviable attention from the media and do-gooders anxious to reform the practice. At the weekend the festival went sour as thousands of pilgrims turned on their tormentors from the press, a group of social workers and the police, forcibly stripped them and paraded them through the dusty village streets.

Renuka takes vengeance against the prudishness of her tormentors by becoming an Outcaste—a social rebel—and by causing *them* to be seen in their nakedness—the nakedness of Jamadagni's projected lust and anger.

Hindu mythology split its women not only at the neck but at the waist, sometimes quite grotesquely, as in a short satire by a contemporary Indian writer, Vilas Sarang:

The Bottom Half of a Woman

[The narrator came upon an island peopled by creatures that were only the lower half of a woman's body:] At first, living with a half-woman was a strange experience. I often had the feeling that there was an invisible upper body floating above her waist like a ghost. Wandering about on heavy feet, she sometimes came and stood before me, and I felt that she was staring at me with invisible eyes. Once, when I was copulating with her in a standing position, I suddenly had the sensation of unseen arms embracing me, and I jumped back in fright.

[The lack of communication was not significant to him, though it was to her.] Whenever I felt the need, I went to her and tapped her on the legs—like tapping at a door, you might say. . . . But she could neither listen nor speak. All she knew was how to open her legs. . . . There was an intelligence, and a certain understanding, in everything she did. . . . She pressed her toes passionately, as if she were desperately trying to tell me something. I too pressed my toes upon hers. This went on with increasing fervour. But it was never clear what she wanted to say. Then in despair she would open her legs and pull me closer with her feet. But I would gently extricate myself and lie quietly beside her.

[The obvious solution occurred to him: he went to a nearby island where there were creatures that consisted of nothing but the upper half of a woman. He tried tying the two halves together with a rope and sleeping with the resulting woman.] It really wasn't very satisfactory. In a way you could make one woman from the halves, but in your heart you knew it wasn't real, you were merely fooling yourself. . . . On one occasion I was heaving up and down on top of the bound bodies, when the rope suddenly slipped and the two halves began to slip apart. . . . They were sliding in opposite directions, pulling me apart. It was like the earth splitting beneath my feet.

[He returned to India, where he married an attractive, passionate, and rich widow named Lakshmi. But:] I didn't like the idea of women with whole bodies. . . . It seems to me that the half, the partial, gives something that the whole, or what appears whole, doesn't. . . . I went down to the blacksmiths' lane and bought myself an axe. I hid it under the bed. That night after Lakshmi had fallen asleep I brought the axe out, and, in the pale glow of the night-lamp, I aimed at her navel. In four or five blows I cut her exactly in two.[23]

Speech, as well as vision, is problematized here: the "invisible eyes" of the half-woman are a wonderful metaphor for the problematized female gaze, reminiscent of the cursed invisibility of Ahalya. The reconstituted woman is rejected not for her mixture of castes but for her mixture of qualities (speech and sexuality) that the speaker would rather keep separate. The ghost of Parashurama, "Rama with the Ax," surely hovers over this tongue-in-cheek revision of the ancient Hindu story of the split woman.

In commenting on the Himalayan goddess whose head becomes Shiva, her body Gauri, Sax remarks that "[t]he motif of a goddess splitting herself in two is common in Hinduism,"[24] and he goes on to suggest:

> So we see that our "split goddess" can be interpreted in at least two ways. She can be interpreted in theological terms as the embodiment of *maya*, whose very nature is to multiply forms. She can also be interpreted in psychological terms as the embodiment of female sexuality in its controlled and uncontrolled (i.e. married and unmarried) manifestations. . . . But this latter explanation is unsatisfying because it is couched almost entirely in terms of male psychology; it centers exclusively on male fears, fantasies, and projections. What do Hindu women have to say about all of this?[25]

In the texts that we have considered, they remain silent, but the texts themselves may be the voices of women.

The story of Renuka/Mariatale found its way into European literature; we have already seen Mariatale through French eyes. Goethe retold it in a form that was known to the great Indologist, Heinrich Zimmer.[26] In 1938, Marguerite Yourcenar published a story called "Kali Beheaded," which she had first published in French (as "Kali Décapitée") in 1928.[27] This was a retelling of the Sonnerat story of Mariatale, but with a difference: The amorous escapades of the goddess Kali with Outcastes lead the gods to decapitate her; eventually they join her head to the body of a prostitute who has been killed for having troubled the meditations of a young Brahmin. The woman thus formed is a creature who becomes "the seducer of children, the inciter of old men, and the ruthless mistress of the young." In the English edition, Yourcenar explains that she rewrote the ending, "to better emphasize certain metaphysical concepts from which this legend is inseparable, and without which, told in a Western manner, it is nothing but a vague erotic tale placed in an Indian setting."[28] This is a very different story indeed, combining Hindu ideas of caste rebellion (Brahmin women sleeping with Outcastes and disturbing male Brahmins) with misogynist European ideas about feminist rebellion (seducing children, inciting old men).

SCYLLA AND CHARYBDIS

A text that offers a Greek parallel to the story of Mariatale is not a narrative, properly speaking, but an episode within the larger narrative of the *Odyssey*, a violent image of two women split in two at the waist (with the inevitable horror of the lower half):

UP TO THE WAIST IN A HOLLOW CAVE

Scylla has twelve feet, which wave in the air, and six heads, each with three rows of deadly teeth, with which she devours dolphins and dogs and men. She is hidden up to the waist in a hollow cave. . . . The other cliff is lower; they lie close together. Below a great fig tree, dense with leaves, Charybdis sucks down the dark water three times a day; you do not want to be there when she sucks it down.[29]

When Scylla actually fishes for six of Odysseus's men, she devours them "screaming and stretching out their hands at her doors."[30] This is misogyny squared: there are two of them (Scylla and Charybdis), and one (Scylla) is herself a pair of nightmare women. Put differently, Scylla is split in half (one half hidden under water, the other half with the devouring heads), and together with Charybdis she constitutes a woman split in half, into two sorts of mouths: Scylla the toothy upper mouth, Charybdis the sucking lower mouth.

Ovid, however, splits Scylla differently and tells a story about her:

GIRDLED BY FIERCE DOGS

Scylla infests the straits of Messina to the east, Charybdis to the west. Charybdis sucks the ships into her depths and spits them up again, while Scylla's waist is strange and dark and girdled by fierce dogs. Yet Scylla has the face of a young girl and she used to be a girl before she suffered her monstrous transformation.

One day, when Scylla was walking on the shore, Glaucus fell in love with her; he was a man above the waist but from the groin down a fish. When she rejected him, he asked Circe for magic to make Scylla love him; but Circe, who was in love with him herself and was enraged when he scorned her, mixed a noxious potion and poisoned the bay where Scylla used to bathe. Scylla plunged in waist-deep and suddenly saw barking dogs around her hips. At first she didn't realize that they were part of her own body, and tried to run away from them; but then she saw that her own thighs, shins, and feet had been replaced by mad dogs like the dogs of Cerberus. Her belly was cut short at the loins, and rested upon the backs of beasts.[31]

Scylla is thus split as a result of the combined forces of the unwanted sexual attentions of a god, who is himself split from the waist down (a kind of merman, half-fish), and the jealousy of another woman, who is also responsible for the metamorphosis of men into animals (pigs). Where, in Homer's text, Scylla devours dogs,[32] here they devour her until they become her.

The image of Scylla casts its shadow upon later English literature. Edmund Spenser's description, in 1590, of Duessa, the witchlike daughter of Deceit and Shame, owes much to Homer:

Duessa's Neather Partes

Her neather partes misshapen, monstruous, / Were hidd in water, that I could not see—/ But they did seeme more foule and hideous / Then womans shape would beleeve to bee . . . / Her neather parts, the shame of all her kind, / My chaster Muse for shame doth blush to write . . . / And eke her feete most monstrous were in sight; / For one of them was like an Eagles claw / With griping talaunts armd to greedy fight; / The other like a beares uneven paw, / More ugly shape yet never living creature saw.[33]

Here, as usual, monster feet* are associated with (though, in this case, not necessarily identified with) the mysterious "nether parts" of monstrous women—the devouring cave.

In Shakespeare's *King Lear* (composed in 1605–6), the king expresses his horror of female sexuality through the image of a female centaur conceived in terms strongly reminiscent of Scylla:

Down from the waist they are Centaurs, / Though women all above: / But to the girdle do the Gods inherit, / Beneath is all the fiend's: there's hell, there's darkness, / There is the sulphurous pit—burning scalding, / Stench, consumption: fie, fie, fie! pah! pah![34]

John Milton, in 1667, added an entire new mythological dimension to this image. He describes Satan's journey to the Gates of Hell, which are guarded by two formidable figures, one on each side. One is Death, Satan's son, a shapeless shadow* black as night; the other, Sin, is described in hideous detail:

The one seem'd Woman to the waist, and fair, / But ended foul in many a scaly fold / Voluminous and vast, a Serpent arm'd / With mortal sting: about her middle round / A cry of Hell Hounds never ceasing bark'd / With wide Cerberean mouths full loud, and rung / A hideous Peal: yet, when they list, would creep, / If aught disturb's their noise, into her womb, / And kennel there, yet there still bark'd and howl'd / Within unseen. Far less abhorr'd than these / Vex'd Scylla bathing in the Sea that parts / Calabria from the hoarse Trinacrian shore.[35]

The guardian of the gates of hell is not Scylla, but she is explicitly compared with Scylla and said to be far worse. This passage owes more to Ovid than to Homer: the creature whose womb is surrounded by dogs and whose legs are made of dogs now becomes one whose womb is a kennel and who is, like Scylla, both "double-form'd" (as Satan calls her) and one half of the team that guards the dangerous gates—that here lead not to safety but to hell.

Moreover, the story of Sin's birth is strongly reminiscent of Scylla's transformation: she was born out of Satan's head, like Athena from Zeus, and then, as she tells Satan, "Thyself in me thy perfect image viewing / Becam'st enamour'd"—and so Satan impregnated Sin with Death. This genealogy stems in part from the Epistle of James (1:15): "Then when lust hath conceived, it bringeth forth sin: and sin, when it is finished, bringeth forth death." But Milton draws an incestuous side onto the triangle, when Satan (taking the place of Lust in James's text) not only brings forth Sin but impregnates Sin with Death. And then the triangle becomes a pentagon, as two more generations commit incest: Sin tells Satan that when Death was born, he tore apart Sin's entrails, deforming her womb; then he came back and raped her to beget the howling dogs—who, in their turn, also go back into her womb, "and howl and gnaw / My Bowels, their repast."[36] Thus the monstrous births in the womb of the "double-form'd" female proliferate.

And they proliferate in Homer too, for Scylla and Charybdis are further doubled by two other sets of female monsters: the Sirens and the crashing rocks, whom Odysseus must pass before he even gets to Scylla and Charybdis. The Sirens hold their weapons in their (upper) mouths, in the form of beautiful, seductive voices; and the beach in front of them is piled high with heaps of the bones of men with their rotten flesh and dried skin.[37] The duplicity of the Sirens consists, therefore, in the contrast between their apparent beauty and their real deadliness. After the Sirens come the rocks that crash together, the Amphitrites (whose name indicates their duality),[38] which Odysseus must pass between. This is yet another image of the woman split in half, perhaps a gross metaphor for the devouring vagina, though it is about far more than sex; it is a literalization of our expression for any inescapable dilemma, "between a rock and a hard place." The images in this passage thus represent female dualism to the fifth power: the unlucky man must pass between the voice and the carnage of the Sirens, then between the rocks, then between the rocks and Scylla-and-Charybdis, then between Scylla and Charybdis, and finally between the two halves of Scylla.

The Inuit tell a story that combines the theme of Mariatale/Renuka with the theme of the Amphitrites. It is about Kiviok, an immortal who is said to have gone south on a ship after the white men arrived in the Arctic but to be ready to come back when he is needed. His most recent manifestation was in around 1979, when a Russian satellite threatened to fall on Baker Lake, a small community on Hudson Bay; Kiviok is said to have harpooned the satellite out of the sky down into northern Manitoba, thus saving the community.[39] Kiviok's mythology comes from the broad geographical area of Asia and the New World connected by the Bering Straits[40] and hence may have dim historical connections with India:

Caught between Mountains and Clams

Kiviok came to a land where there were only two people, an old lady and her daughter. He married the daughter, but one day while he was out hunting the old lady killed the daughter and skinned her head down to the neck. She pulled her daughter's head skin over her head to fool her son-in-law, so she would look like her daughter and could marry Kiviok. When Kiviok approached, the old lady put on the head and walked to meet him, but because her looks didn't really change, she could still be recognized as an old lady. He told her to remove her kamiks, and when she did, her legs were skinny and brown like straw. After she told Kiviok what she had done, Kiviok married the old lady, but not for long. He left her to go back to his parents. On the way he had to pass several obstacles, including two huge mountains that kept crashing together in front of him and almost crushed him (the tail of his shirt was caught and torn off), two giant clams which opened and closed in front of him, two bears that kept fighting in front of him, and a great pot of boiling water that kept moving to block his way. When he reached his parents at last they died from the shock of hearing the good news of Kiviok's arrival.[41]

Kiviok can tell the difference between an old woman and a young one, but he is still caught between them, just as he is caught between the mountains and the clams. The wicked mother who wishes to become her daughter's double, who exchanges skins with her daughter as Mariatale and the Outcaste woman exchange heads, is "doubled" by the various obstacles that try to prevent Kiviok's escape, culminating in the theme of the Amphitrites. In the Winnebago and other Inuit variants of this myth, when the rocks crash together as the hero has almost crawled through, they smash his testicles.[42] Another variant specifies that the old woman creates the obstacles to keep Kivioq (as he is here called) from getting away, and it further elaborates on the obstacles: the two clams are replaced by a great mussel that tries to cut Kivioq's kayak in two but succeeds only in cutting off the stern (the equivalent of the coattails or testicles in other versions). Moreover, two entirely new episodes make nakedly and unmistakably explicit the implicit symbolism of the other obstacles:

> Then Kivioq came to a place where the road was barred by the lower part of a woman's body, a huge big underpart of a woman, that placed itself in front of him with legs wide apart every time he tried to get past. But Kivioq lay with the thing and got away after he had lain with it. . . .
>
> Then Kivioq went on again and came to the house of an old woman with a tail made of iron. When he lay down to sleep, he placed a flat stone on his chest. The old woman could hardly conceal her delight when she saw him making ready to sleep. She sat there laughing all the time, and afterwards, when he pretended to fall asleep, she clambered up on to the sleeping place, jumped up in the air, and came down on top of him, so as to strike his chest with her iron tail. But the iron tail struck the stone, and was driven into the woman's inner parts, so that she gave a deep sigh and fell down dead. After that, Kivioq went on again.[43]

The iron tail of the woman is phallic, a threat to the man; he turns it against her so that she literally fucks herself to death, in a manner reminiscent of Shiva's impalement of the demon Adi* on the knife at the end of his penis.[44] I hardly think that the story of Kivioq's obstacles needs any further gloss.

INTERLUDE: SPLITTING LUCY

The Hindu tale of Mariatale told of the combination of two women, as did the Greek image of Scylla and Charybdis, the latter often reduced, in its later European transformations, to a single woman (Scylla alone) split in half at the waist. This static image of Scylla was then sometimes reinflated, as it were, into a narrative about a woman split into two women, not literally at the waist but figuratively so—into a pure woman (the woman above the waist) and an impure woman (the woman below the waist). Such a woman is Lucy in Bram Stoker's *Dracula*. Like Sita and Helen, Lucy is the image of purity, and to preserve that image it is necessary to construct her impure double, who does all the things that Lucy cannot be allowed to do.

This is not a subtle book, but Stoker masterfully manipulates the myths to mock the Victorian concept of the virtuous woman, and the blatant imagery makes its mythological basis all the more patent and hence all the more useful for our purposes. The plot concerns a young man, Jonathan Harker, who undertakes a secretarial job in the castle of Count Dracula in Transylvania, discovers the vampires, and manages to escape; his fiancée, Mina, nurses him back to health. Mina's best friend, Lucy, is beautiful and as pure as the driven snow; but she has three suitors, one of whom she accepts (the aristocratic Arthur) and two of whom she rejects (a psychiatrist, Dr. Seward, and an American, Quincey Morris). Dracula comes to England, seduces Lucy, and turns her into a vampire. Not fully understanding what is wrong with her, Dr. Seward gets help from his friend Dr. Van Helsing, who is a kind of nineteenth-century ghostbuster, an expert on vampires. Van Helsing is too late to save Lucy, but he manages to save Mina when Dracula attempts to seduce her too, and eventually they succeed in destroying Dracula.

The vampires are doubles: they double for themselves in the coffin and in the flesh, and they double for "nice Victorian women" in the world (our "vamps" are vampires). When Lucy becomes a vampire, she produces a visual double of herself that is not, however, herself, as Dr. Seward makes clear:

THE FOUL THING THAT HAD TAKEN LUCY'S SHAPE

We recognized the features of Lucy Westenra, but yet how changed. . . . I call the thing that was before us Lucy because it bore her shape. . . . Lucy's eyes in form and colour; but Lucy's eyes unclean and full of hell-fire, instead of the pure, gentle orbs we knew. At that moment the remnant of my love passed into hate and loathing; had she then to be killed, I could have done it with savage delight. . . . There was no love in my own heart, nothing but loathing for the foul Thing which had taken Lucy's shape without her soul. . . . She seemed like a nightmare of Lucy as she lay there; the pointed teeth, the bloodstained, voluptuous mouth—which it made one shudder to see—the whole carnal and unspiritual appearance, seeming like a devilish mockery of Lucy's sweet purity.[45]

Since Lucy is defined by her "sweet purity," any time that she is not sweet and pure—but, rather, "unclean and full of hell-fire"—she must be, ipso facto, someone other than Lucy, no matter how much she may resemble Lucy. To the men in the book, Lucy the pure is masquerading as Lucy the impure; to the perceptive reader on the outside, Lucy the impure is masquerading as Lucy the pure. This neatly unfalsifiable argument unmasks the purely visual masquerade: someone who looks like Lucy may not be

Lucy. The doubles persist right up into Whitley Strieber's 1981 novel, *The Hunger,* which describes vampires as "another species, living right here all along. An identical twin." Lucy is her own twin.

Seward too is split in half, between lust and loathing; the grotesque Lucy is his own projection, or Bram Stoker's projection of Seward's projection. We may well assume that he has repressed a considerable hatred for Lucy, who has after all brutally rejected his love; but he can only conceive of this as a loathing for someone whom *he* defines as not-Lucy. He expresses this ambivalence when contemplating the violent mutilations that Van Helsing plans to inflict upon Lucy: Seward at first recoils "to think of so mutilating the body of the woman whom I had loved. And yet the feeling was not so strong as I had expected. I was, in fact, beginning to shudder at the presence of this being, this Un-Dead, as Van Helsing called it, and to loathe it. Is it possible that love is all subjective, or all objective?"[46] The vampire Lucy is Seward's subjective, projective nightmare of the real Lucy. Van Helsing immediately confirms that Lucy's shape is not her soul; when Arthur asks, "Is this really Lucy's body or only a demon in her shape?" Van Helsing replies, "It is her body, and yet not it." And when she has been finally killed for good, Seward loves her again: "There, in the coffin lay no longer the foul Thing that we had so dreaded and grown to hate that the work of her destruction was yielded as a privilege to the one best entitled to it, but Lucy as we had seen her in life, with her face of unequalled sweetness and purity."[47]

But how real is "Lucy's sweet purity"? Lucy's lover, Arthur, is doubled (indeed trebled) by her other lovers, Dr. Seward and Quincey Morris, whose hearts she breaks (metaphorically; in return, they will literally break her heart with a phallic stake). The three lovers of Lucy are balanced by the three vampire women, would-be lovers of Harker, in Dracula's castle. It is no accident that Lucy becomes a vampire: she is a very naughty girl. She writes to Mina: "Why can't they let a girl marry three men, or as many as want her, and save all this trouble? But this is heresy, and I must not say it."[48] Lucy is indeed a heretic, but this is repressed; whenever anyone refers to Lucy in the days before Dracula corrupts her, she is described (by all the men who are in love with her, but also by Mina) as the very image of purity and innocence. No one dares to acknowledge her sexuality—until she is officially transformed into what she has secretly always been. At that point, she becomes entirely mythological and also entirely non-British: the folds of flesh on her brow are likened to "the coils of Medusa's snakes, and the lovely, blood-stained mouth grew to an open square, as in the passion masks of the Greeks and Japanese."[49] Appropriately, therefore, when Arthur hammers her to death he too becomes mythologized: "He looked like a figure of Thor." As her fiancé, Arthur is also given the privilege of de-flowering her in a scene of vivid, perverse sexuality that leaves him fainting:

> His untrembling arm rose and fell, driving deeper and deeper the mercy-bearing stake, whilst the blood from the pierced heart welled and spurted up around it. . . . And then the writhing and quivering of the body became less, and the teeth seemed to champ, and the face to quiver. Finally it lay still. The terrible task was over. The hammer fell from Arthur's hand. He reeled and would have fallen had we not caught him.[50]

But that is not the end: Van Helsing says, of Lucy, "I shall cut off her head and fill her mouth with garlic, and I shall drive a stake through her body." (In fact, he has Arthur stake her first, while he himself beheads her after-ward.) Vampires, like other hypersexual women, as we have seen, can be destroyed permanently only by being beheaded, which is to say desexed. The telltale vampire mouth is what a Freudian would see as a kind of in-verted *vagina dentata,* further analogized to the wolves' "*eye*-teeth." Or rather, through the kind of upward displacement that made possible the substitution of eyes for vaginas on the body of Indra,* we might see the mouth of the vampire as a *dens vaginatus.* That is, since the vampire's head is not her head but is analogized to her sexual organ, there is no need to transpose the teeth from the upper mouth to the lower; the upper mouth *is* the lower mouth. These women, with their lips like vulvas, are the heirs to Long-tongue the canine demoness*—and perhaps the ances-tors of the character portrayed by Linda Lovelace in *Deep Throat,* the woman who had her clitoris in her throat. Since, in real life, beheading causes death, while in mythology it does not, Lucy's beheading is quasi-mythological: it does not kill Lucy's body, which is already dead (staked through the heart), but it frees her soul. Like the ancient Hindus and Greeks, Bram Stoker is telling us that the only way to control a woman's excessive sexuality is to split her—first into a woman and a vampire, and then into a vampire split in two, head and body.

Comparison: Heads You Lose

The woman with the transposed head reappeared in a case before the Massachusetts Supreme Judicial Court in 1995. Sandra Bowman, a candidate for the presidency of her union, sued a male fellow worker who had circulated among their colleagues a photograph of her head superimposed upon the bodies of other women, naked and sometimes in pornographic poses.[51] The upper-class head upon the lower-class body; the intellectual's head upon the whore's body; the public head upon the private body; and, perhaps most vividly, the modest head upon the naked body—where have we seen this before? The image is also enshrined in what has now become a canonic *New York Post* tabloid headline: "Headless Corpse Found in Top-less Bar." The implication is, perhaps, that the lack of a head is simply a few steps farther along the path that begins with the lack of a bra. A more literal reenactment of the Renuka/Lucy scenario was reported by Reuters in 1997, under the intriguing headline, "Head Is Partly Severed and Then Reattached." A surgeon in London did it—but apparently he unimagina-tively reattached the woman's own head.[52] A real-life surgery closer to Mariatale's dilemma involved twenty women (and one man) who, in what one plastic surgeon called a quest for the "ultimate face" (the face of Helen of Troy?), unknowingly participated in an experiment: surgeons performed two different operations on them, using different procedures, one on each half of the face, to see which came out better. The ethical questions raised by this procedure are obvious, as are the mythological resonances: men cutting women into unequal halves, without their con-sent.[53]

The theme of the human with the wrong head (no head, two or more heads, someone else's head, an animal head, and so forth) is incredibly malleable. It is always *about* much the same thing—death, sex, disorder, dichotomy, the irruption of the divine or animal into a human life—but what it says about what it is about is quite different in each instance. *Something* is cut away from something else. But what is that something? What is symbolized by the opposition between the head and the body in the beheadings or bifurcations of these women? Unlike the widespread pattern of myths in which a human head is removed and replaced with the head of an animal,[54] here the exchange is more subtle, a woman's head for a woman's head. Indeed, in the *Mahabharata* version Renuka simply gets back her *own* head again. (A similar reunion may be seen in the story of Catherine of Siena, a saint whose head now resides in Siena, while her headless body lives in Rome; once a year, on a ritual occasion, Catherine's head pays a visit to her body, before the Sienese claim it back again.)[55] Woody Allen nicely expressed this quandary in his description of the mythical beast called the Great Roe, which has the body of a lion and the head of a lion, but not the same lion.[56]

The head often but not always functions as a metaphor for the mind, especially when it parts company with the body. It might appear that Renuka's head is rational and chaste, her body emotional and lustful. Certainly in the Tamil text Mariatale's head is pure, the body polluted. This model assumes that sex is in the genitals, love and lust are in the heart, and the head is the site of nothing but Kantian pure reason. If the head is thus rational and chaste, the body emotional and lustful, beheading might mean that the woman can't *think* (straight) any more, that her sexuality has destroyed her rationality.

But the head, rather than the body, is where semen is stored, according to a belief prominent in Hinduism, as well as in Jewish cabala, medieval Christian alchemy, and elsewhere;[57] and women as well as men have sexual seed that is stored in the head.[58] Ezra Pound once argued that "the brain itself [was] more than likely—only a sort of great clot of genital fluid held in suspense or reserve."[59] (This connection also underlies the Freudian concept of upward displacement from the genitals to the head.) It may well be, therefore, that removing a woman's (sexual) head purifies the *body*. On this model, beheading might make it possible for the woman to think (straight) again, freeing her rationality from her sexuality. (Like all forms of capital [*sic*] punishment, beheading seems to focus the mind wonderfully.) If a literal beheading occurs in a realistic novel, it is of course fatal. Elaine Showalter has remarked upon this:

> Decapitation [is] a remarkably frequent occurrence in male fin-de-siècle writing, from the severed head of Daniel Dravot in "The Man Who Would Be King" to the blackened heads that surround Kurtz's hut in *Heart of Darkness*. It is tempting to see these episodes reflecting the castration anxieties Freud describes in "Medusa's Head": "To decapitate: to castrate." Indeed, when Dr. Seward sees the vampire Lucy, he observes that her brows "were wrinkled as though the folds of the flesh were the coils of Medusa's snakes." But the Freudian equation of decapitation and castration is itself a product of fin-de-siècle culture. The severed head also seems to be a way to control the New Woman by separating the mind from the body. . . . Finally, as in the English inn sign "The Silent Woman," which shows a headless female body, decapitation is a Draconian way to shut women up.[60]

But it is not merely "the New Woman" but also, alas, "the Old Woman" who inspires men to behead her. From ancient myth to contemporary culture the metaphor of beheading has been used to dehumanize and silence women.

In contrast with the silence of the severed female head of Mariatale (and of the mountain goddess described by Sax), the severed horse head of the male horse-god Dadhyanc* is a talking head. As Joseph Nagy remarks of Dadhyanc (and of the Greek, Irish, and Norse parallels with that story), "The symbolic baggage of the severed head. . . . can lend itself to an evaluation of the relationship between written and oral communication."[61] In his view, "the speaking head mediates between the various opposed realities featured in these myths (male-female; human-divine; . . . living-dead) and reintegrates the totality that originally threatened to disintegrate."[62] This integration takes place in the myth of Mariatale too when the women are reunited at the end—but still they remain silent. Here we may also recall the gloss of Samjna as a horse that is a text (with the Shadow her commentary), but does not speak when her husband becomes a horse to cover her. Her silence is reversed (along with so much else) in the Amar Chitra Katha comic book version of the myth, in which, when the Sun searches for his wife, he asks a passerby, "Have you seen a mare go by?" Passerby: "Yes! A quaint one . . . by the river." The Sun: "Why do you call it a quaint one?" Passerby: "I speak the truth, sir. This mare talks!" To which the Sun makes the wonderful reply, "It must be Sanjna." Joseph Nagy goes on to characterize the Indian myth, "where the head of Dadhyanc must be detached and replaced in order for knowledge to spread and tradition to grow," as an instance of a broader theme of "head recovery"[63]—which becomes, in the myth of Samjna, the recovery of the head (which she turns toward her attacker in an attempt to protect her hindquarters) of the lost wife, the feral mare.

The beheaded woman is thoroughly modernized in Carl Reiner's satirical 1983 film about a man who "has" two brains not in the sense of the men in the nineteenth-century French and English novels who combine two male brains,* nor like Baron Frankenstein, who combined one man's brain and another's body,[64] but in the sense that a man "has" a woman—in this case, two women:

THE MAN WITH TWO BRAINS

A brain surgeon, married to a gorgeous but horrid woman, fell in love with a disembodied brain kept alive in a jar filled with fluid, with whom he communicated telepathically. When his wife was killed, he transferred the brain into his wife's body, though he himself was injured in the course of the operation and remained unconscious for six weeks. When he regained consciousness, and was told that his wife was waiting to see him, he asked, "Whose brain does she have?" He saw her, and she was a very fat version of his original wife. "I forgot to tell you," she said, apologetically and nervously, "I got fat." He was delighted, as this was proof that the soul was not that of the horrid glamour girl, but of the sweet brain. "Fat?" he said. "What fat?"

Here, the brain outvotes the body and even transforms the body into a shape that challenges the contemporary American stereotype which equates the good not only with the beautiful but with the thin. Where the Indian myth contrasts a Brahmin woman and an Outcaste, and the French (Sonnerat and Yourcenar) make the Outcaste a prostitute, the Americans simply turn her into their cultural pariah, the fat girl—and elevate her above the cultural ideal, the thin beauty. By transposing his true love's lovely brain into the formerly lovely, now unlovely body of his despised wife, the hero is able to have it all. But this is a unique, and satirical, success story; the Hindu women who are accidentally combined by their men or who accidentally combine their men end up with the worst, not the best, of both worlds.

Conclusion: Put a Bag over Her Head

The vivid similarities among the more grotesque images that I have selected to present in these myths of beheaded women tell us some interesting things. They tell us that several cultures share certain images of evil and terrifying women, nightmares about women, and negative images of the human body, particularly but not only the female body. But we have also found striking correspondences in several cultures between more positive and rational images of women, like Damayanti and Penelope. Both sets of images are culturally mediated of course, but the fact that they are shared across cultures suggests that they grab the human imagination on a level somewhere below the waterline of culture, on the pre- or subcultural level below the waist, as it were.[65]

The women who get other women's heads are in a sense having bags put over their own heads—bags that in this case consist of other heads. But the phrase "Put a bag over her head" generally carries a very different meaning: it is a macho locker room joke, implying that even an ugly woman can be sexually useful in the dark. The trope is occasionally applied to men, but only as a joke, an understood reversal of the normal gender: thus

Anthony Lane compares a beautiful actress, who pretends unconvincingly to be ugly, with the notoriously handsome and virile Gary Cooper: "Yeah, Gary Cooper had the same problem. He used to wear a bag over his head."[66]

The phrase is often attributed to Benjamin Franklin, who actually referred not to a bag but to a basket. He made this suggestion in the course of a letter, written on June 25, 1745, in which he advised a young friend to marry ("A single Man . . . resembles the odd Half of a Pair of Scissors," a violent and split image, from the start) but, failing that, to "prefer old Women to young ones." Franklin gives eight reasons for this preference,[67] some of which exalt mental qualities such as knowledge and truth. But the fifth reason contains the metaphor that concerns us at the moment:

> 5. In every Animal that walks upright, the Deficiency of the Fluids that fill the Muscles appears first in the highest Part. The Face first grows lank and wrinkled; then the Neck; then the Breast and Arms; the lower parts continuing to the last as plump as ever; so that covering all above with a Basket, and regarding only what is below the Girdle, it is impossible of two Women to know an old from a young one. And as in the Dark all Cats are grey, the Pleasure of Corporal Enjoyment with an old Woman is at least equal and frequently superior; every Knack being by Practice capable of improvement.[68]

The fluid analogy implies that as the face dries up, the lower mouth gets wetter. The gray cats are part of a closely related sexist metaphor for the interchangeability of women in bed.[69]

The adventurer in the short story, "Nativity Room," composed by Li Yu in China, in 1657 or 1658,[70] finds his bride, Miss Cao, with a bag over her head, indeed over her entire body:

> The rebels were devilishly cunning. They feared that if they let their captives' faces be seen, the buyers would pick and choose among them, snapping up all the presentable women. To whom would they sell the rejects? With that thought in mind, they set new rules and established a different sales procedure. Bundling the women into sacks, like pickled or rotten fish, they offered people a choice. With no way to tell which sacks held the pickled fish, the customer had to chance his luck. Crammed inside the sacks, the women were sold by weight, not quality, at a uniform tariff. The lucky buyers got a paragon, the unlucky a gorgon—it was undoubtedly the most equitable system of exchange ever devised.
>
> [Yao Ji then thought,] Perhaps by some happy coincidence of their

> marriage destinies he might pick out the girl he loved. But even if he was
> never able to meet her and chose some other girl, so long as she was nice-
> looking and would make a suitable wife for a rich man, he would take her
> in Miss Cao's place. Back home no one would know the facts.[71]

The women are bundled up "like pickled or rotten fish," and, it is implied, have the same smell (a cross-cultural dirty joke: "Not tonight, Josephine"). Thus, as a footnote informs us, "Pickled fish also smelled foul; you had to see the fish to tell the difference." And presumably you had to see the women too to tell the difference. Selling women by weight, like a pasha weighing himself against scales full of gold or Shylock with his pound of flesh, is the ultimate commodification (though it would have to be in- verted to work in present-day America). The brutal metaphor is then translated into human terms when Yao remarks that if he can't get his own true love, Miss Cao, any good-looking girl would do as well. But underly- ing the put-down is another aspect of the male gaze, the fear of looking at a woman who might, like the gorgon Medusa, castrate you; better to keep her in a sack. As the story remarks (at least in this English translation), "The unlucky [man got] a gorgon."

The dishonoring of old women implicit in Franklin's satire lingers in our pejorative synecdoche, "old bag," as in the gigolo's song in Cole Porter's *Kiss Me Kate:* "If my wife has a bag of gold, do I care if the bag be old?" Franklin's parable also gives a new meaning to the "bag lady," who is depersonalized not by her sexuality but by her poverty; here, as so often, we see the conflation of sexual and political-economic forms of oppres- sion.

The fantasy of removing or bagging the head of a woman denies the power of the individual, reducing sexuality to pure animality—like com- paring her to a gray cat. It is a way of gaining power over a woman by im- plying that no one particular woman has power over a man; if a man fears that he may lose his control over a woman if he loves her as an individual, he may wish to deindividualize her. The bag removes both the cultural and the natural evidence of identity. The woman with a bag over her head, who has no personality, no individualism, is the perfect pornographic woman—by definition generic rather than individual, an object rather than a subject. She is always the same, sealed off from reality, seldom a nurturing mother, in contrast with real women who change, decay, and raise children.

F I V E

Transposed Male Heads
and Tales

Transposed Male Heads

A counterpart to the story of Renuka/Mariatale centers upon the beheading of men rather than women. It is found in *The Ocean of the Rivers of Story:*

The Transposed Male Heads

One day a young washerman came to bathe in a lake near the temple of the goddess Gauri and fell in love with a young girl who was bathing there, a girl named Madanasundari. She fell in love with him at first sight too and their parents arranged the marriage. After a while, Madanasundari's brother came to visit them, and the three of them went together to the festival celebrating the victory of the goddess Durga over the demons. In the Durga temple, the washerman was overcome with a desire to sacrifice himself to Durga, and he cut off his head; Madanasundari's brother followed him and did the same.

When Madanasundari saw her husband and her brother beheaded, she resolved to commit suicide, and she prayed to the goddess, "You who occupy half of the body of your husband, Shiva, I beg you; in all my future births, let these two men be my husband and brother." The goddess said, "Do not do anything rash, my daughter. Join the heads of your husband and brother to their bodies, and by my grace they will rise up alive." In her delight and confusion, Madanasundari stuck her husband's head to her brother's body and her brother's head to her husband's body. They came to life, and Madanasundari did not at first know what to do. But the one who had her husband's head was her husband.[1]

The role of the handsome king (or demigod) in the tale of Renuka is here played by the woman's brother, a factor that introduces overtones of incest. But the woman in this story splits and recombines not herself but *them,* the two men—so that there is still only one of her and two of them, but now two of them, each halved and recombined. The human woman's happiness is short-lived, however; her solution is intolerable. For in Hindu India (indeed, in most of Indo-European literature) a woman cannot officially have two men. The tale therefore immediately poses a question (it is one of a set of questions put by a vampire to a king): Which of the two does she belong to? Split between them, she has to choose. And answer came there, predictably: "The one with the husband's head." (A contemporary South Indian village retelling ends when the Goddess asks the woman, "Who do you belong to?" and the new, quasi-feminist answer is "Myself.")[2]

Even though this is a story about two split men, it is told from the point of view of the woman caught between them. There are also echoes of split women in the form of two goddesses—the benevolent golden Gauri who is present at the original love match and the destructive Durga (Kali) who presides over the deaths, two goddesses who were originally a single woman.[3] The goddesses also double human women in that as superhuman women they have the power to bring to actuality what the human woman can only fantasize. In this sense, of course, all gods and goddesses are doubles.

This story about conjoined men has other analogues in classical Sanskrit literature, such as the story in the *Mahabharata* about the joining together of two halves of *one* man, as a result of the splitting of one woman into two:

JARASANDHA

A childless king with twin wives was given a mango consecrated to ensure the birth of a son. He had promised never to favor either wife, and so he gave it to them both; they split it in half, and each gave birth to half a child, each with one eye, arm, leg, and buttock, with half a face and half a belly. The wives, horrified, exposed the two halves, but a demoness *(rakshasi)* who was not a demoness, named Jara ("old age"), found them and tied them together. They became a whole child, whom she returned to the king, who named him Jarasandha ("Joined Together by Old Age").[4]

This story begins, like the *Ramayana,* with a fruit divided between several wives; but where that fruit produced multiple sons, this one produces multiple fragments of a single son. The mother who joins him is the ambivalent female, demonic but not demonic; that is, she is a demoness by birth and diet and is said to live upon flesh and blood, but she has a divine beauty and saves the child (who is one-sided, like the stone-people from Ceram*) instead of devouring him as demonesses usually do.

A child is similarly joined together from two halves in a much later Sanskrit text in which one of two widowed queens eats a dish consecrated to make them pregnant, and the other has intercourse with her "in the manner of a man"; the eldest queen becomes pregnant, and after the usual time brings forth a son, but since the boy has been born without any semen of a man, which provides the hard parts of a child, he has no bones and is just like a ball of flesh.[5] The Sun* too, it may be recalled, was born as a shapeless mass as a result not of his father's absence but of his mother's overaggressive impatience, which amounts to much the same thing: too much of woman in him. Several Hindu gods are born in embryonic fragments and eventually reunited: the wind-gods called the Maruts (born when Indra enters the womb of a demoness and chops the embryo into bits,[6] like Milton's Satan* in the womb of Death), Krishna,[7] and Skanda.[8]

In the famous parable of Solomon (1 Kings 3:16–27), when each of two prostitutes claimed to be the mother of the same living child, Solomon ordained that the child should be split in two, each mother to have a half; the true mother cried out in horror and said that rather than that she would prefer to relinquish her claim and let the other woman have the child. Solomon (as wise as his Hindu counterpart, Mariyatai-Raman*) gave the baby to her. In the story of Jarasandha, each wife apparently would, like the evil prostitute in the story of Solomon, rather have half a loaf than no bread at all. Old Age ties the halves together to make a complete son—the same Old Age who will eventually break him back down into fragments again.

We will soon encounter Greek versions of this vertical splitting. But the Indian story itself became a European story, as the Greek myths did. The story of transposed male heads was one of eleven (of the original twenty-five) that Sir Richard Burton selected from *The Ocean of the Rivers of Story*, more precisely from the Marathi version of a portion of that text, the *Vetalapancavimshati* (Twenty-five tales of a vampire). Burton translated the story—*very* loosely, and greatly expanded—and published it in 1870, under the evocative title: "Showing That a Man's Wife Belongs Not to his Body But to his Head."[9] The tale was also retold by the Indologist Heinrich Zimmer first in a German essay published in 1935 and then, in

English, in a volume published after his death in 1943.[10] Zimmer's translation introduces two significant phrases that are not in the original: he surmises that "the marriage was not particularly happy" and that switching the heads was an "interesting" mistake. But there is no hint in the Sanskrit text that Madanasundari mixed up the heads through any conscious or unconscious desire to have the best of both men.[11]

In 1940, Thomas Mann, a good friend of Zimmer's, published a novella, *The Transposed Heads* (translated into English in 1941),[12] a lengthy, witty, thoroughly European elaboration of the story as retold by Zimmer. Mann expands all the themes—he takes a 115 pages, in the English translation, to tell a story that took half a dozen pages in the original Sanskrit, 17 pages in Burton's expanded version, and a single paragraph in Zimmer's condensation. In Mann's version, the heroine (whom he calls Sita, an appropriate name for a woman who gets mixed up with doubles) thinks she has it all when she puts her husband's upper-class head on his friend's hunky body. But time has the last laugh: the husband's head neglects the friend's body, which eventually becomes just as scrawny as the husband's had been, while the friend's head exercises the husband's body until it becomes magnificent. In this retelling, it is not merely the case that the woman desires to have both men at once; the men too desire one another. (Mann is, after all, the man who wrote *Death in Venice*.) They love one another much more than they love her, and it is their desire, as well as hers, that is fulfilled when they become intermingled.

Girish Karnad used the ancient Indian story of the transposed heads, including some of the overtones introduced by Mann, as the basis of an incident in his play, *Hayavadana:*

THE HORSE HEAD

A woman named Padmini was married to a Brahmin named Devadatta but attracted to a lower-caste man named Kapila. The two men beheaded themselves and were restored to life, but with their heads transposed [the text refers to each by the name of his head]. Each claimed her: Kapila's head insisted that the child she was carrying was the child of Devadatta's body (i.e., now Kapila's body; though, when the baby was born, he had Kapila's mole on his shoulder). But Devadatta's head quoted Hindu law texts (and the Sanskrit text of the story of the transposed human male heads): since the head is what determines the person, she married the head, not the body. And so Padmini was given to Devadatta's head (and Kapila's body), apparently the ideal arrangement. . . . But then Devadatta's

head started to put Devadatta's sandalwood oil on Kapila's body, and she
missed Kapila's sweaty smell as well as his body—for Devadatta's head let
Kapila's body get fat.[13]

Gradually both men changed and reverted to their original selves, their
original smells: the heads overpowered the bodies. As Padmini com-
plained to Kapila, after many years, "The head always wins, doesn't it?" But
the body won in the end: the athlete's body decayed under the care of the intellectual, while the athlete's head became refined under the influence of the
intellectual's body. Thus the men became one another through her.

Bram Stoker's *Dracula** achieves a similar communion of males
through a woman, indeed a split woman, when all of Lucy's suitors give
her blood transfusions to replace the blood drained by Dracula. Arthur,
her fiancé, regards the transfusion as the equivalent of marriage "in the
sight of God," and the others therefore conceal from him the fact that they
too have "married" Lucy by giving her their blood.[14] When Dracula again
drains Lucy's blood (which is now literally Arthur's blood) he is in a very
real sense cuckolding Arthur. At this point, an earlier image of one man
giving his male friend his blood becomes newly relevant: Van Helsing tells
us that Dr. Seward once drank his, Van Helsing's, blood—entirely scientif-
ically of course and, unlike most vampirism, life-giving. This is almost the
first thing we learn about Dr. Van Helsing, in his own mitteleuropäische
words: "Tell your friend that when that time you suck from my wound so
swiftly the poison of the gangrene from that knife that our other friend,
too nervous, let slip."[15] If blood sucking is erotic, this scene is surely homoerotic. Thus Lucy becomes a kind of conduit through which the four
men (five, when we count Dracula) commune sexually, while avoiding any
need for contact with (dangerous) women. She becomes a kind of typhoid
Mary for male homosexuality, a vessel through which they all swear blood
brotherhood like little boys cutting their fingers: it does not affect her, but
they get it from one another through her. Claude Lévi-Strauss expressed
another aspect of this idea when he suggested that a man uses a woman as
a "conduit of a relationship" in which the true partner is a man and the
woman is an object of exchange.[16] This is a concept that takes on new
meaning in the mythology of bisexuality.*

A bizarre variant of the theme of the transposed heads appears in one
episode of Shakespeare's *Cymbeline*. It is a most convoluted play, but the
episode that concerns us might be summarized as follows:

Cymbeline

> King Cymbeline wanted his daughter Imogen to marry Cloten but Imogen
> instead married Posthumus; when Cloten attempted to seduce her she told
> him that Posthumus's "meanest garment / That ever hath but clipped his
> body is dearer / In my respect than all the hairs above thee."[17] The king
> banished Posthumus; Imogen disguised herself as a man and escaped to
> the wild. To take revenge on Imogen for her remark about Posthumus's
> clothing, Cloten stole and put on some of Posthumus's garments, intend-
> ing to rape her while wearing the offending garments and then to murder
> Posthumus "in her eyes," that is while she was watching. The two sons of
> the king, however, killed Cloten and beheaded him; when Imogen saw his
> headless corpse in Posthumus's clothes, she mistook him for Posthumus.

Although the heads of Cloten and Posthumus are not actually exchanged,
Imogen imagines that Cloten's headless body is lacking, as it were, Posthumus's head.

Cloten intends to exchange merely the outer layer of clothing, but he
inadvertently masquerades in the layer below that, the layer of the body—
though, presumably, without Posthumus's head, Cloten's body will not be
able to masquerade as Posthumus's mind or soul. Imogen wrongly assumes that she can tell the men apart without their heads; when she sees
Cloten's headless corpse in Posthumus's clothes, she says, "A headless man!
The garments of Posthumus! / I know the shape of's leg: this is his hand; /
His foot Mercurial; his Martial thigh; / The brawns of Hercules; but his
Jovial face—/ Murder in heaven? How! 'Tis gone." And, finally, "O Posthumus! Alas, / Where is thy head?"[18] Her gruesome error implies that, without the head, all bodies are alike in the dark. We may read this as a cynical
argument against romantic idealism or as supporting evidence for the argument that the soul or mind is where true identity lies, not in the body.

The splitting and recombining in the Hindu myths about men takes a
different form in Vedantic mythology, which contrasts the entire body, the
deha (which contains the heart and the emotions, but also the head and
reason), with the embodied soul, the *dehin* (which literally "possesses the
body"). In Vedantic mythology, therefore, when a magician combines two
people, instead of placing the *head* of one person on the body of another,
he places the *soul* of one person within the body of another.[19] Usually it is
men who do this, often in order to double themselves. For instance, the
Hindu philosopher Shankara once took on the body, but not the soul, of a
king. Engaged in an argument with a king, he was stymied by a question

about sex, since he had always been chaste; asking for time out, he entered the body of a king who had a large harem, to the relief both of the exhausted king and of the unsatisfied women. After a month of pleasant research and fieldwork, he returned to his philosophical body and won the argument.[20] Similarly, the souls of an ascetic and a whore were once transposed into one another's body, with predictably farcical results.[21] Sometimes gender is all that is exchanged, as when a helpful goblin lends his male sex to a woman (Shikhandin/i*) who is masquerading as a man and has to perform on the wedding night or else.

Just as the story of the head split from the body makes sense in a European context (as we saw in Marguérite Yourcenar's French version of the transposed female heads and in Thomas Mann's German retelling of the transposed male heads), so too the story of the transposed souls caught on in Europe. The theme underwent a transformation in nineteenth-century French literature and became so well entrenched that the translator of one of the stories we are about to consider remarked that "[t]he mere transference of the soul of one man to the body of another is not in itself a novelty in fiction, and apart from the possible comical or tragical mistakes to which it may give rise, is not startlingly novel."[22] What is novel, perhaps, is the emphasis: in the myths of Ahalya and Alcmena, as well as in the tale of the transposed male heads, the text focuses on the woman's state of mind in confronting the double men and only secondarily on the motives of the man who becomes the double (Indra or Zeus). The European retellings, by contrast, emphasize the reaction of the man who suddenly confronts a double he did not know he had; and not surprisingly his reaction is far closer to that of Amphitryon (whose state of mind is actually described in some detail by all authors, from Plautus to Kleist and Giraudoux and Behrman) than to Gautama (who simply knows it all and curses everyone).

Indian influence of the Vedantic type is patent in Théophile Gautier's 1856 novella about exchanged souls:

AVATAR

Octavius de Saville was in love with Prascovia, the wife of Count Olaf Labinski; but she, being chaste, rejected him. Doctor Balthazar Cherbonneau, who had studied for many years in India, put Octavius's soul in Olaf's body (now referred to as Octavius–Labinski) and the reverse (Olaf–de Saville)—each now designated in the text by the soul's first name and the body's last name. The wife immediately realized that her husband had someone else's soul in him, precisely because he lusted after her as her husband never did, and she locked him out of the bedroom. Olaf–de Saville challenged Octavius–Labinski to a duel. Each one experienced a wave of terror as he was about to plunge his sword into the body that he had inhabited until the day before, an act that felt like a kind of suicide. But since Olaf–de Saville wanted to destroy the body that might deceive Prascovia, heedless of the danger to himself, he "lunged straight in order to reach, through his own body, his rival's soul and life." Octavius–Labinski, however, eluded Olaf–de Saville's thrust and disarmed him (remarking that Olaf, whose body he wore, was by far the better swordsman), but refused to kill him because, he said, "That death, even though unreal, would plunge my dear mother into the deepest grief."

Then Octavius–Labinski said to Olaf–de Saville, "I am going to restore your body to you, for Prascovia does not love me. Under the appearance of the husband she recognised the lover's soul." They went together to Dr. Cherbonneau, who put Olaf's soul back in Olaf's body. But Dr. Cherbonneau allowed Octavius's soul to escape, so that Octavius died (or, at least, Octavius's body died). Then Cherbonneau made a will, bequeathing all of his property to Octavius de Saville, and put his own soul into Octavius's body, allowing his own senile body to die. Appearing as Octavius de Saville (though, in reality, Balthazar–de Saville), he attended the funeral of Dr. Balthazar Cherbonneau. Olaf Labinski returned to his Countess, who at once recognized her beloved husband.[23]

A heavy aura of Orientalism links this story, which even has a Sanskrit title, directly to the magical Indian stories we have encountered: Doctor Balthazar Cherbonneau speaks of "panels of hieroglyphs on the cryptic walls of Ellora" and of "the slopes of Mount Merou, whence flows the Ganges," where "centenarian Brahmins decipher unknown manuscripts" and "murmur words belonging to tongues that no people has spoken on the surface of the earth for thousands and thousands of years." He claims to have "learned Sanscrit and Pacrit [sic]."[24] His laboratory is decorated with paintings of "Siwa the blue god" and "Durga with his boar's tusks [and] his chaplet of skulls,"[25] and he promises Octavius visions "from the depths of Indra's heaven, where the apsaras surround you in voluptuous groups." We are told that "the mysterious transfer of souls [was] brought about by Dr. Cherbonneau, thanks to the formula of the sannyasi Brahma-Loghum,"[26] and at the end, his will stipulates that his heir, Octavius, should hand over to the Mazarin library his manuscript copy of the Laws of Manu. He also claims to have something like the magic mirror in which Mephistopheles showed the image of Helen to Faust.[27]

The soul gets star billing both in the names, hyphenated not by marriage but by transmigration, and in the plot. The protagonist wants to possess the woman not with his body but with his soul, although, since he also wishes to possess her physically, he also needs his rival's body. Prascovia, however, rejects his soul; because she is pure, she recognizes the impostor for the very reason that he became an impostor: because he wants her. (Ahalya suspected Indra for this reason too, but took it as a cause to receive, not to reject, the false husband.) This rejection so demoralizes Octavius that he spares his rival's life and gives him back his body. Otto Rank views this as a "narcissistic element of forbearance in the suicide of the double."[28] And indeed the story bears a striking resemblance to narcissistic myths such as the tale of Dorian Gray,* in which the protagonist attacks his own portrait. But Dr. Cherbonneau, who had served as a kind of second to them both in the duel, now becomes another sort of second, when he "allows" the soul of world-weary Octavius to escape so that he himself can exchange his old body for a young one, to have more time to carry out his research, as he says, but perhaps, . . . who knows?

The explicit desire both for a woman and for a young body is the motive in another French variant on the theme, Maurice Renard's novel Le docteur Lerne, sous-dieu (1919), which deals not with transposed souls or heads but with the mediating case, transposed brains. An old man, rejected by the young girl he loves, surgically exchanges his brain with that of his young nephew. Again the ruse is detected and there is a duel, but this time the nephew's brain leaves the uncle's body and enters the body of a bull. When the nephew's brain, in the bull's body, sees his own physical body (the nephew's body, with the uncle's brain) embracing the girl, he becomes so jealous that he tries to kill it, precipitating a second duel between what appear to be his animal and human selves. At the critical moment the uncle stops him by exclaiming, "My dear friend, if you do that you will kill yourself!" Here the soul undergoes a series of transformations in a quasi-Vedantic manner,[29] from the body of the young nephew to that of the old man and then to the bull. But once again the double confronts himself and cannot allow his soul to kill his body; once again the doubling that was intended to win something new for the lover (a new, better body, and the object of his love) turns out to deprive him of what he has (his body, and ultimately his life). Cyrano de Bergerac, who presents Roxane with a fictional man composed of Cyrano's mind in the body of the handsome Christian, is one of the great European expressions of this mythology. He transposes the image of the double lovers, himself and Christian, onto that of Amphitryon's twins—and then makes the serpents, not the boys, the twins; he tells Roxane that his love is "a new-born babe, an infant Hercules, strong enough at birth to strangle those two serpents, Doubt and Pride."[30]

The story of the transposed male heads lives on in various Hollywood movies in which men and women exchange minds and/or souls, or parents change places with their children, or black people with white people, rich with poor, or various permutations of all of these. One of the American classics of this nineteenth-century genre found its way into a French film (*Dans histoires extraordinaires* [Spirits of the dead], 1968): Edgar Allan Poe's "William Wilson" (c. 1840), in which the narrator, Wilson, is, like the protagonists in the French stories, intent on seducing another man's wife but is foiled by his double, whom he kills. As in some of the Hindu variants of the transposed heads and the masquerades of Zeus and Indra with Alcmena and Ahalya, these exchanges in films often facilitate adultery: the double sleeps with the wife of the original. A dark example of this genre is the 1991 film *Shattered*.

SHATTERED

A man in San Francisco who had been in a terrible automobile accident woke up without a memory or a face, horribly disfigured in mind and body. His wife, Judith, showed him (and the plastic surgeons) photos of the face, and told him who he was: her husband, Dan Merrick, a wealthy man. They reconstructed his face according to the photos.

But when he found photos of Judith making love to a man whose face was different from his, he became jealous and disturbed; and one day he looked into a mirror and smashed it to bits. He learned that he had treated Judith very badly, that she had been having an affair with a man named Jack Stanton, and that he had wanted a divorce. Finally he realized that *he was Jack Stanton,* that she had killed Dan and persuaded him (Jack) not to call the police but to dump the body and drive away; that when he had told her he was through with her, they had struggled in the car, and crashed. Now, in the present, there was again a struggle in the car, but this time he rolled free and the car exploded, killing her. When people addressed him as Dan, he did not correct them.

The riddle seems at first to be that Judith really does seem to love the reconstructed Dan, though we know she hated her husband and cheated on him. "I don't get it," Dan keeps saying; "why did she do all this?" Why indeed? What is there, beside the mind and the face, that she loves? Is it just the body? Or is it the idea that he is her lover, not her husband? Dan smashes the big mirror because he knows instinctively that what he sees in it isn't his image—it isn't his soul.

Another example of this mythological film genre combines plastic surgery with organ transplants: *Face/Off* (1997), in which Nicolas Cage and John Travolta play a terrorist and an FBI man whose faces (rather than heads) are surgically transposed. This procedure, which is in effect an exchange of masks, leaves souls and/or brains intact:

FACE / OFF

Castor Troy (Nicolas Cage), a terrorist, is in a coma; Sean Archer (John Travolta), whose son Castor has killed, undergoes plastic surgery to switch not only faces with him, but voice and body: "I've implanted a microchip in your larynx," says the doctor, and so Sean can speak with Castor's (that is, Cage's) voice. Then the faceless body of Castor (who comes out of his coma) forces the doctor to give him Sean's spare face.

As Janet Maslin sums it up, in a review neatly entitled "Good and Evil Trade Places, Body and Soul," "Castor is free to wreak havoc with Sean's suburban family and at F.B.I. headquarters. Bingo. . . . Sean once looked like Mr. Travolta, but now he looks like Mr. Cage. That means that he sees the horrible sight of his own son's killer every time he looks in a mirror." When Sean (with Castor's face) sees himself as Castor, he shatters the mirror; at one point, the two men stand on two sides of a double mirror, and shoot at one another through it—each shooting at the image he hates, his own reflection but really the reflection of his enemy, whom he resembles inside, through years of obsessive hatred, as well as outside. This is precisely what happened to Dr. Lerne, as well as to the victim in *Shattered*. The mythology is patent: Castor has a brother named Pollux (the mortal and immortal twins, the Dioscuri,* now twins actually named Troy, as in Helen of) and a son named Adam, while Sean has a wife named Eve (a double woman in both Gnostic texts[31] and Hollywood [*The Three Faces of Eve*]*).

The psychology is equally patent: as usual the evil double (Castor as Sean) sleeps with the wife of the original. When people ask Sean as Castor how he knows so much about Sean, he replies, "I sleep with his wife." This statement winds a crooked road to the truth: the man who seems to be saying it (Castor) is indeed sleeping with Sean's wife—but only as Sean, which Sean alone knows even as he speaks the bitter words through Castor's face; while the man who is really saying it (Sean) has barely avoided sleeping with Castor's wife—but only as Castor. Got it?

The teenage daughter of the FBI agent keeps changing her face too— but she does it with green paint and weird earrings, the usual teenage self-mutilation, and her father asks her, "Who are you supposed to be now?" Hers is another sort of splitting, a bifurcation of identity between child and woman that is the key to another familiar subtheme of doubling, incest: she shoots Sean, mistaking him for Castor, naturally enough, but when Castor (whom she mistakes for Sean, her father) makes sexual advances to her, she stabs him. In the end, Sean and Eve adopt Castor's son, Adam, the surrogate for the son Castor had killed. Maslin remarks that, in terms of films, this is "a gimmick that hasn't been seen before,"[32] but as a myth, it certainly *has* been seen before.

A final touchdown in what passes for reality: Robert J. White, the director of the Brain Research Laboratory at the Case Western Reserve University School of Medicine, has transplanted the severed head of one monkey onto the headless body of another, with qualified success; he believes it is possible to do the same for humans. But he hesitates, saying, "I would like first to have a more ongoing discussion of the moral and ethical aspects of brain transplants, so we could put behind us the notion that one is violating some Judeo-Christian principle." Or Hindu? or Buddhist, perhaps? Arthur Caplan, a bioethicist at the University of Pennsylvania, objects not only to what he calls the high "yuck factor" of White's work, but to its threat to our Cartesian notion of personal identity (and mortality), to the idea that we are (or are not) only our brains.[33] The identity issue arises, as in the myths, when the head "gets" the body, or the body "gets" the head: Who is the person? The mortality issue arises when someone keeps exchanging one head for another and then one body for another; as in the paradox of the knife handle and blade, which are continually and alternatively replaced,[34] we may ask, is it the same person? Who is it that is immortal? Indeed, very few people want this operation; instead, they just want their own bodies fixed up for a little while longer.

Splitting Male Androgynes

In chapter 4 we went from a consideration of Hindu tales of two women whose heads were transposed and pairs of Greek women who were split in half at the waist to the Victorian tale of one woman split in half into two sexually polarized women—one chaste, one lustful. Having considered, in this chapter, Hindu tales of two men whose heads were transposed and European tales of men whose souls were transposed, let us now turn first to the Greek and then to the Victorian tale of one man split into two sexually polarized people—a man and a woman. For androgynes, like the serially bisexual creatures that we will encounter in the next chapter, are no more egalitarian than any other sexual form: they are primarily male. This is certainly the case with the classical instance of this type, Narcissus.

NARCISSUS

Narcissus was born when the river god Cephisus raped the blue nymph Leiriope. The seer Teiresias told Leiriope, "Narcissus will live a long time, as long as he does not know himself." He was so beautiful that many people fell in love with him, but he rejected them all, for he was too proud of his own beauty. One person who fell in love with him was the nymph Echo, who could use her voice only to repeat what someone else said. When Echo tried to embrace Narcissus he repelled her, and she spent the rest of her life pining for him until only her voice remained. Finally, Artemis caused Narcissus to fall in love with his own reflection in a clear spring. Unable to possess the image, he lay gazing helplessly into the pool. Echo stayed beside him and echoed his cries as he plunged a dagger into his breast and died. Out of his blood there grew the narcissus plant.[35]

And out of his story, the name of a psychological syndrome. Pausanias rationalized the story by arguing that Narcissus had an identical twin sister who died; Narcissus was inconsolable until he saw his own reflection.[36] Plutarch tells another variant of the myth in which the protagonist is not Narcissus but Entelidas, who was so delighted by his own reflection in the water that he became ill and lost his beauty.[37] There is a related legend that Dionysus was conceived when Persephone admired herself in a mirror, and that Dionysus, in turn, gazed into a mirror made by Hephaestus, became seduced by the reflection, and created the external world in his own image.[38] With an implicit pun on intellectual knowledge and carnal knowledge, the Greek and Latin myth demonstrates the devastating reflexivity of perverse erotic love, an all too human weakness that makes necessary the creation of empty reflections of sound and sight. The story was mirrored in later Gnostic texts; Adam loses his celestial nature as a result of falling in love with his own image glimpsed in the mirror of water.[39] The Hindu sage Vyasa* too was consoled by the combination of an echo and a shadow* (that is, a reflection) when he lost his son Shuka forever.[40]

There are other Greek stories about this sort of reflexive androgyny, such as the myth related by Aristophanes in Plato's *Symposium,* the story of an original circular creature, half-male and half-female (or, as the case may be, half-male and half-male, or half-female and half-female), split in two and condemned to spend its life trying to get back together with its own other half. This image of wholeness and completion is globular, sated, self-contained; it represents an extreme of self-love, purely physical, that depicts human sexuality in terms of excess (the male-female halves become adulterers and adulteresses, the male-male halves pederasts, and the female-female halves lesbians—all regarded with disdain by Plato).[41]

The image of the androgyne who sleeps with his own better half becomes a joke in Shakespeare's *Merchant of Venice,* when Portia and Nerissa disguise themselves as a lawyer ("civil doctor") and his clerk, in what may be one of the earliest lawyer jokes in English literature. The women in drag trick their fiancés, Bassanio and Gratiano, into giving them the rings that they had promised never to part with; then, appearing as themselves, as women, they accuse the men of infidelity (Portia: "I'll die for't but some woman had the ring" [5.1]). (In fact, there is a sting beneath the joke, a submerged homosexual subplot: one reason why Portia becomes a man is to challenge Bassanio's love for Antonio, which consistently overrides his love for Portia; the ring is proof that Bassanio has in fact betrayed his wife with someone he loves better—not, in this case, the man she pretended to be, but the man for whose sake she ostensibly cross-dressed.) To tease the men, the women threaten to sleep with the doctor and manservant who had gotten the rings—i.e., their own fictional male halves (Portia: "I'll not deny him any thing I have; / No, not my body, nor my husband's bed. . . . I'll have that doctor for my bedfellow"). Then, producing the rings, the women say that they *have* slept with the men, as women usually do when they get the telltale rings (Portia: "By this ring, the doctor lay with me"; and Nerissa: "The doctor's clerk, / In lieu of this last night did lie with me"). When the men finally catch on, they continue to pretend, playfully, that the male personae of Portia and Nerissa are real rivals. As Bassanio says to Portia: "Were you the doctor and I knew you not? . . . Sweet doctor, you shall be my bedfellow. When I am absent, then lie with my wife."

We have seen a kind of Hindu parallel to the tale of Narcissus in the myth of the creator who desires his own reflection.* Hinduism also tells of a male who splits off half of his body in order to make a woman to be his mate, beginning with the famous cosmogony in the *Brihadaranyaka Upanishad* (1.4.3). Such an androgynous bifurcation, vertical rather than horizontal (within the body: that is, cut left from right, rather than top from bottom, like Renuka), though with a different sort of recombination, is described in a contemporary story that A. K. Ramanujan called

THE PRINCE WHO MARRIED HIS OWN LEFT HALF

A prince refused to marry any woman; when his parents insisted that he marry, he commanded that his own body be cut in half; the right half healed and became the full prince, while the left half became a woman, whom he married. The prince kept her in a deserted place, and seldom visited her; but a wizard fell in love with her and became her lover; he entered the palace by taking the form of a snake. One day, the king killed the snake, and she mourned for him, had him cremated, and wore his ashes in a gold talisman tied around her shoulder. Her husband, concerned by her emaciated state, came to see her and questioned her. She said, "You've kept me here in a jail. I get to see your face here only twice a month. How can my heart be happy or content?" The king's son felt very contrite when he heard about her sorrow. "Then I'll stay here all the time, every day," he said, to console her. This was not what she wanted. She made him agree to a riddle: if he answered it, she would throw herself on the fire and die; if he did not, he would do the same. He failed to answer the riddle, which ended: "A husband on the thigh, a lover on the shoulder." So, according to his word, he fell into a fire and killed himself. His wife who was his own left half took another lover and lived happily.[42]

The prince who rejects women by limiting the field of possible suitors to himself is directly descended from the androgyne who splits off from half of his body a woman to be his mate. But this variant develops the darker psychological implications of the theme: the man who will only marry the woman within him neglects her and is in turn rejected and ultimately killed by her. Midway through the text, the story veers off into another, far better known Hindu story: the snake-lover,[43] who is doubled in his animal and human forms and is, in his snake form, symbolically androgynous (masculine as the phallus, feminine as the coiled power). In other variants of that story too, the heroine, like Ahalya, uses a riddle to wriggle out of an adulterous situation. We may hazard a guess that the prince created the woman out of himself and locked her up because he hated and distrusted women and feared that his wife would betray him—a fear that was, as it so often is, a self-fulfilling prophecy.

The world title in this sort of narcissism surely belongs to the sixteenth-century Hindu saint Caitanya, in whom Krishna and Radha became simultaneously incarnate; this happened because Krishna looked into a mirror and said, "How handsome I am! I wish I were a woman and could fall in love with me," and so he became Radha, and was able to make love with himself.[44] The seeds of that transformation lie back in the transformation of Krishna himself, and his worshippers, the cowherd women, or in some cases cowherd men: the cowherd women, abandoned by the teasing Krishna, fantasize that half of them have been sexually transformed into men and make love with one another,[45] while the men wish to become women (and the male worshipers of Krishna sometimes dress as women) in order to make love with Krishna. Similarly, it is said that the men who saw Rama wanted to become women to make love with him, and the women who saw Draupadi wanted to become men to make love with her;[46] and to close the circle, it is said that the men who saw Rama and wanted to become women to make love with him became reincarnate as the cowherd women and made love with him when he had taken the form of another incarnation of Vishnu, Krishna.[47] The Tantric yogi too copulates with the female principle inside his own body (the Kundalini),[48] thus becoming his own sexual partner—a neat but, as we have seen, not a unique trick.

The myth of Narcissus was reworked in the Victorian tales of Dr. Jekyll and Dorian Gray. Robert Louis Stevenson's *Dr. Jekyll and Mr. Hyde* is a story of metaphysical splitting, the splitting of good and evil:

Dr. Jekyll and Mr. Hyde

Dr. Jekyll, composed of a mixture of good and evil, split away the evil part of himself into a man entirely evil, Mr. Hyde, and through him led a double life of depravity until Hyde gradually took over Jekyll's body entirely; Jekyll killed himself, and they died together.

Interesting details come to light once one begins to ask, "What unspeakable thing did Hyde actually do?" The mythological answer is that Hyde is Jekyll's (which is to say Stevenson's) fantasy of a homosexual lover.[49] And since Hyde is a part of Jekyll's own body, a subset of Jekyll, as it were, the fantasy is an instance of a kind of extreme homoerotic narcissism, a Victorian reworking of the Greek tale of Narcissus.* In this sense, Jekyll/Hyde functions like a mythological androgyne, who splits apart and mates with himself.

The fantasy belongs first to the lawyer Utterson, the superego (the counterpart to Hyde as id), the wholly respectable aspect of Jekyll: "As he lay and tossed in the gross darkness of the night and the curtained room . . . he would see a room in a rich house, where his friend lay asleep, dreaming and smiling at his dreams; and then the door of that room would be opened, the curtains of the bed plucked apart, the sleeper recalled, and lo! there would stand by his side a figure to whom power was given, and even at that dead hour, he must rise and do its bidding." Surely this "power" that compels a man to "rise" can only be an erotic imperative, and the fact that Utterson himself is lying in a curtained bed when he imagines Hyde pulling back the curtains of the bed of "his friend" shows that it is a fantasy that Utterson shares with Jekyll (whom he calls "Harry," in suggestive intimacy). Nothing that Utterson has learned about Hyde has implied in the slightest way that Hyde has access to Jekyll's bedroom, merely to his laboratory; Utterson's jealous imagination creates the scene. And the same bedroom fantasy recurs to Utterson just a few pages later: "It turns me cold to think of this creature stealing like a thief to Harry's bedside; poor Harry, what a wakening!"[50] It is an erotic wakening, for Hyde is Jekyll's homosexual lover; Elaine Showalter hinted at this when she wrote, "Unable to pair off with either a woman or another man, Jekyll divides himself, and finds his only mate in his double, Edward Hyde,"[51] but she did not draw out the narrative implications of this statement. If the reader should object that, being a part of Jekyll, Hyde cannot have intercourse with him, one may simply invoke Narcissus,* Caitanya,* and so forth.

But the early reception of the text emphasized not its androgyny (let alone its homosexual subtext) but its moral ambivalence. Stevenson's novel inspired a number of films, once every ten years for a while, which conjured up a double heterosexual female love interest for Jekyll/Hyde—a good girl for Jekyll and a bad girl for Hyde—to replace the more efficient mutual homosexual partnership ruled off-bounds by the film censors of the time.[52] It also inspired a number of literary imitations, including feminist (or at least proto-feminist) imitations that raise questions suggested by Elaine Showalter: "Is the divided self of the fin-de-siècle narrative everybody's fantasy? Can women as well as men have double lives? Can there be a woman in Dr. Jekyll's closet?"[53] Andrew Lang and Rider Haggard, friends of Stevenson, produced a female version of the story in their collaborative novel *The World's Desire*, but "they thought the most improbable part was when 'the hero having gone to bed with Mrs. Jekyll wakes up with Mrs. Hyde.'"[54] Fay Weldon, in *Lives and Loves of a She-Devil*, created "a Hyde heroine who makes herself over into a beautiful Jekyll," and the Scottish novelist Emma Tennant wrote "a brilliant feminist version of Stevenson's novel called *Two Women of London: The Strange Case of Ms. Jekyll and Mrs. Hyde* (1989)."[55] Showalter imagines an American version of Tennant's novel: "Henrietta Jekyll, a distinguished woman scientist in her mid-fifties, unmarried" takes a potion and becomes "a young, tough, sexy" babe with no inhibitions. But then, Showalter continues, "The story pulls up short. Where does Edie Hyde go once she's all dressed up? To look for Mr. Goodbar? To walk in Central Park? To the porn shops and sex shows in Times Square? . . . In order for the Jekyll-Hyde fantasy of liberation to be fully imagined for a woman, Henrietta Jekyll has to turn into a man."[56] Again we must confront the double standard that judges stories about double men differently from those about double women.

These feminist texts change both Jekyll and Hyde into women. But the androgyny that is implicit in the original Stevenson scenario comes out only in two B-film versions, made a quarter century apart, in which Jekyll is male and Hyde is a woman. The first film was *Dr. Jekyll and Sister Hyde*, the Hammer Studios' 1971 horror version, of which Showalter remarks that "the film's mingling of themes of duality and bisexuality, science and religion, is a closer reading of Stevenson's story than the more celebrated Hollywood versions."[57] The film begins with the theme best known from *Frankenstein*, with a male scientist who hates women and attempts to steal the female secret of creating life—or rather, in this film, to postpone death:

DR. JEKYLL AND SISTER HYDE

Dr. Jekyll procured female reproductive organs from the morgue in order to manufacture an elixir to prolong life. He took the potion and became a beautiful woman, his own female double, Sister Hyde. Gradually, however, his female persona began to kill men that got in her way and to take over more and more of the personality; Jekyll therefore had to kill women in order to maintain his supply of the elixir. And *she* responded by becoming Jack the Ripper, eluding the police since they were not looking for a woman. Finally, Jekyll was entirely taken over by Sister Hyde.

The female persona is at first just silly, embarrassing Jekyll with a sudden and irresistible desire to shop, and becoming sexually excited by touching his own new breasts (a scene mirrored in the moment in the movie *Switch* [1991] when a womanizer becomes reincarnate as a woman and gazes with lust at his/her knockers). But then she becomes murderous. . . .

The second androgynous version, *Dr. Jekyll and Ms. Hyde* (1995), names the woman Helen (a highly appropriate name for the woman who is a false double of the man) and develops many of the same clichés in a more slapstick vein:

DR. JEKYLL AND MS. HYDE

When Dr. Richard Jacks is transformed into Helen Hyde, the signs of gender as well as of sex are changed: he sprouts breasts and loses his penis, and his hair and nails grow long. Helen Hyde is at first nicer, or at least better behaved, than her male counterpart: she is considerate to his secretary, whom he had treated with contempt. But then, when her employer fails to promote her simply because she is a woman, she becomes murderous and/or seductive. Eventually, Richard, with the help of his girlfriend, Sarah, finds the formula to make Helen disappear forever.

As Richard and Helen switch back and forth, neither has any memory of the other's actions, and this makes for trouble with Sarah. When Richard is being transformed into Helen, Sarah comes to the locked door; hearing the agonized moans of first a man and then a woman, she mistakes them for orgasmic moans—first his, then hers. Her consequent jealousy prompts Richard to remark, "Who would have thought that, if another woman came between me and Sarah, it would be me?" The homoerotic subtext of the original novel is deflected into a gay subtext: a gay guy who falls for Helen says she is the first woman he's ever been attracted to, and when at last he sees her become transformed into Richard he cries out, "It's Richard! Oh, thank god!" The appearance of breasts is a source of shock and hilarity to one and all, over and over and over again, and in the end the restored Richard pronounces the psychobabble conclusion: "There's a woman in all of us." But sexist clichés abound, capped by Richard's reference to Helen as "my dark side" (a direct throwback to Freud's notorious reference to woman as "the dark continent").[58] I am still waiting for a film in which Jekyll is female, and Hyde is male. . . .

The implications of homosexuality, androgyny, and narcissism in Stevenson's novel became far more overt in a novel published just a few years later, Oscar Wilde's *The Picture of Dorian Gray*:

The Picture of Dorian Gray

A beautiful young man named Dorian Gray was granted his wish to keep
his youthful appearance through the years, while the portrait of him became increasingly ugly as age and the evil that he committed progressively
disfigured it instead of him. In the end, Dorian stabbed the portrait and
died; the portrait was instantaneously restored to its original beauty, and
Dorian's corpse at that moment became hideous.

The portrait* that serves, classically, as a surrogate for a lost lover here becomes a surrogate for a self that the protagonist is happy to lose—his own
morally evil and physically aging self. When Lord Henry first sees the portrait of Dorian Gray (before he has met Dorian Gray in person), he comments, "He is a Narcissus." Much later, Wilde writes of Dorian with his
portrait: "Once, in boyish mockery of Narcissus, he had kissed, or feigned
to kiss, those painted lips that now smiled so cruelly at him. Morning after
morning he had sat before the portrait wondering at its beauty, almost en-
amoured of it, as it seemed to him at times."[59] Even the kiss is feigned,
faked.

This is, like the Stevenson novel, a highly metaphysical myth, especially
in its central image: one person splits into two, not, this time, a good person and an evil person, but a (good) body, captured in the flesh, and an
(evil) soul, captured by art. The book presents, among other things, a
powerful argument for the existence of the soul: the soul that is usually invisible (and sometimes therefore thought not to exist) is here reified, and
we can see that it does in fact exist. Dorian says idly that he would sell his
soul to the devil to stay young, and he does just that, selling it to the devil
incarnate in Lord Henry.

Wilde plays upon the metaphysical problems of change and death and
immortality: what, if anything, is real? What, if anything, lasts forever?
The theme of preserving youth forever is often a subtheme of the myth of
the double (recall the guiltless, ageless Helen of Troy, and the role of "Old
Age" in the Hindu and French tales of split men). Wilde tackles the problem
of physical aging by suggesting three increasingly insupportable hypotheses: first, that when you get old you get old, which no one can deny; second, that when you get old you get ugly, which some might challenge; and,
last, that when you get evil you get ugly, which is highly debatable. But he
quickly reverses all three of these processes by postulating a magical cir-
cumstance in which none of them happens after all: Dorian Gray gets evil
and old, but never ugly and never even visibly old. This reversal is made

possible by the suspension of the normal relationship between appearance and reality: all that is real is appearance—the portrait is the only real thing in the whole book. The portrait is the soul of Dorian Gray, and so it appears that when we sin the soul becomes old and ugly, just as the body normally does whether we sin or not.

The assumptions that normally you do see evil in a face, and that it is sin that makes you not only ugly but old (age and death resulting from the sin in Eden) are stunningly puritanical views for a man often regarded as a superficial libertine. The portrait has the effect of a face-lift, but it also steals Dorian's life force. For the final, unavoidable step in this syllogism comes at the end: you get dead when you get dead.

The Stevenson and Wilde novels often served as paradigms for androgyny in soi-disant real life. The transformed male gazing upon his/her own breasts (that we just noted in two films) is mirrored in an incident described by the journalist James/Jan Morris in her wry and perceptive narration of his transition from male to female. In the course of his sex change surgery, she found herself in a lake in North Wales, "and when, gently wading through the reeds, and feeling the icy water rise past my [male] loins to my trembling breasts, I fell into the pool's embrace, sometimes I thought the fable might well end there, as it would in the best Welsh fairy tales."[60] And Morris remarked, "The change was infinitely gradual. I felt like a slow-motion Jekyll and Hyde."[61] Or, one might suppose, Narcissus.

INTERLUDE: SELF-IMPREGNATING ANDROGYNES

Narcissus, the left-sided prince, and Henry Jekyll fell in love with their other halves but did not procreate with them. This, however, was accomplished by the single parent of the monkey heroes Valin and Sugriva in the *Ramayana*, who is first the father, and then the mother, and then the father again:

THE MONKEY AND HIS REFLECTION

One day a great monkey named Riksharaja saw the reflection of his own face in a lake. Thinking that it was an enemy mocking him, in his monkey foolishness he plunged into the water, but when he came out of the water he was a beautiful woman. The gods Indra and Surya [the Sun] desired her and were overpowered by lust. Indra shed his seed on her head before he actually managed to consummate the act, and then he turned back; but because Indra's seed is never shed in vain, she gave birth to a king of the monkeys;

and because the seed had fallen in her hair *[vala]* he was named Valin. The seed of Surya, when he was overpowered by lust, was sprinkled on her neck; he said not a single good word, but regained control and reined in his lust; Sugriva was born from the semen that had fallen on her neck *[griva]*. Then the two gods went away, and when the sun rose after that night had passed, Riksharaja resumed his own monkey shape and saw his two sons. He suckled them with honey and took them home. Thus the monkey Riksharaja was the father of Valin and Sugriva, and also their mother.[62]

Like Narcissus, the monkey mistakes his reflection for another creature— not, this time, a potential sexual partner, but a mocking enemy. The result is much the same, however: the myth short-circuits the Narcissus connection so that the monkey does not mate with his reflection, as if it were someone of the other sex, but becomes his sexual reflection, as it were— and mates with someone else. (Indeed, he mates with two other males— Indra and Surya, both implicated in other myths of doubling—, who double one another even as his female self doubles his male self; and, like Heracles* and Iphicles, and Helen and the Dioscuri, the twins have two different fathers.)

Since Riksharaja is a serial rather than a simultaneous androgyne, his male and female parts are never able to meet and mate; the gods must descend ex machina to substitute their sperm for that of the usually required male monkey in order to allow him to procreate. The text makes it clear that the seed fell on the upper body, that there was no consummated male homosexual act. Riksharaja simultaneously changes gender and species: a male monkey becomes a human (or at least anthropomorphic) woman. (Indeed, his species is fragile from the beginning: his name means King of the Bears, and he is closely associated with bears in the *Ramayana*.) But his monkeyness prevails: though two gods more or less artificially inseminate a woman, the resulting children are neither gods nor humans, but monkeys, the true, underlying form of the father.

Satan manages not exactly to impregnate himself but to act as a kind of sexual matchmaker between mutually impregnating demons. We learn this from the *Malleus Maleficarum*, the locus classicus for the theology of the incubus and succubus and the medieval Latin handbook for witch-hunters:

THE INCUBUS AND THE SUCCUBUS

It is true that to procreate a man is the act of a living body. But when it is said that devils cannot give life, because that flows formally from the soul, it is true; but materially life springs from the semen, and an Incubus devil can, with God's permission, accomplish this by coition. And the semen does not so much spring from him, as it is another man's semen received by him for this purpose.[63] For the devil is a Succubus to a man, and becomes Incubus to a woman. In just the same way they absorb the seeds of other things for the generating of various things, as S. Augustine says, *de Trinitate* 3.[64]

Thus the devil becomes a succubus to a man, takes his sperm, becomes an incubus, and uses that man's sperm (as the Hindu gods used Riksharaja's) to impregnate a woman that "he" sleeps with. He hands the sperm down the line, just as Bram Stoker's Lucy passes around the blood (itself a metaphor for sperm).

The fantasy of the self-impregnating androgyne came more literally true in an episode reported in that great compendium of modern mythology, with an appropriate name for a reteller or retailer of the great Vedic solar myths, *The Sun*. The story appears under the headline:

SEX-CHANGE WOMAN MAKES SELF PREGNANT!

Gender-switch patient Gilda Raybourne is both a mommy and a daddy to her unborn child after impregnating herself in what stunned docs are calling a "first-of-a-kind" case. Gilda, 28, was supposed to be all woman, but surgeons apparently botched the operation, leaving the transsexual with just enough stuff to raise her own family—single-handedly! "Both her male and female sexual organs were still functioning," explains her personal physician Dr. Clyde Mouche. "The surgeons missed something. These organs were able to join together at some time, whether Gilda knew it or not, and perform in such a way that sexual intercourse occurred. This could have happened, say, during sleep without Gilda's knowledge. The pregnancy followed. She was obviously shocked when she found out. She thought her male sexual organs were completely gone." Gilda—formerly Gaylord Raybourne Morgan—was actually born a hermaphrodite with both male and female organs. However, she was brought up as a man, since her outward male characteristics seemed more dominating than her female features. But as she grew up, she realized she wanted to be a woman. "I was definitely a case of a woman trapped in a man's body," Gilda says. "But in my case I could do something about it since I was halfway there." The heir to a British steel fortune, Gilda, who also has homes in New York and Los Angeles, went to a special clinic outside Paris, France for a sex-change operation. All was well until she began experiencing symptoms not unlike her pregnant women friends. . . . "All her life, her male reproductive system had been dormant," says Dr. Mouche. "The surgeons might have thought they had gotten rid of that function, but they failed. Not only that, but it's possible they unwittingly triggered it to respond for the first time." . . . Dr. Victor Faircloth, a London fertility expert, [said,] " . . . A person having sex with himself and becoming pregnant is the stuff of science fiction. But it actually can happen and brings us a host of other possibilities to study."[65]

Gilda was impregnated during her sleep, like the women impregnated by the satanic succubus, but the real demons are the surgeons, who awakened her long-dormant (i.e., sleeping) masculinity—also during her sleep. This is the stuff not only of contemporary science fiction but of ancient mythology.

Comparison: Victorians and Others

The two great Victorian novels about men that we have just considered— Robert Louis Stevenson's *The Strange Case of Dr. Jekyll and Mr. Hyde* (1887) and Oscar Wilde's *The Picture of Dorian Gray* (1890)—were written within a decade of Bram Stoker's *Dracula* (1897), at a time when questions of science and the early stirrings of psychiatry were in the air. As the religious aspects of moral splitting had been exacerbated, rather than resolved, by the Enlightenment advances of science, these three Victorian novels express a vision of the hybridization of religion and science and a horror of the ways in which science had attempted, in vain, to usurp the privileges of religion.

They suggest three different but closely related ways to split moral evil (particularly but not only sexual evil) away from oneself, three variants of the split-level alibi. Stoker's novel says, "It was not I who did the evil act; it was a dead (or sleeping) form of me." Stevenson's says, "It was not I who did the evil act; it was a drugged form of me." Wilde's says, "It was not I who did the evil act; it was an artistic form of me." This search for freedom from evil was shared by a triad of fin de siècle writers who invented their own ideologies of the splitting of good from evil—Friedrich Nietzsche, Sigmund Freud, and Sir Arthur Conan Doyle. The ideas of these three men, more generally diffused among the reading public before their actual publication, some a few years before, some after, our triad of novels, may well have influenced them or indeed been influenced by them. Doyle published the first Holmes book *(A Study in Scarlet)* in 1887, the same year that Stevenson published *Jekyll and Hyde;* Nietzsche published *Beyond Good and Evil* a year earlier, in 1886; Freud published *The Interpre-*

tation of Dreams in 1899. As George Stade has put it, implicating Doyle and Freud (though not Nietzsche), "Van Helsing is to Dracula as Victor Frankenstein is to his monster, as Holmes is to Moriarty, as Dr. Jekyll is to Mr. Hyde, as Freud's ego is to his id."[66]

Nietzsche strove to erase the entire category of evil, to settle the ultimate boundary dispute once and for all. He poses a theological challenge to Stevenson: if God (and the devil) are dead, there is no specific entity that one might cut off in order to split away one's evil. Freud's idea of the return of the repressed from childhood validates the dreaming self that is the source of evil in *Dracula* (where half of the characters spend most of their time asleep, drunk, or drugged) and the drugged self in *Jekyll and Hyde;* the Freudian argues, "It was not I who did the evil act; it was the child that I used to be, a child who cannot be held responsible." And Sir Arthur Conan Doyle's villains often embody the idea of the return of the repressed from the colonies: the dull, stolid bourgeois British gentleman turns out to have been a brutal creature who sowed his wild oats long ago in Australia, or the American West, or, most often, India (where the equally stolid Dr. Watson, Holmes's narrator and straight man, served for many years).

Indeed, an Oriental (or Orientalist) presence haunts all of these Victorian novels (as, during the same period, it haunted Gautier's *Avatar*). When Hyde tramples down a little girl he is twice referred to as a Juggernaut, and Orientalism and colonialism are manifest in *Dorian Gray* in the form of the oppressive presence of luxurious Oriental spoils—fine china, Persian carpets, Indian emeralds and rubies. (The 1945 film version invents an Egyptian cat who watches the drama with appropriate inscrutability.) Dracula too is an Oriental, who claims descent from the Szekelys, prompting Nina Auerbach to remark: "No human can share the mirror with a lord of lost races whose names Englishmen can't pronounce."[67] This Orientalist presence brings with it a subtext about drugs—opium for Holmes and by implication for Dorian Gray; "tokay" for Dracula; "the drug" for Jekyll; and on the level of the supertext, cocaine for Freud. The drugs are presented with a perverse Orientalism: opium, actually introduced by the British into China, is depicted as introduced into Britain by Chinese, and hashish brought to London by Indians.

The perduring mythological substructure of these novels indicates that, although the more particular paradigms may be confined to the cultural range of Victorian England and Hollywood, the more general problem of splitting away evil ranges far beyond the late nineteenth century and Europe. These tales of splitting are not merely Orientalist; they are Oriental too. One of the earliest expressions of the wish to project responsibility for evil away from the self was recorded in the *Rig Veda,* some three thousand years before the Victorians formulated their responses: "The mischief was not done by my own free will, Varuna; wine, anger, dice, or carelessness led me astray."[68] And at the other end of the temporal spectrum, Robert Jay Lifton's *The Nazi Doctors* documents the ways in which those who perpetrated atrocities split away their moral selves. We have already considered, in chapter 1, another aspect of this splitting in the stories of women who dissociate in reaction to experiencing violence, in contrast with these stories of men who dissociate in reaction to perpetrating violence. And the vampire scenario was curiously resurrected in a recent English legal decision that exculpated women from crimes committed during the premenstrual period in which they are presumed to be insane. (Though, as Mary Douglas notes, "There was a short period recently when women had the possibility of claiming impairment in law due to pre-menstrual tension—but when they considered the implications of allowing themselves to be viewed as less than fully responsible citizens, they abandoned the idea.")[69]

The double standard is patent in these tales of splitting away evil: it makes a difference to have the brains (or in some stories the heads) male instead of female; the whole point of the story is different. The women exchange their heads in reaction to male violence, and they become violent to other men and women; the men do it to avoid death, and they kill one another. The women are beheaded by men who fear women's sexuality; but men who, like Ravana,* persist in raping women are threatened with having their heads explode.[70] The men, more than the women, in these myths come into conflict not only with other men, but with themselves. And isn't it curious that a French woman (Marguerite Yourcenar) chose to write about the story of the split woman, part goddess, part prostitute, while two German men (Heinrich Zimmer and Thomas Mann) chose to write about the woman with the two split men? This is a rare moment in the long history of the theme when we can identify, with confidence, the genders of the authors of different variants. It hardly allows us to speculate about the male or female bias of other, earlier variants; but it is something to think about.

CONCLUSION: MIND AND BODY (AND SOUL)

Many of these myths split the body away from the mind and/or the soul—or from something else. In European mythology, the severing of head from body raises questions of the link between mind and body: Which is real? Which holds one's identity? But some myths go beyond this coarse Cartesian paradigm to pose more subtle questions. Where Descartes, that protostructuralist, divided us into two, other cultures (and other parts of our own culture) divide us into several different sorts of entities: body and soul and heart and mind and memory and morals and affections. These more miscellaneous fragmentations may still be forced onto the Procrustean bed of Cartesian dualism if they are structured through a (Hegelian) dialectic: thus body/soul is mediated by, for example, mind; but mind/action is mediated by speech; or mind may form an opposition with heart, and heart/mind is mediated by loyalty ... ad infinitum.

Many cultures—including Hinduism—do not debate the mind-body question at all; they assume that memory, for instance, is a part of both. Mainstream Hindu philosophies, beginning with the Upanishads in about 600 B.C.E., distinguish the body, which dies, from the soul, which transmigrates. But where is mind located in this paradigm? And where is identity? This is not so clear in the myths. Moreover, this Upanishadic, Vedantic scenario is not the only Hindu paradigm. Girish Karnad's *Hayavadana* locates identity ultimately in the body, and many Hindu texts assume that life is real, the body is real, and the shadow or the soul is an unreal intrusion into that reality. (The word *mey* in Tamil actually means both "real" and "body.") In this more secular, or at least naturalistic, view, the body is more important than the soul, the visible form (the body) is the person, and the invisible form (the soul) is not.

Some myths assume that one can take on the body of someone else without taking on the mind and soul contained in that body. Euripides distinguishes not only between Helen A and Helen B, but between Helen's mind and Helen's body. When someone carelessly remarks to Helen, "You have a body like Helen's but you don't have a mind like hers, no, very different,"[71] Helen becomes furious and makes him retract. But as Norman Austin rightly asks, "Helen's body was transported to Egypt, but who knows where her mind was displaced?"[72] And as Froma Zeitlin points out, Euripides, in his concern for the divided self, posits "an actual double who is the opposite of the real self, who matches her in appearance in every physical, visible detail, in *demas, opsis,* but not in *ethos.*"[73] This is a distinction rarely made in myths of doubling and splitting, which generally assume that the duplication of form and face *(demas* and *opsis)* is all that is needed and seldom refer to the duplication of thought and behavior *(ethos).* When the Hindu philosopher Shankara* took on the body but not the soul of a king, he put on the king's body just as one would put on a costume: inside, he apparently retained his own mind, his own memory, presumably his own soul.

But there are several interesting exceptions to this rule, texts in which the transformed person changes mind and soul along with the changed body, like the mind of a Stanislavskian Method actor who begins to feel the emotion that he mimes. We think that mask is to face as face is to head, but often the mask is not merely a superficial surface but something that encompasses the whole head, and in such cases it is more likely that the wearer would take on the mind as well as the body of the person whose face appears on the mask. Philostratus in the second century wrote that even an image made of nothing but shadow and light *(skia* and *phos),* lacking color and substance, can still convey not only likeness and form, but intelligence, modesty, and bravery.[74]

Sometimes Hollywood cuts this Gordian knot and explicitly excludes the mind from the transposed body, as in the film *Excalibur* (1981), when Merlin has the foresight to say to Uther, "Take on the outer form of the Duke"; or on the other hand, the screenplay may explicitly include the mind in the transplant, as in films about reincarnation *(Chances Are, The Reincarnation of Peter Proud).* The initial dichotomy of mind and body allows both for texts that maintain that dichotomy and for others that challenge it in one way or another.

These issues—the survival of memory and identity when the surface of the body, or the whole body, is transformed—take on a new power and complexity when we introduce into the already rich mix the factor of gender. This happens in the mythology of bisexual transformation, to which we must now turn.

SIX

Bisexual
Transformations

~~✦~~

MALES INTO FEMALES IN INDIA

We have now considered androgynes who split in half in various ways, sometimes to create life and sometimes to kill. In Hindu mythology, gods are more often serially than simultaneously bisexual and more often lethal than fecund. Each of the great gods, Vishnu and Shiva, is transformed into a female in a famous cycle of myths, and the Goddess becomes male in a later and more miscellaneous cycle of texts. We might use the modern term *bisexual* for such deities who are not serially monogamous but serially transsexual. Indeed, serial transformation, which in a sense appears to be horizontal, first one sex and then another, is really vertical: it is an attempt to recover a lost possibility, to express an ambiguity that is present from the start, revealed when it seems to be transformed.

Many Hindu myths involve either transvestism (dressing as someone of the other gender) or transsexuality (transformation into someone of the other sex). But when it comes to mythology at least, it is not always possible or desirable to draw a clean line splitting these two phenomena like the two sides of an androgyne. Many actual transsexuals say that they feel as if they had been born in the wrong body; they feel that they have to change their sex in order *not* to change their gender, to get the two back into synch. By contrast, people who are not transsexuals often argue that transsexuals who undergo surgery are thereby taking on the wrong body. Thus these two views dispute the authenticity of the transsexual body. The *perception* of the self as transsexual (as having a body of one sex and a mind/soul/personality/gender of another) is attested by very early mythological sources, as are transsexual *transformations,* from male to female (MTF) or female to male (FTM).

In real life, such transformations have until recently been limited to the changes wrought by castration and now through more subtle surgery, but the perceptions are attested in a wide range of texts; transsexuality in the sense of perception is a dilemma for which myths of transsexual transformation imagine a solution. That is to say, myths in which gods change their sex are often coded human bisexual or homosexual fantasies. But the myths of transsexual transformation do not precisely represent the self-perception of transsexuals, who feel that they are not changing to a new sex, as the gods seem to do, but changing back to their original sex.

Myths of transsexual transformation are not nearly as common as stories of transformation of gender, changes in the superficial, social trappings of sex, transvestism. In myths of transsexual transformation, I would also distinguish between the sexual transformation of the body and the gendered transformation of the mind, memory, and personality; sometimes both change, but sometimes sex changes while gender remains unchanged. Let us consider the implications of these mythologies, beginning with Vishnu.

In the *Mahabharata*, the gods and demons churn the ocean to obtain the ambrosia, the Soma juice that maintains their immortality, and the demons claim it as theirs. Then, in just three verses (what Americans would call the lite form of the myth), this story is told:

VISHNU THE ENCHANTRESS SEDUCES THE DEMONS

Vishnu took on an enchanting *[mohini]* illusion, the marvelous body of a woman, and he went to the demons. As their minds were bewitched and their hearts set on her, they gave the ambrosia to him in his female form. The goddess who was made of the illusion created by Vishnu gave the ambrosia to the gods but not to the demons. A fight broke out, and Vishnu gave up his incomparable female form and attacked the demons.[1]

Vishnu uses sex to destroy a demonic enemy (an old Hindu trick: celestial nymphs routinely use their wiles to destroy individual powerful ascetics)[2] just as the male trickster god (Zeus) creates and sends Pandora to punish Prometheus* and mankind for the theft of fire (= the elixir).[3] As Nicole Loraux remarked of the Greek variant of this story, "Woman is indeed the 'deceiving female form' of the Indo-European myths studied by Georges Dumézil, with this essential difference, that for the Greeks the 'false woman' is not a man disguised but woman herself."[4] The reference is to Dumézil's *Festin d'immortalité*, in which he cites the story of Vishnu as the enchantress as a parallel to the myth of Pandora and the theft of ambrosia as the parallel to Prometheus's theft of fire. Where the Hindu god is a man masquerading as a woman, the Greek goddess is a goddess masquerading as a mortal and a woman masquerading as a woman. For in the Hindu version of the story, the divine trickster, Vishnu, instead of creating a woman like Pandora, or simply enlisting the aid of one of the always available celestial nymphs, himself masquerades as a woman, collapsing several of the agents in the Greek myth (Prometheus and Pandora) into one—named Mohini, "Enchantress."

An interesting variant of the story of Vishnu as Mohini appears in a Norse text, "The Lay of Thrym" *(Thrymskvidha),* related (like the Irish tale of Etain*) to the Greek and Indian myths of Pandora and Mohini, if one accepts the hypothesis of an Indo-European* cultural system:

THOR IN DRAG SEDUCES THE GIANTS

[Thrym, the lord of giants or Jotuns, stole Thor's hammer and told Loki that he would return it only if Freyja were given to him as his wife. Thor and Loki went to Freyja, and Thor asked her to dress herself in her bridal gown and go with him to Jotunheim, the home of the giants.] Then Freyja was angry and snorted, . . . "Never shall I be so mad for men that I drive with you to Jotunheim." [The gods and goddesses assembled, and Heimdal suggested that they dress Thor in the bridal gown and the great Brising necklace:] "Let keys dangle from his belt, and woman's garments hang to his knees. Place on his head a pretty veil, and on his breast broad stones." Then said Thor, the mighty god: "The gods will call me unmanly if I dress in the bridal gown." Then said Loki, the son of Laufey: "Be silent, Thor; say no such words. The Jotuns will soon abide in Asgard, unless you regain your hammer."

[They dressed Thor in the bridal gown, with the necklace, keys, women's garments, and veil, and Loki went with him as his slave-maiden. In Jotunheim they feasted and drank ale.] Thor alone ate an ox, eight salmon, and all the delicacies that were for the women. [He] drank three tuns of mead. Then said Thrym, the Lord of Giants: "Where was a bride seen to bite more sharply? I never saw a bride whose bite was broader, nor a maiden drink more of the mead." Sitting near by, the wise slave-maiden found the answer to fit the Jotun: "Freyja ate nothing for eight nights, so eager was she for Jotunheim."

Wanting to kiss the bride he bent under the veil, but he fled back to the end of the hall: "Why are Freyja's eyes so fierce? Her eyes, it seems, are like burning fire." [Loki answered that she had not slept for eight nights, in her eagerness. Thrym laid his hammer, Mjolnir, on the lap of "the maiden," and Thor recognized his hammer.] First he killed Thrym, the Lord of Giants, and he slew all the Jotun folk. So Odin's son regained his hammer.[5]

Thor's hammer here replaces the magic object that is the elixir of immortality in the story of Mohini and the knowledge of fire in the myth of Prometheus; in Wagner's version of the more closely related story of the *Ring of the Nibelungen,* Wotan uses Freyja herself to get back the golden ring. But in this Norse text, Thor does not merely *use* Freyja, as Zeus *uses* Pandora; here, Thor *masquerades as* Freyja, as Vishnu becomes Mohini. Thor, however, is not a transsexual, like Mohini, but merely a transvestite, since he seems to change not his body but merely his costume. This accounts for the greater human detail, and the humor, as well as the greater violence, in the myth. The widespread theme of "Grandma, what big teeth you have" (best known, perhaps, from Red Riding Hood) here significantly includes that all-powerful female gaze: "Why are Freyja's eyes so fierce?"

Like Thor, Vishnu presumably takes on merely the outer form of the demon; he never forgets that he is Vishnu; he retains his male memory and his male essence and resumes his own form after returning the Soma to the gods. But when the story is retold and greatly expanded in the *Brahmanda Purana,* about a thousand years after the *Mahabharata,* Vishnu *resumes* his Mohini form at Shiva's express request on a second occasion, and although Vishnu still remembers who he really is, Shiva seems to forget that the enchantress is Vishnu:

Shiva Rapes Vishnu as the Enchantress

When the demons stole the elixir of immortality from the gods, Vishnu meditated on the great Goddess [Maheshvari], and by concentrating on nothing but her he took on her form: a beautiful enchantress. She seduced the demons and returned the ambrosia to the gods. When the sage Narada saw what the enchantress Mohini had done, he went to Mount Kailasa; Nandin, the doorkeeper and son of Shiva, allowed him to go in. Shiva asked Narada, "What has happened to the ambrosia? Who has won it, the gods or the demons? What is Vishnu doing about it?" Narada told him how Vishnu had taken the form of Mohini, deluded the demons, and brought the ambrosia back to the gods. Shiva dismissed Narada and went with Parvati to see Vishnu, unknown to anyone, even Nandin, Skanda, and Ganesha.

Vishnu rose to greet Shiva and Parvati, and Shiva asked Vishnu to show him the form he had taken before, enchanting everyone. Vishnu smiled a little and again meditated single-mindedly on the Goddess; then he vanished, and Shiva saw a gorgeous woman [described in fifteen more or less boilerplate verses]. Immediately Shiva ran after her, abandoning Parvati, who stood with her head lowered in shame and envy, silently. He grabbed her [Mohini] with some difficulty and embraced her again and again; each time she shook him off and ran away, but Shiva grabbed her again, overpowered by lust. From that violent coupling his seed fell upon the ground, and the god Mahashasta was born. The Goddess who enchants everyone disappeared, and Shiva turned back and went to his mountain with Parvati.[6]

Is the "difficulty" with which Shiva catches and embraces Vishnu/Mohini somehow connected with the fact that Vishnu/Mohini is not really a woman? In this text, composed in honor of the Goddess, whose worship had developed during the many centuries after the brief *Mahabharata* story, Vishnu does not have to produce the woman out of his own power of feminine illusion, perhaps an expression of his own feminine nature, but is able to meditate on an already existing goddess, just as in the Greek myth Zeus can create a woman who is separate from himself and who remains an individual—Pandora. This somewhat weakens the original idea that Vishnu himself actually becomes transformed, for unlike Pandora, Mohini does not go on to have an enduring separate existence; she is absorbed back into Vishnu. But the existence of the Goddess as a separate person gives a kind of feminine reality to the creature, who now actually mimics a real female, and perhaps that is what inspires the author to imagine that she inspires Shiva with lust. We may also hear an echo of the earlier and famous episode in the *Bhagavad Gita*, in which Arjuna asks Vishnu to show him his true form, and Vishnu shows him the doomsday form—to Arjuna's terror. The statement that Vishnu "smiled a little" before agreeing to Shiva's request suggests that he too knew that this was one of those boons that the asker quickly comes to regret.

In this and other variants of this myth, Shiva's seed—shed on the ground, with no reference to a male or female partner—gives birth to a child, here called Mahashasta ("The Great Chastiser"), but variously identified as Skanda,[7] Hanuman,[8] Aiyanar,[9] or Hariharaputra ("the son of Vishnu and Shiva").[10] These later texts may have added the quasi-homosexual episode to the Mohini myth precisely in order to justify the theological love child, the quasi androgyne Hariharaputra, to join Vishnu and Shiva in sex as well as in sects. Yet, since Vishnu retains his male memory and his male essence, he can be regarded as having male homosexual relations, playing first the active role with the demons (like the demon Adi, who takes the form of Parvati to seduce Shiva)[11] and then the passive role with Shiva. In this inadvertent masquerade Mohini is the victim rather than the aggressor—though the text is *very* careful to tell us that (as in the case of Riksharaja*) the seed fell short of its goal, perhaps implying that no actual sexual act was consummated, that Mohini/Vishnu was never penetrated. Moreover, Shiva himself expressly loses his memory (though not his sex or gender) in one variant of his seduction of Mohini, in which, at the end, "When the seed was shed, Shiva realized his delusion, became cool, and turned back from his evil act."[12] Is the delusion the loss of control that lets Shiva commit rape, or the loss of the memory of the fact that the woman he is raping is a man, his pal Vishnu? The text does not say. The extreme case of this homosexual agenda occurs in a Telugu variant of the story, in which, when Shiva makes love to Mohini, in the middle of the act Mohini turns back into Vishnu, and Shiva goes on with it—a very rare instance of a consummated, explicit, male homosexual act (seduction or rape) in Hindu mythology.[13] This ambiguity adds yet another nuance to the more general question of the depth of the transformation.

Vishnu—more precisely his avatar, Krishna—engages in transsexual behavior on other occasions too, one of which is used as a charter myth for the Hijras, or transvestite eunuchs, of contemporary India:

Krishna as a Woman

Krishna takes on the form of a female to destroy a demon called Araka. Araka's strength came from his chasteness. He had never set eyes on a woman, so Krishna took on the form of a beautiful woman and married him. After three days of the marriage, there was a battle and Krishna killed the demon. He then revealed himself to the other gods in his true form. Hijras, when they tell this story, say that when Krishna revealed himself he told the other gods that "there will be more like me, neither man nor woman, and whatever words come from the mouths of these people, whether good [blessing] or bad [curses], will come true."[14]

This text owes much to the myth of Mohini: the god becomes female in order to destroy a demon. The vulnerable man "who had never set eyes on a woman" is a theme taken from other sources in Hindu mythology, such as the famous episode in which Rshyashringa mistakes a courtesan for a man who has peculiar but delightful things on his chest.[15]

Another version of the story of the origin of the Hijras makes the demon Araka (here called Aravan) into a virtuous warrior who is a son of Krishna:[16]

> Aravan agreed to sacrifice himself for the sake of the rest of his family, but only after he had been married. The only one willing to be widowed in this way was Krishna, who became a woman, married Aravan, made love to him all night on the wedding night, saw him beheaded at dawn, and, after a brief period of mourning, became a man again.[17]

Aravan thus one-ups Oedipus, by sleeping with (a transformation of) not his mother but his father.

Although Shiva's motives in raping Mohini seem straightforwardly heterosexual, his own connection with androgyny and bisexuality also facilitates these shifts, and when it comes to transsexuality he can see Vishnu and raise him one. The story of a magic forest sacred to Shiva and/or Parvati, in which men become women, undergoes numerous sea changes in many retellings. In some versions, such as the one in the *Bhagavata Purana,* the forest becomes enchanted when someone interrupts the divine couple in their love play:

THE BISEXUAL FOREST OF SHIVA

> One day when Shiva and Parvati were making love, the sages came to see Shiva. Parvati was naked, and when she saw them she became ashamed and arose from Shiva's embrace, tying her waist-cloth around her loins. The sages, seeing that the couple were making love, turned back. Then, to please his beloved, Shiva said, "Whoever enters this place will become a female."[18]

This episode is linked to the myth of Shiva and Mohini by the theme of Parvati's shame, which in that myth is caused by his bisexual infidelity but here inspires him to enchant the forest bisexually. By barging into the divine bedroom, the sages set in motion the curse that makes everyone become female in the magic wood—a classic Freudian enactment of the primal scene. We may see here yet another refraction of the belief that it is dangerous to look at a god—not, in this case, because the god shines too brightly, like the sun,* but because the god's sexuality cannot be violated by the worshiper's gaze, two themes that are conflated in Saranyu's excessive brightness and sexuality and in Freud's hypothesis of the connection between blinding and castration (or in this case loss of masculinity).

In some texts, however, the magic forest is no human's fault at all, merely a sexual land mine that the gods plant; what the intruder interrupts, then, is not the divine love play but the transformative forest itself. In the *Brahma Purana,* the forest is created not by an interruption but merely by the anticipation of a potential interruption, and it is Parvati, not Shiva, who casts the spell on it:

THE BISEXUAL FOREST OF PARVATI

One day when Shiva and Parvati were making love, Parvati said, "It is the nature of women to wish to hide their sexual pleasure. Therefore, give me a special place, called the Forest of Parvati, in which, except for you and Ganesa and Skanda and Nandin [her sons and servants], any man will become a woman."[19]

This text explicitly avoids the awkward possibility that Shiva himself might be transformed into a woman by having Parvati stipulate a list of exceptions—the same exceptions that, as we have seen, are mentioned as people not to be told when Shiva engages in his bisexual adventure with Vishnu/Mohini: the male members of her family. In the *Bhavishya Purana* text that we have just seen, Shiva himself takes the same precaution: "All creatures *but me* will become women."

But in the earliest text that tells this story, the *Ramayana,* Parvati neglects to stipulate any exceptions to the transformation of males into females, and Shiva himself became a woman too. No reason is given for the spell in this version: "When Shiva was making love with Parvati, he took the form of a woman to please Parvati, and everything in the woods, even trees, became female."[20] That is, *first* comes the statement that Shiva turned into a woman, and only afterward, as a *result* of that transformation, does the rest of the forest change gender; all the subsequent texts, which we have just seen, are now revealed to have reversed that causal sequence. The idea that Shiva became a woman and still made love with Parvati, explicit in this text, may well have been implicit in all the others that follow, which specify neither that Shiva was transformed nor that he was not. The tenth-century Vedic commentator, Sayana, for instance, simply says that when making love with Shiva, the goddess said, "Let any man who enters here become a woman,"[21] leaving ambiguous the question of whether Shiva himself becomes a woman while making love with Parvati. The *Brahmanda Purana* is stunningly inconsistent on this point:

Once upon a time, Shanaka and other young boys came to see Shiva, and they saw him making love with the goddess in a hidden place. They all

turned back, embarrassed, and the beloved goddess said to her beloved
god, to do what he would like, "Let any man who enters my ashrama become a woman as beautiful as a celestial courtesan." Then all the creatures, goblins and beasts, became females, sporting with Rudra [Shiva]
like celestial courtesans. Rudra became a woman, together with the goblins.[22]

The first part of this passage imagines Parvati generously supplying Shiva
with a kind of harem, the whole point of which requires that he remain
absolutely male. But then the text says that he too became a female. What
are we to make of this—or for that matter of the paradoxical statement in
the *Ramayana* that Shiva himself becomes a woman while making love
with Parvati? Are we to assume that he goes on making love to her in that
form? Or that he stops?

That he stops making love is suggested by another text, in which, when
the Goddess all by herself creates her peaceable kingdom, no one gets an
erection;[23] of such is the orthodox Hindu kingdom of heaven. But if he
continues, this raises the same ambiguity that we considered in the myth
of Mohini: if Shiva is merely superficially transformed into a female, but
remains essentially male, we might expect him to continue despite the
transformation. This interpretation is supported by one Hindu view of
gender, the view that when the body changes the mind and the memory
remain the same and that gender is not fluid or superficial but embedded
in memory. But if it is a complete transformation, a change of inner
essence, Shiva's continued lovemaking would involve him in a lesbian act,
a rare but not unprecedented situation in Hindu mythology[24] (we saw an
example in a variant of the Jarasandha* story), and a parallel to those variants of the myth of Mohini in which Shiva continues to rape Vishnu/Mo-
hini when he changes back into a man, in inner essence as well as
superficial form. This would support the other Hindu view of gender, as
fluid and superficial, changing completely when the body changes.[25] In
another cycle, the gods or the sage Bhrigu who interrupt the lovemaking
of Shiva and Parvati transform Shiva not into a woman but, on the contrary, into an unequivocally male form: the erect phallus. This may be an
attempt to resolve the uncomfortable ambiguity of Shiva's gender in the
Ramayana version of the story.

Another example of changing sexual horses in midstream, as it were, is
provided by a story popular in Mahayana Buddhism in China and Japan:

UPAGUPTA AS A WOMAN

[Upagupta wanted to reform a monk who had stopped exerting himself. One day the monk met a woman who slipped and fell into a river, crying, "Save me!"] Reflecting that the Buddha *did* allow bhiksus to touch women in order to pull them out of a river when they were drowning, the monk grabbed her. As he held onto her, however, he experienced a moment of desire, and, once they were safely back on shore, this grew into a longing for fornication. Taking her to an isolated spot, the monk was about to satisfy his lustful intentions when he realized that the woman was none other than Upagupta![26] The end of the Japanese version is even more graphic; as the monk is about to rape the woman (who here is not consenting), she turns into Upagupta. The monk tries to pull away, but Upagupta holds him fast between his legs and demands, "Why do you torment an aged priest in such a manner?"[27]

The rapist in the Japanese version presumably stops when he realizes he is in bed with a man; in the myth of Shiva as a female, or with Vishnu as a female, this is not so clear.

On the other hand, the magic forest's antierotic implications for Shiva are supported by yet another variant in which Parvati casts the spell on the forest precisely in order to keep Shiva from making love to her at all:

THE BISEXUAL FORESTS OF SHIVA AND PARVATI

One day when Shiva and Parvati were playing dice, Shiva cheated and Parvati went off in a huff to the Sahya mountain, cursing her birth and without any passion for her husband; she said, "If males enter this divine forest of mine, let them become females." And so ganders turned into geese, stags into does, trees into creepers; men became women as though made of stone, for the forest was made of the female power *(shakti)*. There was a not a sidelong glance, not a double entendre *(vakrokti)*, not a quarrel.

Meanwhile, on Mount Kailasa, Shiva began to miss Parvati. He began to generate ascetic heat, and he said, "If women enter here while I am separated from Parvati, they will be transformed into men." The (f.) moonlight on Shiva's head became the (m.) full moon marked with the hare, and women took on the male *linga* (sign, or penis). Since all the female friends of Parvati had gone to the Sahya mountain, Shiva told all the celestial nymphs to go to heaven, but they cursed their birth on earth and decided to go to the top of Mount Kailasa to become men, saying, "She who be-

comes a man because of a curse will not be an object of lust." And the gods
settled above Kailasa, thinking within their hearts that life without women
is pointless for men.[28]

This version begins with a recurrent problem in Hindu mythology, the
dice game that causes Shiva and Parvati to fight. Here their separation re-
verberates into two polarized genders in the two forests, which in turn inspires various attempts to return to the pre-polarized form.[29] This time,
therefore, when Parvati destroys the symmetry of the sexes, Shiva restores
it by creating a twin unisex forest to match hers. The men who become
women become like stone women, like Ahalya when she is cursed for committing adultery.[30] But all women are cursed, and so they take advantage
of the symmetrical creation of Shiva's forest to escape from the curse, to
become men.

Sometimes Shiva himself becomes female for a different reason:

> The gods begged the goddess Kali to rid the earth of demonic kings, and
> she agreed to become incarnate as Krishna. Shiva prayed to Kali and was
> given permission to become incarnate as Radha, the mistress of Krishna, in
> order to make love in reverse. At Shiva's wish, Radha's husband became im-
> potent immediately after marriage.[31]

There are two simultaneous negative transformations here, vertical and
horizontal: the god becomes both human (vertically worse) and female
(horizontally worse, in the Hindu view). Like the monkey Riksharaja,
Shiva simultaneously changes gender and species. He becomes a
woman—not this time to make love to his wife homoerotically, but on
the contrary to remain heterosexual when she has switched her own sex.
The implication is that Shiva wants to experience not only the reversal
of being female but the reversal of the reversal, that is, to be a woman in
the "reversed" sexual position (reversed from the missionary position),
the man's role, on top.[32] The mortal husband of the transsexual female
half of the androgyne is impotent, so that the apparently mortal wife
can commit adultery with the god who is her true husband, the immortal male who has become yet another incarnation of the immortal female.

Whatever the results of the enchantment may have been for Shiva, it
turns all subsequent male intruders into women. In particular, when King
Ila comes to the forest, he is transformed into a woman (Ilā). Indeed, in

the *Bhavishya Purana*, it is King Ila himself, not the sages, who causes the spell in the first place and then falls into it:

> One day when Shiva and Parvati were making love in a forest, King Ila came there hunting. When he saw that Shiva was naked, he closed his eyes, but Shiva saw that Parvati was embarrassed, and so he said, "In this place, all creatures but me will become women." And as he said this, all male creatures were transformed, and Ila/ā became a princess, and his/her stallion became a mare.[33]

More often, however, King Ila is simply the most famous victim of the curse, a man whose transformation is said to be a kind of accidental fall-out from the more general spell cast in another story.

Ila/ā is both the daughter and the son of Manu, the son of Saranyu.[34] The *Mahabharata* tells us rather cryptically that Manu had many sons and one daughter named Ilā, who gave birth to Pururavas (the ill-fated husband of Urvashi*) and became both his mother and his father.[35] In the *Ramayana*, Ila is said to begin not as the daughter but as the son—not of Manu but of a sage named Kardama, born, significantly, from the *shadow** of Brahma. Ila's birth is sexually ambiguous, and his/her adult sexual life is so problematic that it sometimes becomes convenient, in discussing this myth (and others in this chapter), to use at ambiguous moments the otherwise awkward modern nonsexist pronoun *s/he* to describe a person who is sometimes she, sometimes he—meaning, in this case, not she *or* he but she *and* he:

ILA / Ā IN THE FOREST OF THE GODDESS

When Shiva was making love with Parvati, he had taken the form of a woman to please her, and everything in that part of the woods, even trees, had become female. One day, King Ila, the son of Kardama, went hunting and killed thousands of animals, but still his lust for hunting was unsatisfied. As he came to that place where Shiva was making love with Parvati, he was turned into a woman, and when she approached Shiva to seek relief from her misery, Shiva laughed and said, "Ask for any boon except manhood." Ilā pleaded with Parvati, who said: "Shiva will grant half of your request, and I the other half. In that way you will be half female, half male." Rejoicing at this wonderful boon from the Goddess, Ilā said, "If you, whose form is unrivaled by any copy, are truly pleased with me, let me be a woman for a month, and then a man again for a month." "So be it," said Parvati, "but when you are a man, you will not remember that you were a woman; and when you are a woman, you will not remember that you were a man." "So be it," said the king, and for a month she was the most beautiful woman in the world.

During that first month, she was wandering in the forest [outside the magic grove] with her female attendants who had formerly been men, when she came upon King Budha, the son of the Moon, immersed in a lake and immersed in meditation. She was struck by his stunning good looks, and started splashing the water; he noticed her and was pierced by the arrows of lust. He thought to himself, "I have never seen a woman like this, not among goddesses or snake women or demon women or celestial courtesans. If she is not married, let her be mine." He asked her followers whose she was, and they replied, "This woman with superb hips rules over us; she has no husband and wanders with us in the woods." When he heard this speech, whose meaning was obscure, Budha used his own magic powers and discovered the entire truth of what had happened to the king. He transformed the women into female Quasi-men, and they ran away. Then he smiled and said to Ilā, "I am the son of King Soma; look upon me with loving eyes, and make love with me." In that deserted place, deprived of all her attendant women, she spoke pleasingly to him, saying, "Son of Soma, I am free to do as I wish, and so I place myself in your power. Do with me as you wish." Hearing that astonishing speech from her, the king was thrilled, and he caused Ilā to enjoy the exquisite pleasures of lovemaking, for a month which passed like a moment.

But when the month was full, Ila the son of Kardama awoke in the bed and saw Budha immersed in the water, immersed in meditation. He said to Budha, "Sir, I came to this inaccessible mountain with my attendants. But now I don't see my army; where have all my people gone?" When Budha heard these words from Ila, whose power of recognition had been destroyed, he replied with a persuasive, conciliating speech: "Your servants were all destroyed by a hailstorm, and you were exhausted by your terror of the high winds and fell asleep on the grounds of this hermitage. Don't be afraid; live here in comfort, eating fruits and roots."

Though the wise king Ila was encouraged when he heard those words, he was greatly saddened by the death of his servants, and he said, "I will renounce my own kingdom; I cannot go on for a moment without my servants and wives. Please give me leave to go. My eldest son, named Shashabindu, will inherit my throne." But Budha said, "Please live here. Don't worry. At the end of a year, O son of Kardama, I will do you a great favor." And so Ila decided to stay there.

Then, for a month she was a woman and enjoyed the pleasure of making love ceaselessly, sleeplessly, and then for a month he increased his understanding of dharma, as a man. In the ninth month, Ilā, who had superb hips, brought forth a son fathered by Budha, named Pururavas. And as soon as he was born, she placed him in the hands of Budha, for he looked just like him and seemed to be of the same class. And then when she became a man again, Budha gave him the pleasure of hearing stories about dharma, for a year.

Then Budha summoned a number of sages, including Ila's father, Kardama, and asked them to do what was best for him/her. Kardama suggested that they propitiate Shiva with a horse-sacrifice and ask his help. Shiva was pleased by the horse-sacrifice; he came to them, gave Ila his manhood, and vanished. King Ila ruled in the middle country of Pratishthana, and his son Shashabindu ruled in the country of Bahli.[36]

The story of Ila/ā is told in many of the medieval Sanskrit texts called the Puranas, since s/he founded both of the two great Indian dynasties, the lunar and the solar, and dynastic succession is a central concern of the Puranas. It also comes to be cited as a kind of proof text for other transsexual splittings.[37] The myth tells of the joining of the descendant of the Sun (Ila/ā, the grandchild of Saranyu) with a descendant of the Moon (Budha, son of Soma, the Moon; his son is named Shashabindu, "Hare-marked," an epithet of the Moon, in which the Hindus see a hare where we see a man). The sexual labyrinths of the text may have been generated, at least in part, through a desire to account for the joining of two great dynasties, each claiming descent from a male cosmic body (for both the Sun and the Moon are usually male in Sanskrit), without demoting either partner to the inferior status of a female. The solution: to imagine two cosmic patriarchs, and to turn one—only temporarily, of course—into a woman. (The parallel desire, to have a child born of both the gods Shiva and Vishnu, was resolved by turning Vishnu temporarily into a woman, Mohini.*) On the other hand, the fact that one person, Budha, has the power and the knowledge and undiminished masculinity throughout the episode, while the other, Ilā, does not, would seem to privilege the status of Budha and the lunar dynasty over Ila/ā and the solar dynasty; and that may well have been one of the intentions of this text.

The form of the curse in the *Ramayana* is no accident; the founding of the lunar dynasty is linked by natural association with the monthly vacillation between female and male, a dichotomy doubled, as it were, in the dichotomy between human and equine, as it was in the myth of Saranyu. This monthly time cycle is biological and female, in contrast with the daily and yearly solar cycle that is dharmic and male, that marks the official sacrifices (such as the horse sacrifice at the end of the year). Ila's servants become female Quasi-men (kimpurushis), creatures half-horse and half-human, literally "sort of men." These horse-headed rather than horse-bodied creatures, a kind of inverse centaur, like the Ashvins,* are self-contradictory as well as liminal, since the word for "men" [purusha] defines the male in contrast with the female; to be a female "quasi-man" is thus to be a kind of Irish bull, or at least an Indian mare,[38] a living oxymoron. Thus time (the months) and space (the halves of the body) provide a double response to sexual liminality.

There are scattered references here to the problem of recognition, all refractions of the central problem, namely, that when he is transformed into a woman, Ilā does not recognize himself. One aspect of recognition is resemblance: does one self resemble another? Thus, in praising the Goddess, Ila says that her form is "unrivaled by any copy" (pratima, a reflected image), Budha says that he has never seen "a woman like this," and their child is said to look just like him or to "seem to be of the same class or kind" (sa-varna*). In another variant of this text, when Ila becomes a woman he is said to become an identical shadow.[39] In the Ramayana, when Ila does not recognize himself after he has been restored to his primary form as a man, he is said to be someone whose power of recognition (samjna) has been destroyed; as a woman, in his secondary form, she is not himself, but only his (female) shadow or inverted mirror image (pratima).

But recognition also involves memory, and part of the curse (or is it the boon that balances the curse?) is to make Ila/ā forget one gender when s/he is immersed in another. In the initial transformation, in the enchanted forest, Ilā apparently does retain his memory, for she asks the gods to change her back; at this stage, he would seem to have the body of a woman and the mind of a man. When, however, the transformation is settled into monthly alternations, Ila forgets who he is; her servants tell Budha the story that we must assume Ilā too believes, that she is a woman without a husband, wandering in the woods. Parvati explicitly states that s/he will not remember the altered states; is this because normally one would, or normally one would not, remember? Ila, however, apparently doesn't remember her pleasure in bed when he is a man. Budha doesn't tell Ilā who she is, though he knows this through powers of his own; he withholds Ila/ā's memory from her/him and keeps him/her in his power.

By cutting him/her off from the knowledge of his/her true identity and then seducing him/her, Budha is in effect raping a sleeping woman, engaging in what Hindu law classifies as the "marriage of a ghoul," which "takes place when a man secretly has sex with a girl who is asleep, drunk, or out of her mind."[40] (We too have legal sanctions against the rape of an insane woman.) In this case, she is quite literally out of her mind, and into someone else's, and the text does not rest until s/he is restored to his/her manhood (purushatva) again—this being the "favor" that Budha cryptically promises to do for him at the end of the year.

Ila/ā is disempowered by the loss of both sex and class: in one stroke s/he is deprived of political power, class (servants), and gender. As soon as s/he becomes a woman, even while s/he still has servants (class), s/he loses his/her ownership of his/herself; Budha asks her followers *whose* she is, the standard way of inquiring about a woman's identity in ancient India (to which the standard answer consists of her father's name, if she is unmarried, or her husband's, if she is married; this is the question that the followers answer "obscurely"). And of course s/he also loses his/her political power, both because s/he forgets that s/he is a king and because a woman cannot (except in extraordinary circumstances) be a king. When Budha pulls out from under him/her the one remaining prop, his/her servants, she finds herself alone with him in the middle of the forest, helpless. Naturally, she gives in to his sexual demands.

But even when Ila/ā becomes retransformed into a man, he remains helpless, for reasons of class that remain even when gender has been restored. Thus he remarks, "I cannot live without my servants and wives." He has lost a significant part of his identity by losing his social world. Men, in this worldview, are dependent on women for services, and women are dependent on men for protection. But they are also mutually dependent for sex. We have already been told that Ila is, as it were, "asking for it." We know that she lusted for him before he lusted for her and indeed that even as a man Ila suffered from the fatal and quasi-sexual lust to hunt. (Significantly, Ila/ā's transition to and from her existence as the wife of King Budha takes place when Budha is meditating in the water—precisely the condition of Narada's translation into and out of womanhood,[41] and the place where Renuka and the woman who transposed the male heads felt desire.) One text makes explicit this connection between hunting and gender transformation: "One day, a female goblin [yakshini] who wanted to protect her husband from King Ila took the form of a deer expressly in order to lure him into the magic part of the forest. King Ila entered the wood."[42] It is surely significant that Ila is hunting females—whether demons or deer—when he is lured into the forest where he will be cured, at least temporarily, of his passion for hunting.

Budha keeps Ila/ā captive not only by lying to her but by giving her pleasure, as she gives pleasure to him (the verb for sexual enjoyment, *ram*, is consistently used in the causative both for him and for her). Even when she becomes a man, Budha gives him the pleasure of hearing stories, using the same verb, *ram*, for sexual pleasure and for what Roland Barthes has taught us to call the pleasure of the text. But in this mutual dependence, the woman is far more dependent on sex than the man is. Thus, in a parallel story about a man, Bhangashvana, magically transformed into a female, when Indra asks him/her which sex s/he would like to remain for ever more, s/he says that s/he would prefer to remain a woman, since as a woman s/he had greater pleasure in sex—which also makes her love the children she had as a woman more than the children she had as a man.[43] The Buddhist transsexual, Soreyya, also has children both as male and as female, and prefers the children of his female persona to those of the male. (No one seems to have dared to ask him which way sex was better.)[44] So too the serial bisexual Cudala* says that a woman has eight times as much pleasure as a man, which could also be translated as eight times as much desire,[45] even more threatening to the misogynist mind than female pleasure. Yet, even Ilā's greater pleasure does not ultimately weigh in the scale of gender against the disadvantages of being a woman: he chooses *not* to remain female.

Here, as so often, the myth reifies and embodies a cliché: we often speak of a "single parent" as being "both mother and father" to a child; in Hindu myths, it actually happens, as we have seen in the case of the monkey Riksharaja.* In some variants of this myth, including the *Mahabharata* version, Ila/ā begins life not as a male but as a female, which puts a special spin on the story. Here is how the *Bhagavata Purana* connects Ila with the bisexual forest episode we considered above:

> Ilā's parents had wanted a boy; but the priest had made a mistake, and so a girl was born instead, named Ilā. The priest then rectified his error and she became a man named Ila. One day when Shiva and Parvati were making love the sages came to see Shiva. Parvati was naked and when she saw them she became ashamed and arose from Shiva's embrace, tying her waist-cloth around her loins. Seeing that the couple were making love, the sages turned

back. Then to please his beloved Shiva said, "Whoever enters this place will become a female." Some time later Ila reached this spot and became a woman, and all the men in his/her entourage became women, and all their stallions became mares. Queen Ilā, as she had become again, married and gave birth to King Pururavas. Eventually she begged Shiva to change her back to a man, named Sudyumna, and s/he was allowed to be a woman for one month and a man for one month. S/he went to heaven as someone who had the distinguishing signs of both men and women.[46]

It might be argued that, even here, Ila/ā begins as a male, since it was the original desire of his parents (like all Hindu parents) to have a boy. But since his first physical form is that of a female, his final physical transformation (after he has become a man) is in effect a transformation *back* into her original physical nature. The text therefore constantly fights its way upstream against the current of Ila/ā's tendency to revert to female type, and requires constant interventions from male powers (gods or priests) to keep making her male. Even in heaven, s/he still has both sets of distinguishing marks *[lakshana]*, which here cancel one another out and therefore distinguish nothing.

In all the texts we have seen, Ila/ā (like Narada) is the passive victim of a curse; he loses his memory when he loses his body. But the Sahya mountain variant reverses the force of both memory and gender:

ELA ON THE SAHYA MOUNTAIN

Ela, who would have been king of the lunar dynasty, came to the Sahya mountain, greedy for hunting, but when he entered the forest he became Ilā, an identical shadow of Ela, and when his soldiers saw Ilā from the distance, they fled in terror. Ilā became a female companion and servant of the Goddess Parvati. Though s/he learned that if she bathed in the river as a woman she would be released, Ilā said s/he preferred to be a slave to Ganga [the river Ganges] and Gauri. Ganga and Gauri, however, quickly replied, "To hell with birth as a woman; it's nothing but pain and grief," and so Ilā entered the water and bathed in a special pool and emerged as King Ila, a man. The face that had been as beautiful as the moon was now bearded and deep-voiced, and the female sex that she had acquired through the curse of Parvati was now a male sex *(linga)*.[47]

This text—in which, as we have seen, the celestial nymphs choose to be men to escape the curse of being women—makes brutally explicit the fact that it is a bad thing to be a woman, and clearly implicit the fact that for once Ila/ā is conscious of his male past in the midst of his female present, and therefore able to make a choice. Nevertheless, perhaps for religious reasons that have motivated many devotees of both the Goddess and Krishna in India, he chooses to be a woman, but the women around him quickly enlighten him and he rejoins his true self, his true gender.

A gender masquerade of a different sort is revealed in a contemporary story told by the Hijras, bands of men whose sexuality is liminal in any of several different ways: they may be transvestites, male homosexual prostitutes, or eunuchs (or, indeed, several of these at once):

THE GODDESS AND THE TRANSSEXUAL

Once there was a prince whose parents wanted to get him married. The boy did not want to get married, but his parents insisted. They selected this goddess as his wife, and the marriage took place. He was a very handsome boy, but the Mata was also a very beautiful lady. But after the marriage the husband and wife never joined together. On the first night, leaving the goddess alone in the nuptial room, the prince rode away into the forest. The goddess waited till dawn and felt very angry that her husband had left her. This went on for some months.

The goddess felt very hurt and decided to investigate. So one night she followed him on a path to the forest clearing where the prince had been acting like the Hijras. She was puzzled by what she had seen and returned home. When her husband returned, she said to him, "I want to ask you something, do not get angry at me. Don't you feel that you must have your wife by you?" Then the prince fell at her feet and told her, "Mother, if I had the urge for a wife and children, I wouldn't have left you and gone away. I am neither a man nor a woman, and that is the truth."

The goddess got very angry and said, "They have spoiled my life by hiding the facts, and therefore your life will also be spoiled. Hereafter, people like you should be *nirvan* [undergo emasculation in order to be reborn]." So saying, she cut off his genitals. After cutting off his genitals she said, "People like you, who are going to have this *nirvan*, should call me at that time." After this the prince took on the form of a woman.[48]

The opening episode strongly resembles the corpus of myths (including some versions of the story of Ila/ā,[49] as well as the tale of Amba/Shikhandin*) in which a daughter is raised as a son and fails to consummate the marriage. But the fact that the bridegroom is not actually a woman leads the goddess to transform him not into what s/he appears to be, a woman masquerading as a man, but into what s/he feels she is: a man masquerading as a woman, more precisely a nonhusband mas-

querading as a husband (a masquerade that often has tragic consequences). She is infuriated not by a sexual attack but by the lack of it.
"Hiding the facts," the goddess's complaint, resonates both with the past,
inadvertent masquerade of a "woman" (in the Hindu definition: a man
who does not desire women) as a man and the future, intentional masquerade of a man as a "woman" (a Hijra). Behind this story lies a story far
more basic to Hindu mythology, the myth of the rape of a Brahmin
woman by an Outcaste man.* For an Outcaste who masquerades as a
Brahmin commits a far more serious crime, in the Hindu imagination,
than a nonman who masquerades as a man: in this case, at least, caste
trumps gender. Hence the consequences of the Outcaste's masquerade are
far more serious than those inflicted upon the masquerading proto-Hijra:
many people are devoured by the Goddess into whom his wife is transformed. Yet the *forms* of the two myths are very similar: male is to female
as Brahmin is to Outcaste.

Another story that the Hijras tell about their origins turns upon their
sexual rather social than ambiguity. It is set at the moment when Ram left
Ayodhya to go to the forest:

RAM AND THE TRANSSEXUALS

The whole city followed him because they loved him so. As Ram came to
the banks of the river at the edge of the forest, he turned to the people and
said, "Ladies and gents, please wipe your tears and go away." But those people who were not men and not women did not know what to do. So they
stayed there because Ram did not ask them to go. . . . And so they were
blessed by Ram.[50]

Here the Hijras are so feminized that they play the role of Sita, who always
insists on following Rama to the forest despite his protests, and so liminal
that they slip between the prohibited categories.

The sexually ambiguous Hijras—neither male nor female—are descended from another group of people defined in the same way: the *klibas.*
A *kliba* is not merely an androgyne; where androgyne implies a primarily
male male-female creature of mythological status, with some power and
dignity, a *kliba* is a defective male, a male suffering from failure, distortion,
and lack. This word has traditionally been translated as "eunuch," but it
meant anything but a eunuch (a practice that entered India only centuries
after the word *kliba* became current). Rather, it includes a wide range of
meanings under the general homophobic rubric of "a man who does not

act the way a man should act," a man who fails to be a man. It is a catchall term that a traditional Hindu culture coined to indicate a man who is in their terms sexually dysfunctional (or in ours, sexually challenged), including someone who was sterile, impotent, castrated, a transvestite, a man who committed fellatio, who had anal sex, a man with mutilated or defective sexual organs, a man who produces only female children, or finally a hermaphrodite. This promiscuous spectrum is assumed not only in the *Laws of Manu,* but in the *Kamasutra,* which is generally (but not always) more tolerant of deviance.

An approximate female counterpart to *kliba* (though, as usual, asymmetrical) is the term *apsaras,* which has the same vague sexual range, covering whore, prostitute, courtesan, dancer, water nymph, and so forth. But where the *kliba* is undersexed, in the Hindu view, the *apsaras* is oversexed. When a culture does not want to confront an issue, it produces a haze of obfuscating terms that can be used for a wide range of pejorative purposes. Cultures are often nervous and vague about extremes of sexuality and tend to equate them rather than look closely at them. *Kliba* is such a term. Thus, though it is often correctly pointed out that Hindus recognize a third sex, this fact should not be adduced to imply that Hindus approve of this third sex or use it to counteract what we think of as "Western" dualism and homophobia. Hindu ideas about homosexuality and *kliba*s do not support a gay agenda.

A relatively lighthearted story about a *kliba* is told of the great hero of the *Mahabharata,* Arjuna, though his role as a *kliba* is at least in part a masquerade:

ARJUNA THE ANDROGYNE

The celestial courtesan Urvashi fell in love with Arjuna and propositioned him, but he said she was like a mother to him and clapped his hands over his ears. Furious, the spurned nymph gave him a curse to be a dancer among women, devoid of honor, regarded as a an impotent man *(kliba).* But Indra, the father of Arjuna, softened the curse and promised Arjuna that he would spend only a year as a dancer and then would be a man again. Years later, when it was time for Arjuna and his brothers to go into exile in disguise, Arjuna put on woman's clothing (barely managing to disguise his hairy, brawny arms) and told his brothers: "I will be a *kliba*." He offered his services as a dancing master to the women in the harem of a king. The king was suspicious at first, remarking that Arjuna certainly did not *look* like a *kliba,* but he then ascertained that "her" lack of manhood was indeed firm [*sic*] and so let "her" teach his daughters to dance.[51]

Urvashi here plays the role of the seductive mother, the spurned, vengeful, and incestuous goddess who punishes her unwilling son. Urvashi is not literally Arjuna's mother but she is a female ancestor, the mother of Bharata the eponymous founder of the Bharatas, Arjuna's line. Arjuna's response to Urvashi's threats is to disguise his manhood twice over: he pretends to be a *kliba* pretending to be a transvestite. Since the king determines that he lacks manhood (more precisely, in a double entendre, that he has a firm lack of manhood), his disguise must mean here something more physiological than mere transvestism. But what?

This is a paper-thin masquerade, meant to be funny, because we all *know* how virile he is; Arjuna is, in effect, mimicking a drag queen. His assumed name is a phallic joke ("Big-reed," Brihannala), and there are lots of jokes about his big hairy arms; in fact, Arjuna argues that women's clothing is the only thing that will disguise the bowstring scars on *both* of his arms, which would otherwise reveal his identity as the world's greatest ambidextrous archer (a man who shoots with both hands, a delightful metaphor for a bisexual). Arjuna does no harm when he is in drag because he never approaches any man sexually; his womanliness at the most reflects some true aspect of his macho womanizing in the rest of the epic.

FEMALES INTO MALES IN INDIA

The transformation of women into men is both rarer and far more destructive than the transformation of men into women. The sexist assumption is that every woman is lethal (the poison damsel) and every woman is a fake (the Ahalya/Pandora* scenario). Any woman corrupts; a transvestite woman corrupts absolutely. And where men are usually cursed to become women, women often choose to be men—a not surprising asymmetry, since the culture regards male status as higher than female.

A typically lethal transsexual from the great Sanskrit epic, the *Mahabharata*, is Amba, whose story is told in fragments scattered throughout the long text:

THE REVENGE OF AMBA / SHIKHANDIN/I

Bhishma had gone to find wives for his brother, Vicitryavirya; he took Amba and her three sisters by force. But when he learned that Amba had given her heart to another man who loved her, Bhishma sent her back to her betrothed lover, King Shalva.[52] Shalva, however, refused to accept a woman who had been carried off by another man; caught in the middle, Amba cursed Bhishma and became an ascetic in order to amass the power to kill him. The Ganges, Bhishma's mother, tried at first to dissuade Amba and then cursed her to become a crooked river, dried up except in monsoon and teeming with crocodiles. Amba did become a river, but only with one half of her body; the other half remained a woman and propitiated Shiva, saying, "Because of Bhishma I have come to this eternally miserable state, neither a man nor a woman. I am disgusted with the condition of being a woman and have determined to become a man. I want to pay Bhishma back." Shiva promised her that she would become a man who would kill Bhishma and that she would remember everything when she had taken on a new body. Then she entered the fire and died.[53]

Meanwhile King Drupada, whose wife had had no sons, asked Shiva for a son, but Shiva said, "You will have a male child who is a female." In time the queen gave birth to a daughter, but she and the king pretended it was a son and raised the child as a son, whom they called Shikhandin. Besides the parents only Bhishma knew the truth, from a spy, from Narada's report, from the words of the god [Shiva], and from Amba's asceticism. When the child reached maturity, "he" married a princess; but when the princess found out that her husband was a woman, she was humiliated, and her father waged war on King Drupada. Drupada, who had known all along, pretended that he had been deceived by the queen, and she swore to this.

When Drupada's daughter, Shikhandini, saw the grief and danger she had caused her parents, she resolved to kill herself, and she went into the deserted forest. There she met a goblin [yaksha] named Sthuna ("Pillar") and begged him to use his magic to turn her into a man. The goblin said that he would give her his own sign of manhood [pum-linga] for a short time, if she would promise to return it to him after the armies left the city; meanwhile, he would wear her sign of womanhood [stri-linga]. They made this agreement and exchanged sexual organs. When Drupada learned from Shikhandin what had happened, he rejoiced and sent word to the attacking king that the bridegroom was in fact a man. The king sent some fine young women to learn whether Shikhandin was female or male, and they happily reported that he was absolutely male. The father of Shikhandin's bride rebuked his daughter and went home, and Shikhandini [sic!] was delighted.

Meanwhile, Kubera, the lord of the goblins, found out what had happened and cursed Sthuna to remain female forever and Shikhandin to remain male forever—or rather (in response to Sthuna's pleas) to remain male until Shikhandin's death, when Sthuna would regain his own form.

When Shikhandin returned to Sthuna to keep his part of the bargain, he learned of Kubera's curse and returned to the city, rejoicing.[54]

Now, Bhishma had vowed not to shoot at a woman, anyone who used to be a woman, or had a woman's name, or appeared to be a woman.[55] Shikhandin attacked Bhishma, but Bhishma, regarding him as someone made of a woman [strīmaya], did not return the attack. Arjuna said, "Put Shikhandin in front; Bhishma has said he won't fight with him because he was born a woman."[56] When Shikhandin shot arrows at Bhishma, Bhishma repelled them playfully, laughing as he remembered the femaleness of Shikhandin. But he did not strike Shikhandin, and he [Shikhandin] did not understand. Then Arjuna and the rest of the Pandavas used Shikhandin as a shield in their vanguard, and Bhishma fell under the rain of their arrows.[57]

Later, in the night raid, Shikhandin attacked Ashvatthaman and struck him between his two eyebrows; furious, Ashvatthaman attacked Shikhandin and cut him in half.[58] After Bhishma died, the Ganges, his mother, lamented, "At the self-choice in the city of Benares he conquered the warriors and carried off the women, and no one on earth could equal him. How is it that my heart did not break when I heard that Shikhandin killed him!" Krishna said, "Do not grieve; he was killed by Arjuna, not by Shikhandin."[59]

Amba is caught in limbo between two men, her beloved and the man who abducted her; she is socially, if not physically, raped by Bhishma (for his abduction of her made her second-hand goods from the standpoint of the man she loved) and then rejected by Bhishma as well as by her betrothed lover. In her own view, this makes her neither man nor woman—the phase often used to describe a *kliba;* that is, she equates her liminal sexuality with androgyny.

Amba epitomizes the no-win situation of a woman tossed like a shuttlecock between two men, each of whom ricochets between inflicting sexual excess or sexual rejection upon her. And when she becomes a man, that is precisely the sort of doubly hurtful man she becomes: she is reborn as the child of Drupada, which makes her the sister of the polyandrous Draupadi,* whose hypersexuality stands in dramatic contrast with the reborn Amba's ambiguous sexuality. The liminal Shikhandin/Shikhandini rejects her bride, who is humiliated as Amba had been, and unsexes (and humiliates) a helpful goblin. His/her sexual ambivalence is itself ambivalent, or at least doubled: s/he is a female first masquerading as a male and then transformed into a male. And there are further echoes of Shikhandin's tendency to split in two: before undertaking asceticism herself, Amba chooses as her champion Rama with an Ax, Parashurama, who cut his own mother in two, just as Ashvatthaman cuts Shikhandin in two when he kills him. And Amba is cursed by the motherly river, Ganga, to become a deadly river, devoid of fluids and teeming with toothy crocodiles, and then is further split between that river and the form of a woman. In contrast with Arjuna, who neither harms anyone else nor is harmed himself while he is sexually transformed, because he never actually engages in a sexual act, Amba does engage and is both harmed and harming. The presence of Arjuna at crucial points of Amba's story makes this contrast all the more poignant.

Shikhandin does not seem to remember that s/he was Amba, even though Shiva expressly promises her that she *will* remember (just as Parvati promised Ila/ā that he would *not* remember—is there a significant gendered difference here?). Shikhandin knows he was Shikhandini, but apparently not that he was Amba; indeed, since Shikhandin/i has no voice, we don't really know what s/he knows—s/he can't even act, but is used as a screen. Because s/he doesn't remember, s/he doesn't "understand" when Bhishma won't fight with him/her. Despite Shiva's promise, memory here does not survive rebirth, even rebirth as someone of the same sex (though a different gender!). And the killing of Bhishma by Shikhandin is rather anticlimactic, and further blurred by its diffusion: Shikhandin does not kill Bhishma outright but merely functions as a human bulwark for Arjuna (one androgyne behind another); and Bhishma does not die immediately of his wounds but withdraws and dies long, long afterward. Shikhandin himself takes part in the night raid that violates the injunction against killing someone asleep, just as Budha violates the injunction against violating someone asleep.

But if Shikhandin does not remember, Bhishma certainly does; he has the whip hand over her in this too, though it seems to be more important to him that Shikhandin was born a woman (Shikhandini) in this life than that she was a woman in a former life (Amba), let alone a woman who died cursing his name and vowing to kill him. Bhishma explicitly notes, but no one seems to care, that Shikhandin was Amba. There is something suspiciously idiosyncratic about Bhishma's vow not to "shoot at a woman, anyone who used to be a woman, or has a woman's name, or appears to be a woman."[60] Perhaps he invented the vow to protect her; he changes the wording each time he says it, and he says it often in justifying his refusal to fight with Shikhandin, almost as if he is ad-libbing.

But this vow opens a loophole clause for Bhishma's enemies in his otherwise complete invulnerability: only a woman can kill him, precisely because he regards a woman as so lowly that he would not stoop to defend himself against her. Thus the text implies that Shikhandin retained her female gender when she lost her female sexuality. Indeed, it is imperative for Bhishma that Shikhandin is in essence (in this case, in gender) a woman, despite her outer male form. This mythological loophole is a variant of the observation that men, by ignoring the differences between women (or others whom they dominate), can be tricked and overcome by them, by what James Scott has called the weapons of the weak. It is also related to a theme that appears elsewhere in the Hindu epics (and in epics from other cultures): the villain blackmails the gods into granting him the boon that he can be killed by no one on a list that he formulates, but he omits people beneath his contempt, one of whom, sneaking under the radar of the protective boon, kills him. Thus Ravana failed to specify that he could not be killed by a human (Rama),[61] and closer to our theme, the buffalo-demon Mahisha failed to specify that he could not be killed by a woman (inspiring the gods to create the Goddess, Devi).[62] Similarly, the Hijras validate themselves by filling in, in Rama's injunction to his followers, the unspoken category between men and women. In the case of Bhishma, the perfect solution to his unkillability, a creature with the technical status of a woman but the power of a man, is a murderous transsexual. Bhishma's mother, shamed at the thought of her son's death at the hands of a man-woman, is consoled by being told that Bhishma was killed not by Shikhandin but by another sort of *kliba*, Arjuna.

Amba's connection with Hijras has been appropriated by contemporary Indian politics, as Lawrence Cohen has noted in a cartoon that was plastered onto walls near a big political rally in Benares in 1993:

A male figure representing the common man and labelled the *Sikhandin janata* (*janata* means the people and Sikhandin is the gender-bending warrior from the *Mahabharata* epic, who for most Banarsis is thought to be like a *hijra* or eunuch) is shown bent over and raped at both ends by two other male figures, orally by a *gandu neta* or politician-bugger and anally by a *jhandu pulis* or useless policeman.[63]

This image is classical in two senses. First, it draws upon a political insight couched in sexual language already documented in an ancient Brahmana text about the horse sacrifice, which speaks of a male who "thrusts the pe-

nis into the slit, and the vulva swallows it up," and glosses this statement:
"The slit is the people, and the penis is the royal power, which presses
against the people, and so the one who has royal power is hurtful to the
people."[64] As we would say, the king fucks the people. Second, Shikhandin
himself was, in his previous life as Amba, unraped, as it were—sexually rejected—at both ends: she was raped and rejected by Bhishma, and rejected by her betrothed lover. An apt image indeed, but transformed, like
Shikhandin himself, from the image of a woman to that of a man. Since
the epic is in general more sympathetic to women than is contemporary
Indian culture, to make the metaphor powerful and meaningful the authors of the Banarsi cartoon had to transform the doubly unraped, but
lethally vengeful, Amba into the doubly raped Shikhandin.

Goddesses, always dangerous, become even more dangerous when they
become male. Every year at the festival of Gangamma in Tirupati, people
enact a great myth of transsexual revenge:

GANGAMMA

A Palegadu, a local warrior lord and landowner, was forcing every virgin to
sleep with him the night before her wedding. He terrified everyone. Spying
Gangamma drying her hair, he lusted for her. She decided to teach him the
lesson of his life. But first she needed to discover where he lived. Each day
she and her sister took another guise and went through Tirupati searching
him out. The day before Gangamma killed the Palegadu she took the guise
of an Outcaste Sweeper (Toti) and went from house to house assuring
everyone that they would not be harmed. The day of the killing she took
the guise of a foreign ruler, a "prince from another place" (Dora), and went
to the Palegadu's palace, where he was playing dice with friends. He came
forth to fight the Dora, and Gangamma beheaded him. She revived him for
a few moments to show him her true form (visvarupa), telling him, "This is
what a woman really is." He pleaded for his life, vowing his devotion to her.
Gangamma refused, saying he would be just the way he was before, and
killed him again. Following this she pierced her tongue with a needle to
demonstrate her power. Gangamma instructed the Weavers how to reenact
her story, the guises to take and how to dress and embody them so that she
would return to Tirupati. Then she turned herself into a stone at the Talla-
paka shrine.[65]

Again we see the *Gita* theme (and even the *Gita* form, the *vishvarupa*
doomsday form): at the villain's foolish request, the goddess shows him
not just what she really is, but what every woman is. And as always, he's

sorry he asked. As in the story of Amba/Shikhandin, the villain who intends to force a woman is killed by that woman herself, disguised as a man. Here the woman kills him before he can rape her but she herself becomes, like other hypersexual and/or bisexual women, a stone.

The sexual switches become far more complicated in the ritual, as Don Handelman points out:

> The Goddess uses the appearance of maleness to eliminate the male who perceives only appearance. To do this, the Jatra creates a ritual cosmos that on its surface subordinates women to men, wives to husbands, and that has only males at the apex of hierarchy—the Prince, his Minister, the Palegadu. Then everyone is shown that she is fully conscious of herself, as deliberately and violently she tears this fabrication to shreds. Males have a significant place in this ritual cosmos only so long as disguise does. Males, one may say, are part of the disguise of the Goddess as a meekly married woman. As the absence of her self-awareness gives way to self-revelation, so maleness dissolves into superfluity. The male (Palegadu) perceives his own nature as utterly masculine, and as absolutely superior to the inferior female; and so the male forces from the female what is of value to her (her virginity, her inner state of wholeness). During the casual course of the Jatra, these premises are transformed. The female (Gangamma) emerges into herself through the male (the Weavers) disguised as a female (the guise).[66]

And, as David Shulman sums it up, "Male and female are inside-out images of one another, endowed with countervailing and complementary directionality."[67]

A tale of a woman who becomes a man who becomes a woman is told with labyrinthine Vedantic switchbacks in the *Yogavasishtha,* a Sanskrit text composed in Kashmir around the tenth century C.E. She is a magician (in other times and places, she might have been called a witch) and one of the relatively rare FTMs and even rarer *positive* FTMs in Hindu mythology.

CUDALA

Queen Cudala and her husband King Shikhidhvaja were passionately in love, like two souls in one body. In time, Cudala became enlightened and acquired magic powers, including the ability to fly, but she concealed these powers from her husband, and when she attempted to instruct him he spurned her as a foolish and presumptuous woman. Yet he remarked that she seemed to have regained the bloom of her youth, and he assured her that he would continue to make love to her. Eventually, the king decided to

seek his own enlightenment and withdrew to the forest to meditate; he re-
nounced his throne and refused to let Cudala accompany him, but left her
to govern the kingdom.

After eighteen years she decided to visit him; she took the form of a
young Brahmin boy named Kumbha ("Pot") and was welcomed by the
king, who did not recognize her but remarked that Kumbha looked very
much like his queen, Cudala. Cudala told the king that "he" was named
Kumbha because he had been born when his father, the sage Narada, had
become excited by the sight of a group of divine nymphs sporting in the
water while he was bathing and shed his semen into a pot. After a while,
the king became very fond of Kumbha, who instructed him and enlightened him; and Cudala began to be aroused by her handsome husband.

And so Kumbha/Cudala went away for a while. When she returned, she
told the king that she had encountered the hot-tempered sage Durvasas
hurrying through the sky and had remarked that he looked like a woman
hastening to an illicit rendezvous with her lover. "When the sage heard
this," said Kumbha/Cudala, "he cursed me to become a woman, with
breasts and long hair, every night." That night, before the king's eyes,
Kumbha/Cudala changed into a woman named Madanika, who cried out
in a stammering voice, "I feel as if I am falling, trembling, melting; I am so
ashamed as I see myself becoming a woman. Alas, my chest is sprouting
breasts, and jewelry is growing right out of my body."

Madanika/Kumbha/Cudala slept beside the king every night in the
same bed like a virgin, while Kumbha/Cudala lived with him during the
day as a friend. After a few days Kumbha/Cudala said to him, "Your
majesty, I sleep beside you every night as a woman. I want to behave like a
woman and get good at it. I want to marry you and to enjoy the happiness
of a woman. Since we are both immune to desire, there can be no harm in
this." He consented to this, and so one day Kumbha/Cudala bathed cere-
monially with the king, and that night Madanika/Cudala married him.
And so the couple, whose previous state of marriage was concealed, were
joined together. They lay down on the marriage bed of flowers and made
love all night.

Thus they lived as dear friends during the day and as husband and wife
at night. After they had lived happily in this way for a while, Cudala decided to test the king's detachment. She used her magic powers to create
the illusion of a garden with a beautiful bed, and on that bed lay
Madanika/Kumbha/Cudala making love passionately with a young man
handsomer than the king. The king saw them and turned away, but was unmoved. "Please continue; do not let me interrupt your pleasure," he said to
the flushed and apologetic Madanika/Kumbha/Cudala; "Kumbha and I are

great friends, free from all passion; but you, Madanika, are nothing but a girl created by a sage's curse." Madanika/Kumbha/Cudala said, "Women are fickle by nature; they have eight times as much lust as men. Please don't be angry with me." "I have no anger, my dear girl," said the king; "but— only because good people would disapprove—, I do not want you to be my wife. Let us be good friends, as we were before, without any passion."

Cudala was delighted with the king's immunity to lust and anger, and she changed immediately from Madanika/Kumbha/Cudala to Cudala. The king said, "Who are you and how did you get here? In your body, your movements, your smile, your manner, your grace—you look so much like my wife." "Yes, I am truly Cudala," she said, and then she told him all that she had done. He embraced her passionately, and said, "You are the most wonderful wife who ever lived. The wife is everything to her husband: friend, brother, sympathizer, servant, guru, companion, wealth, happiness, the Vedic canon, abode, and slave. Come, embrace me again." Then he made love to her all night and returned with her to resume his duties as king. He ruled for ten thousand years and finally attained release.[68]

Cudala and the king are said to be passionately in love; there is no conflict here between the personae of the wife and the mistress or the mother and the whore as there are in many myths of this genre. This renunciant text regards as irrelevant the fact that Cudala and the king are childless; she is his lover, a relationship that the text begins by regarding as complete. Therefore, instead of wishing to be both her husband's concubine and the mother of his children like the typical rejected wife, Cudala wishes to be her husband's mistress both in the sense of lover and in the sense of teacher; she has already played the first role but is now denied it; and he refuses to grant her the second role; when he goes off to meditate, god is the other woman. In the Hindu view, Cudala is like a man to begin with: aggressive, resourceful, and wise.

The text tells us that in the beginning Shikhidhvaja and Cudala were like two souls in one body; it is he who splits the souls apart when he goes away, renouncing her. In order to reunite them, she engages in a series of splittings, a series of schizophrenic disguises, that she understands but her husband does not. Does she just change costume or use her magic to change her form? It doesn't seem to matter here; in any case, she is always aware of what is happening and in control of it. First she becomes entirely one-sided, entirely male, a boy who does not even have a mother, having been born from a pot (kumbha). This is almost certainly a satire on the births of so many Indian sages whose fathers have nothing but a pot to put their seed in, the ultimate safe-sex surrogate. The children born of this male parthenogenesis, however, are not usually given the matronymic of "Pot."[69] Perhaps Cudala becomes so unilaterally male because she suspects that on some level the king's need for asceticism is in part a revulsion against her as a woman, an erotic woman, like the revulsion of the potted sages.

This part of the story owes much to the story of Ila/ā as told in the *Ramayana* (and here it may be noted that the *Yogavasishtha* regards itself as a retelling of the *Ramayana*):[70] like Budha and Ila/ā, Shikhidhvaja and Cudala live in the forest, "eating fruits and roots," and in his/her male existence Cudala as Kumbha studies *dharma*, just like Ila. But there is a crucial difference: unlike the *Ramayana*, the antinomian *Yogavasishtha*, composed many centuries after the tale of Ila/ā, is able to imagine a woman who has (male) power and uses it for the benefit of her man. For Ila/ā is accidentally transformed against his will and then tricked into bed by a manipulative, lying man, while Cudala undergoes her transformations on purpose, tricking her husband at every step. Unlike Ila/ā, Cudala always remembers who she is; she is in the outer frame and makes it all happen, while Ila/ā is inside the story, passive, the victim of other forces. When Madanika/Kumbha/Cudala repeats the old saw that women have eight times more desire/pleasure* than men, she is mocking it. Yet we should note that the woman, Cudala, gains power by her transformation into a man, while the man, Ila/ā, loses power by his transformation into a woman; all of the texts agree on that.

But the queen wants to get her husband into bed as well as to enlighten him; the story is, after all, not merely a parable of enlightenment but a very human, very funny story. And the text is not so antinomian as to image a consummated male homosexual relationship. Eventually Cudala manages to enjoy her husband as a male friend by day and as a lover and wife by night. The double woman whom she creates—Madanika/Kumbha/Cudala—is her real self—the negation of the negation of her femininity. And the story that she tells to explain Madanika/Kumbha/Cudala is a reflection of the complex androgyny of Madanika/Kumbha: she is born of a curse given by a man mistaken for a woman—and not just for any woman, but for an erotic, illicit woman, the adulterous woman hurrying to a rendezvous (a conventional theme in Sanskrit court poetry and painting). The words she speaks in her transformation surely conjure up the double entendre of a woman in orgasm ("I am falling, trembling, melting"); they also combine a natural and cultural construction of what it is to be a woman: just as her breasts grow (in a manner echoed by the MTFs in films like *Switch* [1991] and *Dr. Jekyll and Ms. Hyde** [1971]), so her jewelry grows.

This double deception works well enough and may in fact express her full fantasy: to be her husband's intellectual superior under the sun and his erotic partner by moonlight (an alternation that Ila/ā accomplishes too, though she does it month by month instead of day by night, and she doesn't know she is doing it). The story imagines the intimacy that takes place in the daylight (the light in which enlightenment is produced) when the woman, by becoming a man, experiences the friendship that men have with one another in their daytime associations; the sexual intimacy of night is different, though still complementary rather than contradictory to the intellectual companionship of the day. Like the vampire or werewolf or animal-lover who assumes the true form at night, who comes alive at night, or the orthodox Hindu image that tends to split the diurnal and nocturnal images of women, distant by day, intimate by night, Cudala assumes her true sexual form at night.

Unlike both vampires and orthodox Hindu women, Cudala achieves a double intimacy. But since the two roles belong to two different personae, she wants to merge them and to play them both as her original self; she wants to reintegrate herself and abandon her double. To do this and to test the king she creates two more magical doubles: a double of the already double woman Madanika, and a double of the king, her lover. The illusion of the adultery of Madanika mirrors the lie of the adulterous rendezvous of the sage Durvasas. The king passes the test not because he is so far above jealousy as to allow his wife to sleep with another man, but because he realizes that the woman who has betrayed him is not only not really his wife but not even really a woman. As a result of his vision of the adultery of the false Madanika, the king comes to realize the purely illusory nature of the "true" Madanika and rejects her—for being illusory or for being promiscuous? We do not know. Cudala isn't jealous; she watches him make love with another woman—herself—but doesn't mind, while he watches her make love with another man—an illusion—and seems to mind. She is free of jealousy for a number of reasons: she is more enlightened than the king; she knows from the start that none of it is real; she knows that the illusory woman is herself; and the text may still assume the double standard: a woman should not mind, like a man, if her spouse is unfaithful.

The king is still willing to maintain his friendship with Kumbha/Cudala, for he thinks that Kumbha is one step closer to reality than Madanika is (Madanika being a double of what he takes to be the "real" Kumbha). And he is half right: Madanika/Kumbha/Cudala is closer to the original Cudala in gender, but Kumbha/Cudala is closer in intellect. Though the king is not hurt or jealous or angry, he is cut loose from his illusion of Madanika; Cudala has begun to repair the split between him and her real self by revealing the illusory nature of sexual love. The playful juggling of the genders demonstrates both the unreality of appearances and the falsity of the belief that one gender is better than the other.

When the king rejects Madanika/Kumbha/Cudala, Cudala is forced to reveal herself and to tell him the truth. He is overcome with gratitude and delight that it was his wife, of all people, who was his guru—a situation that he found intolerable at the beginning of the story. The wife is everything to him, integrating not (in this case) mother and whore, but guru and slave, and many other human relationships (somewhat reminiscent of the Vaishnava texts that tell us that one may worship Krishna as a friend, brother, child, servant, mother, or lover). Where this might commonly be used as a figure of speech, here Cudala literally becomes his guru and his friend, a person apparently other than herself.

The relationship between Cudala and Shikhidhvaja is never the relationship of a real husband and wife. She functions like a goddess, giving him her grace and leading him up the garden path of enlightenment, setting up a divine illusion and then revealing herself to him as the gods reveal themselves. She can fly, after all, and as Kumbha her feet* do not touch the earth, a sure sign of disguised divinity; she masterminds the whole story. She is even able, like Helen, to remain young. This is a story about a goddess, not a story about a woman. Nor is it a story with an easy feminist reading, let alone a homosexual reading: the woman is wiser than the man, enlightens the man, and so forth, but she has to become a man herself to do it—like a Bodhisattva*—, and she has to become a woman again to sleep with him. Yet the philosophy of illusion, as expressed in the *Yogavasishtha*, demonstrates that there is no difference at all between the male and female forms of Cudala; they are, in a sense, all alike in the dark. In this way, the tension of the myth is resolved, the contradiction is unmasked as purely illusory, and everybody lives happily ever after. But this is hardly a typical solution, for it happens only in an India where a king can rule for ten thousand years.

MALES INTO FEMALES IN GREECE AND EUROPE

The sage Teiresias, who is implicated in other Greek (and Roman) myths of transformation (Amphitryon, Narcissus*), is himself an alternating androgyne:

TEIRESIAS

Teiresias once came upon two huge snakes coupling; when both attacked him, he struck at them with his stick and killed the female; at that moment, he was changed from a man to a woman. But seven years later he came upon two snakes again, struck them again, this time killing the male, and was changed back into a man.

Now, one day, Jupiter, in his cups, was joking with Juno; he asserted that women had greater pleasure from love than men did. She disagreed, and they decided to ask Teiresias to decide for them, since he had made love both as a man and as a woman. Teiresias sided with Jupiter, and Juno was so angry that she condemned him to eternal blindness, while Jupiter, to mitigate her curse, gave him the power to see the future.[71]

Like the Hindu prince/ss Ila/ā, Teiresias is changed into a woman as punishment for interrupting the sexual activity not of a god, like Ila/ā, but of an animal—more precisely, a snake, an animal often implicated in the mythology of androgyny. Looking upon something that should not be looked upon, in this case not divinity but animal sexuality, makes Teiresias first androgynous and then blind. Teiresias's female double, like that of Riksharaja* and other serial androgynes, does not exist simultaneously with his male self, but it functions very much like a double all the same. Some texts add that Teiresias said that women have not just more pleasure, but *nine times* as much pleasure as men[72]—thereby slightly one-upping the ante in comparison with the Hindu story of Cudala,* which calculates the ratio as merely eight to one.

Marjorie Garber asks the right questions about Teiresias:

Is his knowledge finally about his *own* pleasure, or about that of the other? . . . If bisexuality, like Tiresias, is often imagined heterosexually, as the copresence or alternation of "male" and "female" selves each desiring an object of the "other" gender, how does this positing of a heterosexual norm change if we imagine that bisexuality is related to a fantasy about knowing the pleasure of the other? . . . What is at work here is the eroticism of the shifter . . . to use Roman Jakobson's term—words that change their referent with each use, depending on the context. . . . Tiresias himself (or herself) is

a shifter, an index not only of sex and gender instability but of the erotic secret of bisexuality. Does the X chromosome or the Y chromosome, the female or the male, mark the spot?[73]

The mythological creatures who are bisexually transformed are precisely
such shifters (and shape shifters too of course).

It is not possible to make a clear split between surface change of gender
(transvestism, or even the transformation of physical sex without a change
of mind or memory) and the deeper psychological transformation of gender in mind as well as body. If you change your dress, you change your
mind; and, on the other hand, even if you change your body, you may not
change your mind. This point is brilliantly demonstrated by Virginia
Woolf's Orlando, a great serial androgyne:

ORLANDO

Orlando had become a woman—there is no denying it. But in every other
respect, Orlando remained precisely as he had been. The change of sex,
though it altered their future, did nothing whatever to alter their identity.
Their faces remained, as their portraits prove, practically the same. His
memory—but in the future we must, for convention's sake, say "her" for
"his," and "she" for "he"—her memory then, went back through all the
events of her past life without encountering any obstacle.[74]

Here Orlando argues that the changed body did not change the soul, but
later she came to believe the opposite, that the body did change the soul:

[W]hat was said a short time ago about there being no change in Orlando
the man and Orlando the woman, was ceasing to be altogether true. She
was becoming a little more modest, as women are, of her brains, and a little
more vain, as women are, of her person. . . . Thus, there is much to support
the view that it is clothes that wear us and not we them; we may make them
take the mould of arm or breast, but they mould our hearts, our brains,
our tongues to their liking.[75]

What is the relationship between Orlando's mind and her body, on the
one hand, and her clothing, on the other? The change in the inner person
was brought about not merely by the effect that clothing had upon her
own body, her movement, her freedom to swim or leap, but by the effect
that it had upon the bodies of others, the ability to make a sailor lose control and fall off the rigging. Yet if this is true of clothes, how much more
must it be true of the body, the clothing of the mind?

CONCLUSION: MALE AND/OR FEMALE

What conclusions can we draw from this corpus of myths, and from others related to them? How are we to adjudicate the relative influences upon the soul of, on the one hand, an unchanged body in different clothes (transvestism) or, on the other hand, a changed body in the same or different clothes (transsexuality with or without transvestism)? To chart it structurally, we might say that clothes/body = body/mind = mindbody/soul. Judith Butler has argued, along similar lines, that sex is the epiphenomenon, that sex/gender = matter/form,[76] a nice handle by which to grab many of the myths of bisexuality, though to say (as she does) that form is more important than matter is a more Platonic argument than I would wish to make. Matter matters.

There are crucial differences between the implications of the mythologies of bisexual deities and of bisexual humans. The stories about the gods have their human models, of course, and their human moments. To the extent that they are composed by humans and clearly reflect human attitudes, we might, with caution, use them to attempt to formulate hypotheses about ancient Hindu attitudes to homosexual acts, for instance. But myths about transsexual deities are also stories about the way the world is, about the ambiguity of all existence. On that level, they may express a desire that transcends not only appearance but even gender itself, a desire that desires the soul no matter what bits of flesh may be appended to various parts of the body.

Some of the transformations in these myths are temporary: the person undergoing the transformation, willingly or as the result of a curse, ends up as s/he was at the start. But sometimes the transformation lasts forever, and even in stories in which during the period of the transformation there is no memory of the original (and final) state, there is usually at the end a memory of the temporary transformation. Here we must note a significant gender asymmetry: no matter whether a man becomes a woman or a woman a man, the transformed person usually forgets the former gender and identity. But in both cases, there is often *another man present, untransformed, who remembers,* and who therefore has power over the transformed person. For Ila/ā, it is Budha; for Amba, Bhishma.

In some texts, a male is entirely transformed into a female, with a female mentality and memory (aspects of gender rather than of sex), the situation that we might expect from the fluidity of gender; this happens to Ila/ā in most texts (except on the Sahya mountain). Yet other texts, proba-

bly reflecting the dramatic, even grotesque, asymmetry between perceptions of people of different genders in actual life in ancient India, seem to
reflect the very opposite view, a view of gender as astonishingly durable:
the male merely assumes the outer form of the female, retaining his male
essence, his male memory and mentality (as Ila/ā does in the Sahya text
and at the beginning of his transformation in most texts). In the play (the
Bhagavad-Ajjuka) in which a servant of Yama* puts the soul of a courtesan
into the body of a wandering mendicant and vice versa, the poet comments: "The life's breaths of the woman, placed in the body of this Brahmin, will cause a transformation of his essence and his behavior [*sattva,
shila*]."[77] Here gender clearly remains distinct from the transformed body:
the courtesan behaves like a Brahmin, not like a courtesan.

When male deities are magically transformed into women but change
only their superficial physical genitalia, they do so usually in order to kill a
male enemy; this is the case with Vishnu as Mohini. The man retains his
male memory, and it is this male consciousness that kills—or, at least,
fights. Sometimes a man changes back from woman to man to kill in
battle (like Mohini), but sometimes he will stay a woman and kill as a
woman, sexually, like the poison damsel or the demon(ess) with the
vagina dentata. But when the transformation is deeper and the male takes
on a female memory, it is this female consciousness that enjoys sex and
makes love and babies. This is the case in those variants of the myth of
Ila/ā in which the mind and memory change too, change their gender
when the body changes its sex. This pattern reaffirms gender stereotypes:
males kill, females make babies. But it also suggests that male memory is
the killer. Female-to-male transformations reinforce this pattern: when
they are superficial, the retained female memory makes love (as in the
myth of Cudala*); when they are deep, they generally involve the deep
transformation of memory and personality, and so the female-to-male
transsexual becomes murderous (as in the case of Amba).

Yet on the philosophical level these myths often erase what they regard
as a false boundary between the male and the female. This is a philosophical stance shared to some extent by Hinduism and Buddhism but more
explicitly stated by Buddhist texts. For instance, Buddhists tell a story
about the Buddhist monk Soreyya,* who was so taken by the beauty of the
elder Mahakaccayana, whom he glimpsed at the bath, that he wished to
marry him, and his genitals were instantaneously transformed from male
to female.[78] Other Buddhist variants express a related worldview:

SARIPUTRA AND THE GODDESS

A bodhisattva should regard all living beings as a wise man regards the reflection of the moon in water or as magicians regard men created by
magic. . . . like the track of a bird in the sky; like the erection of a eunuch;
like the pregnancy of a barren woman. . . .

The goddess employed her magic power to cause the elder Sariputra to
appear in her form and to cause herself to appear in his form. Then the
goddess, transformed into Sariputra, said to Sariputra, transformed into a
goddess, "Reverend Sariputra, what prevents you from transforming yourself out of your female state?" And Sariputra, transformed into the goddess, replied, "I no longer appear in the form of a male! My body has
changed into the body of a woman! I do not know what to transform!" The
goddess continued, "If the elder could again change out of the female state,
then all women could also change out of their female state. All women appear in the form of women in just the same way as the elder appears in the
form of a woman. While they are not women in reality, they appear in the
form of women. With this in mind, the Buddha said, 'In all things, there is
neither male nor female.'" Then, the goddess released her magical power
and each returned to his or her ordinary form. She then said to him, "Reverend Sariputra, what have you done with your female form?" Sariputra: "I
neither made it nor did I change it." Goddess: "Just so, all things are neither
made nor changed, and that they are not made and not changed, that is the
teaching of the Buddha."[79]

This is the ultimate philosophical support for the fluidity of gender.

Yet gender often proves remarkably tenacious. Buddhist mythology
teaches that to become a Bodhisattva a woman must take on not only the
body but the *mind* of a man—though, since Buddhists do not affirm the
existence of a soul, she can't have the *soul* of a man. Indeed, in Buddhism
women are often reborn as males in order to become enlightened; and the
Tibetan Vinaya casually remarks that anyone who changes sex more than
four times a month can't become a monk.[80] Even the Vedantic theory of
illusion, which disparages the body in favor of the soul, implies that you
may very well remain a male in some essential way even when you happen
to take on a female body; even when memory is transformed the male almost always reverts to his maleness in the end. One might assume that
since these stories were composed within a world in which you probably
were recently and will soon be again someone else, this factor would seem
to contribute to the Hindu view that does not seem to regard sex or gender as an intrinsic part of human identity. But in fact you probably were

not, in your previous existence, someone of another sex or gender. For in Hindu texts (in dramatic contrast with Buddhist texts), very few, if any, gender changes occur in reincarnation; even Amba changes her gender only *after* she has been reborn, with the same gender that she had in her previous life. (An exception is posed by the text in which the men who wanted to become women to make love with Rama became reincarnate as the cowherd women.)[81] This dearth of gender transformations in Hindu stories of rebirth stands in strong contrast to the frequent changes of species that take place in reincarnation in texts like *The Laws of Manu*. Thus a man might more easily be reborn as an ant (presumably a male ant) than as a woman. The two contrasting views of the persistence of gender may be correlated with two contrasting attitudes to women and to homosexual love: the texts that view gender as fluid generally depict the transformed male as happy in her female form, while those in which the gendered memory lags stubbornly behind depict him as miserable in her female form.

We may also interpret the seduction of a woman by a man, transformed into a woman but retaining his male memory, as a homosexual act. Freudians see latent homosexual impulses lurking under the covers even of ostensibly heterosexual acts like cuckolding, which mask a sexual attraction between the man who seduces another man's wife and the man whom he cuckolds. According to this interpretation, which we have already considered in the context of the transposed male heads,* a cuckolder is a man who wants to get at another man through his sexual partner; whether or not he really wants the woman, out of lust or aggression toward her husband he can, as the phrase goes, fuck him or fuck him over. The Hindus speak of weakening a man by destroying the shield constituted by his wife's chastity, rather like the shield that Shikhandin became for the Pandava brothers. The cuckolder takes the indirect route via the woman, who may be regarded as the facilitator in a transaction between two men, as Bram Stoker's Lucy* facilitated the blood transfusions between five men. Whenever one man cuckolds another, therefore, there is a duel between two phalluses, glowing like the magic weapons of Darth Vader and his son, Luke Skywalker. This is hardly a homosexual act in the strict sense of the word, but it does depict a world in which the sexual tension, if not the desire, is between members of the same sex—or indeed within a single person, at war with his or her changing self.

The fact that adultery is often a transaction between men is betrayed

by our term *cuckold,* which means something that one man does to another man—even though it happens when a man and a woman are alone
together and the man who is the object of the verb is usually not present
at all. This is not to deny the wife agency: she has her own fantasies, makes
her choices and is responsible for them—it takes three to tango. But it implies that there is some degree of homosexual desire, conscious or unconscious, in the mind of a cuckolder who knows that his bedmate is married
(even if he thinks he is doing it just to have her). This idea was passed
through Freud and Gayle Rubin to Eve Sedgwick, who rightly points out
that "to cuckold" is "by definition a sexual act, performed on a man, by a
man"[82] and who formulated her concept of an erotic triangle in which the
bond linking the two male rivals is more intense than the bond that leads
either of them to the woman.[83] This romantic triangle is precisely that,
not the V that so often represents it ("John loves Mary and Mary loves
Bob"), leaving one side open. The Freudians closed the triangle with the
hypothesis of closet homosexuality: Bob loves John (or better, John loves
Bob). Garber likens this third leg of the triangle to the missing "fourth
wall" in proscenium theater.[84]

Robert P. Goldman has seen the homosexual scenario at work in certain myths of the transsexual transformation of a man into a woman,
which "takes place as the consequence of a desire to avoid or defuse a potential sexual liaison with a prohibited female seen as the property of a
powerful and revered male and/or the desire to be passively enjoyed sexually by such a male."[85] The repression of a homosexual impulse may account for the violence in so many of these myths: some, such as the stories
of cuckolding, may be motivated not only by lust but by hatred and the
desire for revenge.

Aspects of these myths may express positive homosexual fantasies that
until now only psychoanalysts have read in (or into) more realistic stories.
Parts of the psychoanalytic hypothesis are substantiated by several different sorts of myths: realistic stories in which men dress as women to seduce
other men (like Bhima—with Kicaka—in the *Mahabharata,*[86] or Kaviku-
mar, who dresses as a woman to seduce and kill his brother);[87] fantastic
stories in which men become magically doubled and the homosexual fantasy is enacted in a conveniently simplified form, by eliminating the
woman (indeed any separate partner) altogether (such as the prince who
married his own left half); and magical stories in which the fantasy is actually acted out by a man who transforms himself into a woman and en-

gages in a heterosexual act with the man (Vishnu as Mohini). The most direct variant is also by far the most rare: stories in which men or women, untransformed and undisguised, actually do consummate a homosexual act.[88]

A homophobic society often inspires a closet homosexuality encoded in texts that make it necessary or useful for us to employ a hermeneutics of suspicion if we are to understand them. On a repressed level, available to such a hermeneutics of suspicion, there is a great deal of masked homosexual desire in these myths of transsexuality and narcissism. The homosexual themes in traditional myths are seldom overt, because such myths almost always have, as a latent agenda, the biological and spiritual survival of a particular race, in both senses of the word: race as contest and as species ("us against them"). Such myths regard homosexual acts as potentially subversive of this agenda (or at the very least irrelevant to it, perhaps not part of the problem but certainly no part of the solution). The ascetic aspects of Hinduism create a violent dichotomy between heterosexual marriage, in which sexuality is tolerated for the sake of children, and the renunciant priesthood, in which asceticism is idealized and sexuality entirely rejected, or at least recycled. In this taxonomy, homosexual love represents what Mary Douglas has taught us to recognize as a major category error, something that doesn't fit into any existing conceptual cubbyhole, "matter out of place"—in a word, dirt.[89] Traditional Hindu mythology regards homosexual union not, like heterosexual marriage, as a compromise between two goals in tension (procreation and asceticism), but as a mutually polluting combination of the worst of both worlds (sterility and lust). The myths therefore seldom explicitly depict homosexual unions at all, let alone sympathetically. (Indian Buddhism, by contrast, is far less homophobic.)

But something far more positive is also going on in the Hindu mythology of bisexuality. David Shulman has suggested, on reading Winnicott, that "splitting might be, as even Plato thought (in the Symposium), the internal movement that happens *before* we even achieve a sexual identity at all, as male or female." And he continues:

Were this the case, then sexual doubling within the context of a theoretically mature sexuality—as in the vast majority of our stories—could also be a recursive or regressive form of reconstituted cross-identification, i.e. an attempt to get back to some point before the initial split by identifying with the split-off counter-sex. This would help explain both the amazing inven-

tiveness and creativity around this theme and the somewhat driven quality
so many of these stories have.[90]

By and large, these are not happy stories, nor charters for the affirma-
tion of a polymorphous, psychopompous Jungian androgny. But not all
the homosexual desire in these myths of transvestism is depicted as perverse or destructive. Nor should we be too quick to see homosexual desire
as an evitable component of the myths of sex change. In some of the European texts, and in Hindu texts like the story of Queen Cudala,* the
change may be effected in the service of heterosexuality and occasionally
bisexuality. Some of these myths may be read as tales about bisexual desire
rather than homosexual desire *tout court*. Even the Hindu texts, however
homophobic some of them may be, challenge our own ideas about gender; they tell us that the desire for sexual pleasure both with and as members of both sexes is real, though ultimately unrealizable by all but the
magically gifted—or cursed. Some of them may express a wish for androgyny and offer, in subversion of the dominant homophobic paradigm,
closeted images of a happily expressed and satisfied bisexual desire. The
episodes of Arjuna as the dancing master and of Cudala as the master of
enlightenment, and some variants of the magic forests of Shiva and
Parvati, epitomize, in vivid contrast with the anxious often ugly stories
about sexual transformation, this playful, relaxed attitude toward gender
boundary-jumping.

Some of these stories are also about empathy: what is it like to be the
other? True, empathy can be used as a weapon: "Which way was the sex
better?" they asked Bhangashvana, and answer came there, "As a woman."
But often the transformed characters become far more sympathetic to the
other that they have experienced. It would certainly be simplistic to over-
look the misogynist implications of the argument that women enjoy sex
more than men do, but these texts do tell us that sexual pleasure is a serious goal for both sexes.

To the question posed by these myths—How deep is gender? Is it skin
deep, superficial, or truly deep, essential?—Hinduism answers Yes. It is not
the case that some myths answer "Deep" and others "Shallow." Often a single text will answer "Deep and shallow." Indeed, given the intertextuality
of the Hindu tradition, even the texts that say "Deep" are well aware of
others that say "Shallow." This unresolved paradox, constantly repeated
and transformed through the complexity of the textual tradition, tells us

that Hindus found this an important question, one to which they did not know the answer but that was so pressing that they could not stop trying to find an answer. The corpus of these stories therefore reminds us of two truths in tension, a paradox: one Hindu view of gender makes it as easy to slough off as a pair of pants (or a dress), but this view is often challenged by myths in which skin is more than skin deep, in which the soul and the memory too are gendered, an intrinsic part of the mortal coil that is not quite so easily shuffled off.

The Shadow of Gender

꘍

Is it possible to draw general conclusions about all the stories that we have considered throughout this book? Do we gain new insights into the stories about women by considering similar stories about men, and the reverse? And do the Hindu stories give us new insights into Greek stories, and the reverse? I find that the more general the statement, the less interesting it is, but I am willing to take a stab at it. Let us consider first the contrast in cultures and then the contrast in genders.

If we trace the variants of a myth within a single culture (Hinduism or ancient Greece) we find new twists and reversals. And if we go on to compare those two cultures, we find even more significant variants and reversals; often the different cultures will draw radically different, even opposite, conclusions from the same plot.[1] From the very start, we can see a difference in the genre, the tone, the style of the Hindu and Greek texts. The Hindu texts span a far greater period, ancient to modern (an imbalance that we have somewhat artificially leveled by placing in the other scale later European retellings of Greek stories). Even the Sanskrit tellings are closer to Indian folk and oral traditions than are the ancient Greek to their modern parallels, and they are further supplemented by retellings in Indian vernacular languages. These relative Hindu excesses in sheer quantity are further multiplied by excesses in style, which seem to answer, to the sober Greek "Nothing too much [meden agan]," "Everything too much!" The Hindu texts are more rococo, often sexier, sometimes more violent, than the Greek. Erich Auerbach noted in *Mimesis* that the stark genre of the Hebrew Bible leaves silences, gaps, in stories that other traditions, such as the longer-winded, elaborated genre of the Greeks, tell in greater detail.[2] I would go Auerbach one better and argue that when it comes to myth, Hindu is to Greek as Greek is to Hebrew.

But the tellings from the two cultures often objectify women in strikingly similar ways, and these similarities may be there because the texts were by and large composed by men, and men in different cultures depict women in similar ways (and as different from men). We must, however, note the voices of those relatively rare women who do actually speak in our texts, and we may also listen for women's voices behind the silences in texts transmitted by men, for those texts may capture the fantasies of both men and women. The texts tell us that a man may double himself as two different men or split a woman into two different women so that he can enjoy both his permitted woman and the forbidden woman for each of his various purposes. But a woman may do this too, doubling herself to enjoy different men for different purposes—as Helen does, in some readings, and Bram Stoker's Lucy—or splitting her man into two different men—as Alcmena and Ahalya do, if we read them that way.

Moreover, the same myth may be for him a doubling to achieve a sexual union and for her a splitting to avoid it, and these two forms of the same story may be combined to present simultaneously two views of the same situation, his and hers. For instance, some of these stories tell us that women flee from this world to otherworldly lovers, while other stories tell us that they prefer this world and their human husbands. We have seen some of the reasons for the preference for the human, which apply more often to women than to men; but the contrasting theme, the flight from the human world, may express a male point of view (that women are from the start inhuman) or a female point of view (that women are treated inhumanly by men). To this extent at least, it does not matter whether the author of a specific telling is male or female: the myth, which preserves both points of view, allows readers of both genders to find their meanings in it.[3] Because both men and women may be authors of the text and both may be in the audience, one myth often has two different gendered meanings.

But the bigendered authorship and/or interpretation of a single myth does not produce a corpus of mythology in which genders are portrayed as the same or even equal; far from it. We may isolate certain asymmetrical patterns in the behavior of men and women in comparable situations, especially if we focus on the depiction of women as objects and isolate for comparison the specific themes that have been the concern of this book (which means, of course, ignoring many other factors that are more culturally specific.)[4] Both Hindu and Greek texts reflect a double standard for the sexual roles and constructed genders of men and women in each society. That is, the same stories are told about men and about women within each culture, but the plot takes a different turn when a woman is the subject; the things that happen to the men and women in two stories where women do in one what men do in the other are radically different; the same acts have different consequences when men or women engage in them.

We might venture a few tentative generalizations about the relative frequency of certain patterns. Stories in which women split to avoid a sexual encounter (Sita, Helen) are more common than stories in which men avoid a sexual encounter (Odysseus with Calypso—after seven years), and stories in which women seek a sexual encounter (Shurpanakha) are not as common as stories in which men double themselves to seduce women (Indra, Zeus). This may be because both biology and society conspire to produce situations in which men, more often than women, double themselves in order to seek sexual encounters aggressively—women are more often raped than raping. But our texts can tell us only that *stories* emphasize male seduction over female seduction. Rarely does a man get another man to replace him in order to avoid a sexually threatening woman, though women often resort to this measure to avoid men who overpower them physically or politically. Thus women more often than men produce doubles in order to get away from the men who pursue them, in order not to be in a particular bed, while men (Indra, Zeus) more often than women double themselves in order to get into a bed where they are not wanted.

And although the initial premise is the same in variants where women or men double—a man wishes to sleep with a woman against her will—, when *she* splits off the double she avoids the encounter (because she outnumbers him two to one), while when *he* produces the double (often by masquerading as some other man) she is tricked into the encounter (because he outnumbers her two to one). The myths tell us that a man wishes to be a shining moment in the lives of as many women as possible while a woman tries to be all things to one man. The texts assume from the start that men have different women for different purposes and that the women do *not* have this privilege and must generate strategies either to take it from the men or (more rarely) to win it for themselves. By and large, men split women in two to dichotomize them and women create doubles to protect themselves from sexual violence. Where the woman is forced to have two different men only one of whom she desires, she splits off a double of herself to sleep with the man she does not love in order to keep her true self for the man she does love. In this way his doubling forces her splitting. We might surmise that the male tellers of these stories tell them in order to exalt their lineages and to encourage the fidelity of their women, while the women tell them to find ways to live with themselves after rape or simply under ongoing harassment or sexual alienation.

A woman's identity is constructed in these stories as far more fatally dependent upon the identity of her man than his is dependent upon hers. Where Nala and Odysseus must prove who they are through their knowledge and behavior, their wives, Damayanti and Penelope, must prove their identities primarily in terms of their fidelity to their husbands. The double standard in myths reflects the practice of most societies, which endorse the man's fantasy of having two different women but not the woman's fantasy of having two different men, making the consequences for men when women are fooled—cuckolding, illegitimate children, and so forth—far more serious than the consequences for women when men are fooled—humiliation and rejection. The man can indulge in his fantasy without casting doubt on the parentage of his heirs, while she cannot. Yet the biology of sex is also constructed, not anatomically but physiologically; that is, the fact that a man has a penis (his anatomy) is not socially constructed, but how he uses it (his physiology, matters such as impotence, not to mention castration) is. This cultural construction of biology leads to what Allan Grapard has nicely termed the "biodegradable" attitude to women.[5]

Marjorie Garber locates the double standard not in biological difference but in the arena of sexual politics. Noting how Eve Sedgwick, in *Between Men*, "redrew the erotic triangle to show that it was not symmetrical," she comments:

> Because males and females do not, historically, have equivalent cultural powers in most societies, and because, whatever the prevailing rhetoric of "opposites" or "complementarity" (the "opposite sex," the "other half"), "one gender is treated as a marginalized subset rather than an equal alternative to the other," bonds between men will be seen as different from bonds between women.[6]

And these bonds are depicted differently in different texts.

Ian Hacking noted a different sort of double standard for the genders of the protagonists in romantic fiction about doubling, on the one hand, and on the other, not the authors but the actual people who experienced the sorts of psychotic fantasies of doubling that we have seen expressed in many of our ancient texts: "most instances of double consciousness were girls or women, and most romantic doubles were men."[7] But then questions rise to the mind, certainly to the female mind: Who diagnosed these cases? Who recorded them? Who tabulated them? And for the mythologist, What was the relationship between the fiction and the psychosis? Which inspired which?

Elaine Showalter accounts for the prevalence of female mental disorders in the medical literature of divided consciousness by reminding us that the authors of the texts that we have were men:

> The impossibility of actualized double lives for women did not mean that women were not as divided by fantasies, longings, and unrealized desires as men. Women as well as men were "truly two." . . . Yet medical literature of the *fin de siècle* reveals that observed clinical cases of multiple personality were predominantly female and that in life rather than art, hysterical self-fragmentation was more likely to be a feminine than a masculine response to social pressures. . . . While Victorian men could get through the week on a mere two personalities, Victorian women seemed to need at least three.[8]

Thus men had more opportunity both to actualize their fantasies of multiple personalities and to publish them; most women could only imagine them, sometimes to the point of psychosis.

This brings us back to the question of agency: Who splits whom? The women in most of the myths we have considered are split by men in order to contain the evil that the men perceive in them; or in reaction to abuse by others (usually men) they split themselves rather than their abusers. By contrast, the men in the stories usually split themselves in reaction to their perception of the evil (or more often, inadequacy) within themselves; while in reaction to their perception of the evil (particularly the sexual danger to men) within women, they split the women. But the agency of men is subject to many of the limits that the women experience; a man (even a man-god like Rama) may find that someone else has split his woman, and a man (Amphitryon, Gautama, Count Olaf Labinski) may suddenly encounter a double he didn't know he had. And some women, such as Saranyu and Damayanti, have some degree of agency and subjectivity; different cultures at different times allow longer leashes to their women than others at other times. Nevertheless, in the end the cultural paradigms of gender raise their ugly heads and women must submit to men's powers—or subvert them.

For there are many ways in which having—or recognizing that you have—"at least three" personalities is a strength, not a weakness. Against the background of men's negative images of women, our texts also celebrate a more positive sort of self-image that women have of themselves and a different image that men have of them. Even where the male authors meant to depict women as dishonest, we can read these same women as clever and subversive, not victimized but resourceful, not sexually voracious but desiring even as they desire to be desired, both transforming and transformed, wiser than men in their ability to see through the illusion to the reality, in their ability to recognize both their partners and themselves. As Ann Gold has remarked, "Folklore persuasively offers images of female nature that includes a sexuality not rampantly destructive but seeking mutuality with males. The erotic imagination . . . suggests a relish for sexual encounter on both sides that is more human than demonic."[9] These stories testify to the inventiveness with which women have both split themselves in order to circumvent men's agendas and circumvented men's tendencies to split women for those same (and other) agendas. They testify, moreover, to women's ability to consummate these subversions under the very noses of the male authors of the texts, to insert their agendas and their strategies even in texts composed by men literally to demonize them. In the texts under consideration here, women (such as Sita and Helen, Mariatale and Lucy) use these strategies more often to flee or retaliate than to attack or subvert; but in the closely related stories of the bedtrick, women are often more aggressive,[10] and we may see some of those more active agendas even here in subplots of the tales of Ahalya and Alcmena, Damayanti and Penelope.

Thus, both in their objectification by male authors and in their own subjective strategies of subversion, women in Hindu stories are more like women in Greek stories than they are like men in Hindu stories. Mariatale is more like the Greek Scylla than she is like the men with the transposed heads from her own culture. Penelope in confronting Odysseus resembles Damayanti confronting Nala far more than she resembles another Greek, a male Greek like Menelaus confronting Helen. A Hindu story about a doubled woman more closely resembles a Greek story about a doubled woman than a tale of a doubled woman in Greece or Hinduism resembles a tale of a doubled man in the same culture. That is, gender transcends culture in establishing lines of convergences between texts in different cultures that tell the same sorts of stories about men and women. Women resemble one another across cultures in certain ways more than they resemble the men within their own cultures. Differences in gender are more significant than differences in culture; gender trumps culture. We began by suggesting that the two sets of texts, Hindu and Greek, were shadows of one another; and we may conclude by noting that in each set of texts, culture is the shadow of gender.

The androgyny of the text also makes it possible for both Greek and Hindu men and women—in ways colored differently by gender and culture—to tell these stories for positive purposes. They tell them to achieve the joyous and creative life that William Butler Yeats said depended on "the energy to assume the mask of some other self . . . created in a moment and perpetually renewed."[11] They tell them to validate the many, not just two, parts of themselves and to construct other selves into which they may move in their lived lives, fueled by the power of the stories that express their fantasies and those of their partners. They tell and listen to these stories both to revise their past histories and to express their imaginative view of possible futures. They tell them to celebrate the infinite variety of ways in which men and women have used storytelling to storm the oppressive barricades of gender and culture.

NOTES

ACKNOWLEDGMENTS

1. Wendy Doniger O'Flaherty, *Other Peoples' Myths.*

2. See Wendy Doniger, "From Great Neck to Swift Hall: Confessions of a Reluctant Historian of Religions"—and, someday, my novel, *Horses for Lovers, Dogs for Husbands.*

PRELUDE

1. I should state at the outset that the word *India* has different connotations in different chronological periods. In general, it is a shorter way of referring to what is now generally called *South Asia,* though that latter term usually includes Sri Lanka in the ancient period and Pakistan and Bangla Desh in the modern period, areas from which I have drawn almost no materials. The reason for this is that I am dealing almost exclusively with Hindu materials, and after the most ancient period of all, the Vedic (in which our only Indian texts are the Vedas, the Hindu canon), India and Hinduism ceased to be coterminous: ancient Sri Lanka became the site of Buddhism, modern Pakistan and, to some extent, Bangla Desh the site of Islam. Thus, where India technically should only be compared with another country, like Greece or England, Hinduism should be compared only with another religion, like Greek religion or Islam or Buddhism. I will therefore in general refer to Hindu, rather than Indian, stories. But there are times when I do wish to include the entire geographic area, and sometimes to touch specifically upon interactions of Hinduism with Buddhism and Islam, and on those occasions I will refer to Indian rather than Hindu phenomena.

2. I am indebted to David Tracy for this insight.

3. Maurice Olender, "Gender, Sex, and Mythology in Greece and Rome," 1–2.

4. For a further justification of this comparative method, see Wendy Doniger, *The Implied Spider.*

5. I am grateful to Gregory Nagy for persuading me that this distinction, as well as the more basic distinction between historical and morphological comparison, has to be clarified and stated from the start.

6. The arguments for and against Dumézil's theories are complex, and need not concern us here. See Bruce Lincoln, *Death, War, and Sacrifice,* and my introduction to that work (ix–xi).

7. Sheldon Pollock, "Literary History, Region, and Nation in South Asia," 136.

8. Wendy Doniger O'Flaherty, *Other Peoples' Myths;* Wendy Doniger, *The Implied Spider.*

CHAPTER ONE

1. *Ramayana* 6.103.15–25.

2. Euripides, *Trojan Women,* 865.

3. Paula Richman, *Many Ramayanas.*

4. *Ramayana* of Valmiki, 6.103–6; Wendy Doniger O'Flaherty, *Dreams, Illusion, and Other Realities,* 92; Wendy Doniger O'Flaherty, *Hindu Myths,* 198–204.

5. I have translated all the Sanskrit and Greek texts from the original, but have not reproduced them verbatim as I did in my Penguin editions; I have abbreviated them by cutting words and passages that are not essential to the tale I wish to tell; readers who wish to read the full text are referred to full English translations where they are available. Texts in other languages I have, in general, quoted verbatim from translations by other scholars and marked with the usual convention of quotation marks or (for long passages) indentation. Where I have summarized and reworded such translations, I have so indicated in the bibliographic notes. And where I have partly summarized and partly cited verbatim, I have separated my own summary with brackets and left un-bracketed the passages quoted verbatim; in the case of direct speech quoted verbatim, I have simply used quotation marks. I have taken these liberties only with stories in-dented as source texts; quotations within the body of my text are cited with the usual conventions. So, too, I have given titles to all the stories that I have translated myself and to stories that others translated without giving them a title, but I have kept other translators' titles where they exist (and identified them as "original titles" in the notes).

6. *Ramayana* 7.26.8–47, plus the verse excised from the critical edition after verse 47.

7. Ibid., 6, appendix 1, no. 3, ll. 249–59.

8. Ibid., 7.17.1–31.

9. Ibid., lines 6–10 excised after 6.48.7.

10. This may be as good a place as any to acknowledge my debt to Freud in many of my analyses of these texts. Though I do not find all Freudian approaches to all texts useful, I find it impossible to ignore certain basic Freudian ideas about symbolism, such as overdetermination (the ability of a symbol to stand for several valences at once), the Freudian error (an unconscious slip that reveals a deeper truth), the di-chotomy between the madonna or virgin and the whore (the chaste mother and the promiscuous mistress), and displacement, particularly upward displacement (the belief that parts of the body often stand in, as it were, like doubles, for other parts; in partic-ular that the genitals are often displaced upward to the head, mouth, or eyes).

11. *Brahmavaivarta Purana* 2.14.1–59.

12. *Ramayana* 3.42.14; 3.43.1–10, 21–23.

13. J. W. de Jong, *The Story of Rama in Tibet,* 153–62.

14. *Adhyatma-ramayana* 3.7.1–10.

15. There may be an ancient connection between the myth of Sita protected by fire and the Norse myth of Brunnhilde, whose virginity is protected when her father puts her to sleep within a circle of fire.

16. *Adhyatma-ramayana* 6.8.21.

17. Frank Whaling, *The Rise of the Religious Significance of Rama,* 138; Linda Hess, "Rejecting Sita."

18. *Ramacaritamanasa* of Tulsi Das, 3.23–24, 6.107–8.

19. *Ramacaritamanasa* of Tulsi Das 6.108.7.

20. Whaling, *The Rise of the Religious Significance of Rama,* 248.

21. David Shulman, "On Being a Stone: A Reading of the Tirupati *Puranas*," 13.

22. This docetic story was reported by Ireneus in the name of Basilides (Ireneus, Adv. Haer. 1.24.4) and was repeated in the *Second Treatise of the Great Seth,* one of the Gnostic texts found at Nag Hammadi (CG VII, 55.9–56.19). See Guy Stroumsa, "Madness and Divination in Early Christian Monasticism," 20.

23. *Brahmavaivarta Purana* 2.14.1–59.

24. *Mahabharata* 1.175.

25. *Sri Venkateca Mahatmiyam,* chap. 3, 11–12; trans. Norman Cutler.

26. Shulman, "On Being a Stone: A Reading of the Tirupati *Puranas*," 13, citing I. Munucaminayutu, *Tiruppati tirumalai yattirai . . .* (Cittur, 1928), 22.

27. *Ramacaritamanasa* of Tulsi Das, 1.49–53, 56–7, 97 (trans. Prasad).

28. Wendy Doniger O'Flaherty, *Siva, The Erotic Ascetic,* 298–99.

29. *Mahabhagavata Purana* 9–11.

30. David Shulman, *Tamil Temple Myths,* 324–5, citing *Tiruvarancaram* 5–7. I have simplified some of the names.

31. *Ramayana* 3.17.

32. *Ramayana* of Kamban, 2888–91; also summarized by David Shulman, "Sita and Satakantharavana," 12–16.

33. *Ramayana* of Kamban 2918.

34. *Ramankanatika* of Dharmagupta, also known as the *Balavagisvarakavi.* I am grateful to Deepak Sharma for this text, which he received from his aunt, Prof. Sita Nambiar, who believed it to have been composed in the fourteenth century. The palm leaf manuscript is described in the catalogue of the Buddhist Sanskrit Manuscripts in the University Library, Cambridge, by Cecil Bendall, 1883, p. 87, item 1409; and in the *Puratattvaprakasanamala* 5, Nepalarajakiya virapustakalayasthahastalikhilapustakanam brhatsuccipatram, 3.56. This is my summary of Prof. Nambiar's detailed synopsis of the contents of act 1, pp. 24–28.

35. The actual incident of fetching the *parijata* flower could have been inspired by the *Mahabharata,* where Draupadi (who is, as we have seen, an alter ego of Sita) asks one of her husbands to get her a special flower [*Mahabharata* 3.146], or from the episode in the *Ramayana* of Valmiki in which Hanuman is sent to bring back a magic herb to revive Rama and Lakshmana when they have fallen in battle [*Ramayana* 6.61].

36. R. K. Narayan, *The Ramayana,* 83–84.

37. *Ramayana* of Kamban 3309–15; see also the note on verse 3314 in Hart and Heifetz, *The Forest Book,* 359.

38. Denys Lombard and Christian Pelras, "The Ramayana in Indonesia," 957.

39. J. W. de Jong, *The Story of Rama in Tibet,* 368–86.

40. Ibid., 386–92.

41. Sheldon Pollock, "Ramayana and Political Imagination in India," 283.

42. *Ramayana* 6.106.15–16 *(pradharshayitum);* 3.50.9 *(pradharshitayam).*

43. *Shatapatha Brahmana* 2.1.2.4–5.

44. *Mahabharata* 3.213–15.

45. *Shiva Purana, Dharmasamhita,* 11.28–35.

46. For a discussion of the ambiguity of the oblation into fire as symbolic either of the male semen = fire placed in the woman = water or of melted butter = semen placed in a female = fire, see Wendy Doniger O'Flaherty, *Women, Androgynes, and Other Mythical Beasts,* 20–25.

47. *Harivamsha* 47–48; O'Flaherty, *Hindu Myths,* 204–13.

48. *Bhagavata Purana* 10.33.38.

49. Jiva Gosvamin, *Krishna Sandarbha,* 177, p. 101, cited by J. K. Brzezinski, "Does Krsna Marry?," 25.

50. Jiva Gosvamin, citing the *Kurma Purana* version of the story; cited by J. K. Brzezinski, "Does Krsna Marry?," 25.

51. Rupa Gosvamin, *Lalita-Madhava,* 1.54–5, 15, cited by J. K. Brzezinski, "Does Krsna Marry?," 26.

52. Edward C. Dimock, personal communication. This is a tradition in later Bengali commentaries.

53. Kirin Narayan, *Mondays on the Dark Night of the Moon,* 86; a propos of story 11, "Honi."

54. Whaling, *The Rise of the Religious Significance of Rama,* 126, 150.

55. See Camille J. Bulcke, *Ram-Katha: Utpatti aur Vikas* (Allahabad: Hindi Parisad Visvavidyala, 1950), 345, as cited by Whaling, *The Rise of the Religious Significance of Rama,* 126.

56. *Ramayana* 6.68.1–28.

57. Ibid., 7.89.4.

58. *Uttararamacarita* of Bhavabhuti, act 3.

59. O'Flaherty, *Dreams,* 92–97.

60. David Shulman, "Sita and Satakantharavana."

61. E. V. Ramasami, cited by Lloyd Rudolph, "Urban Life and Populist Radicalism," 288.

62. I cannot hope to add anything to the enormous volume of classical scholarship on this subject; I will merely summarize it, particularly the excellent analyses by Froma Zeitlin, Norman Austin, and Roberto Calasso, selecting the parts that seem to provide the most vivid parallels and contrasts to the Hindu material that is my own contribution to this comparison.

63. Homer, *Odyssey,* 4.276.

64. Froma Zeitlin, "The Lady Vanishes," 1.

65. Linda Lee Clader, *Helen,* 71.

66. Roberto Calasso, *The Marriage of Cadmus and Harmony,* 122–23, 139, 130.

67. Aeschylus, *Agamemnon,* 416–24 (trans. Grene and O'Flaherty).

68. Herodotus, *History,* 2.112–20 (trans. Grene).

69. Herodotus, *History,* 1.119.

70. Herodotus, *History,* 1.4 (trans. Grene).

71. Hesiod, fragment 358 M-W. See Gregory Nagy, *Greek Mythology,* 419.

72. Plato, *Phaedrus* 243a.

73. Plato, *Republic* 586 C [2.365 C]; cf. *Republic* 598 B 6 ff.

74. Pausanias, *Description of Greece,* 3 (Laconia), 19.13–20.1.

75. Ibid., 4 (Messenia), 33.7.

76. Gregory Nagy, *Greek Mythology,* 420.

77. Norman Austin, *Helen,* 10.

78. Froma Zeitlin, "Travesties of Gender and Genre," 202.

79. Austin, *Helen,* 99.

80. Euripides, *Helen,* 31–67, 1218–19.

81. Ibid., 425.

82. Homer, *Odyssey,* 1.15, 12.82.

83. Euripides, *Helen,* 582–8; Froma Zeitlin, "The Lady Vanishes," 29.

84. Austin, *Helen,* 167.

85. Ibid., 162.

86. Euripides, *Helen,* 165, 703.

87. Austin, *Helen,* 161.

88. Ibid., 622, 575.

89. Aristophanes, *Thesmophoriazousae,* 850 ff.

90. Zeitlin, "Travesties of Gender," 194, 208.

91. Austin, *Helen,* 138.

92. Euripides, *Helen,* 43.

93. Hugo von Hofmannsthal, "Die ägyptische Helena," 473.

94. Hugo von Hofmannsthal, *Die ägyptische Helena,* libretto.

95. Homer, *Odyssey,* 4.229.

96. Scholiast on Aristeides, *Orations,* 3.150.

97. Austin, *Helen,* 98.

98. Zeitlin, "The Lady Vanishes," 17.

99. Plato, *Republic* 586 C [2.365 C]; cf. 598 B 6.

100. For other mythological challenges to Plato's caves, see O'Flaherty, *Other Peoples' Myths,* 33–37.

101. E. Panofsky, *Idea,* 161.

102. Apollodorus, *Epitome* 3.5.

103. Pindar, *Pythian* 2.21–48 in *The Odes of Pindar* (trans. Lattimore).

104. Apollodorus, *Epitome* 1.20. The Loeb editor also cites Pindar, *Pythian,* 2.21(39)–48(88); and various commentaries of Scholiasts on Euripides, *Phoenissae* (1185), Homer, *Odyssey,* 21.303; Apollonius of Rhodes, *Argon,* 3.62; Hyginus, *Fab.* 62; Servis on Virgil's *Aeneid* 6.286.

105. Hesiod, *Catalogue of Women,* fr. 148 Rz, 260 M-W; cited by Zeitlin, "The Lady Vanishes," 3.

106. Hellanicus, FGH 4 F 23; Conon, FGR 26 Fl. 21; cited by Zeitlin, "The Lady Vanishes," 3.

107. Plutarch, *Moralia,* fr. 157, 1 (Sandbach).

108. Calasso, *The Marriage of Cadmus and Harmony,* 295.

109. Sophocles' lost play, the *Lacedaemonian Women,* and the pseudo-Euripidean *Rhesos,* cited by Zeitlin, "The Lady Vanishes," 21.

110. Euripides, *Trojan Women,* 525; Antisthenes the Sophist, *Odysseus,* cited by Zeitlin, "The Lady Vanishes," 21.

111. Michel Woronoff, cited in Zeitlin, "The Lady Vanishes," 21–22.

112. Calasso, *The Marriage of Cadmus and Harmony,* 228.

113. Ibid., 229.

114. Euripides, *Helen,* 260–63.

115. Calasso, *The Marriage of Cadmus and Harmony,* 151.

116. Ibid., 122.

117. Shakespeare, *Midsummer Night's Dream,* 5.1.

118. Goethe, *Faust,* part 2, act 3, 8879–81.

119. Shakespeare, *All's Well That Ends Well,* 5.3, 1.3; and Shakespeare, *Troilus and Cressida,* 2.2.

120. Christopher Marlowe, *Dr. Faustus,* scene 14.

121. Cited by Matthew Adkins at the memorial service for Arthur Adkins, Rockefeller Memorial Chapel, the University of Chicago, March 13, 1996.

122. Doniger, *The Implied Spider*, chaps. 1 and 4.

123. John Erskine, *The Private Life of Helen of Troy*, 43, 263, 55.

124. James Branch Cabell, *Jurgen*, 160.

125. Wendy Doniger O'Flaherty, "Myths and Methods in the Dark."

126. Iris Murdoch, *The Sea, The Sea*, 175, 352–53, 491–92.

127. Jeffrey Toobin, "The Trouble with Sex," 48. Earlier he had remarked that, "In legal if not Biblical terms, Paula begat Monica." I wonder if he meant to imply here that Monica was the shadow double of Paula—or that a war was going to be fought and lost for the sake of a woman who was in every significant sense unreal.

128. The date of the *Rig Veda* is much debated, but it is generally localized somewhere between 1500 and 900 B.C.E.

129. *Rig Veda* 10.17.1–2.

130. Maurice Bloomfield, "Contributions," 172.

131. She is briefly called Surenu in the *Skanda Purana* [7.1.11.75] and the *Bhavishya Purana*, and Sarenu in the *Samba Purana* version cited by Hazra, *Studies*, 1:42.

132. *Harivamsha* 8.1–48.

133. *Rig Veda* 10.72.8–9; Wendy Doniger O'Flaherty, *The Rig Veda*, 37–39.

134. *Shatapatha Brahmana* 3.1.3.3; see O'Flaherty, *Women*, 174–76.

135. *Harivamsha* 8.4.

136. *Markandeya Purana* 102.12–19.

137. *Skanda Purana* 7.1.11.79. The *Samba Purana* has the opposite reading: "The Sun in the old days took on a human form to make love [rantum]."

138. *Samba Purana* 11.4b–5a, cited in Hazra, *Studies*, 1:42.

139. *Mahabharata* 1.104; 3.290–94; 5.138–42.

140. *Rig Veda* 10.14.2, 10.13.4; *Atharva Veda* 18.3.13, 8.3.137; Bruce Lincoln, *Priests, Warriors, and Cattle*, 82.

141. Reading *adhrishya* (unable to be raped) for *adrishya* (unable to be looked at). *Harivamsha* 1.8.36.

142. *Markandeya Purana* 105.1–13.

143. O'Flaherty, *Women, Androgynes*, 211–12.

144. *Markandeya Purana* 74.8 and 23.

145. *Amar Chitra Katha*, "Surya."

146. Maurice Bloomfield, "Contributions," 177–78.

147. O'Flaherty, *Women, Androgynes*, 149{endash}282.

148. *Harivamsha*, four verses excised from the critical edition after 8.14.

149. O'Flaherty, *Women, Androgynes*, 213–37.

150. *The Laws of Manu* 5.148; *The Laws of Manu* (trans. Doniger and Smith), 115.

151. *Nirukta* of Yaska, 12.10. This is also the version told by Shaunaka in the *Brihaddevata*, 6.162–3, 7.1–6.

152. *Gopatha Brahmana* 1.3.

153. *Rig Veda* 10.95; O'Flaherty, *The Rig Veda*, 253–56.

154. *Shatapatha Brahmana* 11.5.1.1–17; O'Flaherty, *Women, Androgynes*, 180–81.

155. Barbara Fass Leavy, *In Search of the Swan Maiden*, 101.

156. *Matsya Purana* 11.1–39.

157. *Skanda Purana* 7.1.11.77.

158. *Bhagavata Purana* 8.13.8–10.

159. Vettam Mani's gloss of the *Vishnu Purana* variant, 485.

160. Personal communication from Kirin Narayan, July 1997. The image of Ran-

dhal-ma, from an old poster in the collection of Kirin Narayan's grandmother, is on the cover of this book.

161. *Rig Veda* 8.10.2, 10.63.7, 10.70.8; 1.112.16, 1.112.18, 3.60.3, 9.96.12, 10.76.3, 1.68.7.

162. Gregory Nagy, *Greek Mythology*, 111.

163. Saranyu's equine textual connection finds a curious parallel in English, which refers to a very literal translation used as a commentary, or as an illegal aid on exams, as a "pony" or a "trot."

164. Stella Kramrisch, "Two," 130, 134–35.

165. O'Flaherty, *Dreams*. It is this heavier meaning of "resemblance" that Goethe may have had in mind when he wrote the closing lines of *Faust:* "All that is transient is just a likeness *(Gleichnis)*. . . . The eternal female draws us on." Chaya is the "likeness" of Saranyu the Eternal (or, at least, ur) Female.

166. Herman Lommel, "Vedische Einzelstudien," 243–57.

167. Bloomfield, "The Marriage of Saranyu," 181; Albrecht Weber, *Indische Studien* 17, 310 ff. Adalbert Kuhn ("Saranyu-Erinnus," 448) interpreted *Rig Veda* 10.17.1 to say not that Vivasvant was giving a wedding *for* his daughter, but that he was marrying her himself. Kuhn suggested that "the anger of the gods regarding the wedding of the father and the daughter also explains why the gods hide Saranyu and slip a look-like under Vivasvant."

168. See Bruce Lincoln, *Myth, Cosmos, and Society,* for "man" and "twin"; and Lincoln, *Priests, Warriors,* 80–82, and Nagy, *Greek Mythology,* 111, for Manu and Yama as twins.

169. *Rig Veda* 8.52.1, 10.62.9, 11. The tenth-century commentator Sayana glosses *savarni* as *savarnaputra,* "son of the resembling *male.*" *Rig Veda* 8.51.1 calls Manu the son of Samvarana—a man whom later tradition regards as the husband of Tapati, a daughter of Saranyu's Shadow.

170. *Nirukta* of Yaska, 12.10.

171. Bruce Lincoln, *Myth, Cosmos, and Society.*

172. The *Markandeya Purana,* in particular, devotes many chapters to the multiple Manus.

173. *Harivamsha* 8.1–48.

174. *Bhagavata Purana* 8.13.8–10.

175. *Mahabharata* 1.160–63.

176. *Matsya Purana* 11.1–39.

177. *Vishnu Purana* 3.2.1–20; *Markandeya Purana* 74–75, 103–5.

178. Kramrisch, "Two," 135–36.

179. O'Flaherty, *Siva,* 211–12; O'Flaherty, *Women,* 27.

180. O'Flaherty, *Siva,* 303.

181. *Markandeya Purana* 81. Kirin Narayan tells me that her family's guru used to say that if you recite the first verse of the Durga Saptashati, it is as good as the whole book. Personal communication, December 1997.

182. O'Flaherty, *Other Peoples' Myths,* chap. 3.

183. Hesiod and Aeschylus, for instance, regarded Zeus with far more awe and reverence than did their contemporaries Homer and Sophocles, respectively.

184. Homer, *Odyssey,* 4.796.

185. Homer, *Iliad,* 22.227–95; 3.381–83; 5.311, 449.

186. Homer, *Odyssey,* 4.121.

187. Ibid., 4.273–77.

188. Eustatius on Homer, *Odyssey,* 23.218.

189. Sarah B. Pomeroy, *Goddesses, Whores, Wives, and Slaves,* 17, 20–21.

190. Sheldon Pollock, "Ramayana and Political Imagination in India."

191. Otto Skutsch, "Helen," 189, citing J. Ehni in 1890 and V. Pisani in 1928.

192. A. H. Krappe, "Lancelot et Guenièvre."

193. Cristiano Grottanelli, "The King's Grace and the Helpless Woman."

194. Cornelia Dimmitt, "Sita: Mother Goddess and Sakti."

195. *Ramayana* 6.106.3.

196. See O'Flaherty, *Women, Androgynes,* and Barbara Fass Leavy, *In Search of the Swan Maiden.*

197. *Ramayana* 6.103.17.

198. Ibid., 6.106.17–18.

199. Paul Friedrich, *The Meaning of Aphrodite.*

200. Greek *dios thugater,* Sanskrit *divas duhitar.*

201. Linda Lee Clader, *Helen,* 81.

202. Ptolemy Chennos, preserved in Phtoios's *Bibliotheke* 149a, cited by Otto Skutsch, "Helen: Her Name and Nature," 189.

203. Linda Lee Clader suggests a number of other etymologies, but they seem equally dubious to me.

204. Skutsch, "Helen: Her Name and Nature," 189.

205. Adalbert Kuhn, "Saranyu-Erinnus"; Pausanias, *Description of Greece,* 8.25; and O'Flaherty, *Women, Androgynes,* 190–91.

206. Pausanias, *Description of Greece,* 8.25.4–8; O'Flaherty, *Women, Androgynes,* 190–91.

207. Homer, *Odyssey,* 4.273–77.

208. Skutsch, "Helen: Her Name and Nature," 189.

209. Gregory Nagy, "Phaethon, Sappho's Phaon, and the White Rock of Leukas."

210. Clader, *Helen,* 50.

211. Ibid., 62.

212. Ibid., 72.

213. Ibid., 82.

214. *Markandeya Purana* 74.1–7; *Skanda Purana* 7.1.11.81.

215. When the woman whom Vyasa is sent to impregnate closes her eyes, Vyasa curses her child, Dhritarashtra, to be blind. (*Mahabharata* 1.99–100); see Doniger and Spinner, "Misconceptions."

216. *Markandeya Purana* 105.15–17.

217. In Christian mythology, it is God himself, no longer the sun, who is associated with the eye, as Meister Eckhart notes: "The eye with which I see God is the same as the eye with which God sees me" (Meister Eckhart, *An Anthology of Sermons,* 288).

218. *Rig Veda* 10.16.3; O'Flaherty, *The Rig Veda,* 49.

219. European mythology reverses the argument, saying that we *can* look at the sun because it is an eye. Thus Goethe: "If the eye were not of the sun, It could not see the sun" [Wär nicht das Auge sonnenhaft—Die Sonne könnt es nie erblicken].

220. Doniger, *The Implied Spider,* chap. 1.

221. O'Flaherty, *Other Peoples' Myths,* 157; Robert Jungk, *Heller als tausend Sonnen,* 211 (*Brighter Than a Thousand Suns,* 202).

222. *Bhagavad Gita* 11.25–29.

223. Plato, *Republic,* 6:508B–D.

224. Plato, *The Sophist,* 239 D, 266 B–C.

225. Ibid., 254 A.

226. Sigmund Freud, "Medusa's Head."

227. De la Rouchefoucald, *Maximes et réflexions morales,* 8, maxim 26; Georges Bataille, "The Solar Anus," 8.

228. Marina Warner, "Stolen Shadows," 41.

229. Charles Malamoud, "Les dieux n'ont pas d'ombre," 242; translated, rather differently, by David White, 196–97.

230. *Shatapatha Brahmana*

231. *Brihaddevata* of Shaunaka, 6.162–63, 7.1–6.

232. Malamoud, "Les dieux n'ont pas d'ombre," 243.

233. *Ramayana* 9.36.10.

234. In Tennessee Williams's play *The Night of the Iguana,* when Shannon sardonically remarks, "Don't tell me you have a dark side to your nature," Hannah replies, "I'm sure I don't have to tell a man as experienced and knowledgeable as you, Mr. Shannon, that everything has its shadowy side? . . . Everything in the whole solar system has a shadowy side to it except the sun itself—the sun is the single exception" (p. 353).

235. Sayana, in his tenth-century C.E. commentary on *Rig Veda* 1.84.14–15, explains:

> The cow of Tvastr—who is the blazing sun—is a traveler in the house— that is, the orb—of the moon. Her own name—that is, the energy of the sun—is hidden—disappearing at night. But they recognize her by her rays, for the sun's rays are reflected in the clear circle of the moon, which is made of water, and these rays reflected there create a sign or image that looks the same even when cast upon the moon. This is the meaning. When the solar energy that disappears at night enters the circle of the moon, then, dispelling the darkness of night, it illuminates everything as if it were day. The sun, which has this kind of energy, is Indra himself.

See also O'Flaherty, *Hindu Myths,* 59.

236. Ann Gold, "Spirit Possession Perceived and Performed in Rural Rajasthan," 38.

237. Giraudoux, *Amphitryon,* 58.

238. Otto Rank, "The Double as Immortal Self," in *Beyond Psychology,* 74.

239. Sigmund Freud, "Psycho-analytic Notes on an Autobiographical Account of a Case of Paranoia (Dementia Paranoides)," 54, 384.

240. Ibid., 80.

241. Salomon Reinach, *Cultes, mythes, et religions,* 3.80.

242. Otto Keller, *Thiere des classischen Alterthums,* 268. In 447 n. 295, Keller cites Aristotle, *Historia Animalium* 9.34, as well as Lucan, 9.902–6, Pliny, *Natural History* 10.10 and 15, W. Antigonus c. 46, 52, and Physiologus c. 6. Keller, who refers to the myth as "a probably Egyptian fable" and an "Oriental fable," says that the eagle is able to look right at the Sun without blinking and that "he also expects this ability in his young, and if not, he regards them as false brood *(falsches Brut)."*

243. Aristotle, *Historia Animalium,* 9.34, 620a. The editor supplies a footnote on the phrase "looking at the sun" *(pros ton helion blepein):* "An Egyptian myth: cf. Horap 1.6 . . . Plin. 10.3; Antigonus, Mirab. 46 (52); Ael. 2.26; Phile, 1.14; etc."

244. Isak Dinesen (in "The Monkey," 136) draws a similar connection between

looking at the Sun and distinguishing between legitimate and illegitimate children: "The peasants of our province have the saying that no child born in wedlock can look straight at the sun; only bastards are capable of it." Does this mean that only the child of the false Sun goddess, the shadow, can look at the Sun? And does this mean, in turn, that we normal mortals, who cannot look at the Sun, are the true offspring of Saranyu after all?

245. *Rig Veda* 10.10.8–9.

246. Ibid., 1.35.7.

247. Ibid., 2.27.9.

248. Ibid., 10.10.8–9.

249. Sigmund Freud, *Totem and Taboo,* "The Omnipotence of Thought," 122.

250. O'Flaherty, "The Interaction of Saguna and Nirguna Images of Deity."

251. David Shulman, "Concave and Full," 6, 8.

252. Arlene Mazak, "Multidimensionality," 400.

253. Gold, "Spirit Possession Perceived and Performed in Rural Rajasthan," 38.

254. John Strong, *The Legend and Cult of Upagupta,* 29, 31.

255. Samuel Beal, *Si-Yu-Ki,* 1.93–94.

256. Pierre Blanchard, *Le plutarque de la jeunesse.*

257. Lorraine Daston, response to an early draft of chapter 8 of this book, at the Einstein Forum, Berlin, December 9, 1997.

258. Marina Warner, "Stolen Shadows, Lost Souls," 49. Warner adds (58) that the ancient belief that the shadow/sculpture preserves the soul resurfaces as the myth, perpetuated by anthropologists, that "natives" believe that the (anthropologist's) camera steals their souls.

259. *Kamasutra* 2.3.28–29.

260. *Mahabharata* 12.320.1–40; Doniger, "Echoes of the *Mahabharata,*" 48–50.

261. Rostand, *Cyrano de Bergerac,* 110. In Steve Martin's film version, *Roxanne,* the Cyrano character says, "It was as though I had looked at the sun too long. I could close my eyes and see."

262. Pindar, *Pythian* 8.95–97.

263. Gregory Nagy, *Pindar's Homer,* 195.

264. Richard F. Gombrich, "The Consecration of a Buddha Image."

265. Strabo, *Geography,* 6.1.14.

266. Euripides, *Iphigeneia at Tauris,* 1165–70.

267. Calasso, *The Marriage of Cadmus and Harmony,* 229.

268. Pliny the Elder, *Natural History,* 160.

269. Erskine, *The Private Life,* 55, 147.

270. Homer, *Iliad,* 1.590.

271. Homer, *Odyssey,* 8.

272. *Uttaratantra* of Maitreya, cited in A. K. Coomaraswamy, "The Interior Image," 16–17. Also *Divyavadana* 547, cited by Coomaraswamy, "Chaya," 279.

273. *Shrishriramakrishnalilaprasanga* 2.7.4.

274. Personal communication from Jeffrey Kripal, January 1993.

275. Marina Warner, "Stolen Shadows, Lost Souls," 49.

276. E. H. Gombrich, *Art and Illusion;* O'Flaherty, *Dreams,* 279–83.

277. François Flahault, "Imagination and Mythology in Contemporary Literature (Tolkien, Lovecraft) and Science Fiction," 790.

278. *Kamasutra* 5.6.24–25.

279. Advertisement in the *New Yorker*, September 30, 1991, 59.

280. *Kojiki*, bk. 1, chaps. 4–17, pp. 50–86, plus chap. 39, pp. 139–40.

281. This is documented in *Rig Veda* 10.10; a significant difference: the Indian siblings do *not* commit incest; she tries in vain to persuade him.

282. O'Flaherty, *Women*, 246–62.

283. *Kojiki*, Philippi, 85.

284. Doniger, *The Implied Spider*, chap. 5.

285. O'Flaherty, *Dreams*, 95–96.

286. Joyce Wadler, "Public Lives; Ex-Stripper Reveals Herself, in a Memoir," *New York Times*, July 24, 1998, B2.

287. Elaine Scarry, *The Body in Pain*, 48–49.

288. Cathy Winkler, "Rape Trauma: Contexts of Meaning."

289. Ian Hacking, "Double Consciousness in Britain, 1814–1875," 137, citing Robert MacNish.

290. Ian Hacking, "Double Consciousness," 137, citing S. L. Mitchill, *The Medical Repository of Original Essays*, 185–86.

291. Ian Hacking, "Double Consciousness," 140, citing Pierre Janet, *The Major Symptoms of Hysteria*.

292. Corbett H. Thigpen and Hervey M. Cleckley, *The Three Faces of Eve*, 23.

293. Ibid., 35.

294. Ibid., 35–37.

295. Ibid., 86, 91.

296. Ibid., 195–97.

297. Ralph Slovenko, "The Multiple Personality," 701.

298. R. G. Blumenthal, "After All These Years, Here Is the Fourth Face of Eve: Plaintiff"; see also " 'Faces of Eve' Woman Settles Film Co. Lawsuit," *New York City Tribune*, June 21, 1990, 5.

299. Arnold, "Whose Life Is It, Anyway?"

300. Jeanine Basinger, *How Hollywood Spoke to Women*, 100.

301. "Sister Charged with Murder, and Identity Switch," *New York Times*, July 17, 1997, A16.

302. Richard Winnington, cited by Leslie Halliwell, *Halliwell's Film Guide*, s.v. "*Stolen Life, A.*"

303. Elaine Showalter, *Sexual Anarchy*, 125.

304. Hugo Williams, "Commentary," *Times Literary Supplement*, February 25, 1994, 14.

305. Homer, *Odyssey*, 10.

306. I thought this was in Milan Kundera's *The Unbearable Lightness of Being*, but it's not.

307. Doniger, *The Bedtrick*.

308. *Lancelot*, part 3, 2:245–80.

309. William Butler Yeats, *The Autobiography of William Butler Yeats*, 340.

Chapter Two

1. *Harivamsha* 111.11–29, discussed in O'Flaherty, *Other Peoples' Myths*, 102–3.

2. Medhatithi, commenting on *The Laws of Manu* 11.106 (104 in the Dave edition). See *The Laws of Manu*, 261 (trans. Doniger and Smith).

3. *Shatapatha Brahmana* 3.3.4.18; see O'Flaherty, "The Case of the Stallion's Wife."

4. *Ramayana* 7.30.17–36.

5. Ibid., 7.26.8–47, plus the verse excised from the critical edition after verse 47.

6. *Kamasutra* 1.2.36.

7. Thomas Laqueur, *Making Sex.*

8. *Taittiriya Samhita* 2.5.1; O'Flaherty, *Origins of Evil,* 157, and chap. 6.

9. O'Flaherty, "The Case of the Stallion's Wife."

10. *Ramayana* 1.47.15–31.

11. Ibid., verses excised after 7.30.36.

12. *Padma Purana* 1.56.15–53.

13. R. K. Narayan, *The Ramayana,* 21.

14. *Brahmavaivarta Purana* 4.61.

15. *Skanda Purana* 5.3.136.

16. Personal communication from Serena Niles, October 27, 1996. This is true of Hindu brides in Sri Lanka; whether it is also true in India I have yet to ascertain.

17. Ibn Battuta, *Travels in Asia and Africa, 1325–1354,* 156. Thanks to Shantanu Phukan for this citation.

18. *Brahma Purana* 87.

19. *Ganesha Purana, Upasana Khanda,* chaps. 30, 32–33.

20. Homer, *Iliad,* 14.223.

21. *Kathasaritsagara* 17.137–148 (2.46 in Tawney trans.).

22. Kamban, *Ramayana,* cited and trans. by A. K. Ramanujan, "Three Hundred Ramayanas," 29.

23. R. K. Narayan, *The Ramayana,* 21.

24. A. K. Ramanujan, "Three Hundred Ramayanas," 29.

25. *Ahalyasankrandanamu* of Samukhamu Venkata Krsnappa Nayakudu (Madras, 1927), translated by David Shulman in Shulman, Rao, and Subrahmanyam, *Symbols of Substance,* 145–68, and by V. Narayana Rao in a later, unpublished MS. The version here borrows from both; I have somewhat condensed and reworded the story.

26. Shulman, Rao, and Subrahmanyam, *Symbols of Substance,* 148.

27. *Adhyatma-ramayana* 2.4.77–78; see O'Flaherty, *Dreams,* 130.

28. Shulman, Rao, and Subrahmanyam, *Symbols of Substance,* 159.

29. *Yogavasishtha* 3.89–90; see O'Flaherty, *Dreams,* 226.

30. *Ramayana* 7.30.17–36.

31. *Mahabharata* 12.329.14.1.

32. *Shatapatha Brahmana* 3.3.4.18; 12.7.1.10–12; 5.2.3.8.

33. *Mahabharata* 12.329.14.2.

34. *Ramayana* 1.47.15–31.

35. *Mahabharata* 13.41.21.

36. *The Laws of Manu,* 8.352, 9.237.

37. *Deshopadesha* of Kshemendra, act 2.

38. R. K. Narayan, *The Ramayana,* 21.

39. *Ganesha Purana, Upasana Khanda,* chap. 31.

40. R. K. Narayan, *The Ramayana,* 21.

41. *Taittiriya Samhita* 2.5.1; O'Flaherty, *Origins of Evil,* 157.

42. Personal communication from Arjun Mahey, November 1994.

43. *Padma Purana* 1.56.15–53.

44. *Kathasaritsagara* 17.147–48.

45. *Mahabharata* 1.203.15–26.

46. Cf. Agni, at *Rig Veda* 1.79.12; cf. also *Rig Veda* 10.90.1; 10.81.3; 10.121.1; O'Flaherty, *The Rig Veda*, 30, 35, 199.

47. *Brahmavaivarta Purana* 4.47.31–32 *(netrayoni)*.

48. O'Flaherty, "When a Lingam Is Just a Good Cigar."

49. *Jaiminiya Brahmana* 1.161–3, 2.440–42; O'Flaherty, *Tales of Sex and Violence*, 102–3, 97–100.

50. Maurice Olender, "Gender, Sex, and Mythology in Greece and Rome," 3.

51. *Kaushitaki Brahmana* 23.7.5–12.

52. Compare the more famous Shunahshepha, "Dog-penis," in the *Aitareya Brahmana* 7.13–18.

53. *Kaushitaki Brahmana* 23.7.5–12, with commentary, the *Vyakhya* of Udaya, 3:521.

54. Geza Roheim, "Aphrodite, or the Woman with a Penis."

55. *Rig Veda* 10.108; O'Flaherty, *The Rig Veda*, 156–58.

56. For the demon with teeth in his vagina, see *Padma Purana* 1.46.1–32, 47–108, 119–21; *Skanda Purana* 1.2.27–29 (the version translated in O'Flaherty, *Hindu Myths*, 251–61); *Matsya Purana* 154–57; Doniger, *The Bedtrick*; and Don Handelman and David Shulman, *God Inside Out*, 154–58. For the demon Blood-seed, see *Vamana Purana* 44.30–38; *Markandeya Purana* 88.39–61; *Matsya Purana* 179.1–86; O'Flaherty, *Women*, 34.

57. Otto Rank, *The Double*, 14.

58. Charles Passage, preface to Passage and Mantinband, *Amphitryon*, final page.

59. Homer, *Odyssey*, 2.266–68; Homer, *Iliad*, 14.323; Herodotus, *History*, 2.43–45.

60. Nauck, *Tragicorum Graecorum Fragmenta*, 156, 386 ff.

61. Homer, *Odyssey*, 2.266–68.

62. Homer, *Iliad*, 14.323.

63. Herodotus, *History*, 2.43–45.

64. Ovid, *Metamorphoses*, 6.112; for the Latin *cepit*, the Loeb translator gives "cheated." The word more literally means "captured, won over."

65. Hesiod, *Shield of Hercules* 11 ff. and 79 ff.

66. Apollodorus, *Library*, 2.4.5–8.

67. Clader, *Helen*, 47–48.

68. Roberto Calasso, *The Marriage*, 126.

69. *Bhagavata Purana* 9.20.34–38.

70. Plautus, *Amphitruo*, lines 103–10, 480–94, pp. 43, 61.

71. Jean Giraudoux, *Amphitryon*, 38.

72. Passage, preface to Passage and Mantinband, *Amphitryon*, 11.

73. I owe this metaphor to Ginger Griffin; personal communication, December 1996.

74. Molière, *Amphitryon*, ll. 1691 ff., pp. 183–84.

75. Kleist, *Amphitryon*, 3.11.

76. Jean Giraudoux, *Amphitryon*, 62.

77. Ibid., 24–25.

78. Ibid., 5–7.

79. Ibid., 88.

80. Kleist, *Amphitryon*, 2.5.

81. Homer, *Iliad*, 14.323.

82. Behrman, *Amphitryon 38*, 12.

83. Wendy Doniger, *The Bedtrick.*

84. Kleist, *Amphitryon*, 2.5.

85. Ibid., 2.2.

86. Ibid., 3.11

87. In French, *sosie* means "a person who bears a perfect resemblance to someone else" (*Le petit Robert*, s.v. "sosie": "de Sosie, nom de l'esclave d'Amphitryon dont Mercure prend l'aspect. Personne qui a une parfaite ressemblance avec une autre").

88. The term occurs in J. de Rotrou's *Les Sosies*, in 1638 (*Le petit Robert*, s.v. "sosie").

89. Molière, *Amphitryon*, ll. 1470 ff., p. 176.

90. Kleist, *Amphitryon*, 2.4.

91. Ibid., 3.1.

92. Molière, *Amphitryon*, ll. 1200 ff., p. 165.

93. Kleist, *Amphitryon*, 3.5.

94. Ibid., 3.10.

95. Doniger, *The Bedtrick.*

96. Kleist, *Amphitryon*, 3.11.

97. In S. N. Behrman's telling she says: "If I were you, Leda, I'd revenge myself. He didn't even make an honest legend of you" (2.2, p. 125).

98. In Behrman's version: "Jupiter will enter your bedroom and you'll never know the difference" (2.2, p. 129).

99. Hesiod tells the story twice, in the *Theogony* and the *Works and Days*. I have taken the passage from the *Works and Days* 57–104.

100. Froma Zeitlin, "Travesties of Gender," 202.

101. Nicole Loraux, "Origins of Mankind in Greek Myths," 391.

102. Ibid., 392.

103. Stephanie Nelson, private communication, January 1994.

104. Rudolf Otto, *The Idea of the Holy.*

105. Jean-Paul Vernant, "Greek Cosmogonic Myths," 123.

106. Marie-Hélène Huet, *Monstrous Imagination*, 38.

107. Walter Ruben, *Krsna: Konkordanz und Kommentar der Motive seines Heldenlebens.*

108. Giraudoux, *Amphitryon*, 74.

109. Apollodorus, *Library*, 2.10.

110. Herodotus, *History*, 6.61–69 (trans. Grene).

111. Nagy, *Pindar's Homer*, 336–37, points out the slurs on Demaratus's legitimacy and Ariston's fertility.

112. Euripides, *Bacchae.*

113. Pseudo-Callisthenes, "Alexander Romance," 653.

114. Ibid., 654.

115. Ibid., 650–735; my condensation.

116. A. K. Ramanujan, "Towards a Counter-system: Women's Tales," 47–54.

117. Wendy Doniger, "Playing the Field."

118. Nathalie Zemon Davis remarks of one reading of the case of Martin Guerre, whose wife Bertrande did or did not recognize his impostor: "It also casts Bertrande as a dupe, understandable given 'the weakness of her sex, easily deceived by the cunning and craftiness of men.' " Yet, in Davis's opinion, Bertrande "had to manipulate the image of the woman-easily-deceived, a skill that women often displayed before officers of

justice any time it was to their advantage." Nathalie Zemon Davis, *The Return of Martin Guerre,* 109–10, 68.

119. For a comprehensive discussion of ways in which men and women do and do not recognize impostors in their beds, see Doniger, *The Bedtrick.*

120. R. Howard Bloch, *Medieval Misogyny,* 22, citing Schopenhauer.

121. John Le Carré, *The Little Drummer Girl,* 139.

122. Ann Gold, personal communication, June 1996.

Chapter Three

1. *Rig Veda* 1.116.10.

2. *Jaiminiya Brahmana* 3.120–29; O'Flaherty, *Tales of Sex and Violence,* 64–66.

3. *Shatapatha Brahmana* 4.1.4.1–14. See O'Flaherty, *Tales of Sex and Violence.*

4. *Mahabharata* 3.122–24.

5. *Devi Purana* 7.2.53.

6. *Amar Chitra Katha,* "The Story of Sukanya."

7. *Mahabharata* 3.122.1–27.

8. *Bhagavata Purana* 9.3.16–23.

9. *Devi Purana* 7.2.3–65, 3.1–64.

10. Ibid., 7.4.1–56, 5.1–59.

11. I owe the insights in this paragraph to a personal communication from David Shulman, July 20, 1993.

12. O'Flaherty, "Horses and Snakes."

13. *Mahabharata* 3.52–54.

14. From Nannaya's *Nalopakhyanamu,* in Telugu, translation by David Shulman and Velcheru Narayana Rao. Personal communication, August 1996.

15. *Padma Purana* 1.56.15–53.

16. *The Laws of Manu* 5.96 lists eight World-Protectors.

17. Introduction to the *Kusha Jataka,* no. 531.

18. *Kathasaritsagara* 56 [9.6].271.

19. Malamoud emends the text when he adds the phrase "they have no shadow at all," in his article expressly devoted to the shadowlessness of the gods.

20. *Markandeya Purana* 58–61. See Doniger, *The Bedtrick.*

21. Allasani Peddana, *prabandha* about Manu Svarocisha, based on the *Markandeya Purana;* portions translated and annotated by David Shulman in "First Man, Forest Mother," 141–42.

22. David Shulman, "First Man," translating verse 2.33, 149–50.

23. O'Flaherty, *Dreams,* chap. 6.

24. Shulman, "First Man," 150.

25. *Naishadiyacarita* 13.2–8, 14.18–22, 14.46–47.

26. Ibid. 1.30, 1.38, 2.104.

27. Ibid. 5.66, 6.14–15, 21, 33, 35, 41–44, 74.

28. Ibid. 6.48–54.

29. Ibid. 8.16, 18, 29, 31, 46.

30. Ibid. 9.137.

31. Ibid. 10.18–20, 23, 33–34.

32. Ibid. 10.36, 42; 14.18–24.

33. See Doniger, *The Bedtrick.*

34. David Shulman, "On Being Human in the Sanskrit Epic."

35. *Naishadiyacarita* 20.12–13.

36. Susan S. Wadley, "Raja Nal, Motini, Damayanti, and the Dice Game" and "Bubbling Kings and Trickster Goddesses in the North Indian Epic Dhola." My summary, supplemented by personal communications from Susan Wadley.

37. A. K. Ramanujan, "Adventures of a Disobedient Son," *Folktales from India*, 284.

38. *Mahabharata* 3.68–75.

39. See *Rig Veda* 1.154; O'Flaherty, *The Rig Veda*, 225; O'Flaherty, *Hindu Myths*, 175; and Doniger, *The Bedtrick*.

40. Giraudoux, *Amphitryon*, 18, 25; cf. Behrman, *Amphitryon 38*, 39, 55.

41. Giraudoux, *Amphitryon*, 63; cf. Behrman, *Amphitryon 38*, 132.

42. Ann Grodzins Gold and Lindsey Harlan, "Raja Nal's Story."

43. Susan S. Wadley, "Raja Nal, Motini, Damayanti, and the Dice Game" and "Bubbling Kings and Trickster Goddesses in the North Indian Epic Dhola." My summary, supplemented by personal communications from Susan Wadley.

44. The episode of the horses is tantalizingly sketched here; does Nala use Jaldariya, Indra's magical horse, to get there in that time, or does he revive the old nags?

45. Sigmund Freud, "Family Romances."

46. Homer, *Odyssey*, 17.300; 19.215–25, 250, 358, 381, 385, 389, 409, 468, 475, 516, 594; 21.218; 23.7, 73–75, 95, 113–15, 166, 202, 206, 225, 229, 254, 310.

47. See Gregory Nagy, *Greek Mythology and Poetics*, 202, 220.

48. Aristotle, *Physics*, 2.13–16.

49. Froma Zeitlin, "Figuring Fidelity," 20.

50. *Mahabharata* 1.176.10–12; 179.15–25.

51. *Ramayana* 1.66.17.

52. I am indebted to Stephanie Nelson for pointing out to me the relevance of the bow contest to Penelope's testing of Odysseus.

53. Homer, *Odyssey*, 17.143.

54. Ibid., 19.560.

55. Norman Austin, *Helen of Troy*, 140.

56. Euripides, *Helen*, 290.

57. Ibid., 540.

58. Austin, *Helen of Troy*, 161.

59. Zeitlin, "Figuring Fidelity," 23–25.

60. Ibid., 48.

61. Rostand, *Cyrano de Bergerac*, 160.

62. Johannes Th. Kakridis, *Homer Revisited*, 154.

63. Ibid., 152–53, citing the variant given by Nikolaus Politis (no. 84).

64. Ibid., 154.

65. Ibid., 155.

66. Ibid., 160.

67. Ibid., 161.

68. Homer, *Odyssey*, 1.13–15.

69. Ibid., 5.215–20; cf. 7.250–60.

70. Kleist, *Amphitryon*, 2.5, p. 133.

71. *Ganesha Purana, Upasana Khanda*, chaps. 30–33.

72. Homer, *Odyssey*, 1.215–16.

73. Zeitlin, "Figuring Fidelity," 24.

74. Ibid., 31–32.

75. Ovid, *Metamorphoses,* 13.162.

76. Claude Lévi-Strauss, *The Elementary Structures of Kinship,* 496.

77. Mihoko Suzuki, *The Metamorphoses of Helen,* 88.

78. Jeffrey Gantz, *Early Irish Myths and Sagas,* 48–51, 55–59.

79. Nathalie Zemon Davis, *The Return of Martin Guerre.*

80. Doniger, *The Bedtrick.*

81. Wendy Doniger, "The Man Who Committed Adultery with His Own Wife."

82. Jean Giraudoux, *Amphitryon,* 22.

83. Ibid., 64.

84. Lal Behari Day, *Folk-tales of Bengal,* 198.

85. Jean Giraudoux, *Ondine,* 182.

86. Clifford Geertz, *Local Knowledge,* 206, citing Ludo Rocher, "Father Bouchet's Letter on the Administration of Hindu Law", citing P. Ramachandra Rao, *Tales of Mariada Raman,* and a seventeenth-century Jesuit minister, Jean Bouchet.

87. Stuart Blackburn gave me this wonderful version in London, on October 30, 1996. It is a bow song that he collected, between 1977 and 1979, near the city of Nagercoil and the great temple complex of Sucindram—whose name means, significantly, "The Purification of Indra."

88. Marina Warner, *From the Beast to the Blonde,* 115.

89. Wendy Doniger, "The Mythology of Masquerading Animals."

90. Norman E. Brown, *The Indian and Christian Miracles of Walking on Water.*

91. *Mahabharata* 3.53.6.

92. This criterion also appears in a contemporary European fairy tale, in which a fairy changeling visits the mortal world and a soldier says, "I've drunk too much wine. I could have sworn her feet did not touch the ground while she walked." Marjorie Fischer, *Red Feather,* 78.

93. Harsha, *Naishadiyacarita* 6.44.

94. S. Baring-Gould, *Curious Myths,* 470–79.

95. *Brihadaranyaka Upanishad* 1.4.7.

96. David Shulman, *Tamil Temple Myths,* 324–25, citing *Tiruvarancaram* 5–7.

97. *Adhyatma-ramayana,* cited by Kathleen Erndl, "The Mutilation of Surpanakha," 76.

98. Shulman, "Sita and Satakantharavana," 22; O'Flaherty, *Dreams,* 94.

99. David Shulman, "Concave and Full," 5–7.

100. *Abhijnanashakuntalam* of Kalidasa, 7.2.

101. Clifford Geertz, *After the Fact,* 167.

102. Carlo Ginzburg, "Morelli, Freud, and Sherlock Holmes."

103. G. Cuvier, *Récherches sur les ossements fossiles* (Paris, 1834), 1:185, cited by R. Messac, *Le 'detective novel' et l'influence de la pensée scientifique* (Paris, 1929), 34–35, cited by Ginzburg, "Morelli," 23 n. 73.

104. Aristotle attempts to correlate criteria like the number of feet with the mode of birth (viviparous, oviparous), fur or lack thereof, placement of breasts, and so forth. See *De motu anim.,* chap. 5; *De generatione anim.,* 732a25–732b35; *De partibus anim.,* 642b5–644a12; 687a2–688a11; *Historia anim.,* bk. 2, chap. 1. I am grateful to Lorraine Daston for these citations.

105. *Rig Veda* 1.114.1; O'Flaherty, *The Rig Veda*, 224. Other Indian texts supplement this simple rule by more complex criteria, not unlike Aristotle's; *The Laws of Manu* (1.42–45), for instance, distinguishes creatures born from an embryonic sac (mammals, humans, ogres, and ghouls) from those born from eggs (including birds, snakes, and fish) and from sweat (insects).

106. George Orwell, *Animal Farm*, 33, 40–41, 122.

107. Carlo Ginzburg, *Ecstasies*, 241, 280.

108. Jonathan Swift, *Gulliver's Travels*, pt. 4, chap. 2, 199, 204–5.

109. Giraudoux, *Amphitryon*, 48.

110. *Mary of Nimmegen*, cited by Warner, *From the Beast*, 121.

111. Sudhir Kakar, *Shamans, Mystics, and Doctors*, 27–28.

112. The tale of Yavakri, told in the *Jaiminiya Brahmana* 2.269–70; O'Flaherty, *Tales of Sex and Violence*, 105–7.

113. James Boswell, *Life of Samuel Johnson*, 287.

114. Warner, *From the Beast*, 121, 124–25.

115. *Rig Veda* 10.90; O'Flaherty, *The Rig Veda*, 29–32.

116. Sander Gilman, *The Case of Sigmund Freud*, vii.

117. Warner, *From the Beast*, 121.

118. Gilman, *The Case*, 113.

119. Oskar Panizza, *The Council of Love*, 79, 91–92; cited by Gilman, *The Case*, 115.

120. Walter Hofmann, *Lacht ihn tot!* 23; cited by Gilman, *The Case*, 261.

121. Hermann Schaaffhausen, "Die Physiognomik," 337; cited by Gilman, *The Case*, 116.

122. Bruce Lincoln, "Rewriting the German War-God."

123. For Fenris, Lincoln, "Rewriting," cites *Gylfaginning*; for Egil, *Egilssaga einhendr*; and for Guntharius, *Waltharius*.

124. E. M. Cioran, *Tears and Saints*, 31.

125. See Doniger, *The Implied Spider*, 93–95.

126. Euripides, *Phoenicians*, 41–42.

127. Hyginus, *Fabulae*, 67.

128. Claude Lévi-Strauss, "The Structural Study of Myth," 206–31.

129. Alan Dundes, "The Hero Pattern and the Life of Jesus."

130. *The Laws of Manu* 1.81–82.

131. *The Laws of Manu* 8.16, 5.76; Wendy Doniger, "Three (or More) Forms of the Three (or More)–Fold Path in Hinduism."

132. Euripides, *Trojan Women*, 518.

133. Or peacock or lizard: *krikavaku*.

134. *Matsya Purana* 11.1–39.

135. *Kaushitaki Brahmana* 23.7.5–12.

136. *Matsya Purana* 11.1–39.

137. *Matsya Purana* 11.30–33; *Samba Purana* 15, cited by Rajendra Chandra Hazra, *Studies in the Upapuranas*, 1:44.

138. *Mahabharata* 16.31.

139. Hans Christian Andersen, "The Mermaid."

140. Oscar Wilde, "The Fisherman and His Soul."

141. Saul Bellow, *The Adventures of Augie March*, 78.

142. Otto Fenichel, "Elements of a Psychoanalytic Theory of Anti-Semitism," 25; cited by Gilman, *The Case*, 118.

143. Richard Wagner, *The Art-work of the Future*, 210–13.

144. David Shulman, "On Being Human," 4.

145. Jean Giraudoux, *Amphitryon*, 49.

146. Giraudoux, *Amphitryon*, 33; cf. Behrman, *Amphitryon 38*, 78–79.

147. Garrison Keillor, "Zeus the Lutheran," 34.

148. Seneca, *Hercules on Mount Oeta*, 1343–981.

149. Thus the Pandavas are called precisely that, the children of Pandu, named after their human father, and sometimes even after their human mother: Arjuna is Kaunteya, the son of Kunti.

150. Paul Friedrich, *The Meaning of Aphrodite*.

151. Homer, *Homeric Hymn to Aphrodite*.

152. *Amphekalupsen:* Homer, *Odyssey*. 4.180.

153. See James Scott, *Weapons of the Weak*.

154. Larry Niven, "Man of Steel," 223–26.

155. Giraudoux, *Amphitryon*, 88.

156. David Tracy, *On Naming the Present*, 16.

157. O'Flaherty, *The Origins of Evil*, chap. 7.

158. Ibid., chap. 8.

159. Giraudoux, *Amphitryon*, 42.

160. Robert A. Johnson, *Femininity Lost and Regained*, 69–70.

161. *Mahabharata* 3, appendix 1.6.36–162; then 4.2.20 and 4.10. See also O'Flaherty, *Women*, 298.

162. Nick Allen, in "The Hero's Five Relationships," argues for a general parallel between the Arjuna and Odysseus cycles, though he does not single out Calypso as a direct parallel to Urvashi, as I wish to do.

163. Ovid, *Metamorphoses* 7.700–865.

164. This rather Cartesian tradition of mythology, denying the body to affirm the soul, stands in contrast to a dominant strain in Christian theology, which argues, as Caroline Walker Bynum has so brilliantly demonstrated (in *The Resurrection of the Body in Western Christianity, 200–1336*), that the body, too, is immortal. But I am limiting myself here to the mythology.

165. Jean Giraudoux, *Ondine*, 237.

166. Paracelsus, "A Book on Nymphs, Sylphs, Pygmies, and Salamanders."

167. S. Baring-Gould, *Curious Myths*, 470–79.

168. Paracelsus, "A Book on Nymphs," 246–47.

169. Quoted in Alexander H. Krappe, "Far Eastern Fox Lore," 138.

170. Otto Weininger, *Sex and Character*, cited in Marjorie Garber, *Vested Interests*, 224.

171. Jean Giraudoux, *Amphitryon*, 44; Behrman, *Amphitryon 38*, 172.

172. Soren Kierkegaard, *Frygt og Baeven* (Fear and trembling), in *Samlede Voerker* (Copenhagen: Gyldendal, 1982), 5:86–87; cited in Per Jacobsen and Barbara Fass Leavy, *Ibsen*, 115.

173. Jacobsen and Leavy, *Ibsen*, 18.

174. Personal communication from Marie Koo, August 1994.

175. Gregory Nagy, "The Name of Apollo," 6.

176. Giraudoux, *Ondine*, 259.

177. Barbara Fass Leavy, *In Search of the Swan Maiden*, 277.

178. Barbara Fass, *La Belle Dame*, 35.

179. *Ramayana* 3.4.14.

180. Angela Carter, "The Tiger's Bride," 53.

181. Giraudoux, *Amphitryon*, 22.

182. Ibid., 62.

183. Roberto Calasso, *The Marriage*, 125.

184. Doniger, "Myths and Methods in the Dark."

185. Wei-yi Li, "On Becoming a Fish."

186. Homer, *Homeric Hymn to Demeter*.

187. This evocative phrase was suggested by Robert J. Lifton, personal communication, July 27, 1993.

188. This lovely phrase was coined by the singer Phyllis Curtin, in her response to an early variant of this chapter, in Boston on April 12, 1995.

189. A. C. Krujit, "De legenden der Poso-Alfoeren aangaande de erste menschen," *Mededeelingen van wege het Nederlandsche Zendelinggenootschap*, 38 (1894): 340, quoted in J. G. Frazer, *The Belief in Immortality*, 1:74–75.

190. Giraudoux, *Amphitryon*, 41–42.

191. Hesiod, *Theogony*, 453–506.

192. Giraudoux, *Amphitryon*, 38.

193. *Naishadiyacarita* 6.95, 99, 105.

194. Claude Lévi-Strauss, *The Jealous Potter*, 71.

195. Carlo Ginzburg, *Ecstasies*, 241, citing A. Szabo, "Der halbe Mensch und der biblische Sündenfall," *Paideuma* 2 (1942–43): 95–100, and faulting him for comparing this story with the myth of Plato's symposium.

196. Chiri Masashibo, *Chiri Masashibo Chosakshu* (Selected works) (Tokyo: Kibonsha, 1973), 2:196. I am grateful to James Ketelaar for giving me this text, and translating it for me.

197. Homer, *Homeric Hymn to Demeter*.

198. *Katha Upanishad*.

199. Joel C. Kuipers, *Power and Performance*, 36.

200. Salman Rushdie, *The Wizard of Oz*, 57.

CHAPTER FOUR

1. A. K. Ramanujan, "Two Realms of Kannada Folklore," 58–61.

2. A. K. Ramanujan, *Speaking of Siva*, 24.

3. Pierre Sonnerat, *Voyages aux Indes Orientales*, 245–47. The Tamil version was also translated into English by B. G. Babington, in *The Vedala Cadai*. See also *Vishnu Purana* 4.7.35, and N. Ramesan, *Temples and Legends of Andhra Pradesh*, 35 ff.

4. Edward Cameron Dimock, "A Theology of the Repulsive."

5. Rudolf Otto, *The Idea of the Holy*.

6. Eveline Meyer, *Ankala*, 16.

7. A. K. Ramanujan, "Two Realms of Kannada Folklore," 58–61.

8. *Kovalan Katai*, as analyzed by Sally Noble in "The Tamil Story of the Anklet."

9. *Mahabharata* 3.116.1–20.

10. *Brahma Purana* 87.

11. *Laws of Manu* 11.174.

12. O'Flaherty, *Women, Androgynes*, pt. 1.

13. An interesting Greek parallel is offered by a story from Epidauros, best accessible in the edition and commentary by Lynn R. LiDonnici, *The Epidaurian Miracle In-*

scription, 102 (Stele B, lines 10–19). In this story, a woman's sons behead her and then try in vain to put her head back. I am indebted to Frits Graf for this text.

14. See Robert P. Goldman, "Fathers, Sons, and Gurus," on the Oedipal implications of Parashurama's relations with his father and mother.

15. *Mahabharata* 3.116.20–25.

16. Meyer, *Ankala*, 16.

17. *Mahabharata* 3.117.1–10.

18. *Kancippuranam*, chaps. 45–46; Shulman, *The King and the Clown*, 120–29. I quote it here in Shulman's translation.

19. O'Flaherty, *The Origins of Evil*, 277–86.

20. Shulman, *The King and the Clown*, 127.

21. William S. Sax, *Mountain Goddess*, 22.

22. Ibid., 34.

23. Vilas Sarang, "An Interview with M. Chakko."

24. Sax, *Mountain Goddess*, 28.

25. Ibid., 32.

26. Goethe, working apparently from Iken's translation of a Persian version of the story, used it in his *Legende*, 1:266–67. He was, however, working from a translation of the Tamil version of the story, with the telltale element of the water that freezes and then melts back into its element. See Dorothy Figueira, "To Lose One's Head for Love" and "Heinrich Zimmer and Thomas Mann."

27. Marguerite Yourcenar, "Kali Beheaded."

28. Yourcenar, "Kali Beheaded," 146 n.

29. Homer, *Odyssey*, 12.85–110.

30. Ibid., 12.245–258 *(autou d' eini thureisi)*.

31. Ovid, *Metamorphoses*, 13.730–39, 900–968, 14.1–70.

32. Some scholars say they are just dogfish.

33. Edmund Spenser, *The Faerie Queene*, cantos II, XLI, 1, 41.

34. Shakespeare, *King Lear*, 4.6.

35. Milton, *Paradise Lost*, 2.650–61.

36. Ibid., 2.752–809.

37. Homer, *Odyssey*, 12.45–46.

38. Ibid., 12.60–72. They are also called the Symplagades or Planktae.

39. Personal communication from Robin McGrath, April, 1990.

40. Alan Dundes, "Earth-Diver."

41. Mark Kalluak, *How Kablomat Became and Other Legends*, 18–21; my summary.

42. Bernard Saladin d'Anglure, "The Mythology of the Inuit of the Central Arctic."

43. Knud Rasmussen, *Observations on the Intellectual Culture of the Caribou Eskimos.*

44. *Skanda Purana* 1.2.27–29; O'Flaherty, *Hindu Myths*, 251–61.

45. Stoker, *Dracula*, 223 and 225.

46. Stoker, *Dracula*, 221.

47. Ibid., 228.

48. Ibid., 62.

49. Ibid., 223.

50. Ibid., 228.

51. Thanks to Tony Doniger, my brother the lawyer, for this case.

52. *New York Times*, September 14, 1997, A17.

53. Philip J. Hilts, "Study or Human Experiment? Face-Lift Project Stirs Ethical Concerns," *New York Times,* June 21, 1998, A25. The study was published in *Plastic and Reconstructive Surgery,* December 1996.

54. O'Flaherty, *Other Peoples' Myths,* chap. 4.

55. Personal communication from David Tracy, Rome, 1995.

56. Woody Allen, "Fabulous Tales and Mythical Beasts."

57. Gananath Obeyesekere, *Medusa's Head.*

58. O'Flaherty, *Women,* 18, 21, 45–46, 87, 255–56.

59. Ezra Pound, postscript to his translation of Gourmont's *The Natural Philosophy of Love,* cited by Bram Dijkstra, *Idols of Perversity,* 178.

60. Elaine Showalter, *Sexual Anarchy,* 181. Here she cites O'Flaherty, *Women,* on Freudian head-shrinking.

61. Joseph Falaky Nagy, "Hierarchy, Heroes, and Heads," 221.

62. Ibid., 220.

63. Ibid., 225.

64. See also *Young Frankenstein* (1974), the parody by Carl Reiner's old partner in crime, Mel Brooks.

65. Doniger, *The Implied Spider,* chap. 2.

66. Anthony Lane, "Romantic Triangle."

67. The other reasons are as follows:
   1. Because they have more Knowledge of the world. . . .
   2. Because when Women cease to be handsome, they study to be good. . . .
   3. Because there is no hazard of children, which irregularly produced may be attended with much inconvenience. . . .
   4. Because through more Experience they are more prudent and discreet in conducting an Intrigue to prevent Suspicion. . . . and . . . if the Affair should happen to be known, considerate People might be inclined to excuse an old Woman, who would kindly take care of a young Man. . . .
   6. Because the sin is less. The Debauching of a Virgin may be her Ruin, and make her for Life unhappy. . . .
   7. Because the Compunction is less. The having made a young Girl *miserable* may give you frequent bitter Reflections; none of which can attend making an old Woman *happy.*
   8. They are so grateful!!!

68. Franklin, "Benjamin Franklin Urges a Young Friend to Take an Old Mistress."

69. Doniger, "Myths and Methods in the Dark," and *The Bedtrick.*

70. It was composed right after *The Carnal Prayer Mat* and was later reworked into Li Yu's play, *The Ingenious Finale.*

71. Li Yu, "Nativity Room."

CHAPTER FIVE

1. *Kathasaritsagara* 12.130 (163) (Tawney and Penzer, 6.204 ff.; notes on 276–77). This is the sixth of the "Twenty-five Tales of a Vampire" *(Vetalapancavimsati);* it is also told in the *Bhavishya Purana.* Zimmer, *The King and the Corpse,* 217 n, supplies good notes on sources of many versions of the transposed heads.

2. Personal communication from Imhasly, January 1996.

3. *Skanda Purana* 1.2.27–29; O'Flaherty, *Hindu Myths,* 251–61; Doniger, *The Bedtrick.*

4. *Mahabharata* 2.16–17.

5. *Padma Purana, Svarga Khanda* 16.6–24; O'Flaherty, *Textual Sources,* 98.

6. *Mahabharata* 9.37.28–31; *Vamana Purana* 46.

7. *Harivamsha* 47–48.

8. O'Flaherty, *Siva,* 267–71.

9. Richard F. Burton, *Vikram and the Vampire, or Tales of Hindu Devilry,* 203–16.

10. Heinrich Zimmer, "Die Geschichte vom indischen König mit dem Leichnam" (1935); *The King and the Corpse* (posthumous 1948), 210 ff.

11. This "psychological editing," as Dorothy Figueira rightly calls it, did not appear in Zimmer's first retelling of the story in 1938, and was presumably added either by Zimmer or (more likely) by Joseph Campbell in the final posthumous editing of Zimmer's text. See Figueira, "To Lose One's Head for Love," and O'Flaherty, "The King and the Corpse and the Rabbi and the Talk-Show Star."

12. Thomas Mann, *Die vertauschten Köpfe* (1940); *The Transposed Heads* (1941).

13. Girish Karnad, *Hayavadana;* my summary.

14. Stoker, *Dracula,* 182.

15. Ibid., 119.

16. Claude Lévi-Strauss, "Language and the Analysis of Social Laws."

17. Shakespeare, *Cymbeline,* 2.3.

18. Ibid., 4.2.

19. Maurice Bloomfield, "On Entering Another's Body." See also O'Flaherty, *Other Peoples' Myths,* chap. 1.

20. *Shankara-dig-vijaya* of Madhavacarya, chap. 9; *Shankara-vijaya* of Anandagiri, 58–59; Ravicandra's commentary on Amaru, cited in Lee Siegel, *Fires of Love/Waters of Peace,* 4–5.

21. *Deshopadesha* of Kshemendra.

22. Théophile Gautier, *Avatar,* 7–8.

23. Gautier, *Avatar.*

24. Ibid., 57, 59, 61.

25. Ibid., 171. Gautier has it all wrong: Krishna, not Shiva, is the blue god, and Durga, a goddess rather than a god, has no boar's tusks; that's Vishnu.

26. Another error: Brahma-loka is the heavenly world *(loka)* of the god Brahma, not the name of a person.

27. Gautier, *Avatar,* 82.

28. Otto Rank, *The Double,* 80 n. 20.

29. *Yogavasishtha* 6.1.62–69; O'Flaherty, *Dreams,* 207; O'Flaherty, "The Dream Narrative and the Indian Doctrine of Illusion."

30. Rostand, *Cyrano,* act 3.

31. *Hypostasis of the Archons,* 87, 89.20–30 (trans. Robinson, 163–64).

32. Maslin, "Good and Evil Trade Places." She continues: "High-tech identity tricks are nothing new ('Terminator 2,' 'Total Recall,' etc.) but they aren't usually presented with the acting ingenuity of 'Face/Off.'"

33. Lou Jacobson, "A Mind Is a Terrible Thing to Waste," 7.

34. Doniger, *The Implied Spider,* 47–52.

35. Ovid, *Metamorphoses* 3.341–510.

36. Pausanias, *Description of Greece,* 9.31.6.

37. Plutarch, *Moralia, quest. conv.,* 5.7.3.

38. Proclues, cited by Otto Rank, *Beyond Psychology,* and Jean Richer, "The Androgyne."

39. Richer, "The Androgyne."

40. *Mahabharata* 12.320.1–40; O'Flaherty, "Echoes of the *Mahabharata*," 48–50.

41. Plato, *Symposium*, 189E-191E.

42. A. K. Ramanujan, "The Prince Who Married His Own Left Side"; and Ramanujan, *The Flowering Tree*, 142–45. I have somewhat condensed the story.

43. A. K. Ramanujan, "Towards a Counter-system: Women's Tales," 47–54; Sudhir Kakar, *Intimate Relations*, 52–59; and Girish Karnad, *Naga-Mandala: Play with a Cobra*. See also Doniger, *The Bedtrick*.

44. *Caitanyacaritamrita* of Krishnadasa; my paraphrase.

45. *Bhagavata Purana* 10.30.

46. Govindaraja on *Ramayana* 2.3.39, cited by Robert P. Goldman, "Transsexualism," 383.

47. *Padma Purana* 6.272.165–67.

48. O'Flaherty, *Women*, 295–96. Cf. also Ruru and Jaratkaru in the *Mahabharata*.

49. William Veeder's insightful essay, "Children of the Night," does not argue that Hyde himself is Jekyll's lover, but illuminates a more general homoerotic setting for the story as a whole and points out many telling homoerotic double entendres in the symbolism.

50. Robert Louis Stevenson, *The Strange Case*, 42, 51.

51. Elaine Showalter, *Sexual Anarchy*, 109.

52. William Veeder and Gordon Hirsch, eds., *Dr. Jekyll and Mr. Hyde after One Hundred Years*. The most famous are the 1921 version with John Barrymore and Nita Naldi; the 1931 version, directed by Rouben Mamoulian, with Frederic March, Miriam Hopkins, and Angela Lansbury; and the 1941 version, with Spencer Tracy, Ingrid Bergman, and Lana Turner.

53. Showalter, *Sexual Anarchy*, 118. Susan Sontag wrote a short story entitled "Doctor Jekyll" (1978), which Showalter (p. 124) calls "a clever postmodernist version set in contemporary Manhattan. Jekyll is a successful surgeon, Hyde a delinquent addict. Hyde finally persuades Jekyll to try some violence in his own right, and Jekyll goes to prison for the attempted murder of Hyde."

54. Jenni Calder, *Robert Louis Stevenson*, 118, cited in Showalter, *Sexual Anarchy*, 116.

55. Showalter, *Sexual Anarchy*, 124.

56. Ibid., 125–26.

57. Ibid., 118.

58. Doniger, "Myths and Methods in the Dark."

59. Wilde, *The Picture of Dorian Gray*, 45, 76. Donald L. Lawler's critical edition for Norton includes both the original 1890 edition and the edition published a year later, which added much material but also muted some of the stronger implications of homosexuality that were present in the first edition. My references, unless otherwise noted, will be to the first edition.

60. Jan Morris, *Conundrum*, 103.

61. Ibid., 100.

62. *Ramayana* 7.37.28–44, 57; excised verses.

63. Saint Thomas, *De Trinitate*, I. 51, art. 3.

64. *Malleus Maleficarum* 1.3 (trans. Kramer and Sprenger, 26).

65. Fred Sleeves, "Sex-Change Woman Makes Self Pregnant!" *The Sun*, April 15, 1997, 14.

66. George Stade, "Dracula's Women," 38.

67. Auerbach, *Our Vampires,* 112.

68. *Rig Veda* 7.86.6.

69. Mary Douglas, "The Cloud God and the Shadow Self," 85.

70. Stanley Insler, "The Shattered Head Split and the Epic Tale of Sakuntala."

71. Euripides, *Helen,* 160.

72. Austin, *Helen of Troy,* 154.

73. Froma Zeitlin, "The Lady Vanishes," 13.

74. Marina Warner, "Stolen Shadows, Lost Souls," 49.

Chapter Six

1. *Mahabharata* 1.16.39–40, 1.17.8; O'Flaherty, *Hindu Myths,* 274–80.

2. Wendy Doniger O'Flaherty, *Siva,* 87–90.

3. Hesiod tells the story twice, in the *Theogony* and the *Works and Days* (57–104).

4. Nicole Loraux, "Origins of Mankind in Greek Myths: Born to Die."

5. "The Lay of Thrym," from the Elder Edda, in Hallberg Hallmundsson, *An Anthology of Scandinavian Literature,* 187–92; my summary. Thanks to Ben Thomas for this text.

6. *Brahmanda Purana* 4.10.41–77. See O'Flaherty, *Siva,* 228–29.

7. R. Dessigane and Jean Filliozat, *Les légendes çivaites de Kancipuram,* 76–77.

8. *Shiva Purana,* 3.20.3–7.

9. *Bhagavata Purana* 10.88.14–36.

10. R. Dessigane and P. Z. Pattabiramin, *La légende de Skanda selon le Kanchipuranam Tamoul et l'iconographie,* 84–85 (2.32.6–47).

11. Doniger, *The Bedtrick.*

12. *Bhagavata Purana* 8.12.12–35; *Agni Purana* 3.17–20.

13. Personal communication from V. Narayana Rao, March 1995.

14. Serena Nanda, *Neither Man Nor Woman,* 20–21.

15. O'Flaherty, *Siva,* 42–51.

16. See also Don Handelman and David Shulman, *God Inside Out,* 154.

17. Kavita Shetty, "Eunuchs: A Bawdy Festival," in *India Today,* June 15, 1990, 50–55.

18. *Bhagavata Purana* 9.1.25–42; see also *Devibhagavata Purana* 1.12.1–35; etc. See O'Flaherty, *Siva,* 304–5.

19. *Brahma Purana* 108.26–30.

20. *Ramayana* 7.87–90.

21. Sayana on *Rig Veda* 10.95.

22. *Brahmanda Purana* 2.3.60.23–27.

23. *Skanda Purana* 1.3.1.10.1–69. See O'Flaherty, *Hindu Myths,* 245.

24. See also *Laws of Manu* 8.369–70.

25. O'Flaherty, *Siva,* 304–8.

26. John Strong, *The Legend and Cult of Upagupta,* 131–32.

27. Ibid., 212 n. 32, citing *Ashokarajavadana* 50:124c–25a. See D. E. Mills, *A Collection of Tales from Uji,* 397.

28. *Shivalaya Mahatmya* of the *Sahyadrikhanda* of the *Skanda Purana,* chaps. 3–9. I have rephrased and retranslated, working from Micaela Soar's text.

29. See Handelman and Shulman, *God Inside Out.*

30. *Brahmavaivarta Purana* 4.61.

31. *Mahabhagavata Purana* 49–58, cited in Rajendra Chandra Hazra, *Studies in the Upapuranas*, 2:272–73.

32. O'Flaherty, *Women*, 116.

33. *Bhavishya Purana* 3.4.17.23–27.

34. This story has been much studied, principally by Hertel, A. B. Keith, W. Norman Brown, and Robert Goldman (1993), who cites the earlier essays.

35. *Mahabharata* 1.70.16.

36. *Ramayana* 7.87–90.

37. *Kathasaritsagara*, chap. 89 [12.15] (Penzer and Tawney, 7:41 ff.).

38. O'Flaherty, *Women*, 172, 246–59.

39. *Shivalaya Mahatmya* of the *Sahyadrikhanda* of the *Skanda Purana*, 8.39.

40. *The Laws of Manu* 3.34.

41. O'Flaherty, *Dreams*, 81–89.

42. *Brahma Purana* 108.26–30.

43. *Mahabharata* 13.12.1–49; see also O'Flaherty, *Women*, 305–6.

44. *Dhammatthakatha* 3.9, on *Dhammapada* 43, cited in Goldman, "Transsexualism."

45. *Garuda Purana* 109.33.

46. *Bhagavata Purana* with the commentary of Sridhara, 9.1.18–42. See also *Devibhagavata Purana* 1.12.1–35; *Linga Purana* 1.65.19–20; and Wendy Doniger O'Flaherty, *Siva*, 304–5.

47. *Shivalaya Mahatmya* of the *Sahyadrikhanda* of the *Skanda Purana*, chaps. 3–9. I have rephrased and retranslated, working from Micaela Soar's text.

48. Serena Nanda, *Neither Man Nor Woman*, 25–26.

49. *Linga Purana* 1.65.19–20; *Bhagavata Purana* 9.1.18–42; see also *Devibhagavata Purana* 1.12.1–35.

50. Nanda, *Neither Man Nor Woman*, 13.

51. *Mahabharata* 3, appendix 1.6.36–162; then 4.2.20 and 4.10. See also O'Flaherty, *Women, Androgynes*, 298.

52. *Mahabharata* 1.96.45–53.

53. Ibid. 5.170–187.

54. Ibid. 5.188–93.

55. Ibid. 5.193.60–65.

56. Ibid. 6.99.4–7; 6.103.100.

57. Ibid. 6.112.80.

58. Ibid. 10.8.58–9.

59. Ibid. 13.154.19–29.

60. Ibid. 5.193.60–65.

61. *Ramayana* of Valmiki, 1.14.11.

62. *Markandeya Purana*, Devi Mahatmya.

63. Lawrence Cohen, "Semen Gain," 3; published as "Holi in Banaras," 410.

64. *Shatapatha Brahmana* 13.2.9.6–9; O'Flaherty, *Textual Sources*, 17.

65. Don Handelman, "The Guises of the Goddess," 288–89.

66. Ibid., 43, 42, 46.

67. David Shulman, "On Being a Stone," 14.

68. *Yogavasishtha* 6.1.85–108; O'Flaherty, *Dreams*, 280–81.

69. An important exception is Drona, in the *Mahabharata*.

70. Its full name is the *Yogavasishtha-maha-ramayana;* see O'Flaherty, *Dreams.*

71. Apollodorus, *The Library,* 3.6.7; Ovid, *Metamorphoses,* 3.315–40.

72. Apollodorus, *The Library,* 3.6.7; Hyginus, *Fabulae,* 75; Pindar, *Nemean Odes,* 1.91; Tzetzes, *On Lycophron,* 682; Callimachus, *The Bathing of Pallas.*

73. Marjorie Garber, *Vice Versa,* 161–63.

74. Virginia Woolf, *Orlando,* 138.

75. Ibid., 188.

76. Judith Butler, *Gender Trouble.*

77. *Bhagavad-Ajjuka Prahasanam,* verse 32.

78. *Dhammatthakatha* 3.9, on *Dhammapada* 43, cited by Goldman, "Transsexualism," 384.

79. *Vimalakirti,* 56, 61–62.

80. Personal communication from Janet Gyatso, April 1998.

81. *Padma Purana* 6.272.165–67.

82. Eve Sedgwick, *Between Men,* 49.

83. Ibid., 26.

84. Ibid., 433.

85. Goldman, "Transsexualism," 391.

86. *Mahabharata* 4.21.1–67.

87. *Bodhisattvabadanakalpalata,* of Kshemendra.

88. *Padma Purana, Svarga Khanda* 16.6–24, trans. in O'Flaherty, *Textual Sources for the Study of Hinduism,* 98–100.

89. Mary Douglas, *Purity and Danger.*

90. David Shulman, personal communication, April 27, 1993.

Postlude

1. Doniger, *The Implied Spider,* chap. 4.

2. Erich Auerbach, *Mimesis,* 11.

3. Doniger, *The Implied Spider,* chap. 5.

4. For the issue of the author's bias in selecting some themes for comparison at the expense of others, see Doniger, *The Implied Spider,* chap. 2.

5. Allan Grapard, "Visions of Excess."

6. Marjorie Garber, *Vice Versa,* 425.

7. Ian Hacking, "Double Consciousness in Britain, 1814–1875," 136.

8. Elaine Showalter, *Sexual Anarchy,* 119, 121.

9. Ann Grodzins Gold, "Sexuality, Fertility, and Erotic Imagination," 66.

10. Doniger, *The Bedtrick.*

11. William Butler Yeats, *The Autobiography of William Butler Yeats,* 340.

BIBLIOGRAPHY

PRINTED TEXTS

Sanskrit, Tamil, Hindi, and Bengali Texts (by title)

Abhijnanashakuntalam (Shakuntala), of Kalidasa, with the commentary of Raghava. Bombay: Nirnaya Sagara Press, 1958.

Adhyatma-Ramayana, with the commentaries of Narottama, Ramavarman, and Gopala Chakravarti. Calcutta Sanskrit series, no. 11. Calcutta: Metropolitan Printing and Publishing House, 1935.

Adhyatmaramayana. Trans. Rai Bahadur Nala Baij Nath. Allahabad: The Sacred Books of the Hindus, the Panini Office, 1913.

Agni Purana. Poona: Anandasrama Sanskrit Series, 1957.

Atharva Veda, with the commentary of Sayana. 5 vols. Hoshiarpur: Vishveshvaranand Vedic Research Institute, 1960.

Bhagavad-Ajjuka Prahasanam (The Farce of the Saint-Courtesan). Ed. P. Anujan. Trichur, India: Mangalodayam Press, 1925.

———. Trans. Michael Lockwood and A. Vishnu Bhat. In *Metatheater and Sanskrit Drama.* Madras: Tambaram Research Associates, 1994.

Bhagavad Gita. In the *Mahabharata,* Poona ed.

Bhagavata Purana, with the commentary of Shridhara. Benares: Pandita Pustakalaya, 1972.

Bhavishya Purana. Bombay: Venkateshvara Sagara Press, 1959.

Bodhisattvabadanakalpalata, of Kshemendra. Trans. into Bengali by Saratcandra Dasa. Calcutta: Lipika, 1979.

Brahmanda Purana. Bombay: Venkateshvara Steam Press, 1857.

Brahma Purana. Calcutta: Gurumandala Series, no. 11, 1954.

Brahmavaivarta Purana. Poona: Anandasrama Sanskrit Series, no. 102, 1935.

Brihadaranyaka Upanishad. In *One Hundred and Eight Upanishads,* Bombay: Nirnaya Sagara Press, 1913.

Brihaddevata of Shaunaka. Text, with a trans. by A. A. Macdonell. HOS, no. 5. Cambridge: Harvard University Press, 1904.

Caitanyacaritamrita of Krishnadasa. Trans. Edward Cameron Dimock. Cambridge: Harvard University Press, in press.

Deshopadesha of Kshemendra. Ed. Madhusudan Kaul Shastri. Poona: Aryabhusan, 1923.

Devibhagavata Purana. Benares: Pandita Pustakalaya, 1960.

Devi Purana. Calcutta: Gurumandala Press, 1896.

Ganesha Purana. Bombay: Venkateshvara Steam Press, 1892.

Garuda Purana. Benares: Pandita Pustakalaya, 1969.

Gopatha Brahmana of the Atharva Veda. Ed. Rajendra Lal Mitra. Bibliotheca Indica. Delhi: Indological Book House, 1972.

Harivamsha. Poona: Bhandarkar Oriental Research Institute, 1969.

Jaiminiya Brahmana. Ed. Raghu Vira and Lokesha Chandra. Nagpur: Sarasvati-vihara Series, no. 31, 1954.

Kamasutra of Vatsyayana, with the commentary of Shri Yashodhara. Bombay: Lakshmivenkateshvara Steam Press, 1856.

Kathasaritsagara (The Ocean of the Rivers of Story). Bombay: Nirnaya Sagara Press, 1930.

———. *The Ocean of Story*. Ed. N. M. Penzer, trans. C. W. Tawney. 10 vols. London: Chas. J. Sawyer, 1924.

Katha Upanishad. In *One Hundred and Eight Upanishads*. Bombay: Nirnaya Sagara Press, 1913.

Kaushitaki Brahmana. With commentary, the *Vyakhya* of Udaya. Ed. H. Bhattacarya. 3 vols. Calcutta, 1970.

Kusha Jataka. In *Jataka Stories*. Ed. E. B. Cowell. London: Pali Text Society, 1973.

The Laws of Manu [Manusmrti]. Ed. Harikrishna Jayantakrishna Dave. Bombay: Bharatiya Vidya Series, vol. 29 ff., 1972–1978.

———. Trans. Wendy Doniger, with Brian K. Smith. Harmondsworth: Penguin, 1991.

Linga Purana. Calcutta: Sri Arunodaraya, 1812.

Mahabhagavata Purana. Bombay: Venkateshvara Steam Press, 1913.

Mahabharata. Critical Edition. Poona: Bhandarkar Oriental Research Institute, 1933–69.

Markandeya Purana. Bombay: Venkateshvara Steam Press, 1890.

Matsya Purana. Poona: Anandasrama Sanskrit Series, no. 54, 1907.

———. English translation, ed. Jamna Das Akhtar. 2 vols. Delhi: Oriental Publishers, 1972.

Naishadiyacarita of Shri Harsha. Bombay: Nirnaya Sagara Press, 1986.

Nirukta of Yaska. Ed. Lakshman Sarup. 2 vols. London and New York: Oxford University Press, 1920–27.

Padma Purana. Poona: Anandasrama Sanskrit Series, no. 131, 1893.

Padma Purana, Svarga Khanda (The Svarga Khanda of the Skanda Purana). Ed. A. C. Shastri. Benares: All-India Kashiraj Trust, 1972.

Ramacaritamanasa of Tulsi Das *(The Holy Lake of the Acts of Rama)*. Trans. R. C. Prasad. Delhi: Motilal Banarsidass, 1990.

Ramayana of Kamban. See Hart and Heifetz, *Forest Book*.

Ramayana of Valmiki. Critical ed. Baroda: Oriental Institute, 1960–75.

Rig Veda, with the commentary of Sayana. 6 vols. London: Oxford University Press, 1890–92.

Shakuntala. See *Abhijnanashakuntalam*.

Shankara-dig-vijaya of Madhavacarya. Poona: Bhandarkar Oriental Research Institute, 1915.

Shankara-vijaya of Anandagiri. Calcutta: Bibliotheca Indica, 1868.

Shatapatha Brahmana. Benares: Chowkhamba Sanskrit Series, no. 96, 1964.

Shivalaya Mahatmya of the *Sahyadrikhanda* of the *Skanda Purana.* Ms. in the library of the Royal Asiatic Society in Bombay. Transcribed and trans. by Micaela Soar. 1996.

Shiva Purana. Benares: Pandita Pustakalaya, 1964.

Shiva Purana, Dharmasamhita. Bombay, 1884.

Shrishriramakrishnalilaprasanga of Swami Saradananda. Calcutta: Udbdhan Karjalay, 1986.

Skanda Purana. Bombay: Venkateshvara Steam Press, 1867.

Sri Venkateca Mahatmiyam of N. C. Teyvacikamani. Madras: Pilot Publications, 1976.

Taittiriya Samhita of the Black Yajur Veda, with the commentary of Madhava. Calcutta: Bibliotheca Indica, 1860.

Uttararamacarita of Bhavabhuti. Ed. P. V. Kane. Delhi: Motilal Banarsidass, 1971.

Vamana Purana. Benares: All-India Kashiraj Trust, 1968.

Vimalakirti. The Holy Teachings of Vimalakirti. Trans. Robert A. F. Thurman. University Park: Pennsylvania State University Press, 1976.

Vishnu Purana, with the commentary of Shridhara. Calcutta: Sanatana Sastra, 1972.

———. Trans. Horace Hayman Wilson. 3d ed. London, 1840. Reprint, Calcutta: Punthi Pustak, 1961.

Yogavasishtha [*Yogavasishtha-Maha-Ramayana* of Valmiki]. Ed. W. L. S. Pansikar. 2 vols. Bombay: Nirnaya Sagara Press, 1918.

Japanese Text

Kojiki. Trans. with an introduction and notes by Donald L. Philippi. Tokyo: University of Tokyo Press, 1968.

Greek and Latin Texts

Aeschylus. *Agamemnon.* In *Oresteia.* Trans. David Grene and Wendy Doniger O'Flaherty. Chicago: University of Chicago Press, 1988.

Apollodorus. *The Library,* and *Epitome.* Text, with a trans. by J. G. Frazer. 2 vols. Cambridge: Loeb Library, Harvard University Press, 1921.

Aristophanes. *Lysistrata* and *Thesmophoriazusae.* Text, with a trans. by Benjamin Bickley Rogers. Cambridge: Loeb Library, Harvard University Press, 1924.

Aristotle. *Historia Animalium.* Vol. 4 of *The Works of Aristotle.* Ed. and trans. J. A. Smith and W. D. Ross. Oxford: Clarendon Press, 1919.

———. *Physics.* Text, with a trans. by Philip H. Wicksteed and Francis M. Cornford. Cambridge: Loeb Library, Harvard University Press, 1957.

Callimachus. *The Bathing of Pallas.* In K. J. McKay, *The Poet at Play: Kallimachos, The Bath of Pallas.* Leiden: E. J. Brill, 1962.

Euripides. *Bacchae.* Ed. E. R. Dodds. Oxford: Clarendon Press, 1960.

———. *Helen.* Text, with a trans. by Arthur S. Way. Cambridge: Loeb Library, Harvard University Press, 1966.

———. *Iphigenia at Aulis* and *Iphigenia at Tauris*. Text, with a trans. by Arthur S. Way. Cambridge: Loeb Library, Harvard University Press, 1912.

———. *Phoenicians*. Text, with a trans. by Arthur S. Way. Cambridge: Loeb Library, Harvard University Press, 1912.

———. *The Trojan Women*. Text, with a trans. by Arthur S. Way. Cambridge: Loeb Library, Harvard University Press, 1912.

Herodotus. *History*. Trans. David Grene. Chicago: University of Chicago Press, 1987.

Hesiod. *Shield of Heracles; Theogony; Works and Days*. Text, with a trans. by Hugh G. Evelyn-White. Cambridge: Loeb Library, Harvard University Press, 1914.

Homer. *Homeric Hymn to Aphrodite* and *Homeric Hymn to Demeter*. Text, with a trans. by Hugh G. Evelyn-White. Cambridge: Loeb Library, Harvard University Press, 1914.

———. *Iliad*. Text, with a trans. by A. T. Murray. Cambridge: Loeb Library, Harvard University Press, 1924.

———. *Odyssey*. Text, with a trans. by A. T. Murray. Cambridge: Loeb Library, Harvard University Press, 1919.

Hyginus. *Fabulae*. In H. J. Rose, *Hygenini Fabulae*. Lugduni Batavorum: A. W. Sythoff, 1963.

Hypostasis of the Archons. In *The Nag Hammadi Library in English*. Trans. J. M. Robinson. Rev. ed. New York: Harper and Row, 1988.

Nauck, A., ed. *Tragicorum Graecorum Fragmenta*. 2d ed. Leipzig: B. G. Teubner, 1889.

Ovid. *Metamorphoses*. Text, with a trans. by Frank Justus Miller. Cambridge: Loeb Library, Harvard University Press, 1977.

Pausanias. *Description of Greece*. Text, with a trans. by W. H. S. Jones and H. A. Ormerod. Cambridge: Loeb Library, Harvard University Press, 1926.

Pindar. *The Odes of Pindar*. Text, with a trans. by John Sandys. Cambridge: Loeb Library, Harvard University Press, 1961.

———. *The Odes of Pindar*. Trans. by Richmond Lattimore. Chicago: University of Chicago Press, 1947.

Plato. *Phaedrus* [Euthyphro, Apology, Crito, Phaedo, Phaedrus]. Text, with a trans. by Harold North Fowler. 1914. Reprint, Cambridge: Harvard University Press, 1990.

———. *Republic*. Text, with a trans. by Paul Shorey. 1930–35. Reprint, Cambridge: Harvard University Press, 1982.

———. *Sophist*. [Theaetetus, Sophist]. Text, with a trans. by Harold North Fowler. Cambridge: Harvard University Press, 1987.

Plautus. *Amphitruo*. Trans. James H. Mantinband. In Passage Mantinband, 39–108.

Pliny the Elder. *Natural History*. *Pliny's Natural History: An Account by a Roman of What Romans Knew and Did and Valued*. Ed. Loyd Haberly. New York: Frederick Ungar, 1957.

Plutarch. *Moralia*. Text, with a trans. by F. C. Babbitt. Cambridge: Loeb Library, Harvard University Press, 1936.

Pseudo-Callisthenes. "Alexander Romance." Trans. Ken Dowden. In *Collected Ancient Greek Novels*. Ed. B. P. Reardon. Berkeley and Los Angeles: University of California Press, 1989.

Seneca. *Hercules on Mount Oeta*. In *Seneca's Tragedies*. Text, with a trans. by Frank Justus Miller. Cambridge: Loeb Library, Harvard University Press, 1938.

Strabo. *Geography*. Text, with a trans. by Horace Leonard Jones. Cambridge: Loeb Library, Harvard University Press, 1960.

Tzetzes. *On Lycophron*. Oxford: Sheldonian Theatre, 1697.

Texts in Modern European Languages

Aarne, Antti. *The Types of the Folk-Tale: A Classification and Bibliography*. FF Communications, no. 74. Ann Arbor: Edwards Brothers, 1928.

Aarne, Antti, and Stith Thompson. *The Types of the Folk-Tale*. FF Communications, no. 184. Helsinki: Academia Scientiarum Fennica, 1961.

Allen, Nick. "The Hero's Five Relationships: A Proto-Indo-European Story." In Leslie, 15–30.

Allen, Woody. "Fabulous Tales and Mythical Beasts." In *Without Feathers*. New York: Random House, 1976.

Amar Chitra Katha, no. 58. "Surya." Ed. Anant Pai, retold ("from the Markandeya Purana") by Mayah Balse. Bombay, n.d.

———, no. 63. "The Story of Sukanya." Retold by Shanta Iyer. Bombay, n.d.

Andersen, Hans Christian. "The Mermaid." In *Hans Christian Andersen: The Complete Fairy Tales and Stories,* 250–70. Trans. Erik Christian Haugaard. New York: Doubleday, 1974.

Arnold, Beth. "Whose Life Is It, Anyway?" *American Way* (American Airlines), May 1990, 52–56.

Auerbach, Nina. *Our Vampires, Ourselves*. Chicago: University of Chicago Press, 1995.

Austin, Norman. *Helen of Troy and Her Shameless Phantom*. Ithaca: Cornell University Press, 1994.

Babington, B. G. *The Vedala Cadai, Being the Tamul Version of a Collection of Ancient Tales in the Sanscrit Language*. London, 1831.

Baring-Gould, S. *Curious Myths of the Middle Ages*. Ed. Edward Hardy. New York: Oxford University Press, 1978.

Basinger, Jeanine. *How Hollywood Spoke to Women, 1930–1960*. New York: Knopf, 1993.

Bataille, Georges. "The Solar Anus." In *Visions of Excess: Selected Writings: 1927–1939*. Trans. and ed. Allan Stoekl. Minneapolis: University of Minnesota Press, 1989.

Battuta, Ibn. *Travels in Asia and Africa, 1325–1354*. Trans. and ed. Hamilton Gibb. Delhi: Saeed International, 1990.

Beal, Samuel, trans. *Si-Yu-Ki: Buddhist Records of the Western World. Translated from the Chinese of Hiuen Tsiang (A.D. 629)*. London, 1884.

Behrman. S. N. *Amphitryon 38: A Comedy in a Prologue and Three Acts, by Jean Giraudoux*. Adapted from the French by S. N. Behrman. New York: Random House, 1938.

Bellow, Saul. *The Adventures of Augie March*. New York: Avon, 1977.

Blanchard, Pierre. *Le plutarque de la jeunesse*. Paris: Morizot, 1864.

Bloch, R. Howard. *Medieval Misogyny and the Invention of Western Romantic Love*. Chicago: University of Chicago Press, 1991.

Bloomfield, Maurice. "Contributions to the Interpretation of the Veda III: The Marriage of Saranyu, Tvastar's daughter." *Journal of the American Oriental Society* 15 (1893): 172–88.

———. "On Entering Another's Body." *American Journal of Philology* 44 (1923): 193–229.

Blumenthal, R. G. "After All These Years, Here Is the Fourth Face of Eve: Plaintiff." *Wall Street Journal,* February 1, 1989, B-1.

Boas, Franz, and George Hunt. "Kwakiutl Texts." *Memoirs of the American Museum of Natural History* 5 (1902): 1–270.

Bonnefoy, Yves, ed. *Mythologies.* English translation ed. Wendy Doniger. 2 vols. Chicago: University of Chicago Press, 1991.

Boswell, James. *Life of Samuel Johnson.* 2 vols. New York: Everyman, 1930.

Brown, Norman E. *The Indian and Christian Miracles of Walking on Water.* Chicago: Open Court Publishing, 1928.

Brzezinski, J. K. "Does Krsna Marry the Gopis in the End? The Svakiya-Parakiya Controversy in Gaudiya Vaisnavism." In Leslie, 30–45.

Buck, William. *The Ramayana.* Berkeley and Los Angeles: University of California Press, 1976.

Burton, Richard F. *Vikram and the Vampire, or Tales of Hindu Devilry.* London, 1870. Memorial ed. Ed. Isabel Burton, London, 1893. Reprint, New York: Dover, 1969.

Butler, Judith. *Gender Trouble: Feminism and the Subversion of Ideas.* New York: Routledge, 1990.

Bynum, Caroline Walker. *The Resurrection of the Body in Western Christianity, 200–1336.* New York: Columbia University Press, 1995.

Cabell, James Branch. *Jurgen: A Comedy of Justice.* Harmondsworth: Penguin, 1946.

Calasso, Roberto. *The Marriage of Cadmus and Harmony.* New York: Knopf, 1993.

Carter, Angela. "The Tiger's Bride." In *The Bloody Chamber and Other Stories.* London: Victor Gollancz, 1979; Harmondsworth, Penguin, 1981.

———. *Wise Children.* New York: Farrar Straus Giroux, 1991.

Cioran, E. M. *Tears and Saints.* Trans. Ilinca Sarifopol-Johnston. Chicago: University of Chicago Press, 1995.

Clader, Linda Lee. *Helen: The Evolution from Divine to Heroic in Greek Epic Tradition. Mnemosyne: Bibliotheca Classica Batava,* supplement 42. Leiden: E. J. Brill, 1976.

Cohen, Lawrence. "Semen Gain, Holi Modernity, and the Logic of Street Hustlers." Paper presented at the annual meeting of the Association of Asian Studies, Boston, March 25, 1994. Revised version published as "Holi in Banaras and the *Mahaland* of Modernity." *GLQ: A Journal of Lesbian and Gay Studies* 2 (1995): 399–424.

Coomaraswamy, A. K. "Chaya." *Journal of the American Oriental Society* 55 (1935): 278–83.

———. "The Interior Image." *Parabola,* summer 1986, 16–17.

d'Anglure, Bernard Saladin. "The Mythology of the Inuit of the Central Arctic." In Bonnefoy, 2:1145–52.

Davis, Nathalie Zemon. *The Return of Martin Guerre.* Cambridge: Harvard University Press, 1983.

Day, Lal Behari. *Folk-tales of Bengal.* London: Macmillan, 1885.

de Jong, J. W. "An Old Tibetan Version of the Ramayana." *T'oung Pao* 58 (1972): 190–202.

———. *The Story of Rama in Tibet: Text and Translation of the Tun-huang Manuscripts.* Stuttgart: Franz Steiner Verlag, 1989.

de la Rouchefoucald, Duc. *Maximes et réflexions morales.* Paris: De l'imprimerie de Monsieur, 1782.

Dessigane, R., and Jean Filliozat. *Les légendes çivaites de Kancipuram.* Pondicherry: Institut Français d'Indologie, 1964.

Dessigane, R., and P. Z. Pattabiramin. *La légende de Skanda selon le Kanchipuranam Tamoul et l'iconographie.* Pondicherry: Institut Français d'Indologie, 1967.

Dijkstra, Bram. *Idols of Perversity: Fantasies of Feminine Evil in Fin-de-Siecle Culture.* New York: Oxford University Press, 1986.

Dimmitt, Cornelia. "Sita: Mother Goddess and Sakti." In *The Divine Consort: Radha and the Goddesses of India.* Ed. Donna Wulff and John Stratton Hawley, 210–23. Berkeley: Berkeley Religious Studies Series, 1982.

Dimock, Edward Cameron. "A Theology of the Repulsive: The Myth of the Goddess Sitala." In *The Sound of Silent Guns, and Other Essays,* 130–49. Delhi: Oxford University Press, 1989.

Doniger, Wendy. *The Bedtrick: Telling the Difference.* Chicago: University of Chicago Press, forthcoming.

———. "Echoes of the *Mahabharata:* The Parrot as Narrator of the *Bhagavata Purana.*" In *Purana Perennis: Reciprocity and Transformation in Hindu and Jaina Texts.* Ed. Wendy Doniger, 31–58. Albany: SUNY Press, 1993.

———. "From Great Neck to Swift Hall: Confessions of a Reluctant Historian of Religions." In *The Craft of Religious Studies.* Ed. Jonathan R. Stone, 36–51. London: Macmillan; New York: St. Martin's Press, 1998.

———. "Gender and Myth." In *Critical Terms for the Study of Gender.* Ed. Gil Herdt. Chicago: University of Chicago Press, forthcoming.

———. *The Implied Spider: Politics and Theology in Myth.* New York: Columbia University Press, 1998.

———. "The Man Who Committed Adultery with His Own Wife." In *The Longing for Home.* Ed. Leroy S. Rouner, 128–37. Notre Dame: University of Notre Dame Press, 1997.

———. "The Mythology of Masquerading Animals, or, Bestiality." In *In the Company of Animals. Social Research* 62, no. 3 (1995): 751–72.

———. "Myths and Methods in the Dark." *Journal of Religion* 76, no. 4 (1996): 531–47.

———. "Playing the Field: Adultery as Claim-Jumping." In *The Sense of Adharma,* by Ariel Glucklich, 169–88. New York: Oxford University Press, 1994.

———. " 'Put a Bag over Her Head': Beheading Mythological Women." In *Off with Her Head! The Denial of Women's Identity in Myth, Religion, and Culture.* Ed. Howard Eilberg-Schwartz, 14–31. Berkeley and Los Angeles: University of California Press, 1995.

————. "Saranyu/Samjna: The Sun and the Shadow." In *Devi: Goddesses of India*. Ed. John Stratton Hawley and Donna Wulff, 154–72. Berkeley and Los Angeles: University of California Press, 1996.

————. "Sexual Masquerades in Hindu Myths: Aspects of the Transmission of Knowledge in Ancient India." In *The Transmission of Knowledge in South Asia*. Ed. Nigel Crook, 28–48. Delhi: Oxford University Press, 1996.

————. "Three (or More) Forms of the Three (or More)–Fold Path in Hinduism." *Graven Images* (1996, no. 3): 201–12.

Doniger, Wendy, and Gregory Spinner. "Misconceptions: Female Imaginations and Male Fantasies in Parental Imprinting." *Daedalus* 127, no. 1 (winter 1998): 97–130.

Douglas, Mary. "The Cloud God and the Shadow Self." *Social Anthropology* 3 (1995): 83–94.

————. *Purity and Danger: An Analysis of Concepts of Pollution and Taboo*. London: Routledge, 1966.

Dundes, Alan. "Earth-Diver: Creation of the Mythopoeic Male." In *Sacred Narrative*. Ed. Alan Dundes, 270–94. Berkeley and Los Angeles: University of California Press, 1984.

————. "The Hero Pattern and the Life of Jesus." In *In Quest of the Hero*, by Otto Rank et al., 179–223. Princeton: Princeton University Press, 1990.

Eckhart, Meister. *An Anthology of Sermons*. Trans. James M. Clark. London: Thomas Nelson, 1957.

Epstein, Edward Jay. "Dept. of Spin." *New Yorker*, June 22 and 29, 1998, 41.

Erndl, Kathleen M. "The Mutilation of Surpanakha." In Richman, 67–88.

Erskine, John. *The Private Life of Helen of Troy*. Indianapolis: Bobbs-Merrill, 1925.

Fass, Barbara. *La Belle Dame sans Merci and the Aesthetics of Romanticism*. Detroit: Wayne State University Press, 1974.

Figueira, Dorothy. "Heinrich Zimmer and Thomas Mann: The Illusion of Authorship." Unpublished ms., 1994.

————. "To Lose One's Head for Love: The Myth of the Transposed Heads in Thomas Mann and Marguerite Yourcenar." *Rivista de letterature moderne e comparate* 3 (1987): 161–73.

Fischer, Marjorie. *Red Feather*. New York: Modern Age Books, 1937.

Flahault, François. "Imagination and Mythology in Contemporary Literature (Tolkien, Lovecraft) and Science Fiction." In Bonnefoy, 2:790–91.

Franklin, Benjamin. "Benjamin Franklin Urges a Young Friend to Take an Old Mistress." In *A Treasury of the World's Great Letters*. Ed. M. Lincoln Schuster, 159–62. New York: Simon and Schuster, 1940.

Frazer, J. G. *The Belief in Immortality*. 3 vols. London: Macmillan, 1913.

Freeman, John Richardson. "Purity and Violence: Sacred Power in the Teyyam Worship of Malabar." Ph.D. diss., University of Pennsylvania, 1991.

Freud, Sigmund. *Collected Papers*. Ed. James Strachey. 5 vols. London: Hogarth Press, 1950.

————. "Family Romances." In *Collected Papers* 5:74–78.

————. "Medusa's Head." In *Collected Papers* 5:105–6.

———. "Psycho-analytic Notes on an Autobiographical Account of a Case of Paranoia (Dementia Paranoides)" ("The Case of Schreber"). In *Standard Edition* 12:3–84.

———. *Standard Edition of the Complete Psychological Works.* Ed. James Strachey. 24 vols. London: Hogarth Press, 1953–74.

———. *Totem and Taboo.* Trans. A. A. Brill. New York: Vintage, 1918.

Friedrich, Paul. *The Meaning of Aphrodite.* Chicago: University of Chicago Press, 1978.

Gantz, Jeffrey, trans. *Early Irish Myths and Sagas.* New York: Penguin, 1981.

Garber, Marjorie. *Vested Interests: Cross-Dressing and Cultural Anxiety.* New York: Routledge, 1992.

———. *Vice Versa: The Bisexuality of Every Life.* New York: Simon and Schuster, 1995.

Gautier, Théophile. "Avatar." In *Avatar et autres récits fantastiques,* 1–89. Verviers, Belgium: Marabout Géant, 1856–57.

———. *Avatar, Jettatura, The Water Pavilion.* In *The Works of Théophile Gautier.* Trans. and ed. F. C. de Sumichrast, 15:11–181. New York: George D. Sproul, 1902.

Geertz, Clifford. *After the Fact: Two Countries, Four Decades, One Anthropologist.* Cambridge: Harvard University Press, 1995.

———. *Local Knowledge: Further Essays in Interpretive Anthropology.* New York: Basic Books, 1983.

Gilman, Sander. *The Case of Sigmund Freud: Medicine and Identity at the Fin de Siècle.* Baltimore: Johns Hopkins University Press, 1993.

Ginzburg, Carlo. *Ecstasies: Deciphering the Witches' Sabbath.* Trans. Raymond Rosenthal. New York: Pantheon Books, 1991.

———. "Morelli, Freud, and Sherlock Holmes: Clues and Scientific Method." *History Workshop* 9 (1980): 5–36.

Giraudoux, Jean. *Amphitryon.* In *Three Plays,* 1–91.

———. *Amphitryon 38.* In *Théâtre complet,* 113–195. Ed. Jacques Body. Paris: Gallimard, 1982.

———. *Ondine.* In *Three Plays,* 177–273.

———. *Three Plays: Amphitryon, Intermezzo, Ondine.* Trans. Roger Gellert. New York: Oxford University Press, 1967.

Goethe, Johann Wolfgang von. *Faust.* Hamburg: Christian Wegner Verlag, 1959.

———. *Legende.* In *Die Zeit der Klassik,* vol. 1 of *Werke.* Ed. Erich Trunz, 157–303. Hamburg: Christian Wegner Verlag, 1964.

Gold, Ann Grodzins. "Sexuality, Fertility, and Erotic Imagination." In *Listen to the Heron's Words: Reimagining Gender and Kinship in North India,* by Gloria Goodwin Raheja and Ann Grodzins Gold, 30–72. Berkeley and Los Angeles: University of California Press, 1994.

———. "Spirit Possession Perceived and Performed in Rural Rajasthan." *Contributions to Indian Sociology* 22 (1988): 35–63.

Gold, Ann Grodzins, and Lindsey Harlan. "Raja Nal's Story." Paper presented at the South Asia conference in Madison, November 7, 1993.

Goldman, Robert P. "Fathers, Sons, and Gurus: Oedipal Conflict in the Sanskrit Epics." *Journal of Indian Philosophy* 6 (1978): 325–92.

————. "Transsexualism, Gender, and Anxiety in Traditional India." *Journal of the American Oriental Society* 113 (1993): 374–401.

Gombrich, Ernst. *Art and Illusion.* New York: Pantheon Books, 1961.

Gombrich, Richard F. "The Consecration of a Buddha Image." *Journal of Asian Studies* 26 (1966): 23–36.

Grapard, Allan. "Visions of Excess and Excesses of Vision: Women and Transgression in Japanese Myth." *Japanese Journal of Religious Studies* 18 (March 1991): 3–22.

Grottanelli, Cristiano. "The King's Grace and the Helpless Woman: A Comparative Study of the Stories of Ruth, Charila, Sita." *History of Religions* 22 (1982): 1–24.

Hacking, Ian. "Double Consciousness in Britain, 1814–1875." *Dissociation* 4 (1991): 134–46.

Halliwell, Leslie. *Halliwell's Film Guide.* Ed. John Walker. New York: Harper, 1995.

Hallmundsson, Hallberg. *An Anthology of Scandinavian Literature.* New York: Collier Books, 1965.

Handelman, Don. "The Guises of the Goddess and the Transformation of the Male: Gangamma's Visit to Tirupati, and the Continuum of Gender." In *Syllables of Sky: Studies in South Indian Civilization, In Honour of Velcheru Narayana Rao.* Ed. David Shulman, 283–337. Delhi: Oxford University Press, 1995.

Handelman, Don, and David Shulman. *God Inside Out: Siva's Game of Dice.* New York: Oxford University Press, 1997.

Harper, Ralph. *On Presence: Variations and Reflections.* Philadelphia: Trinity Press International, 1991.

Hart, George, and Hank Heifetz. trans. *The Forest Book of the Ramayana* [of Kamban]. Berkeley and Los Angeles: University of California Press, 1988.

Hazra, Rajendra Chandra. *Studies in the Upapuranas.* 2 vols. Calcutta: University of Calcutta, 1958–63.

Hess, Linda. "Rejecting Sita: Indian Responses to the Ideal Man's Cruel Treatment of His Ideal Wife." *Journal of the American Academy of Religion* 67, no. 1 (1991): 1–32.

Hirth, Friedrich. "Chinese Metallic Mirrors." In *Boas Anniversary Volume.* Ed. Berthold Laufer, 208–56. New York: G. E. Stechert, 1906.

Hoffmann, E. T. A. "The Sandman." In *The Tales of E. T. A. Hoffmann.* Ed. and trans. Leonard J. Kent and Elizabeth C. Knight. Chicago: University of Chicago Press, 1969.

Hofmannsthal, Hugo von. "Die ägyptische Helena" (1928). In *Gesammelte Werke.* Vol. 4, *Dramen.* Ed. H. Steiner, 473–76. Frankfurt: S. Fischer, 1958.

————. *Die ägyptische Helena.* Libretto. 1926.

Huet, Marie-Hélène. *Monstrous Imagination.* Cambridge: Harvard University Press, 1993.

Hughes, Robert. *Nothing If Not Critical.* New York: Knopf, 1990; Harmondsworth: Penguin, 1992.

Insler, Stanley. "The Shattered Head Split and the Epic Tale of Sakuntala." *Bulletin d'études indiennes,* nos. 7–8 (1989–90), 97–139.

Iyengar, K. R. Srinivasa. *Sitayana: Epic of the Earth-Born.* Madras: Samata Books, 1987.

Jacobsen, Per S., and Barbara Fass Leavy. *Ibsen's Forsaken Merman: Folklore in the Late Plays.* New York: NYU Press, 1988.

Jacobson, Lou. "A Mind Is a Terrible Thing to Waste." *Lingua Franca*, August 1997, 6–7.

Johnson, Robert A. *Femininity Lost and Regained*. New York: Harper and Row, 1990.

Jungk, Robert. *Heller als tausend Sonnen: Das Schicksal der Atomforscher*. Bern: A. Scherz, 1956 (*Brighter Than a Thousand Suns: The Moral and Political History of the Atomic Scientists*. Trans. James Cleugh. London: Gollancz, 1958).

Kakar, Sudhir. *Intimate Relations: Exploring Indian Sexuality*. Chicago: University of Chicago Press, 1990.

———. *Shamans, Mystics, and Doctors*. New York: Knopf, 1982.

Kakridis, Johannes Th. *Homer Revisited*. Lund: New Society of Letters at Lund, 1971.

Kalluak, Mark, ed. *How Kablomat Became and Other Legends*. Ottawa: Program Development, Department of Education, Canada, 1974.

Karnad, Girish. *Hayavadana*. In *Three Plays*, 67–140.

———. *Naga-Mandala: Play with a Cobra*. In *Three Plays*, 19–66.

———. *Three Plays: Naga-Mandala, Hayavadana, Tughlaq*. Delhi: Oxford University Press, 1995.

Keillor, Garrison. "Zeus the Lutheran." *New Yorker*, October 29, 1990, 32–37.

Keller, Otto. *Thiere des classischen Alterthums in culturgeschichtlicher Beziehung*. Innsbruck: Verlag der Wagner'schen Universitäts-Buchhandlung, 1887.

Kleist, Heinrich von. *Amphitryon*. Trans. Charles E. Passage. In *Plays*, ed. Walter Hinderer, 91–164. New York: Continuum, 1982. Also in Passage and Mantinband, 209–81.

Kramer, Heinrich, and James Sprenger. *The Malleus Maleficarum*. Trans. Montague Summers. New York: Dover, 1971.

Kramrisch, Stella. "Two: Its Significance in the Rgveda." *Indological Studies in Honor of W. Norman Brown*, 109–36. Ed. Ernest Bender. New Haven: American Oriental Society, 1962.

Krappe, Alexander H. "Far Eastern Fox Lore." *California Folklore Quarterly* 3 (1944): 124–47.

———. "Lancelot et Guenièvre." *Revue celtique* 48 (1931): 92–123.

Kuhn, Adalbert. "Saranyu-Erinnus." *Zeitschrift für vergleichende Sprachforschung*, ed. Theodor Aufrecht and Adalbert Kuhn, I, Berlin, 1852, 439–70.

Kuipers, Joel C. *Power and Performance: The Creation of Textual Authority in Weyewa Ritual Speech*. Philadelphia: University of Pennsylvania Press, 1990.

Kundera, Milan. *The Unbearable Lightness of Being*. New York: Harper and Row, 1984.

Lancelot and *Merlin*. In *Lancelot-Grail: The Old French Arthurian Vulgate and Post-Vulgate in Translation*. Ed. Norris J. Lacy. 2. vols. Vol. 1: *The Story of Merlin*, trans. Rupert T. Pickens. Vol. 2: *Lancelot*, parts 1–3, trans. Samuel N. Rosenberg, Carleton W. Carroll, and Samuel N. Rosenberg. New York: Garland, 1993.

Lancaster, Evelyn. *See* Sizemore.

Lane, Anthony. "Romantic Triangle" (review of *While You Were Sleeping*). *New Yorker*, May 22, 1995, 96.

Laqueur, Thomas. *Making Sex: Body and Gender from the Greeks to Freud*. Cambridge: Harvard University Press, 1990.

Leavy, Barbara Fass. *In Search of the Swan Maiden: A Narrative on Folklore and Gender*. New York: New York University Press, 1994.

————. *La Belle Dame sans Merci and the Aesthetics of Romanticism.* See Fass.

Le Carré, John. *The Little Drummer Girl.* New York: Alfred Knopf, 1983.

Leslie, Julia, ed. *Myth and Mythmaking: Continuous Evolution in Indian Tradition.* Richmond, Surrey: Curzon Press, 1966.

Lévi-Strauss, Claude. *The Elementary Structures of Kinship.* Trans. J. H. Bell, ed. Rodney Needham. Boston: Beacon Press, 1969.

————. *The Jealous Potter.* Chicago: University of Chicago Press, 1988.

————. "Language and the Analysis of Social Laws." In *Structural Anthropology,* 55–66.

————. *Structural Anthropology.* Trans. Claire Jacobson and Brooke Grundfest Schoepf. Harmondsworth: Penguin, 1963.

————. "The Structural Study of Myth." In *Structural Anthropology,* 206–32.

Lewis, Janet. *The Wife of Martin Guerre.* Denver: Alan Swallow, 1941.

Li, Wei-yi. "On Becoming a Fish: Paradoxes of Immortality and Enlightenment in Chinese Literature." Paper presented at the Einstein Forum conference on "Transformations of the Self," at Kibbutz Genosar, April 5–8, 1998.

LiDonnici, Lynn R. *The Epidaurian Miracle Inscription.* Atlanta: Scholars Press, 1995.

Lifton, Robert Jay. *The Nazi Doctors: Medical Killing and the Psychology of Genocide.* New York: Basic Books, 1986.

Lincoln, Bruce. *Death, War, and Sacrifice: Studies in Ideology and Practice.* Chicago: University of Chicago Press, 1991.

————. *Myth, Cosmos, and Society.* Cambridge: Harvard University Press, 1986.

————. *Priests, Warriors, and Cattle: A Study in the Ecology of Religions.* Berkeley and Los Angeles: University of California Press, 1981.

————. "Rewriting the German War-God: Georges Dumézil, Politics, and Scholarship in the Late 1930s." *History of Religions* 37, no. 3 (February 1998): 87–208.

Lombard, Denys, and Christian Pelras. "The Ramayana in Indonesia." In Bonnefoy, 2:957–58.

Lommel, Herman. "Vedische Einzelstudien." In *Zeitschrift der Deutschen Morgenlandischen Gesellschaft* 99 (1949): 225–57.

Loraux, Nicole. "Origins of Mankind in Greek Myths." In Bonnefoy, 1:390–94.

Malamoud, Charles. "Les dieux n'ont pas d'ombre: Remarques sur la langue secrète des dieux dans l'Inde ancienne." In *Cuire le monde: rite et pensée dans l'inde ancienne,* 241–52. Paris: Éditions la Découverte, 1989. ("The Gods Have No Shadows: Reflections on the Secret Language of the Gods in Ancient India." In *Cooking the World: Ritual and Thought in Ancient India.* Trans. David White, 195–206. Delhi: Oxford University Press, 1996.)

Mani, Vettam. *Puranic Encyclopedia.* Delhi: Motilal Banarsidass, 1975.

Mann, Thomas. *The Transposed Heads: A Legend of India.* Trans. H. T. Lowe-Porter. New York: Vintage Books, 1941.

Marlowe, Christopher. *Dr. Faustus.* New York: Dover/Constable, 1994.

Maslin, Janet. "Good and Evil Trade Places, Body and Soul." *New York Times,* June 27, 1997, C1, C14.

Mazak, Arlene. "Multidimensionality and Integral Self-Realization in Kundalini Yoga." Ph.D. diss., University of Chicago, 1993.

Meyer, Eveline. *Ankalaparamecuvari: A Goddess of Tamilnadu: Her Myths and Cult.* Beiträge zur Südasienforschung Südasien-institut, Universität Heidelberg, vol. 107. Wiesbaden: Steiner Verlag, 1986.

Mills, D. E. *A Collection of Tales from Uji.* Cambridge: Cambridge University Press, 1970.

Molière. *Amphitryon.* Trans. Charles E. Passage. In Passage and Mantinband, 131–91.

Morris, Jan. *Conundrum.* London: Faber and Faber, 1974.

Mulvey, Laura. "Pandora: Topographies of the Mask and Curiosity." In *Sexuality and Space.* Ed. Beatriz Colomina, 53–72. Princeton: Princeton Architectural Press, 1992.

Murdoch, Iris. *The Sea, The Sea.* New York: Viking Press, 1978.

Nagy, Gregory. *Greek Mythology and Poetics.* Ithaca: Cornell University Press, 1990.

———. "The Name of Apollo." In *Apollo: Origins and Influences.* Ed. J. Solomon, 3–7. Tucson: University of Arizona Press, 1994.

———. "Phaethon, Sappho's Phaon, and the White Rock of Leukas." *Harvard Studies in Classical Philology* 77 (1973): 137–77.

———. *Pindar's Homer: The Lyric Possession of an Epic Past.* Baltimore: Johns Hopkins University Press, 1990.

Nagy, Joseph Falaky. "Hierarchy, Heroes, and Heads: Indo-European Structures in Greek Myth." In *Approaches to Greek Myth.* Ed. Lowell Edmunds, 200–238. Baltimore: Johns Hopkins University Press, 1990.

Nanda, Serena. *Neither Man Nor Woman: The Hijras of India.* Belmont, Calif.: Wadsworth, 1990.

Narayan, Kirin. *Mondays on the Dark Night of the Moon: Himalayan Foothill Folktales told by Urmila Devi.* New York: Oxford University Press, 1997.

Narayan, R. K. *The Ramayana.* London: Chatto and Windus, 1973.

Nietzsche, Friedrich. *Also Sprach Zarathustra.* Trans. Thomas Common. New York: Modern Library, 1917.

———. *Beyond Good and Evil: Prelude to a Philosophy of the Future.* Trans. Walter Kaufmann. New York: Vintage Books, 1966.

———. *The Birth of Tragedy* and *The Case of Wagner.* Trans. Walter Kaufmann. New York: Vintage Books, 1967.

———. *The Gay Science.* Trans. Walter Kaufmann. New York: Random House, 1974.

Niven, Larry. "Man of Steel, Woman of Kleenex." In *N-Space,* 223–32. New York: Tom Doherty Associates, 1994.

Noble, Sally. "The Tamil Story of the Anklet: Classical and Contemporary Tellings of Cilappatikaram." Ph.D. diss., University of Chicago, 1990.

Obeyesekere, Gananath. *Medusa's Hair: An Essay on Personal Symbols and Religious Experience.* Chicago: University of Chicago Press, 1981.

O'Flaherty, Wendy Doniger. "The Case of the Stallion's Wife: Indra and Vrsanasva in the Rg Veda and the Brahmanas." *Journal of the American Oriental Society* 105 (1985): 485–98.

———. "The Dream Narrative and the Indian Doctrine of Illusion." *Daedalus,* summer 1982, 93–113.

————. *Dreams, Illusion, and Other Realities*. Chicago: University of Chicago Press, 1984.

————. *Hindu Myths*. Harmondsworth: Penguin, 1975.

————. "Horses and Snakes in the *Adi Parvan* of the *Mahabharata*." In *Aspects of India: Essays in Honor of Edward Cameron Dimock*. Ed. Margaret Case and N. Gerald Barrier, 16–44. New Delhi: American Institute of Indian Studies, 1986.

————. "The Interaction of Saguna and Nirguna Images of Deity." In *The Sants: Studies in a Devotional Tradition of India*. Ed. Karine Schomer and Hew McLeod, 47–52. Berkeley: Berkeley Religious Studies Series; Delhi: Motilal Banarsidass, 1987.

————. "The King and the Corpse and the Rabbi and the Talk-Show Star: Heinrich Zimmer's Legacy to Mythologists and Indologists." In *Heinrich Zimmer, Coming into His Own*. Ed. Margaret H. Case), 49–60. Princeton: Princeton University Press, 1994.

————. "Myths and Methods in the Dark." *Journal of Religion* 76 (1996): 531–47.

————. *The Origins of Evil in Hindu Mythology*. Berkeley and Los Angeles: University of California Press, 1976.

————. *Other Peoples' Myths: The Cave of Echoes*. Chicago: University of Chicago Press, 1995.

————. *The Rig Veda: An Anthology*. Harmondsworth: Penguin, 1981.

————. *Siva: The Erotic Ascetic*. London: Oxford University Press, 1973.

————. "Speaking in Tongues: Deceptive Stories about Sexual Deception," *Journal of Religion* 74 (1994): 320–37.

————. *Tales of Sex and Violence: Folklore, Sacrifice, and Danger in the Jaiminiya Brahmana*. Chicago: University of Chicago Press, 1985.

————. *Textual Sources for the Study of Hinduism*. Chicago: University of Chicago Press, 1990.

————. "When a Lingam Is Just a Good Cigar: Psychoanalysis and Hindu Sexual Fantasies." In *The Psychoanalytic Study of Society: Essays in Honor of Alan Dundes*. Ed. L. Bryce Boyer et al., 81–104. Hillside, N.J.: Analytic Press, 1993.

————. *Women, Androgynes, and Mythical Beasts*. Chicago: University of Chicago Press, 1981.

Olender, Maurice. "Gender, Sex, and Mythology in Greece and Rome: Priapos and Baubo." Paper presented at the conference on "the Sexual Divide: Human and Divine," at Mishkenot Sha'ananim, April 11–19, 1998.

Ortner, Sherry. "Is Female to Male as Nature Is to Culture?" In *Women, Culture, and Society*. Ed. M. Rosaldo and L. Lamphere, 67–87. Stanford: Stanford University Press, 1974.

Orwell, George. *Animal Farm*. New York: Harcourt Brace, 1946.

Otto, Rudolph. *The Idea of the Holy*. Trans. John W. Harvey. New York: Oxford University Press, 1958.

Panofsky, E. *Idea: A Concept in Art Theory*. Trans. Joseph J. S. Peake. New York: Harper and Row, 1975.

Paracelsus. "A Book on Nymphs, Sylphs, Pygmies, and Salamanders, and on the Other Spirits." Trans. with an introduction by Henry E. Sigerist. *Four Treatises of*

Theophrastus von Hohenheim: Called Paracelsus. Baltimore: Johns Hopkins University Press, 1941.

Passage, Charles, and James H. Mantinband, eds. and trans. *Amphitryon: Three Plays in New Verse Translation (Plautus, Molière, Kleist), Together with a Comprehensive Account of the Evolution of the Legend and Its Subsequent History on the Stage.* Chapel Hill: University of North Carolina Press, 1974.

Poe, Edgar Allan. "William Wilson." In *Complete Stories and Poems of Edgar Allan Poe.* Garden City, N.Y.: Doubleday, 1966.

Pollock, Sheldon. "Literary History, Region, and Nation in South Asia." *Social Scientist* 23 (1995): 112–42.

———. "Ramayana and Political Imagination in India." *Journal of Asian Studies* 52 (1993): 261–97.

Pomeroy, Sarah B. *Goddesses, Whores, Wives, and Slaves: Women in Classical Antiquity.* New York: Schocken Books, 1975.

Ramanujan, A. K. *The Flowering Tree, and Other Oral tales from India.* Ed. Stuart Blackburn and Alan Dundes. Berkeley and Los Angeles: University of California Press, 1997.

———. *Folktales from India.* New York: Pantheon Books, 1992.

———. "The Prince Who Married His Own Left Side." In *Aspects of India: Essays in Honor of Edward Cameron Dimock.* Ed. Margaret Case and N. Gerald Barrier, 1–16. New Delhi: American Institute of Indian Studies, 1986. Also in *The Flowering Tree,* 142–45.

———. *Speaking of Siva.* Baltimore: Penguin, 1973.

———. "Three Hundred Ramayanas: Five Examples and Three Thoughts on Translation." In Richman, 22–49.

———. "Towards a Counter-system: Women's Tales." In *Gender, Discourse, and Power in South Asia.* Ed. Arjun Appadurai et al., 33–55. Philadelphia: University of Pennsylvania Press, 1991.

———. "Two Realms of Kannada Folklore." In *Another Harmony: New Essays on the Folklore of India.* Ed. Stuart Blackburn and A. K. Ramanujan, 41–75. Berkeley and Los Angeles: University of California Press, 1986.

Ramesan, N. *Temples and Legends of Andhra Pradesh.* Bombay: Bharatiya Vidya Bhavan, 1962.

Rank, Otto. *Beyond Psychology.* New York: Dover, 1958.

———. *The Double: A Psychoanalytic Study.* Trans. and ed. Harry Tucker Jr. New York: New American Library, 1971.

Rasmussen, Knud. *Observations on the Intellectual Culture of the Caribou Eskimos.* Trans. W. E. Calvert. 1930; reprint, New York, AMS Press, 1976.

Reinach, Salomon. *Cultes, mythes, et religions.* Paris: Ernest Leroux, 1905–12.

Renard, Maurice. *Le docteur Lerne, sous-dieu.* Paris: Cres, 1919.

Richer, Jean. "The Androgyne, the Double, and the Reflection: A Few Myths of Romanticism." In Bonnefoy, 1:765–66.

Richman, Paula, ed. *Many Ramayanas: The Diversity of Narrative Traditions in South Asia.* Berkeley and Los Angeles: University of California Press, 1991.

Roheim, Geza. "Aphrodite, or the Woman with a Penis." In *The Panic of the Gods and Other Essays.* New York: Harper and Row, 1972.

Rostand, Edmond. *Cyrano de Bergerac.* Trans. into English verse by Brian Hooker. New York: Bantam Books, 1950.

Ruben, Walter. *Krsna: Konkordanz und Kommentar der Motive seines Heldenlebens.* Leiden: Internationales Archiv für Ethnographie, 1939.

Rudolph, Lloyd. "Urban Life and Populist Radicalism: Dravidian Politics in Madras." *Journal of Asian Studies* 20 (1961): 280–90.

Rushdie, Salman. *The Wizard of Oz.* London: British Film Institute, 1992.

Sarang, Vilas. "An Interview with M. Chakko." In *Fair Tree of the Void: Stories,* 89–98. With an introduction by Adil Jussawalla. Harmondsworth: Penguin, 1990.

Sax, William S. *Mountain Goddess: Gender and Politics in a Himalayan Pilgrimage.* New York: Oxford University Press, 1991.

Scarry, Elaine. *The Body in Pain: The Making and Unmaking of the World.* New York: Oxford University Press, 1985.

Scott, James. *Weapons of the Weak: Everyday Forms of Peasant Resistance.* New Haven: Yale University Press, 1985.

Sedgwick, Eve Kosofsky. *Between Men: English Literature and Male Homosexual Desire.* New York: Columbia University Press, 1985.

Shakespeare, William. *The Complete Works of Shakespeare.* Ed. David Bevington. New York: Harper Collins, 1992.

Showalter, Elaine. *Sexual Anarchy: Gender and Culture at the Fin de Siècle.* New York: Penguin, 1990.

Shulman, David. "Concave and Full: Making the Mirrored Deity at Lepaksi." In a forthcoming memorial volume for Sondheimer.

———. "First Man, Forest Mother: Telugu Humanism in the Age of Krsnadevaraya." In *Syllables of Sky,* 133–64.

———. *The King and the Clown in South Indian Myth and Poetry.* Princeton: Princeton University Press, 1985.

———. "On Being a Stone: A Reading of the Tirupati *Puranas.*" Unpublished MS.

———. "On Being Human in the Sanskrit Epic: The Riddle of Nala." *Journal of Indian Philosophy* 22 (1994): 1–29.

———. "Sita and Satakantharavana in a Tamil Folk Narrative." *Journal of Indian Folkloristics* 2 (1979): 1–26.

———, ed. *Syllables of Sky: Studies in South Indian Civilization, In Honour of Velcheru Narayana Rao.* Delhi: Oxford University Press, 1995.

———. *Tamil Temple Myths.* Princeton: Princeton University Press, 1980.

Shulman, David, Velcheru Narayana Rao, and Sanjay Subrahmanyam. *Symbols of Substance: Court and State in Nayaka Period Tamil Nadu.* Delhi: Oxford University Press, 1992.

Siegel, Lee. *Fires of Love/Waters of Peace: Passion and Renunciation in Indian Culture.* Honolulu: University of Hawaii Press, 1983.

Sizemore, Chris Costner. As Evelyn Lancaster, with James Poling. *The Final Face of Eve.* New York: McGraw-Hill, 1958.

————. With Elen Sain Pittilo. *I'm Eve*. New York: Jove, 1978.

————. *A Mind of My Own*. New York: William Morrow and Co., Inc., 1989.

Skutsch, Otto. "Helen: Her Name and Nature." *Journal of Hellenic Studies* 102 (1987): 188–93.

Söhnen-Thieme, Renata, "The Ahalya Story through the Ages." In Leslie, 39–62.

Sonnerat, Pierre. *Voyages aux Indes Orientales et a la Chine: fait par ordre du roi, depuis 1774 jusqu'en 1781: dans lequel on traite des moeurs de la religion, des sciences & des arts des Indiens, des Chinois, des Pegouins & des Madegasses: suivi d'observations sur le cap de Bonne-Esperance, les isles de France & de Bourbon, les Maldives, Ceylan, Malacca, les Philippines & les Moluques, & de recherches sur l'histoire naturelle de ces pays*. Paris: published by the author, 1782.

Spenser, Edmund. *The Faerie Queene*. Ed. J. W. Hales. 2 vols. London: Dent, 1965; New York: Dutton, 1966.

Stade, George. "Dracula's Women, and Why Men Love to Hate Them." In *The Psychology of Men: New Psychoanalytic Perspectives*. Ed. Gerald I. Fogel et al., 25–48. New York: Basic Books, 1986.

Stevenson, Robert Louis. *The Strange Case of Dr. Jekyll and Mr. Hyde* (London, 1887). Ed. Donald L. Lawler. Critical ed. New York: Norton, 1988.

Stoker, Bram. *Dracula* (London, 1897). With an introduction by George Stade. New York: Bantam, 1981.

Strong, John. *The Legend and Cult of Upagupta: Sanskrit Buddhism in North India and Southeast Asia*. Princeton: Princeton University Press, 1992.

Stroumsa, Guy. "Madness and Divination in Early Christian Monasticism." Conference on Transformations of the Self, Galilee, 1998.

Suzuki, Mihoko. *The Metamorphoses of Helen: Authority, Difference, and the Epic*. Ithaca: Cornell University Press, 1989.

Swift, Jonathan. *Gulliver's Travels*. Ed. Robert A. Greenberg. Critical ed. New York: W. W. Norton, 1970.

Syrkin, Alexander. "Chernoye Solntse." *Kratkiye Soobshcheniya Instituta Narodov Azii* 80 (1965): 20–32.

Thigpen, Corbett H., and Hervey M. Cleckley. *The Three Faces of Eve*. New York: McGraw-Hill, 1957.

Thomas, F. W. "A Ramayana Story in Tibetan from Chinese Turkestan." In *Indian Studies in Honor of Charles Rockwell Lanman*, 193–212. Cambridge: Harvard University Press, 1929.

Toobin, Jeffrey. "The Trouble with Sex: Why the Law of Sexual Harassment Has Never Worked." *New Yorker*, February 9, 1998, 48–55.

Tracy, David. *On Naming the Present: Reflections on God, Hermeneutics, and Church*. Maryknoll, N.Y.: Orbis Books, 1994.

Veeder, William. "Children of the Night: Stevenson and Patriarchy." In *Dr. Jekyll and Mr. Hyde after One Hundred Years*. Ed. William Veeder and Gordon Hirsch, 107–60. Chicago: University of Chicago Press, 1988.

Vernant, Jean-Paul. "Greek Cosmogonic Myths." In Bonnefoy, 1:366–74.

————. "Sacrifice in Greek Myths" (part 1). In Bonnefoy, 1:422–27.

———. "Theogony and Myths of Sovereignty in Greece." In Bonnefoy, 1 : 375–78.

Wadler, Joyce. "Public Lives; Ex-Stripper Reveals Herself, in a Memoir." *New York Times,* July 24, 1998, B2.

Wadley, Susan S. "Bubbling Kings and Trickster Goddesses in the North Indian Epic Dhola." Paper presented at Columbia University, April 1996.

———. "Raja Nal, Motini, Damayanti, and the Dice Game: Some Preliminary Thoughts." Paper presented at the Annual South Asian Conference, November 1993.

Wagner, Richard. *The Art-Work of the Future.* In *The Art-Work of the Future and Other Works.* Trans. William Ashton Ellis, 69–213. Lincoln: University of Nebraska Press, 1993.

Warner, Marina. *From the Beast to the Blonde: On Fairy Tales and Their Tellers.* London: Chatto and Windus, 1995.

———. "Stolen Shadows, Lost Souls." *Raritan,* fall 1995, 35–58.

Weber, Albrecht, ed. *Indische Studien: Zeitschrift für die Kunde des indischen Alterthums.* 18 vols. Berlin: Georg Olms Verlag, 1850–98.

Whaling, Frank. *The Rise of the Religious Significance of Rama.* Delhi: Motilal Banarsidass, 1980.

Wilde, Oscar. "The Fisherman and His Soul." In *The Pomegranate House.* Reprinted in *Complete Shorter Fiction,* 203–36. Oxford: Oxford University Press, 1979.

———. *The Picture of Dorian Gray.* Ed. Donald L. Lawler. New York: Norton, 1988.

Williams, Tennessee. *The Night of the Iguana.* In *The Theatre of Tennessee Williams.* Vol. 4. New York: New Directions, 1972.

Wilson, Edmund. *The Wound and the Bow: Seven Studies in Literature.* New York: Oxford University Press, 1959.

Wilson, H. H., trans. *The Vishnu Purana.* 3d ed. Calcutta: Punthi Pustak, 1961.

Winkler, Cathy. "Rape Trauma: Contexts of Meaning." In *Embodiment and Experience: The Existential Ground of Culture and Self.* Ed. Thomas Csordas, 69–96. Cambridge: Cambridge University Press, 1994.

Woolf, Virginia. *Orlando: A Biography.* New York: Harcourt Brace, 1928.

Yeats, William Butler. *The Autobiography of William Butler Yeats.* New York: Doubleday, 1958.

Yourcenar, Marguerite. "Kali Beheaded." In *Oriental Tales.* Trans. Alberto Manguel, 119–28. New York: Farrar Strauss, 1938.

Yu, Li. "Nativity Room." In *A Tower for the Summer Heat.* Trans. Patrick Hanan, 221–49. New York: Ballantine, 1992.

Zeitlin, Froma. "Figuring Fidelity in Homer's *Odyssey.*" In *Playing the Other: Gender and Society in Classical Greek Texts,* 19–52. Chicago: University of Chicago Press, 1996.

———. "The Lady Vanishes: Helen and Her Phantom in Euripides' *Helen* and *Orestes.*" Second Sather lecture, Berkeley, 1996, unpublished draft.

———. "Travesties of Gender and Genre in Aristophanes' *Thesmophoriazousae.*" In *Representations of Women in Antiquity.* Ed. Helene Foley, 169–217. New York: Gordon and Breach, 1981.

Zimmer, Heinrich. *The King and the Corpse: Tales of the Soul's Conquest of Evil.* Ed. Joseph Campbell. Princeton: Bollingen, 1948.

FILMS

Anna Karenina, 1948, w[written by] Jean Anouilh et al.; d[directed by] Julian Duvivier; s[starring] Vivien Leigh, Ralph Richardson.

Chances Are, 1989, w Perry Howze, Randy Howze; d Emile Ardolino; s Cybill Shepherd, Robert Downey Jr., Ryan O'Neal, Mary Stewart Masterson.

Dark Mirror, 1946, w Nunnally Johnson, from a story by Vladimir Pozner; d Robert Siodmak; s Olivia de Havilland, Lew Ayres.

Dead Ringer, 1964, w Albert Beich, Oscar Millard; d Paul Henreid; s Bette Davis, Peter Lawford, Karl Malden.

Dead Ringers, 1988, wd David Cronenberg; s Jeremy Irons, Genevieve Bujold.

The Divorce of Lady X, 1938, w Lajos Biro, Arthur Wimperis, Ian Dalrymple, from Gilbert Wakefield's play, *Counsel's Opinion;* d Tim Whelan; s Merle Oberon, Laurence Olivier, Ralph Richardson.

Dr. Jekyll and Mr. Hyde, 1931, w Samuel Hoffenstein, Percy Heath, from the novel by Robert Louis Stevenson; d Rouben Mamoulian; s Frederic March, Miriam Hopkins.

Dr. Jekyll and Ms. Hyde, 1995, w Tim John Oliver Butcher, from a story by David Price; d Jerry Leider; s Tim Daly, Sean Young.

Dr. Jekyll and Sister Hyde, 1971, w Brian Clemens; d Roy Ward Baker; s Ralph Bates, Martine Beswick, Gerald Sim.

Double Impact, 1991, wd Sheldon Lettich, Jean-Claude Van Damme; s Jean-Claude Van Damme.

Double Indemnity, 1944, w Billy Wilder, Raymond Chandler, from the novel by James M. Cain; d Billy Wilder; s Fred MacMurray, Barbara Stanwyck, Edward G. Robinson.

Excalibur, 1981, w Rospo Pallenberg, John Boorman; d John Boorman; s Nigel Terry, Helen Mirren, Nicol Williamson.

Face/Off, 1997, w Mike Werb and Michael Colleary; d John Woo; s Nicolas Cage, John Travolta.

Hercules, 1997, w John Musker, Ron Clements et al.; d John Musker and Ron Clements.

The Importance of Being Ernest, 1952, w Anthony Asquith, from the play by Oscar Wilde; d Anthony Asquith; s Michael Redgrave, Edith Evans, Margaret Rutherford, Joan Greenwood, Dorothy Tutin.

The Man with Two Brains, 1983, w Carl Reiner, Steve Martin, George Gipe; d Carl Reiner; s Steve Martin, Kathleen Turner, Sissy Spacek.

Mighty Aphrodite, 1996, wd Woody Allen; s Woody Allen, Mira Sorvino.

Multiplicity, 1996, w Chris Miller, Mary Hale, Lowell Ganz, Babaloo Mandel, based on a short story by Chris Miller; d Harold Ramis; s Michael Keaton, Andie MacDowell.

Never on Sunday, 1959, wd Jules Dassin; s Melina Mercouri.

The Picture of Dorian Gray, 1945; wd Albert Lewin; s George Sanders, Hurd Hatfield, Donna Reed, Angela Lansbury, Peter Lawford.

The Reincarnation of Peter Proud, 1974, w Max Ehrlich, from his novel; d J. Lee-Thompson; s Michael Sarrazin, Margot Kidder, Jennifer O'Neill.

The Return of Martin Guerre, 1982, w Jean-Claude Carrière, Daniel Vigne; d Daniel Vigne; s Gérard Depardieu, Nathalie Baye.

Roxanne, 1987, w Steve Martin; d Fred Schepisi; s Steve Martin, Daryl Hannah.

Shattered, 1991, w Wolfgang Petersen, from Richard Neely's novel, *The Plastic Nightmare;* d Wolfgang Petersen; s Tom Berenger, Greta Scacchi, Bob Hoskins.

Sommersby, 1993, w Nicholas Meyer, Sarah Kernochan; d Jon Amiel; s Richard Gere, Jodie Foster, James Earl Jones.

Spirits of the Dead, 1968. "William Wilson" segment, w Louis Malle, based on the tale by Edgar Allan Poe; d Louis Malle; s Brigitte Bardot, Alain Delon.

A Stolen Life, 1946, w Catherine Turney, based on the 1939 film; d Curtis Bernhardt; s Bette Davis, Glenn Ford. (Also 1939, w Margaret Kennedy, George Barraud, from the novel by Karel J. Benes; d Paul Czinner; s Elizabeth Bergner, Michael Redgrave.)

Superman, 1978, w Mario Puzo et al.; d Richard Donner; s Christopher Reeve, Margot Kidder.

Switch, 1991, wd Blake Edwards; s Ellen Barkin.

The Three Faces of Eve, 1957, w Nunnally Johnson, from the book by Corbett H. Thigpen and Hervey M. Cleckley; d Nunnally Johnson; s Joanne Woodward, Lee J. Cobb, David Wayne.

Total Recall, 1990, w Ronald Shusett, Dan O'Bannon, Gary Goldman, from Philip K. Dick's short story, "We Can Remember It for You Wholesale"; d Paul Verhoeven; s Arnold Schwarzenegger, Rachel Ticotin, Sharon Stone.

The Truth about Cats and Dogs, 1996, w Audrey Wells; d Michael Lehmann; w Uma Thurman, Janeane Garofalo, Ben Chaplin.

Two-Faced Woman, 1941, w S. N. Behrman, Salka Viertel, George Oppenheimer, from the play by Ludwig Fulda; d George Cukor; s Greta Garbo, Melvyn Douglas.

Two Much, 1996, w Fernando Trueba, based on the novel by Donald E. Westlake; d Fernando Trueba; s Antonio Banderas, Melanie Griffith, Daryl Hannah.

Young Frankenstein, 1974, w Gene Wilder, Mel Brooks; d Mel Brooks; s Gene Wilder, Marty Feldman, Madeleine Kahn, Peter Boyle.

INDEX